Handbook of persuasive tactics

Handbook of persuasive tactics

A practical language guide

Joan Mulholland

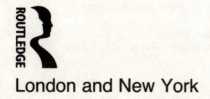

London and New York

First published 1994
By Routledge
11 New Fetter Lane, London EC4P 4EE
29 West 35th Street, New York, NY 10001

© 1994 Joan Mulholland

Typeset in 10/12pt Times Linotron 300 by Florencetype Ltd, Kewstoke, Avon
Printed in Great Britain by Clays Ltd, St Ives plc

British Library Cataloguing-in-Publication Data
A catalogue record for this book is available from the British Library

Library of Congress Cataloging-in-Publication Data
A catalog record for this book is available from the Library of Congress

ISBN 0-415-08930-1

For J.L.
with thanks

Contents

Acknowledgments

In preparing this collection of persuasive tactics, I have consulted a great many sources of language usage—research reports on composition, rhetoric, and discourse analysis, and grammatical and lexical studies. Many of these are listed in the Further Reading list and Bibliography at the end of the book. I would, however, wish to acknowledge here my debt to Randolph Quirk, and his team from the Survey of English Usage, University College London, whose *Comprehensive Grammar of the English Language* has made life a good deal easier for scholars in this field, and I would also like to express my indebtedness to the seminal work done on politeness by Penelope Brown and Stephen Levinson.

Aim of this book

The aim of this book is to present a catalog of the most important persuasive tactics in language. Some 300 of them have been drawn from scholarly studies on rhetoric, and from research studies in communication, linguistics, pragmatics and related fields. Each one has been adapted for practical use either in speech or writing. For each tactic suggestions are offered about the communication tasks for which it is suitable, a descriptive account is given which shows how it works tactically; and a demonstration is given of the ways in which it can be used to good effect by both writers and speakers as they produce communications. Also, of course, by studying the tactics and their persuasive values, readers can equip themselves to enhance their ability to read the communications of others, to improve their interpretation of spoken and written interaction, and to make sense of the communication practices that surround them in their daily lives.

The assumptions on which the book is based are as follows.

(a) Most people spend a very high percentage of their waking life in communication with others.
(b) Every communication has a goal or a set of goals that it tries to achieve.
(c) Everyone communicating with a purpose in mind can use language tactics to try to do it effectively.
(d) Every act of communication, no matter how apparently trivial or brief, has an effect on others.
(e) Every communication imposes to a greater or lesser extent on those who receive it.

How to use this book

There are several ways in which this book can be used.

METHOD I

(a) As an intending writer or speaker, work out what persuasive tasks you have to perform in your next important communication, and think of the problems you might have.
(b) To help you make the best estimate of your tasks and problems, read the Table of Tasks.
(c) Follow the references given in the table to the relevant tactics in the alphabetically listed Collection of Tactics.
(d) Read any you have time for, and then consider how best to use the tactics in the particular circumstances of your communication.

For example

(a) You work out that you need to apologize to a senior colleague for some fault he or she blames on you, but which was not in fact your fault, while at the same time criticizing the person responsible for the fault.
(b) The Table of Tasks could suggest to you that you need to think about these tasks—to apologize, not to lose face, to inform the colleague that there has been a mistake, and to do so with no loss of face to him or her, and to criticize some person for the fault.
(c) Follow the references given in the Table of Tasks to the relevant tactics in the alphabetically listed Collection of Tactics.
(d) Read any you have time for. Then consider how best to use the tactics in the particular circumstances of your communication.

METHOD II

(a) As an intending writer or speaker, work out what persuasive tasks you have to perform in your next important communication, and think of the problems you might have.
(b) Go straight to the Index to Collection of Tactics and check any which appear to be useful.
(c) Turn to the Collection of Tactics and read the useful ones.
(d) Consider how best to use them in the particular circumstances of your communication.

For example

(a) You know you have to put a proposal to your colleagues which they will resist unless you allow them to make some input into it.
(b) On looking through the Index to Collection Tactics you might think some of the following might prove useful—Argument: choose; Explain; Genre: choose; Handle a difficult topic; Impartiality: present; Leave matter incomplete; Moderation: display; Politeness: make action joint; Self-defense; Sociable language; and Understatement.
(c) The tactic 'Argument: choose' shows what a polarized situation you would set up if you put your proposal as an argument. If this seems a bad idea, then settle for the tactic 'Explain,' which makes less of an imposition on those hearing it, and allows more input from them.
(d) Consider how best to word your proposal so that it avoids argument as much as possible, and aims to be more of an explanation.

METHOD III

The *Handbook* can be used as a general checklist of communication features if the reader skims through the whole Table of Tasks, or the whole Collection of Tactics.

METHOD IV

Students or teachers engaged in communication studies could use the *Handbook* as a course programme.

Introduction

THE POWER OF COMMUNICATION

Many people are prepared to accept that they spend a good deal of time each day in talking with and writing to others, as well as in listening, reading, and replying. They are often less prepared to accept that each of these social encounters is done with some purpose in mind, and that each person involved is trying to achieve some goal. They have no difficulty in recognizing that there is persuasive intent in the language of an advertiser or a politician, and can analyze some of the tactics that are used, but they give much less attention to and even deny the existence of their own purposes and tactics as they meet and talk with friends, as they discuss matters at work, and as they engage in their recreational pastimes.

This dismissal of purpose and tactics in individual communications may have come about because, throughout its long and honored history, rhetorical analysis has focussed on the persuasive tactics of political and legal language, and not on the conversations and discussions, the birthday letters and business memos, that form the bulk of most people's communicational practice, and so for many it is unusual to see these taken seriously, and they may be unclear what method to use to analyze them.

Another reason for resisting the analysis of informal communications may be that the purposes of everyday interaction seem trivial in contrast with the goals of those involved in public life. It would be unfortunate if this were so, since everyday interactions and their purposes form the bulk of most people's experience. To deny the importance of one's daily happenings is to deny one's own importance. It would also be foolish because such happenings make a major contribution to people's understanding of the world, the establishment of their value systems, and their behavioral conduct. The persuasive power of communication in interpersonal relations has effects which last just as long, if not longer, than those of the mass media. For example, harsh words from a teacher at primary school can be remembered (and have an effect) long after the ad for soap powder has been forgotten. It is at least as important to an individual that he or she can establish a good working relationship with a colleague as that he or she is told that Smith's soap is the best on the market. It is more important that he or she can communicate well with members of the family and create strong bonds with them than that one politician or another is given support in an election.

The important purposes of everyday life include forming group identities, associating well with others, acquiring a sense of one's own identity from the way one communicates with others, and from the ways others communicate with and about one. And to these should be added the more obvious purposes of having one's information accepted, achieving cooperation in getting things done, passing exams and performing well at job interviews, and so on. Persuasive communications make a major contribution to all of these. Some few people, like politicians and advertisers, may use communication to influence masses of people, but for most people communication has a much more reduced domain than this. This fact should not, however, prevent an understanding that ordinary talk and writing has as many persuasive tactics in it as are used in political or advertising language.

It may also be difficult to accept that ordinary talk and writing are tactically rich, because they are denied social value, and attention, in the courses of study in Western education systems. But also it may be difficult because they are so familiar people hardly notice the detail of their production.

Some people even consider that it is unnecessary to analyze ordinary communications because they believe that if an idea is good enough in itself, this alone will persuade others to accept it, and it needs no persuasive 'embellishment.' But it is not true that having a good idea means that it will win approval and support in and of itself without any persuasive planning to produce it in the best possible way, and taking advantage of what is known of the other person's preferences, habits of mind, and opinions. For example, any good idea which is new, and which needs to be substituted for a familar old one, will have to be very well expressed, and repeated often, before it is accepted. Equally it is not true that a good person's qualities are always recognized and his or her word valued as a consequence; it is necessary to work hard at acquiring a good reputation, and this includes presenting oneself well.

And finally, people resist analyzing ordinary talk because they fear that analysis could mean they would be inhibited from taking part in it as 'naturally' as before. Certainly it is likely that on first looking into the nature of ordinary talk, there could be a period of awkwardness and self-consciousness, but once that stage has passed people would be left with an increase in knowledge about the communicative practices of their daily lives, and an enhanced potential to communicate successfully. This is surely a good goal and worth a little initial discomfort.

If it seems that analysis might destroy the spontaneity or naturalness of ordinary talk, then perhaps it is right that it should do so, if only because the spontaneity is often only apparent and not real, and it is certainly not an indication of untactical language, but rather just a sign that the tactics used are very familiar to all concerned.

Ordinary talk and writing, then, are worth close scrutiny, however awkward it may seem. And this is particularly so because whether people like it or not, others are using persuasive tactics on them, and these should be studied in order to know how to counter them or whether to agree to them. Power, sometimes mildly and sometimes strongly, in some form, is exercised in every communication: for example, in the ways in which some people dominate the speaking role and so force others to listen; or the way they set the tone of an interaction and make it difficult for others to change it; as well as the way they assert strong opinions and thereby influence others to agree with them; and so on. Speakers and writers involved in ordinary engagements can constrain other people's actions, affect others' interpretations of things, they can set up discussions and close them, start embarrassing topics, and so on.

The power of such everyday persuasions can be felt in the strength of feelings that can arise from them. So, for example, a failure to get a straight answer to a straight question from a friend in a casual chat can cause the questioner severe and lasting irritation. Or there could be feelings that last for years because as a child one was hurt by unkind words. A knowledge of the tactical possibilities of language can lead to the empowerment of anyone as a communicator. The more people know of what can be done through language, the more they can try to do with it; and the more knowledge they have about what is being done to them through language, the more they can make informed decisions to accept or reject it. Such tactical knowledge will only have a bad result, and lead to the unacceptable manipulation of others, or to personal hypocrisy, if a person makes a deliberate decision to use it in this way: it is not inherent in the knowledge itself.

THE NATURE OF PERSUASION

'Persuasion' for some people is associated with the misuse of powerful tactics and the exerting of improper influence over others at a mass national, or cultural, level. It is seen as manipulation of others' minds and therefore as unethical. People perceive of it as 'the manufacturing of consent,' that is, an artificial activity, and one which covertly limits the options of those receiving it. (Note that the artificiality of the notion is made persuasive by the metaphor of 'manufacturing.') These associations are, however, more suitably applied to propaganda than to persuasion.

Propaganda uses strong and mainly covert tactics, and hardly allows for resistance to its influence, and has as its goal an absolute imposition of its own wishes on others. If it meets with opposition it simply increases the pressure on others to accept what it seeks. It insists that its message be accepted, and further that it be acted on. It can and does fail if its tactics are inappropriate or badly used, but in the hands of experts it more often succeeds than not. It can work quickly, as in agitation propagandas which seek an instant result, or it can permeate social life slowly as in integration propagandas which are used to impose a steady long-term adherence to a certain view of life.

Persuasion is quite a different activity. It differs in its aims, in the means it uses, in the pressure it exerts, and in the range of people it affects. Persuasion is a factor of ordinary everyday life, and it is what can make people feel more or less comfortable, improve or weaken cooperation between colleagues and friends, and maintain relations with family and the community. By persuasion one may be able to avoid an unpleasant task, or to arrange a better one; one can win a point at a meeting, or one can be the life and soul of a party. Persuasion certainly seeks to achieve the goals of the person using it, but unlike propaganda, if it proves unsuccessful or meets too much opposition, the persuasion may be withdrawn. Also, persuasion acts rather to encourage the other person to share the view of the user, than to insist on imposing it; the persuader simply presents the best case possible, and then leaves it to the other to accept or reject it. Moreover, persuasion will take into account and allow for differences in viewpoint. Unlike propaganda which either succeeds or fails, persuasion can be partially successful. Like propaganda, persuasion can either work quickly or can only gradually increase its influence, but unlike propaganda, persuasion can be quite open and aboveboard in the tactics it uses (though it can employ covert tactics as well).

When the more overt tactics are used in persuasion they provide an opportunity for all participants to recognize that persuasion is intended, and indeed it may be useful at times to let people know what one wants: 'I want you all to come to dinner on Saturday.' The more covert tactics can work towards subtler goals, as when one person wants to know just how a friend judges a meeting they have just been to, while the other person will not reveal this without some expression of judgment by the first person.

It is very important to understand that persuasion can be a joint activity as people with similar aims work together to achieve them: it is not just what one person does to another. One such joint maneuver might occur in the case of a teenager, just returning home from college, who uses a baby voice to ask Mommy's permission to take a cookie, just as she did in the distant past when she was a child. She adopts this role not just to get the cookie, but because she knows Mommy enjoys it when her daughter acts persuasively in this way, and can herself respond as she did in the past, and the whole interaction evokes happy memories. This could be the daughter's aim in setting it up, and her mother's in joining in, forming a joint exercise in reinforcing the family bond which is at risk by the daughter's absence from home.

The joint nature of persuasive activity, and the sophisticated maneuvering it can cause in interactions, is an important truth about its character, and one which can be overlooked if the only persuasions studied are the one-way enticements of the mass media. Joint persuasion, as in conversation, can use delicate discriminations in language to aim for a particular goal at any one time, or in order to build up slowly the quality and kind of relationship with someone which can be used, as a pre-persuasion, for other attempts at influence in future interactions.

Persuasion also has other qualities which are often absent from communication analyses. Where the mass media is taken as the model of social influence it sets up a slant of thought which focusses on its agents—the advertisers and politicians, and on its audience—the passive masses. This is a poor model and mode of thought to use on the very different daily interactions of ordinary life. First, in daily talk, quite ordinary people can be the agents of persuasion and influence. Second, the use of everyday-talk persuasive tactics can occasionally rebound on the users, and can even cause them to change their own views even as they are in the process of imposing them on others. This can happen because the process of putting one's ideas into words so that others can see their value may reveal that the ideas have some faults in logic, or some inconsistencies, or a lack of evidence, or even a lack of value, and so the communicator is forced to rethink or withdraw his or her support for them.

A third aspect of persuasion which is often ignored by analysts, is the fact that not one but many tactics can be employed at a time to achieve influence. And in many cases the use of multiple tactics can be more successful than using just one. And lastly, in talk, tactics have to be constantly adjusted during an interaction. Though at the start one tactic may appear to be working well, this is no guarantee that it will continue to do so. This is because of the interactive quality of daily talk: the copresence of others as communicators ensures that it will often happen that tactics have to be adjusted in the light of developing circumstances.

Though persuasion can and does exert a powerful influence on all aspects of life, neither in mass communications nor in individual interactions can it alter people's fixed prejudices or long-term habits, nor can it easily modify a belief to which someone has been committed for a long time. But it can influence them, for example, it can influence the cultural perception of suitable matters for communication so as to exclude the topics or actions which support the habits of such people, for example, it can make the expression of some prejudices quite unacceptable in public communication, and so can prevent such people from representing their opinions. For example, though many men still hold a poor opinion of women, and will not change it, it has become less socially acceptable to utter this view in public. If it remains unsaid, perhaps one day, because it has not been heard for a long time, people will forget that it was ever current.

PERSUASION AND LANGUAGE

One major tool in the achievement of persuasion is language. It is not the only one, of course, because people can be persuaded by bribery, by family affection, by high-status social influence, and so on, but it is certainly important even for those able to bribe people, or utilize family affection or social influence that they be able to handle the persuasive qualities of language as they do it, a badly communicated bribe may not be correctly recognized.

Language is influential because of the many powers it has: it can represent any single thing in many different ways; it can vary the mental representations of matters in the world to suit people's beliefs; it can mention or omit things, or repeat them till they are accepted as normal (and perhaps true); and hence can construct matters in a way which suits the user's purposes. Many of the most influential aspects of life—people's beliefs, ideologies, assumptions, and values—depend for their construction and maintenance on language. So language can influence thought itself, and can also be used to offer opinions, state facts, suggest attitudes, create moods, attack or defend views, and so on, any of which could be persuasively used for some purpose.

Language also has the power to bring about and affect personal relationships, to set up good interactions, or bad ones, to damage, or repair damage to social interactivity, and to terminate friendships. In short, language can supply people with both the means to interpret the world, and a set of methods by which to influence their own and others' perceptions of the world; and it can help them to manage the interactions they have with others.

Every aspect of language use can represent the world and also form and sustain relationships. Our concepts are selected and represented in language. Our language structures ideas into texts, by grammatical and compositional strategies. Our attitudes to the world and emotions about it are expressed through words, grammar, and such extra-language factors as voice qualities and body language. And our use of language enables us to interpret the communications we receive. Many of the most important actions and interactions of people's life are found in the exchanges of speech and the speech acts they perform in communication.

PERSUASION AND RHETORIC

For the Ancient Greeks the name for persuasion in communication was 'rhetoric,' and during Greek and Roman times the study of rhetoric as the means by which a person could achieve his or her persuasive goals was held in high regard, and used as a foundation course in education. The main aspects of persuasion as they saw it were: the finding of ideas 'invention,' the arrangement of materials into compositions, selection of an appropriate style, retaining the ideas and the arrangement in mind 'memory,' and delivery of the communication. But after Roman times, as rhetorical studies continued through the medieval period, the focus narrowed dramatically to only the first three of these, and in some cases to only style. Within style it became an exercise in classification of grammatical arrangments (called 'figures'), and the selection of words and ideas (called 'tropes'). As it lost touch with practical applications, it lost strength as a study, and the term 'rhetoric' itself lost status.

In this century, however, and particularly in the U.S.A., there has been a revitalization of rhetoric, an increase of flexibility in its use, and a return to the original breadth of the subject, though the term itself has not altogether regained its original high status in the perception of the general public. Today's rhetoric has developed its own special characteristics, in each of the classical areas of study using the developments in contemporary sociological, psychological, and language studies to enhance the rhetorical enterprise; allowing greater flexibility in the use of tactics than was permitted in the rigid models of the classical period, and shifting the focus of study from those of classical times.

For example, 'invention' now incorporates an understanding that the choice of materials involves an adjustment and re-presentation of them; and now covers not only the search for ideas and arguments, but also the choice of genres and media, and the implications of choosing one or another of them. It also covers far more of the context in which a communication occurs, since we now recognize the power exerted by situation on an individual communicator, and we know it is important to consider the involvement of one communication with those which precede it, both for a communicator, and his or her audience. We also know that context is not just brought into texts by, for example, an explicit reference to an external authority's support for one's argument, but that it could be implicitly incorporated into a text through the pervasive use of, for example, a stereotype found in the media. 'Arrangement' now includes the design of informal speech and writing where classical rhetoric focussed exclusively on formality. And it has had to come to terms with studying dialog in addition to treating the classical monolog.

'Style' has broadened its scope considerably. While language is still a very important aspect of rhetoric study, and even the sometimes dry categorization of 'tropes' and 'figures' is still studied, for example, in ads, poetry, and political speeches; there is much more awareness of the importance of language choice as it is affected by and affects the relationship between the communicator and his or her audience. This has given rise to major studies on tact and politeness, gender, and cross-cultural communications.

'Memory,' always an under-examined aspect of communication, is now receiving attention from the cognitive scientists and those who work in artificial intelligence, and new insights have been found to show how meanings are made in the mind, which will eventually prove useful for the analysis of communicational rhetoric.

'Delivery' has flourished as students have explored the minutiae of body language and non-verbal communications, and the intonational and pro-nunciational features of vocal communications.

Many of these areas of study are no longer called 'rhetoric,' passing now as linguistics, psychology, speech and drama, cultural studies, literature, or English studies, but they rightfully belong to the study of the means of achieving good communication. Ideas on the persuasive use of language from all of them have been incorporated here as they were found relevant.

And it is very much a twentieth-century view that sees this as a proper way to present rhetorical tactics. Nowadays, at least in democratic socie-ties, ordinary people have many occasions in which they need to be persuasive, and they should be supplied with the language tools to help them do so. It is no longer a world in which rhetorical tools, and the rights to use them, belong only to the rich and powerful.

The Collection of Tactics presented in this book includes some which have been credentialled by centuries of rhetorical study and others which are quite newly seen as rhetorical. In some cases the presentation in this book is the first articulation of a tactic, as in the instance of 'Minimalism,' or 'Reveal thought processes.' In others it is the first presentation of a mass tactic, like gatekeeping, Stereotyping, or Slogans, for use by individuals, showing how a tactic used by the powerful communicators can be adapted to empower ordinary folk. The tactics are a distillation from classical rhetoric and pragmatic studies, and from contemporary research into language, cognition, discourse analysis, and communication and cultural studies. In every case, the pragmatic information on each tactic's value for communication has been stripped down to its essentials, and is here presented in such a form that any reader who has to perform persuasive work can make use of them. They come with practical examples, collected from real-life instances, to show the tactics in operation and provide a comprehensive means of dealing with a wide spectrum of persuasive aims in the ordinary occasions of practical life. Together they form a compre-hensive coverage of the most important persuasive tactics that could be used in spoken and written communications.

(Should any reader wish for more information about a particular tactic than is supplied in the Collection of Tactics, suggestions for further reading are offered, and a reference list is appended.)

While other texts on communication list language tactics, some of them do no more than name them, as, for example, 'be brief,' 'do not use technical terms;' and those which do describe the tactics in more detail do not explain how they might work in specific cases, nor do they give examples. Other texts on language in communication totally ignore the social value of the tactics; while yet others issue rules for the use of a tactic which imply that a tactic could work anywhere and anytime. This text differs significantly from these in that it comprehensively names and describes the tactics, states the persuasive tasks for which they are suited, explains their persuasive value(s), and gives examples of the different ways in which they could be used.

The book supplies information about the persuasive potential of some 300 language tactics which might be of use, and also provides an index to the tasks for which they could be used. The tasks cover three basic aspects of persuasive communication.

(a) The preparation of material.
(b) The production of a well-constructed text.
(c) Considerations of the relationship between the persuader and his or her audience.

There are tactics which can assist in the choice of genre, for example, explaining the relative pragmatic merits of account, argument, or description, since these set up a particular framework which influences the whole way a person reads or listens to the ensuing communication. There are tactics on the best way to take advantage of the special qualities of speech or writing as a mode of persuasion. There are tactics on the best way to present a topic, how to introduce it, or to change it if it seems to be harmful to the persuasive intention, and how to avoid others' topics. Some tactical rules for interpreting the communications of others are supplied. Useful tactics for the management of personal presentation, the achievement of a good working relationship, are given, and ways of successfully managing some of the most persuasively difficult speech acts, such as apologize, request, and reprimand, are offered. And ways of using words and grammar, figures of speech, and logical argument to the best advantage are presented.

THE READER

Readers of this book, it is assumed, are already practicing communicators, and have some experience in communication, though they may lack experience in the analysis of communication. The book is designed to give them help to examine their own practice, and that of the others they work with or who share their daily lives. They can discover the factors involved in persuasion and the means by which it can be successfully produced, and so can use the tactics in their own practice. The book assumes that readers want practical information and advice on persuasive matters, but neither particular instruction nor rigid rules. So this book will not declare any tactics to be the 'correct' ones for a particular encounter or goal. Nor should it do so, since this can only be done when all the details of the specific circumstances—the participants, their relationships with one another, the changing moods and attitudes of the people involved in an encounter—are known, and only a participant can hope to be the best judge of these factors, and so decide which tactic should be used.

The book has had to take the tactics out of their contexts to some degree in order to show that their applicability is wide ranging, and that their uses can be multiple, but concrete and contextualized examples are supplied which should remind readers of circumstances in their own lives where the tactics could be applicable, so that in this way they can be restored to a contextual reality.

The *Handbook*, then, has been designed to allow readers to make their own decisions about what might prove useful in the many different communication situations they encounter. Indeed, this writer recognizes that the first task for any communicator is to consider the particularities of a situation and its communication needs and only then to examine what tactics the language can offer to achieve the desired results. What this book supplies is a repertory of tactics to be called on when needed. All the tactics are here because they could be valuable for anyone with a persuasive task to perform.

Design of this *Handbook*

The *Handbook* has the following sections:

1 *Table of Tasks*

From page 1 to page 15 the Table of Tasks lists the persuasive tasks which the reader might need to do. It is arranged in an order which reflects as far as possible the way such tasks might occur during the chronology of the communication process. It proceeds roughly from macro matters to micro ones; that is, it begins with general considerations of the communication as a whole, and to what kind of audience it is directed, and continues by giving specific attention to the details of presentation in words and sentences.

2 *Index to the Collection of Tactics*

From page 17 to page 21 is a standard, alphabetized, index to the tactics.

3 *Collection of Tactics*

Beginning on page 23, the tactics are arranged in alphabetical order. Each tactic begins by naming some of the tasks for which it may be useful. Then follows a description of the use of the tactic. To help the reader understand the particular use to which such tactics can be put, examples are supplied showing the tactic in use. For some tactics warnings are given of the dangers involved in handling the tactic badly. Cross-references to other relevant tactics, and suggestions for further reading, are supplied.

Table of tasks

INTRODUCTION

This table offers a comprehensive taxonomic plan for designing and executing communications. It does so by naming the important tasks that are involved in preparing for a communication. For each task the table then refers the reader to at least one tactic from the Collection of Tactics which could improve the performance of that task.

The table could be used in several ways. For example, the reader who wishes to make a general study of the elements of communication could use it as a guide to matters of significance, slowly working through all the tasks mentioned; while the reader who has a specific communication to prepare could search through it for those relevant to the occasion.

Goal	Task	Tactic
1 General issues in communication		
1.1 Supporting one's communication in general ways	Match another's style	Accommodation
	Observe the conventions about who has a right to communicate, who has a right to choose a topic	Communication conventions tactics
	Consider the context features	Communication context
	Adapt one's style to others	Compensation
	Use educated language	Elaborated code
	Decide whether matters should be presented	Information control
	Observe the conventions that one should be clear, concise, and tidy, that one should tell the truth, that one should give the right amount of information, and which should be relevant	Social conventions tactics
	Use one's life as support for material	Testimony of own experience
	Do not make others work hard at interpretation	Principle of least effort
	Consider the general goals of communication	Rapport versus report: choose
	Understand the process of reading communications	Reading: use
	Use the language of close relationship	Restricted code
	Choose an interesting topic	Tellable topic: choose
	Use language primarily for bonding	Sociable language
	Select best topic for bonding	Sociable language: topics
	Consider the topic options involved	Topic
	Note what gives an impression of weakness	Weak expressions
	Consider the word options involved	Word choice
1.2 Finding useful support from outside oneself in general social and community considerations	Impress others with wit and language knowledge	Archaisms
	Put people at ease	Clichés
	Put matters in familiar terms	Metaphor
	Set a hidden agenda	
	Discover a hidden agenda	
	Assess the information others offer	Information: assess

1.3 Using genre (or type) of communication

- Bring general cultural support for one's ideas
  - Myth
  - Quotation
  - Proverbs
- Direct attention to useful matters
  - Reference to texts
  - Referring terms: external
- Bring cultural support for one's ideas
  - Slogans
  - Stereotypes
- Bring figures as evidence for one's ideas
  - Statistical support
- Indicate the degree of reliability of one's material
- Show how firmly one believes in one's material
- Show how generally applicable one's material is
  - Validation of material
- Set a way of reading for one's communications
  - Genre: choose
  - Account: choose
  - Argument: choose
  - Casual chat: choose
- Choose a suitable type of communication
  - Explain
  - Explanation: choose
  - Information: choose
  - Lecture: choose
  - Narrative: choose
- Insert an argument into another type of communication
  - Argument insertion
- Prepare others that one is about to argue
  - Argument preamble
- Choose to aim primarily at friendliness and cooperation
  - Casual chat: choose
- Choose to create a definition
  - Definition
- Create a description which is covertly subjective
  - Describe subjectively
- Reduce or increase others' uncertainty
  - Informing
- Form one's material into a narrative design
  - Narrative: design
- Convert one's material into communicable elements
  - Narrative: elements
- Make a report
  - Reporting
  - Report speech tactics

Goal	Task	Tactic
	Choose to use a particular act	Command/request
		Questioning
		State
	Respond to another's interviewing tactics	Interview: respond to
	Use one's gestures, movements, bodily orientation, and distance from others to create meaning	Body language
1.4 Using the mode of communication	Using the phone, make a good beginning	Greeting: by phone
	Interrupt another person	Interruption of other
	Use one's voice to support one's meaning	Intonation
	Use pause effectively	Intonation: pause
	Use one's voice pitch to support one's meaning	Intonation: pitch choice
	Use one's voice to give emphasis to one's material	Intonation: tone units
		Intonation: voice stress
	Understand how the listening process works	Listening: use
	Prepare a text to be easily listened to	Lecture: design
	Demonstrate emotion	
	Add emphasis by using the voice	Voice quality
	Hold an audience interested	
	Correct oneself with least damage	Self-interruption
	Avoid unfriendly silence	Silence
	Understand the silence of others	
	Make one's words and sentences echo the meaning	Sounds and sense
	Understand the social values of spoken communication	Spoken communication: choose
	Maintain smooth exchange of turns at speaking	Turntaking
	Avoid silence	
	Use one's turn to control who speaks next	Turn: select next speaker
	Hold onto one's speaking turn	Turn: refuse
	Try to gain a speaking turn	Turn: request

1.5 Considering matters of cooperative bonding with others

- Give up one's turn at speaking — Turn: yield
- Understand the social values of written communication — Written communication: choose
- Avoid risking cooperative bond with others — Politeness tactics / Politeness indirection tactics
- Preserve one's self-image — Face: sustain / Face threats: recognize
- Support others in their self-image
- Avoid endangering the self-esteem of others — Face: sustain / Face threats: recognize
- Avoid intruding on another's freedom of action
- Avoid damage to another's self-esteem — Politeness tactics
- Understand how social acts can be best performed through language
- Interpret the communication of others — Cooperative principle

2 Designing a communication structure

2.1 Overall structuring of the interaction, and of one's own communication

- Perform greetings to advantage — Greeting / Greeting: by phone
- Begin an interaction to advantage — Interaction: begin
- Design one's speech or writing to advantage — Spoken communication: design / Written communication: design
- Handle a complex argument — Argument: complex propositions
- Design an interview — Interview: conduct
- Design one's narrative to begin to one's advantage — Narrative: begin
- Arrange points to be argued to best advantage — Argument design tactics
- End a speech interaction to advantage — Interaction closure: spoken
- Maintain the bond with others beyond an interaction — Interaction closure tactics
- Influence others' memories of one's contribution
- Maintain the bond with others beyond an interaction
- Influence others' memories of one's contribution

Goal	Task	Tactic
2.2 Middle-level structuring	End a written interaction to advantage	Interaction closure: written
	Design one's narrative to end to one's advantage	Narrative: end
	Handle the movement of topic through an interaction	Topic movement
	Mark the change of topic	Topic: change
	Present one's material to end on a high note	Climax: create
	Divide one's material to suit one's purposes	Division of material: create
	Highlight one item of one's material	Emphasis
	Focus attention on some matters other than others	Foregrounding
	Arrange one's ideas to best advantage	Idea arrangement
	Ensure that others can handle the amount of information one wishes to give	Information flow
	Adjust the pace of one's information if it is too fast or slow for others	Information flow: adjustments
	Interrupt oneself to adjust what one is saying	Self-interruption
	Interrupt another person with least damage to bonding	Interruption of other
	Arrange one's material in paragraphs and link them	Paragraph design tactics
	Arrange one's material in sentences	Sentence structure tactics
	Effect a change in activity in the interaction	Phase change
	Provide a brief, and persuasive summary of a complex matter	Sum up
	Keep to the subject, and keep others to it	Topic coherence tactics
	Use words that belong together and will be easily understood	Word combinations
2.3 Micro-level structuring	Clarify reference to other parts of the text	Concord
	Use 'the' to advantage	Definite article 'the'
	Address one's audience to effect	Direct address
	Understand the importance of individual speech exchanges	Exchange of speech
	Pack complexity of information, opinion, and self-presentation into the written sentence form	Information: add

Avoid fallacies and note when others use them

Use 'a'/'an' to advantage

Introduce matters into a spoken interaction

Initiate a speech action

Influence others to respond as one wishes

Clarify a matter before proceeding further

Distinguish non-literal language

Signal that extra attention to the language is needed

Close an exchange of speech with oneself in charge

Respond relevantly and with due recognition of the initiator's goals

Prevent loss of face when doing a difficult act, like request, or invite, which involve face threat

Present matters in swift sequences so that they impress with their quantity

Design one's sentence structure to advantage when making a command or request

Avoid making an immediate response

Change the topic or speech activity of a talk

Digress in talk

Take care when using the adjacent words which have complex meaning

---

Begging the question
'Either–or' fallacy

Indefinite article 'a'/'an'

Initiating move

Preferred response

Inserted sequence

Metaphor

Metonymy

Metaphor markers

Move: follow up

Preferred response

Preferred response: types

Presequences

Rapid sequences

Command/request

Side sequences

'By the way'
'Even'
'From . . . to'
'Next'
'Oh'
'Therefore'
'Unless'
'Well'
'Y'know'

Goal	Task	Tactic
3 Representing one's subject matter		
3.1 Ordering the different parts of the material	Persuade by sheer weight of evidence	Accumulation
	Arrange one's ideas to best advantage	Idea arrangement
	Show there are links between the matters one presents to one's advantage	Link material tactics
3.2 Ranking the elements of the material	Bring together two opposed ideas to give each one a richer meaning	Antithesis
	Admit a fault in one's argument, but neutralize its effect by balancing it with a virtue	Balanced representation
	Criticize, but neutralize its effect with praise	
	Put together two contrary ideas in such a way that their opposition seems reduced	Bring contraries together
	Show strong feeling	Emphasis
	Show some matters are more important than others	Foregrounding
	Choose the information most likely to be accepted	Information: choose
	Show importance of material	Ironic understatement/overstatement
	Show there are links within one's subject matter, to one's advantage	Link material
	Present matters as separate items linked into a set	Link material: addition
	Have a matter accepted as being two or more alternatives	Link material: alternatives
	Present a set of matters ranked in importance	Link material: rank matters as they are added
	Have a matter and one's explanation of it accepted	Link material: subject and explanation
	Present a matter in two or more versions to have it properly understood	Link material: substitution
	Bring two things into a reciprocal relationship to enrich their meaning	Reciprocals

3.3 Expanding on or reducing the material

- Highlight some matter — Repetition
- Present some things as important — Generic 'the'
- Refer coherently to matters in the communication — Referring terms: internal
- Produce a brief covering comment on a matter to one's advantage — Sum up
- Make a comparison of one matter with another — Analogy
- Supply one's own comment on a matter — Adverbs: add comments
- Supply the causes of a matter where these are to one's advantage — Adverbs: state causes
- Supply detail of the frequency of a matter's occurrence, where this is to one's advantage — Adverbs: state frequency
- Show the manner in which the matter occurred — Adverbs: state manner
- Show the instrument or means by which a matter came about — Adverbs: state means
- Show the time of the matter's occurrence — Adverbs: state time
- Present two versions of a thing side by side so that the two are accepted as joined and equivalent in meaning — Apposition
- Prioritize points to suit oneself — Apposition: types
- Be accurate and specific in stating the basis of one's argument — Argument proposition: form
- Give details of qualities a thing has, to suit one's purposes — Attribute degree of quality
- Compare and contrast two matters for effect — Comparison
- Provide examples to support one's points — Exemplification
- Leave a matter incomplete as the best way of stating it to one's advantage — Leave matter incomplete
- Avoid naming who did an act so as to avoid something against one's purposes — Omit agent
- Avoid naming the process by which something occurred to suit one's purposes — Omit process
- Avoid mention of the results of an act, to suit one's purposes — Omit results
- Subordinate a matter to others — Parenthesis
- Downgrade some people to suit one's purposes — People presented as things

Goal	Task	Tactic
	Show whether one is being general or specific in attributing a meaning to something	Restrictive meaning
	Avoid a damaging silence	Silence
	Understand the meaning of a silence	
	Make a point obliquely	Understatement
3.4 Selecting names for the material	Influence others' perceptions of matters	Naming
		Naming: text
	Influence others' perceptions of people	Naming: people
		Naming: substitute phrase
		Substitutes for names
	Influence how people interpret one's text	Title choice
3.5 Enriching and elaborating on the material	Describe obliquely or covertly	Describe subjectively
		Descriptive phrases
	Build a whole section of one's text on a metaphor for covert influence	Metaphor: extended
	Lighten the mood of an interaction	Humor
		Jokes
	Present a matter without penalty	Hypothesize
	Make covert meaning in one's communication	Irony
		Ironic understatement/ overstatement
	Appear to involve another person	Questions: rhetorical
	Set or influence the agenda	Reflexive comment
	Enrich one's meaning and influence the interpretation of one's material	Metaphor
	Understand something communicated to one	Metaquestions
	Select the best way to represent some matter	Metonymy
	Guide the answer to one's question	Questions: closed
		Questions: negative
	Show an attitude of annoyance by a question	Questions: negative

3.6 Adding one's attitude to the material

- Show an attitude of annoyance by a question — Questions: negative
- Introduce an attitude or judgment covertly ⎤
- Find the covert attitudes of others ⎦ — Personification
- Add one's attitudes covertly in a way which is hard to reject — Preposed adjectives
- Lighten the mood of one's communication — Puns
- Influence others to accept one's ideas as they are presented — Set a refrain
- Make one's words echo one's meaning — Sounds and sense
- Ensure that people know when one is ending a section of one's communication — Triplets

- Make explicit the degree of accuracy with which the material is being presented — Accuracy: show degree of
- Have people accept something without it actually being put into words — Oblique representation
- Express one's detachment from a matter for effect ⎤ — Express personal detachment
  - ⎦ — Postponement tactics
- Express strong feeling ⎤ — Express emotion
  - ⎦ — Exclaim
- Express strong feeling without naming it — Questions: rhetorical
- Focus one's mind ⎤
- Check one's memory ⎥
- Have a dialog with oneself as a way of sharing oneself with another ⎦ — Questions: self-addressed

4 Presenting oneself

4.1 Presenting oneself to advantage

- Name oneself to best advantage — Naming: oneself
- Show that one is attending to another — Listening: active
- Improve the chance of a generalization being accepted by acknowledging some exceptions — Exception: allow
- Reduce the chances of others objecting to one's material by anticipating and answering potential objections — Objections: anticipate
- Avoid commitment to a view being expressed ⎤ — Avoid responsibility
  - ⎦ — Impartiality: present

Goal	Task	Tactic
	Notice when others try to avoid blame	Avoid responsibility
	Use one's gestures, movements, bodily orientation, and distance from others to support one's meaning	Body language
	Avoid trouble by claiming that one communicates by necessity	Claim necessity
	Avoid trouble when performing a difficult social act	Codeswitching: role-playing in difficult tasks
		Concession
	Concede points that cannot be won	
	Concede the good points of others	
	Show that one is objective in what one says	Express personal detachment
		Impartiality: present
		Postponement tactics
	Show that one is thoroughly involved in what one says	Express personal involvement
	Present oneself as a guardian of information, keeping others out or letting them in	Information: control
	Avoid upsetting the susceptibilities of others	Grammatical 'errors'
		Humor
	Present oneself as witty and entertaining	Jokes
		Jokes: types
	Show that one is moderate	Moderation: display
	Counter extremism in others	
	Present oneself to suit one's purposes	Naming: oneself
	Avoid damage to another's self-esteem when performing socially difficult tasks	Politeness tactics
	Understand the ways in which people interpret communications	Principle of least effort
	Understand the social role of bluntness	Bluntness: choose
	Share one's thoughts with others, to effect	Reveal thought processes
	Correct oneself to suggest one is being honest	Self-correction
	Anticipate when others might correct one, and prevent it	Self-repair
	Support one's views	Testimony of own experience
	Reveal oneself for bonding purposes	

5 Achieving cooperation and bonding

5.1 General bonding

- Note the adverse effect of not paying attention to others' self-esteem — Politeness: principle and tactics / Bluntness: choose
- Communicate in a style which matches another's — Accommodation
- Choose a way of communication that bonds some people and excludes others — Antilanguage
- Show where one's opponents are wrong, without damage to bonding — Attack opponent's argument
- Select language that does not offend — Words: acceptability / Euphemism / Minimalism
- Show that one is not antisocial — Name: call
- Note when others are being antisocial
- Get the attention of a person without offense
- Select questions that will not cause offense — Questions: closed / Questions: open / Questions: tag
- Use casual chat and friendly language to support and maintain one's bond's with others — Sociable language / Sociable language: types
- Present a matter in a way which prevents potential trouble — Handle a difficult topic
- Handle any conflict of topic to good effect — Topic conflict
- Select the right response to another — Preferred response / Responses

5.2 Preserving the self-esteem ('face') of others

- Attend to one's self-esteem, and that of others — Face: sustain
- Notice the acts which involve face threats to oneself or to others — Face threats: recognize
- Avoid intruding on another's freedom of action — Politeness tactics
- Show recognition of another's self-esteem

6 Performing socially difficult communication acts

6.1 Performing difficult communication acts

- Raising a matter of wrongdoing — Accusation: choose
- Bring a claim of wrongdoing against someone — Accuse

Goal	Task	Tactic
	Give counsel to someone	Advise
	Indicate that a course of action is good or bad	
	Express regret for a past action	Apologize
	Avoid blame for a future act	Appeal
	Seek help to prevent something bad happening	
	State something good about oneself	Boast
	Praise oneself	
	Seek to have someone do something or to cause something to be done	Command/request
	Express unease, dissatisfaction, or censure	Complain
	Communicate something bad about oneself without loss of face	Confess
	Criticize other people, ideas, opinions	Criticize
	Claim that something that someone else has said is not true	Deny
	Claim that something bad attributed to oneself is not true	
	Prevent people believing something bad about one is true	
	Require someone to not do something	Forbid
	Influence others indirectly to be critical of something by contrasting it with an ideal or by suggesting it has the wrong priorities	Indirect criticism
	Persuade someone to think something bad about a matter, without noticing how this has happened	Insinuate
	Be critical without others noticing	
	Communicate obliquely as a test of bonding	Irony
	Communicate ironically	
	Present something for acceptance or rejection	Offer
	Make another person feel good	Praise: use
	Present oneself as generous spirited	

Give some praise to another person	
Make someone pleased with one, and with life	Praising another person
Present oneself as generous natured	
Declare a commitment to undertake some action	Promise
Ask a question	Questioning
Refuse to do something requested of one without damage to bonding	Refuse
Reject advice without giving offense	Reject advice
Offer a serious adverse judgment to another	Reprimand
Note what caused a complaint	
Respond appropriately to a complaint	Respond to complaint
Defend oneself against real or expected attacks	Self-defense
Produce an opinion, idea, or fact, which is formulated as a statement to be accepted as true information	State
Show fellow feeling with others over some trouble they have	Sympathize

Index to collection of tactics

17

Definition
Deny
Describe subjectively
Descriptive phrase
Direct address
Division of material: create

'Either–or' fallacy
Elaborated code
Emphasis
Euphemism
'Even'
Exception: allow
Exchange of speech
Exclaim
Exemplification
Explain
Explanation: choose
Express emotion
Express personal detachment
Express personal involvement

Face: sustain
Face threats: recognize
Forbid
Foregrounding
'From . . . to'

Generic 'the'
Genre: choose
Grammatical 'errors'
Greeting
Greeting by phone

Handle a difficult topic
Humor
Hypothesize

Idea arrangement
Impartiality: present
Indefinite article 'a'/'an'
Indirect criticism
Information:
   add

assess
choose
control
Information flow
Information flow: adjustments
Informing
Initiating move
Inserted sequences
Insinuate
Interaction: begin
Interaction closure:
   spoken
   written
Interruption of other
Interview:
   conduct
   respond to
Intonation
Intonation:
   pause
   pitch choice
   tone units
   voice stress
Ironic understatement/
   overstatement
Irony

Jokes
Jokes: types

Leave matter incomplete
Lecture:
   choose
   design
Link material
Link material:
   addition
   alternatives
   rank matters as they are added
   subject and explanation
   substitution
Listening:
   active

Terms employed in the text

C.=The communicator

A.=The reader or hearer

F.T.A.=Face-threatening act

Within the text of the Collection of Tactics subjects in **bold face** are cross-references to other tactics in the section.

Collection of tactics

ACCOMMODATION

Task

To create and maintain bonding.

Description

When people communicate they often accommodate themselves in some degree to the language and associated communicative behaviors of the other, adjusting their words and grammar, pace, pronunciation, pauses and turn length to resemble the way the other participants act. There is a strong need for accommodation when communicating with children, people from other cultures, members of the other sex, superiors or inferiors, etc. All communicators should be able to adjust their communication in this way; it is a sign of a wish to be cooperative and help others understand.

Persuasive value

Accommodation occurs because there is a perceived need to decrease any discrepancies between people if good communication (and persuasion) are to take place. There is a lot of evidence that people dislike divergence, as witness such critical phrases as 'She doesn't talk like people round here,' 'He's always trying to be different,' or 'We never seem to be on the same wave length.' It can be based on differences in grammatical usage, in sentence structure, the use of technical or lay language, the wrong tone, and an unspecified sense of difference.

Accommodating one's communicating style to the other person improves an interaction because C.s try to put themselves in the other's place, and use the language in ways the other is likeliest to understand.

Persuasion can occur because C.s can show they 'belong' to the same world of experience as A. Consequently A. will be attracted to them as persons, and more inclined to heed what they say. The more A. is attracted by the general familiarity of what they say or how they say it the more likely he or she is to agree with it. 'He's just like me and he says the book is good so I'll read it.'

Though the similarities that are created by accommodation may only reside in the superficial aspects of language—word choice, pronunciations, etc., their depth of effect belies this.

Contrary tactic   Sometimes people can be persuaded not by similarity but by difference, because it is exciting, glamorous, or startlingly new. In such cases their awareness of difference prepares them to listen attentively, and this can result in a fuller adherence to what C. offers.

Further reading   Giles and Smith (1979)

ACCOUNT: CHOOSE

Tasks

To have an interpretation of an event accepted as true.
To present a communication as if C.'s goal is only to inform.

Description

An account presents information about an event. It differs from explanation in that C.s do not always understand everything about the material, do not vouch for its validity, but, as far as it is within their power to do so, give an honest account of something they have experienced. C.s can present themselves as merely a conduit through which information is passed: 'It's no use asking me what it means, I am just telling you what I experienced.' C.'s understanding of the material of the account can range from total certainty to puzzlement—so C. could give an account of a meal eaten, accurately, detail by detail, or could speak of a car accident: 'All I know is one minute I was driving along and then wham, and I woke up in hospital. I think the brakes must have failed, or perhaps the steering went.'

C.s can indicate their own involvement in what is being stated, that is, how far they are prepared to vouch for the account material, or they can leave the material to stand by itself.

Persuasive value

Since an account should be informative it will be well received the more it is organized. Its various parts should each be signalled as they begin and end, and any matters which are to be foregrounded should be clearly shown as such.

If it appears to have no other goal than to have A.s know what C. has experienced, then it is likely to be accepted. It will help if it does not seem too unusual or unlike what the A.s already know, either personally or through previous communications.

An account can persuade since it just appears to call for acceptance, and not full agreement. All that it seems to ask of A.s is that they understand that something happened as C. tells it. Yet in fact to do this is to add the matter of the account to A.s' experience where it will form part of their 'knowledge' and as such perhaps cause them to resist a later communication because it does not fit with the present account.

An account can also be persuasive if C.s show signs of thoughtful choice in language, for example, by hesitating before selecting a word, or using a word then explicitly rejecting it in favor of another, as in

Ex. 1 'It was, er a joint activity. Well no, I suppose it was more of a shared activity, with Bill in control.'

If C.s overtly express their concern to be accurate: 'as far as I could tell, it was . . .' and if they already have a truthful reputation, the account is likely to be accepted.

However, it should be noted that an account does not validate what happened; all that it does is supply a truthful representation of C.'s interpretation of the event. As information, therefore, accounts should be taken very carefully, and A.s should carefully examine any possibility that C. might have any persuasive goals beyond that of just passing on information.

See also **Explain; Express personal involvement**

Further reading Chaffee (1991); Dillon (1981); Freadman and Macdonald (1992); Nash (1980)

ACCUMULATION

Task

To persuade by sheer weight of evidence.

Description

C. can supply a vast number of details to support a view.

Persuasive value

1 By presenting so many details C. shows him or herself to be thoroughly prepared, knowledgeable, and a good researcher. All of these constitute a C. worth attending to, and being persuaded by.

2 The details themselves can present overwhelming evidence that the matter should be accepted.
3 While absorbing so many details, particularly if they follow closely on one another, A. has little time to find any item problematic, or to find any counterevidence to it.

The presentation of the items may take several forms.

(a) It may be a list which assumes all items are of equivalent value; but A. might find it hard to understand what constitutes equivalence and so be unable to object that any single item lacks it.
(b) It may be a list with the items in some order, for example, where the last item is a grand amalgam of the whole set.

> Ex. 1 We have a problem with . . ., we have a difficulty about . . ., in short, our whole operation is at grave risk of failure.

but A.s could fail to note that the last matter is not the sum of the others.
4 If it seems probable that one item may be noticed as out of place in the list, C. could explicitly recognize this, as in

> Ex. 2 There is X, and there is Y, and we could include here Z as well, though it is not quite the same as the others.

This could prevent someone else from objecting to the item. It also shows C. is taking care when claiming similarity for the items, and knows when one is different from the others. Such apparent care and fair-mindedness can be persuasive.

See also **Link material** tactics

Further reading   Sonnino (1968)

ACCURACY: SHOW DEGREE OF

Task

To make explicit the degree of accuracy with which C. presents the material.

Description

In both speech and writing, when C.s are not absolutely sure they have got the right term for what they wish to represent, they can indicate this by using a 'hedging' term, for example, 'sort of,' 'kind of,' 'more or less,' or 'roughly.'

Persuasive value

1 In speech, because of the swiftness with which it is produced, C.s know errors can happen when they present material. They often therefore overtly show the extent to which they assess themselves as accurate, and so avoid attack if others know more than they do. Or they may show their commitment to the accuracy of what they present, and so make it hard for A. to quarrel with it. In the first case, there may well be a large number of 'hedges' used, as in

Ex. 1 It was sort of pink.

Ex. 2 We were kind of relieved when we heard.

In informal speech it is also possible to add '-ish' to a term C. wishes to hedge, as in

Ex. 3 She looked sad-ish.

Such terms may or may not be accompanied by a qualification like 'I thought,' as in

Ex. 4 She looked happy, I thought.

Where C. is firmly convinced of the accuracy of his or her representation this can be indicated by such terms as 'absolutely,' 'positively,' as in

Ex. 5 She was positively radiant.

Ex. 6 It was an absolutely disastrous evening.

A.s should note these indications of C.'s commitment, and be wary of objecting if they do not wish to quarrel.

2 In written communications it is also possible to represent degrees of accuracy, but different 'hedges' must be used. In the most formal kinds of writing any uncertainty about accuracy is supposed to be edited out before the text is produced. Writing assumes that C.s have carefully presented the material to include only what they can vouch for. However, if it is still necessary to imply a reservation about accuracy; the acceptable hedges include 'more or less,' 'roughly' or 'to a degree,' as in

Ex. 7 The problem is one of, roughly, personnel.

Ex. 8 The lecture was more of a self-indulgence than anything.

Ex. 9 We found it was what one could call a personnel problem.

In the written form, such hedges would be more noticeable than in speech, and their existence will draw attention to the worry about accuracy. If this focus is not in C.'s interest hedges should not be used; A. may well interpret their presence to mean C. wants to put the accuracy on the interactional agenda.

Further reading Antaki (1988); Sonnino (1968)

ACCUSATION: CHOOSE

Task

To raise a matter of wrongdoing.

Description

In choosing accusation, a C. raises matters of guilt, blame, judgment, and standards. Once these are on the agenda they may have divisive effects, and can create oppositions. A useful accusation seeks not only to have blame attributed to the guilty, but also to begin the process of putting the situation right.

Persuasive value

Making an accusation, whether deserved or not, has several important persuasive consequences.
1 It risks interpersonal cooperation, not only between C. and the accused, but also with any others who might have a negative response to the accusation, so this act should be worth the risk.
2 It reveals C.'s attitudes to the matter under judgment (e.g. to lateness, to inefficiency) and shows how strongly these are held.
3 If made too strongly it can rebound on C. by causing others to sympathize with the accused.

N.B. If C. makes the accusation claiming that it is on behalf of others as well as him- or herself, the others must have agreed to it beforehand, or they may disclaim involvement and make C.'s position weak.

N.B. Accusation can be a useful mode of self-defense, as in 'You say I should stick to the point, but it is you who keep digressing from it.'

See also **Accuse**

Further reading Mulholland (1991)

ACCUSE

Task

To bring a claim of wrongdoing against someone.

Description

To accuse is to say that someone has done something which C. feels is wrong. In making an accusation C. should intend not only to have blame attributed to the guilty one, but also to begin the process of putting the situation right.

Persuasive value

An accusation is often made without proof, and may be improper or inaccurate in detail or attribution of blame; it should therefore include a quality of tentativeness, and begin in general terms, so that C. can withdraw it if necessary with little loss of face.

The following examples show how selecting different modes of tentativeness can vary the strength of an accusation, beginning with the weakest version.

1 Allow that there may be no fault, and so provide a loophole in case withdrawal of the accusation is necessary:

Ex. 1 I notice there's no sign of your report yet.

(i.e. there may be some problem in report delivery or it may be that you have not done it—if the first is true, no accusation would follow).

2 Do not directly name the accused:

Ex. 2 Someone has left the door open

3 Be non-specific about the nature of the fault:

Ex. 3 This report has not been done well.

4 Show only mild feeling about the matter that is wrong, and the accused's role in it, as in both Examples 2 and 3.

5 Accuse the group of which A. is a member, rather than A. in person:

Ex. 4 Your service division has been slack about deliveries lately.

6 Name a consequence of the fault, which heightens it:

Ex. 5 Your section of the report is late, and has delayed the whole program.

7 Directly address the accused, show strong feeling, be specific, note that it is not a first offense, and name the consequences:

Ex. 6 Bill, your damned report is a week late, again, so we are all held up: this is quite unacceptable.

See also **Accusation: choose**

Further reading   Mulholland (1991); Wierzbicka (1987)

ADVERBS: ADD COMMENTS

Task

To offer (or avoid) explicit comments which show one's attitude to the matter being represented.

Description

One can add clauses of comment to reveal one's attitude to some matter being represented. These clauses do not add to the representation of the matter, but indicate how the communicator regards it, as in:

Ex. 1 And to make matters worse, we lost our travellers' checks.

Ex. 2 It was, you know, really awful to see.

Ex. 3 To be absolutely frank, I would have to say that I found your play boring.

Ex. 4 I suppose we ought to be pleased that things are not worse.

Ex. 5 It was, I believe, his first film.

Equally, one can delete such clauses if it is important to conceal an attitude.

Persuasive value

The comments which are added can perform quite different roles, though they all make it clear to A. how C. regards the material.

In Ex. 1, C. says that the loss made matters worse. Since any loss of this kind would be bad, and A. is unlikely to disagree, all that this comment could be meant to do is to make a dramatic matter out of the loss. It shows that C. feels strongly about the loss, and also, perhaps, is trying to design a good narrative. The comment itself has little new or useful meaning for A. other than this.

In Ex. 2, 'you know' is not calling on A. to remember how awful 'it' was, but rather sounds like a comment which substitutes for careful description, saving C. effort, and asking A. to agree that C. can do this. (However, there are many other meanings for **'y'know'**.)

In Ex. 3, the comment is a warning that a face-threatening act will follow. This is one way to modify the impact of the act, and so to save the face of those involved with the play.

In Ex. 4, C.'s comment 'I suppose' is a way of expressing an unhappiness with the following statement. It lets A. know that C. feels obliged to sound optimistic (there is a convention that this is better social behavior than pessimism) but does not really believe the optimistic view.

In Ex. 5, C. indicates an uncertainty about the truth of what he or she is saying. Given that this is so, one could ask why C. bothered to say it at all, except that ordinary talk is full of such uncertainties, and people find them quite acceptable.

See also **Face threats: recognize**

Further reading Leech and Svartvik (1975); Quirk, Greenbaum, Leech, and Svartvik (1985)

ADVERBS: STATE CAUSES

Tasks

To specify the causes or reasons or purposes for some matter.
To judge that something is a cause or reason for something else.

Description

Adverbial phrases can indicate what causes some matter, as in

Ex. 1 If she signs the contract, then we will be able to go ahead.

Ex. 2 He applied for the job out of interest.

Ex. 3 She arrived late because she likes to make a dramatic entrance.

Persuasive value

In Ex. 1, the adverbial clause, 'if she signs the contract' appears just to be a factual proposition which leads to another, 'then we will go ahead.' However, in Ex. 2, while the main part of the sentence states a (provable) fact, 'he applied for the job,' the adverbial phrase then adds what could be an equally factual account of the cause of the job application, 'out of interest.' But this might be not factual at all, and just be the opinion of the speaker. By presenting this in an adverbial phrase attached unobtrusively to the sentence, C. may hope that his or her opinion may be accepted as a fact, just as the first part of the sentence is. It may not matter whether the phrase 'out of interest' is opinion or not, since it is a positive thing to say, but C. might have said 'He applied for the job out of sheer boredom,' which is much more negative, and if accepted could damage the man's chance of employment. A.s should test such statements to see just how true they are: 'How do you know he did?'

In Ex. 3, the clause adds an opinion, one which reflects badly on the woman. It adds to the fact of her being late, an egotistic reason for it. A.s should again test such statements to see just what evidence there is for them.

Further reading   Leech and Svartvik (1975); Quirk, Greenbaum, Leech, and Svartvik (1985)

ADVERBS: STATE FREQUENCY

Tasks

To indicate the frequency with which something is done.
To show the significance of the frequency with which something is done.

Description

It is possible to indicate the frequency with which something happens by using adverbs, or adverb phrases and clauses. It can be an absolute frequency, as in

Ex. 1 People often take irrational dislikes to others.

or one expressed in relative terms, as in

Ex. 2 We go to the beach every weekend.

Persuasive value

The kinds of absolute frequency with which a thing can be done can range from very frequent—represented by 'usually,' 'normally,' 'generally,'—through less frequent—'often,' 'sometimes,' 'occasionally,'—to the least frequent—'seldom,' 'rarely,' 'hardly ever.' Relatively, one can relate the frequency to a measure of time, as in 'once a week,' 'every few days,' 'monthly,' 'annually,' 'twice a year,' 'every other day.'

   The persuasive significance of indicating frequency in the first, absolute, way is that it reveals the patterns of behavior of C., as in 'We normally have supper about 6 P.M..' These can be used by those hearing them to form an impression. If it matches with their own behavior, it can form common ground, and be used directly in persuasion.

   Another significance is that terms like 'normally' suggest that there is a norm of behavior, usually the one C. follows, so that anyone who does not follow it is 'abnormal.'

   The absolute frequency terms can be misleading, precisely because they do not specify a measure of time; for example, at a job interview one should be wary of a question like:

Ex. 3 Do you accept the need to work late on a regular basis?

'Regular' could mean once a week, once a month, or every other night. While if a child one is babysitting says

Ex. 4 Mommy lets me stay up to watch T.V.

with no frequency signal, one should ask how often: it may turn out to be once a year on the child's birthday. Or if one asked a colleague to help with a report and she replied 'O.K., I've done this kind of report before, no trouble,' one might need to ask 'How often?' before accepting the help.

Further reading   Leech and Svartvik (1975); Quirk, Greenbaum, Leech, and Svartvik (1985)

ADVERBS: STATE MANNER

Tasks

To indicate the manner in which something is done.
To show one's attitude to the manner in which something is done.

Description

It is possible to indicate how something happens, that is, in what manner it occurs, by using adverbs, or adverb phrases and clauses, as in:

Ex. 1 She has finished the report very efficiently.

Ex. 2 He did the work like an experienced executive.

Ex. 3 He did his teaching the way he always does.

Ex. 4 She delivered that message as if she was running for a train.

Persuasive value

In Ex. 1 there is no real need to offer information about the manner in which something is done: it would be quite acceptable to end the sentence with 'the report.' By adding the manner, one can add a personal judgment. This happens to be a positive judgment, but it could equally be a negative one, as in 'She finished the report in a mad dash,' or 'without checking her facts,' etc. Manner phrases like these allow scope for opinion to masquerade as fact.

In Ex. 2, the manner is also represented positively, at least if one approves of (a) experienced executives, and (b) this man working as if he were one. It might, for instance, be a negative judgment if 'he' were a young child behaving in a manner much older than his years. The manner in this example is represented by analogy.

In Ex. 3, the manner is expressed vaguely, that is, to understand its meaning one would have to know about the man's previous history. C. might be trying to exclude others from understanding what is being offered, or might be deliberately using the shared bond with others to reinforce it.

In Ex. 4, the manner represented is clearly negative: one is not supposed to deliver messages in a hurried way. So just by using this brief phrase C. can imply the woman's lack of knowledge of social conventions.

Further reading   Leech and Svartvik (1975); Quirk, Greenbaum, Leech, and Svartvik (1985)

ADVERBS: STATE MEANS

Tasks

To indicate by what means something happened.
To show one's opinion about the means by which something happened.

Description

C.s can show how some event or act or happening came about, by naming its means or instrument, as in:

Ex. 1 This came by mail today.

Ex. 2 The villain was caught by means of fingerprints.

Ex. 3 We decided on the final grades for the course by using an average of the marks.

Persuasive value

In each of these examples, the first part of the sentence is apparently factual, while the second, which states the instrument or means by which the thing happened, may be opinion rather than fact. So, in Ex. 1, it can presumably be proved that 'this' arrived, and it may be possible to prove that it came by mail, but this may not be as easily provable as its arrival.

In Ex. 2, it is more possible that the second part 'by means of fingerprints' is not as factually true as the first part, that 'the villain has been caught.' One could easily guess that other strategies were adopted in the search for the villain, and that fingerprints were perhaps only the final proof. But this form of words omits any mention of all the other instruments used—one might wonder why.

In Ex. 3, the means by which a final grade for a course is determined could be of considerable interest to students, yet in indicating the means by which this was determined, a good deal is left unsaid. What does it mean to say that 'an average' was used? By what process was the average worked out? Is it the average for each individual student which is worked out to produce a grade for that student, or is it that the average of all the students' marks is worked out to produce a grade for each student?

Further reading   Leech and Svartvik (1975); Quirk, Greenbaum, Leech, and Svartvik (1985)

ADVERBS: STATE TIME

Task

To indicate the time at which something happened.

Description

It is possible to represent the time as a fixed point, as in

Ex. 1 She went there last month.

Ex. 2 He saw it on the l6th.

But time can also indicate a period of time, as in

Ex. 3 I saw it during the month.

Ex. 4 It happened while I was working on the essay.

Persuasive value

C.s have a choice as to whether they designate time precisely, or loosely, as in

Ex. 5 I saw it last month.

Ex. 6 I saw it on the l5th of June.

Ex. 7 I haven't seen it for ages, oh it must be several weeks ago.

By being vague and non-specific, as in Ex. 5, C.s tell little about the time of the event, but do reveal that they think in terms of months as units of time. Others may more incline to see time as sailors do, in terms of tides, or as students do, in terms of weeks or semesters. This might be useful information, for example if wanting to get this C. to perform some task; one could be fairly sure that it would not be finished quickly. On the other hand, the C. of Ex. 6 could be predicted to name a precise date and to meet it.

The speaker in Ex. 7 reveals that he or she thinks that a few weeks is 'ages' (i.e. an appreciable time). Others might think that only a year or a decade is an appreciable amount of time, but this person thinks in weeks. By noting this one can see whether the speaker shares the same sense of time as oneself. This could be of importance in any matter of joint action, timekeeping, arranging meetings, etc., and it is something that often causes trouble in sociability – for example when one friend is always late because she thinks in large sweeps of time, while the other is always early because he thinks in smaller sweeps. Such differences could be exacerbated in communicating across cultures.

See also **Sociable language**

Further reading Leech and Svartvik (1975); Quirk, Greenbaum, Leech, and Svartvik (1985)

ADVISE

Tasks

To give counsel to someone.
To indicate that a course of action is good or bad.

Description

Advisers assume (a) that the hearer needs to be advised about something; (b) what it is that the hearer needs to be advised about; and (c) that they have the right to offer advice. Each of these assumptions could be erroneous.

Alternatively, if advice is requested, C.s should note (a) the terms in which the request was made; (b) what exactly is required; and (c) what A. has already been done about the matter, so that the advice can be relevant, timely and useful.

Persuasive value

Advising is a dominant act because C. tries to direct A.'s future behavior, perhaps by recommending particular acts. Certainly C.s will imply these are good for A., but this means C.s know what is best for A.

An adviser might use one of the following forms:

Ex. 1 I always do X . . ., you might find it useful too.

Ex. 2 If I were you, I would ask Bill to organize that.

Ex. 3 Why don't you ask Bill?

Ex. 4 You must ask Bill to organize that: he's the expert.

Ex. 1 reveals C.'s own behavior and suggests that A. share it. It does not presume too much, and phrases the suggestion mildly: 'You might find it useful.' Ex. 2 assumes a likeness between C. and A. and builds C.'s advice on this. It is only mildly authoritative and should not arouse hostility. If either of these kinds of advice is rejected, the only damage will be to stress difference between the two participants.

In Ex. 3 the advice is minimally influential, but it still constrains A.s (to give a reason if they wish to reject the advice) and may make them feel awkward if, for example, they wish to say 'I think I know more than Bill.'

A stronger version is Ex. 4 which insists that A. takes the advice ('you must'), and although it supplies a reason ('he's the expert'), the phrasing is an oblique criticism of A. ('you are not an expert'), and offers double advice: that A. ask Bill, and also recognize Bill as an expert.

Even if given good advice, A. may reject C.'s dominance in giving it.

N.B.   The timing of advice needs care, particularly when writing. The (good) advice, 'You should always buy the best equipment,' is annoying if too late, and received when A.'s equipment has already broken down.

N.B.   Some people seek advice when what they really want is support for what they have done.

Further reading   Mulholland (1991); Wierzbicka (1987)

ANALOGY

Tasks

To explain something new.
To persuade A. to a new attitude about a point.

Description

Analogy is a comparison of one matter with another, indicating that they greatly resemble each other.

Analogy can be used to explain some matter new to A., by suggesting that it is like something well known to A., and that therefore the new thing should be taken to have a similar meaning (e.g. a computer could be explained as being like a mechanical brain).

Persuasive value

When used to persuade A. to take a desired attitude about one matter, C.s should choose a matter for comparison about which A. already holds the desired attitude, and suggest that since the two resemble each other, they should be accepted in the same way. Analogy can fail if A. does not think that there is enough similarity between the two matters.

1 If, for example, C. wanted to show how John Smith is clumsy in personal relations with his colleagues, it could be done by analogy. For example, he could be compared to a 'bull in a china shop.' This familiar phrase would bring to A.'s mind a whole set of behaviors—the equivalent of a bull breaking things and spoiling things in the china shop—and make A. see John Smith as like the bull. However, this particular analogy has a problem, because it compares physical with psychological acts, and they are very different. But it is a cliché that has been so frequently used that A.'s memory probably holds a stock of instances where it has been used much like it is in the present example. So the chances are that this analogy would work to show A. 'that John Smith among people at work behaves psychologically much like a bull in a china shop behaves physically.'

2 An analogy used to support a point in argument needs to rest on a better comparison than this, as in:

Ex. 1 Some people claim that women incite sexual assault because they dress provocatively, but these same people do not claim that men who drive fancy cars provoke car theft.

Here the analogy is used to argue that if A. agrees about the lack of blame in the second part, he or she should show the same attitude to women over provocative dress, since the two things are here made closely comparable. Such analogies will fail if A. can see more differences than similarities between the two matters, or if A. were to believe that men who drive fancy cars do provoke theft.

To work well, the comparison should be highly relevant to the point at issue, and should have nothing extra in it which might cause distraction.

Further reading   Corbett (1977, 1990); Sonnino (1968)

ANTILANGUAGE

Tasks

To exclude people from a group.
To include people in an atypical group.

Description

The term describes language which is used deliberately to show difference or deviation (e.g. Cockney rhyming slang, rap, and the private language of drug addicts). In extreme cases, the language shows opposition to the norms of society. While antilanguage is likely to be found mainly in restricted circles—'subcultures' or 'countercultures'—there is one kind of antilanguage which is more common. It takes the form of an excess of colloquialities and swearwords where the general community would find them inappropriate, and, particularly, it focusses on bluntness, and a refusal to use politeness.

Persuasive value

1 Antilanguage creates an in-group solidarity of great strength, especially as it is based on opposition to others, not just difference from them. Using it as a sign of group solidarity can bring influence to bear on the group who employ it. However, the best way to do this is not to pretend to be a member of the group but simply to show that their (anti)language is known and accepted.

2 In some cases antilanguage indicates to others that those using it see themselves as in rebellion or in revolutionary mode with respect to society; where this is so, any tactics which appeal to the norms of society, its beliefs, standards, etc., will make only a negative impact.

3 Where it is used by the atypical group in an attempt to get attention from the community, it is often because they feel they are unfairly ignored or given insufficient freedom to be the group and individuals they wish to be. Where this appears to be the case, the most persuasive tactics may be to acknowledge their presence, their individuality, and their difference, and to build on these.

See also **Politeness tactics**

Further reading   Halliday (1978)

ANTITHESIS

Tasks

To bring together two opposed ideas to give each one a richer meaning.
To give an impression of wit and cleverness.

Description

Antithesis is the juxtaposition of two contrasting or opposed ideas to focus the mind on some aspect of their meanings which is of value to the communication. The juxtaposition usually involves using parallel grammatical structures for the two different ideas so that the comparison between them is easily seen.

Persuasive value

1 The tactic can be used to bring together two ideas which are not in fact opposed, and suggest that they are, as in

Ex. 1 Cunning students despise study; foolish students worship it.

Here a false opposition between cunning and foolishness is created, partly by the grammatical similarity between the two clauses, and partly because the two verbs 'despise' and 'worship' are rationally opposed. However, the rational opposite of cunning is naivety, and of foolishness is wisdom, but this may be concealed and mislead any A.s who accept the antithesis. Further, the grammatical parallel between the two clauses, and hence its aphoristic appearance, suggests that the whole of the issue of student types and attitudes to study is covered in the sentence, and this is surely not so.
2 Where there is a juxtaposition of true opposites, C. can intend that something special about the meaning of each will be drawn out by the act of juxtaposition. So, for example in

Ex. 2 The faculty thought him an unproductive colleague; the students
        thought him an inspiring teacher.

The fact that his colleagues and his students varied so much in their judgments of him is worth mention for its own sake, but C. has tried to make a stronger point than this, to suggest that being an inspiring teacher is precisely what would make colleagues think him unproductive: that his colleagues think it a bad thing to be a good teacher. And so rouse A. to an understanding of the opposed judgments about the same thing.
3 The use of antithesis shows C. to be skilled at language use, aware of the relative values of different sentence structurings, and would win C. a reputation for wit.

Further reading   Corbett (1977, 1990); Sonnino (1968)

APOLOGIZE

Tasks

To express regret for a past action.
To avoid blame for a future act.

Description

1 Apologizing involves a face-threatening act for C.s, because it acknowledges that they have performed an act which others (may) condemn. (Since it depends on other's recognition that a regrettable event has occurred, it is possible to apologize mistakenly.) It is important to analyze one's actions for possible faults, and note any signs of condemnation in others, so that an apology can rectify the situation. An unnecessary apology is better than no apology.
2 An apology can acknowledge that a future act is likely to attract blame

and so may be a pre-emptive attempt to reduce the blame. It often takes the form 'I'm sorry but I will have to . . .' or 'I'm sorry if it causes problems, but we simply must deal with . . .' These justify the act by claiming necessity, and suggesting that some unspecified force is prompting the action rather than the personal whim of C.

Persuasive value

Apologies can take any of these forms.
1 Pure formality, as in 'We deeply regret the inconvenience . . .' or 'It is incumbent on me to accept responsibility on behalf of my staff . . .' Such apologies are not taken as personal expressions of regret.
2 An admission that an offense has been committed, as in 'There has been an office relocation, and some things have gone astray, including your file.' This is a very minimal apology, containing no regret, and accepting no blame. It will be sufficient for minor faults, or where people often have to apologize to each other.
3 An admission that C. has personally committed an offense, as in 'I've lost your file,' or 'We have lost your file, and I must take some of the blame for that.' Beyond the acceptance of blame there is no regret or explanation. How this is received will depend on how important the loss is for A.
4 An apology with expressions of regret, from 'I've lost your pen, I'm afraid,' to 'I'm terribly sorry, but I've lost your pen.' If the degree of regret matches A.'s sense of loss, this will work well.
5 An offer to make restitution, as in 'I've lost your pen, but I will replace it with a new one,' with no recognition of blame, no regret, no explanation. Most people are content enough with restitution, and indeed if it is not included in an apology may feel it is insufficient.

Further reading   Mulholland (1991); Owen (1983); Wierzbicka (1987)

APPEAL

Tasks

To seek help to prevent something bad happening.
To have someone do something that C. wants done.

Description

To appeal to someone is to seek to cause him or her to bring about a good situation, or to prevent a bad one. To appeal to someone is to ask that they consider doing something, but in doing this the appealer knows that no compulsion can be brought to bear, that it must be left to the good will of the person who is appealed to. Appealing to someone is usually done as a public act, either spoken before witnesses, or in writing which could be shown to others. It is also public in that it is often addressed to someone in their public role, so a taxpayer could appeal to the Mayor to get the streets cleaned.

Persuasive value

For an appeal to work, C. must be certain that the person appealed to is someone who can really help.

C.s must also consider the implications of their own position when they appeal to someone. The act of appealing automatically puts C. into a position of low authority, that of one who wants to have something happen but who cannot make it happen, that is, as powerless but wanting power.

An appeal is made by someone who cannot force the other person to do anything. Its success therefore will rest entirely on the amount of persuasion C. can bring to it. Most appeals use emotion to influence the person: this happens in two ways: C. makes the appeal somewhat emotionally, and/or appeals to the emotions of the other person. Both are present in:

Ex. 1 Dear Mayor Smith,
        I appeal to you on behalf of our furry friends, the cats of this fine city of ours, to set up a program to force cat-owners to have their pets vaccinated. You love cats I know, and must hate, as I do, to see them suffer unnecessarily. Could you please use your powers to stamp out these dreadful cat diseases? It needs a national attack, and you could lead the way on this.

C.s must carefully consider whether they wish to be observed in this emotional condition, and whether therefore it is better not to perform the act of appealing, but to choose one of the other possible acts to bring about their goals: arguing, demanding, asking, etc.

Further reading   Wierzbicka (1987)

APPOSITION

Tasks

To present two versions of a thing side by side so that the two are accepted as joined and equivalent in meaning.

To have C.'s judgment of a matter accepted.
To add extra detail on a matter and have it accepted.

Description

Apposition is the presentation side by side of two versions of a common referent, as in 'Our parent company, // Smith International, has posted a good profit.'

Persuasive values

Because it is routinely used as here, where the second part is just a reformulation of the first, and the words 'namely/that is/in other words,' could be used between the two versions, it can suggest in other instances that two dissimilar matters are identical. This is supported by the close juxtaposition of the two versions: by the way each one could act grammatically in place of the other in the sentence structure, and by the way the relation between the two versions is left unstated, as if it were unnecessary because they are identical.

Ex. 1 John Brown, the well-known utopian, is visiting Boston.

1 Here the word 'utopian' is an opinion, an adverse judgment of the worth of John Brown, presented as if it were just a synonym for his name. Other terms with less bias could have been used, for example, 'scientist,' or 'writer,' if John Brown is in these professions; but C. can hope that the appositional form will cause A. not to notice the bias in the judgment. It will, however, only work if the bias is not too obvious; A. would be more likely to notice if C. used the term 'fanatic' or 'day-dreamer.'
2 Using the appositional form to present two versions of the same thing makes the bias not only difficult to see but also difficult to argue against, as in:

Ex. 2 Be assertive, leave home and find yourself.

where, if A. notices at all that these two things are not identical, and so wishes to object to them being equated, then he or she would need (a) to effect a reformulation, and (b) to find a grammatical way to express it: perhaps 'No, leaving home is not a matter of being assertive, it's something different. . . .' This involves a deal of cognitive work, and it is likely that A. will only take the trouble if he or she strongly contests the point. It also might take so long to achieve that C. might have moved on to another matter before A. manages it, and thus it may be out of place and interruptive to raise it.
3 Contrast the form of Ex. 1 with the non-appositional form used in

Ex. 3 John Brown is a well-known visionary.

Here the form makes it clear that C. is presenting a proposition, and so it could be more easily contested: A. could easily retort 'No, he is not.' This version also provides a grammatical structuring which A. could easily echo in a response, 'No, he's a well-known scientist.' The easier it is for A. to produce an argumentative response, the more A. is likely to do it.

See also **Apposition: types**

Further reading   Leech and Svartvik (1975); Quirk, Greenbaum, Leech, and Svartvik (1985)

APPOSITION: TYPES

Tasks

To strengthen or emphasize a point.
To substitute one's own version of matter.
To alter A.'s point.
To prioritize points to suit oneself.
To present two versions of a thing side by side so that the two are accepted as joined and equivalent in meaning.
To have C.'s judgment of a matter accepted,
To add extra detail on a matter and have it accepted.

Description

Apposition is the presentation side by side of two versions of a common referent, as in 'Our parent company, // Smith International, has posted a good profit.'

Persuasive value

1 A point can be strengthened or emphasized by juxtaposing a factor which supports it, as in

Ex. 1 My sister, // a lawyer, considers we should do this.

Ex. 2 Company Regulations, // C.R. Item 23.45, permit this.

Using the appositional form means that the support is offered so quickly after the point is first raised that it is hard for A. to separate the two: he or she receives the point almost simultaneously with a reason for agreeing with it, and this makes it hard to resist. So just when A. might be preparing to resist the 'sister's' advice, C. strengthens its value by adding that it is a legal opinion. C. can also emphasize a point by using a second term which repeats the first, but with extra detail, as in

Ex. 3 Our meeting, and // a most fruitful meeting it was, produced the following plan.

A point can also be strengthened by adding as second term a correction of the first, as in

Ex. 4 The whole team, that is, // all those involved in this project, agreed on this.

N.B. Such self-corrections appear to be a sign of C.'s honesty and accuracy, or at least that C. holds honesty and accuracy to be important.

2 By using the appositional form, C.s can represent a matter to suit their views. Typically an abstract word—idea, decision, plan—is used as first term, and then a specific summary is added as second term, as in

Ex. 5 The plan // that we should cooperate was well received.

For example, here C. represents the plan as being 'that we should cooperate,' though this could be a very partial or biassed account of the 'plan,' while C. also represents 'that we should cooperate' as being a 'plan' where others might see it as a 'policy' or 'routine behavior,' etc.

3 C. can produce a version of a matter which gives priority or importance to his or her opinion, as in:

Ex. 6 Our prime concern, // the allocation of space to office staff, is receiving attention.

It may be only C. who sees this as a 'prime' concern, but the form again makes it difficult for A. both to recognize the partiality of the view expressed and to object to it. Another way to give priority to C.'s own views is, for example,

Ex. 7 The time has come to choose between our options // to stagnate or to expand.

Here the options offered may set the agenda that C. wants, unless A. quickly notices that there could be other options (or notice the bias expressed in the word 'stagnate').

N.B. Such appositions are often criticized as tautological in using both the general term (e.g. 'plan') and the specific (e.g. 'that we should cooperate),' but this is to ignore the way they can be used to persuasive effect.

Further reading   Leech and Svartvik (1975); Quirk, Greenbaum, Leech, and Svartvik (1985)

ARCHAISMS

Tasks

To bring wit to support an idea.
To impress others with one's language knowledge.

Description

Archaisms are words and phrases which are not in current or recent usage. They can be (a) still current forms which differ in meaning from what they represented in the past; or (b) the use of clearly non-current words or phrases.

Persuasive value

1 To use currently used words for their historical meanings is to use terms which others are unlikely to share; indeed the tactic suggests that C. uses them precisely for this reason, to show that he or she has different (and more?) knowledge than those he or she is communicating with. It is a dangerous tactic because it will not only cause confusion, but it may not even be noticed that confusion has occurred. A.s would assume the word had its current meaning and not question it. For example, it would be foolish to use 'pretend' in its eighteenth-century meaning of 'having pretensions to something,' (as in 'The Old Pretender'), since the modern meaning of the word, 'to be false in some deed,' is both like and unlike the old one, and the confusion could be serious.

2 To use words or phrases which are recognizably archaisms must be in the hope that A.s will be awed by C.'s historical knowledge of language, or C.'s wide reading. However, they are likely to give much less weight to this awe if they sense that C. is deliberately using a word they cannot be expected to understand.

Ex. 1 Certes, i'faith, we are twixt the devil and the deep blue sea, me-
    thinks, are you with me?

In this instance, however, the antique flavor might be quite acceptable, as humorous, since nothing of importance is represented through it, and it contains another kind of old-fashioned language, a **proverb**, which is known. It also has an ending in which C. gives the impression of losing control of the archaic language, and therefore presents as less skilled and more like A.

Further reading   Sonnino (1968)

ARGUMENT: CHOOSE

Tasks

To have others accept a viewpoint which is debatable.
To have others reject an accepted viewpoint.

Description

To argue is to take a position on a contentious matter and to use reason and supporting evidence, etc., to have others share the position. Once started it is difficult to stop an argument, so ask whether an argument would be a better tactic than using another genre (e.g. account, description, assertion or persuasion).
Factors to consider:
   1 If it is reasonable to assume agreement or only a mild disagreement on the issue, argument is unnecessary and pointless.
   2 Consider the consequences of winning or losing the argument – would they be desirable in the long run? For example, one can win an argument but in the process damage a friendly relationship with those who lose it.
   3 Consider whether it is possible to win, even if the best reasons are marshalled in support of a viewpoint. And ask who would support the case; if they would be inappropriate allies it might be better to forgo the argument than be associated with them.
   4 Consider whether it would be possible to live with losing the argument. And whether the desired aims could be better achieved by other means.
   5 Constant arguers are seen as unpleasant and difficult to work with, so C. should pick the occasion for argument well, make clear that it has operational value, and should monitor the number of arguments that he or she initiates.

Persuasive value

1 Since an argument by its nature recognizes the existence of a different view from that held by C., it can act to entrench that difference rather than to abolish it. It allows A. to consolidate his or her views on the matter in order to defeat C.'s position. It sets up an opposition in the process of trying to diminish it, and so can be counterproductive.

2 Argument sets the structure of the interaction as adversarial, and this may have both immediate and residual effects.

3 Choosing argument stops the interaction from moving to easy compromise or a gradual maneuvering towards acceptance or rejection, because its goals and its approach work to have one view prevail to the exclusion of another. It also requires one to show a public acceptance of another's conquest, which involves loss of face.

4 In arguing, C. discloses both a viewpoint, and a strength of commitment to it, and as the argument proceeds other aspects of his or her opinions, attitudes, even feelings, which might better remain covert, can be revealed in the heat of battle .

5 As an argument proceeds, it may actually cause disagreement where none previously existed, because as details are added, or reasons are adduced, A. may realize that he or she opposes these, though in agreement with the basic proposition which began the argument.

6 The initiator who starts by assuming an opposition and then finds there is none will be be revealed as a bad judge of A.'s views.

The best ways to handle the initiation of an argument are:

(a) to begin by raising the point and seeing whether there is need for argument;
(b) to suggest that the argument is merely being reported (i.e. belongs to someone unspecified, so leaving the way open to attribute responsibility elsewhere if the argument becomes unproductive);
(c) to suggest it is being raised solely as a basis for discussion, without commitment.

See also the other **Argument** tactics; **Genre: choose**; **Idea arrangement**

Further reading   Jacobs and Jackson (1981); Schiffrin (1985, 1991)

ARGUMENT: COMPLEX PROPOSITIONS

Task

To focus attention on main points of a complex proposition in argument.

Description

There are two main types of complex propositions.

1 Hypothetical propositions, of the kind: 'If X then Y.'

Ex. 1 If we find the workload is too great, then we must reallocate it.

2 Double propositions, of the kind: 'Either X or Y happened,' or 'Either we do X or we do Y.'

> Ex. 2 Either we insist on a policy of voluntary retirement or we start laying off people.

Both present problems, which could lead to non-productive outcomes for C.

Persuasive value

1 This type can cause debate about the projected possibility before the main point is tackled, and it may make the main point worthless. C. could be seen as unprepared or disorganized because the proposition was not well-enough handled for a useful debate. A better version would be 'Is the workload too great?' and after that was settled, if it was still relevant, 'a reallocation is necessary' could be offered.
2 This type can cause A.s to deal simultaneously with 'voluntary retirement' and 'lay-off' (i.e., two different arguments could begin, without a joint focus, and C. may be held responsible for the confusion).

Sometimes such double propositions are necessary and useful. For this to be true, there must only be the two named alternatives. If there is a third, the proposition is easily defeated, as being incomplete, and C. as being ill prepared. For example, the following is a bad double proposition:

> Ex. 3 Feminists should stop trying to change the language and should try to change job inequalities instead.

because A. could retort 'Why not do both?' or 'There is another change needed—free childcare provision.'

Further reading   Corbett (1990); Jacobs and Jackson (1981); Schiffrin (1985)

ARGUMENT DESIGN

Task

To arrange the points to their best advantage.

Description

An arguer needs to consider how best to marshall his or her points, emphases, examples, and rebuttals of the opposing view. They need to be incorporated into the standard argument design, which comprises preamble, proposition, main body of the points, and conclusion.

Persuasive value

1. C. should consider the following questions:

(a) What is the justification for the argument? (This should go into the preamble, and an escape route should be left in case argument turns out to be an inappropriate activity.)
(b) What is the precise proposition to be argued?
(c) What main and subordinate points are to be used?

2 All terms should be chosen with A. in mind, and clarified to prevent misunderstanding.

3 Care should be taken to state only what is useful with no distracting details or digressions; not to descend to personalities; and not to become unsuitably emotional.

4 The main line of argument should be easily summarized, the main points should be clearly distinguished from minor ones, and all the points should be quite separable from examples and illustrations. The ideas should be linked. This can be done by:

(a) articulating a master plan for the order of ideas in an early sentence and then following it, as in:

  Ex. 1 There are *three* reasons for a change in policy . . . *First*, . . . *Second*, . . . *Third*, . . .

(b) repeating a word from one sentence to another, as in

  Ex. 2 We know that policy has lately been a *problem*. It's a *problem* of management, but *we* are not alone in this. *Others* play a part, since their work affects the *implementation* of policy. And policy without the possibility of *implementation* is of little value.

(c) or by repeating grammatical patterns, as in

  Ex. 3 *It is a matter of* policy. *It is* also *a matter of* management . . . *It is* finally *a matter of* personnel . . .

(d) good use of connective words, as in

  Ex. 4 It is *not only* a case of policy . . . *but also* a matter which needs treatment . . . *Therefore* we must do . . . *However*, there are exceptions . . . *On the one hand* . . ., and *on the other hand* . . .

The conclusion of an argument needs careful planning, since A.s remember best the first and last points in an argument, and are less likely to recall the middle points (unless one provokes strong debate).

See also the other **Argument** tactics; **Link material**

Further reading   Dillon (1981); Jacobs and Jackson (1981); Schiffrin (1985)

ARGUMENT DESIGN: SPOKEN

Task

To arrange the points to their best advantage.

Description

An arguer needs to consider how best to marshall his or her points, emphases, examples, or rebuttals of the opposing view. They need to be incorporated into the standard argument design, which comprises preamble, proposition, main body of the points, and conclusion.

Persuasive value

If the argument is in spoken form, C. must recognize that at any phrase or sentence end, even of the first articulation of the proposition, A. could interrupt with some point. This must be dealt with, and if possible the original plan should then be continued (a summary of the progress so far may be useful to both C. and A.) though A.'s intervention may mean serious disruption to the plan, and important adjustments may need to be made. To prevent this being too difficult to handle, C.'s preparation for an argument with A. should include using memories of previous argument encounters with A. so as to predict both when and with what objections A. will interrupt.

Since losing a spoken argument involves immediate loss of face, opportunities should be provided to allow A. to withdraw his or her opposition without too much indignity. For example, C.s should accept any signs of agreement without making an adverse comment; or they should allow A. a minor victory before he or she loses the war. (People often respond to losing an argument by such petty acts as correcting C.'s misuse of a word, or the ungrammaticality of a sentence; C.s would be wise to accept this and not retort or raise objections.)

More positively, C.s should allow for different ways of accepting the argument, and therefore give A. some freedom of choice in his or her response. Or they should give A. an opportunity to gain face afterwards, as in

Ex. 1   So, O.K., we are agreed this sounds reasonable. The next thing we need to consider is whether to do X or to do Y. Sam, you're the expert, what do you think?

See also **Argument preamble**; **Argument proposition: form**; **Face: sustain**

Further reading   Jacobs and Jackson (1981); Schiffrin (1985)

ARGUMENT INSERTION

Task

To insert an argument into an interaction.

Description

Argument is an oppositional activity with potential to damage the bonding between those involved, and so it should not be started lightly. Its starting point, as it is inserted into the interaction, should be signalled clearly.

Persuasive value

The start should be signalled so that those who do not wish to engage in argument have a chance to escape from it before it gets underway. It should also include some sign that C. knows of its dangers, has important reasons for starting it, and has good intentions in so doing.
1 This could be done, for example, by beginning with a summary of the discussion to that point, which shows (truly or not) that an argument has been incipient for some time. This acts to make C. simply the one who has recognized the need to have an argument:

Ex. 1 So far, as I understand it, we seem to be saying two quite different
        things; that . . . and that . . . We need to get this settled before we
        go on.

Note the loopholes left for the others to resist the argument: they could claim that C. has not 'understood' it, or that they had not been 'saying two different things,' or that even if all this were true, there is no need to settle matters at this stage.
2 An argument can be signalled as both acceptance and partial resistance to a view previously expressed, this shows a link to what has gone before, and shows the argument to be an outcome rather than a new event. This again shows C. in a better light than as one who deliberately starts a divisive activity.

Ex. 2 I agree when you say . . . but I can't accept your point about . . ., so
        I would argue [a modified view of what has gone before].

3. An argument can be inserted as showing that others have so far neglected some major aspect of the situation, so that they are to blame for not facing up to an inherent argument, not C. for having the sense to recognize this.

Ex. 3 That is O.K., as far as it goes, but what about the basic point?

Ex. 4 So far we have been discussing X, but the purpose of our meeting
        was to do Y., and so far we have not done this.

N.B.   To ensure as little resistance as possible to the argument insertion, C. should use tact, as in

Ex. 5 I agree with your main points, of course, but I am concerned when you say . . . It seems more a matter of . . . So I would want to argue . . .

Also, the correct tone should be used: not too serious, not too emphatic, emotionally charged, or jocular.

Further reading   Jacobs and Jackson (1981)

ARGUMENT PREAMBLE

Tasks

To prepare ground for having an argument.
To indicate argument goals.

Description

A preamble is an optional preparatory section, useful if initiating an argument, but also of value if responding with a counterargument. For example, it can give C.'s reasons for arguing, as in 'I need to raise/we need to settle a serious issue,' or 'We need a decision on X,' or 'The current situation is such that I want to change it.'

Persuasive value

1 It can make clear that what follows is to be understood as the start of an argument, and not as just a statement of a contrary opinion. Unless this is done A. might take a while to understand how to treat what C. offers. Without a preamble, A. would have to adjust while C. is dealing with the substance of the argument, and could miss it.
2 It can justify the coming argument, for example, by showing its operational value, or its relevance to the goals of the interaction, or its necessity at this time and in this place. Unless C. does this, the others may not be prepared even to hear let alone accept any reasons which might be offered.
3 It can indicate C.'s attitude to the coming argument, for example, whether serious, whether disinterested or not, whether C. personally holds the views to be expressed or is acting on behalf of others, or is acting as devil's advocate. This will enable the others to prepare their own attitudes in response.
4 It can justify C.'s role as an arguer by indicating what right he or she has

to require an argument of the others, for example, that C. will be in charge of the implementation of some matter which needs settling.

5 It can set the kind of language to be used: technical, specific, emotionally loaded, logical, casual, etc. This prepares the others to respond in kind, or to show they want the preamble changed, and do so before the first argument points are made.

6 It can explain or justify any terms to be used which may prove problematic in the coming argument.

7 If offered in response to a communication by another, it can be necessary if the other seems not to anticipate any opposition. It serves as a warning that objection is beginning, so the other has time to prepare him or herself to hear and understand the coming argument.

Further reading   Jacobs and Jackson (1981); Schiffrin (1985)

ARGUMENT PROPOSITION: FORM

Task

To be accurate and specific in making a main point.

Description

A good proposition is an independent, rational, statement, which contains only what the proposer wants to argue, and what is suitable to his or her goals, and no more. Moreover, it should address future possibilities rather than rehash past disagreements, though it may of course arise from a past matter. It should attract debate, but should not be likely to be defeated in a given interaction.

Persuasive value

1 An independent proposition is one which can be argued without A. having to accept a prior view. A bad proposition depends on another, so that the very grounds of the proposition will cause debate, and its thrust will be lost.

Ex. 1 We need to consider whether the new computer we have budgeted for is really necessary.

This would be a dependent proposition if A. could retort 'Before we do that we need to reexamine our budgeting priorities in general.' A better version would be:

Ex. 2 Is a new computer really necessary?

2 Propositions should be rational in tone and words; if they are emotionally provocative they provoke strong resistance rather than reasoned debate, and they rarely result in agreement.

3 Extraneous matters (e.g. qualifying statements and exceptions) should be left out of the proposition. They can distract A.'s thinking from the main focus that C. intends.

Ex. 3 Our budget surplus this year, if we have one, should be spent on a new computer.

This could lead A. to discuss the likelihood of a surplus, and distract everyone from discussing a new computer.

N.B.   A proposition should not contain matters solely to anticipate objections by A.; to put them here gives them a higher priority than is sensible; it is better to set a proposition which A. would find difficult to resist.

4 A proposition which deals only with past business will rarely be useful, unless something new has changed the perception of the past and this needs to be communicated.

5 Propositions should be statements which are debatable opinions or hypotheses, not just factual comments or truisms.

See also **Argument: complex propositions**; the other **Argument** tactics

Further reading   Jacobs and Jackson (1981); Schiffrin (1985)

ATTACK OPPONENT'S ARGUMENT

Task

To take note of and deal with an argument expressed in opposition.

Description

An opponent's arguments can be opposed in several ways. They can be ignored; or attacked in general terms or in specific detail; or the person offering the argument can be attacked for raising it.

Persuasive value

1 They can be mentioned as wrong, but no further comment be given, as in

Ex. 1 A: I think the course needs some new set text if it is to work; we are all tired of the old ones.
       B: No, no, that's not true. What we need to do is to get more staff to teach it.

This is attack by dismissal, implying that the argument is not worth attention. To pay any attention at all to an argument is to give it credible status, to imply that it has to be attacked or the argument could be lost. A better tactic may just be silence.

2 The opposing arguments can be put into one's own words and then given counterarguments to reject them. In the process of using one's own words to report the argument it is possible to change some element of the meaning to one better suited to one's own argument, as in

Ex. 2 A: No one who has marked student essays could ever think that students know how to write.
   B: Well, anyone who has marked first-year students might find it a bit hard to understand what they have been taught at school about writing, but at least they try hard and put a lot of effort into their writing.

3 An opposing argument can be attacked for its illogicality, its inconsistency, its weakness of detail, or its inapplicability to the situation. All are respectable reasons for rejecting an argument.

4 It is regarded as poor argument to attack the person who offers an opposing view rather than the view itself, though it often happens. If C.s must for some reason attack the person, then they can reasonably blame the person for ignorance of detail, lack of awareness of complexity of the substance of the argument, or inconsistency with views previously expressed.

See also the **Argument** tactics

Further reading   Corbett (1977, 1990); Jacobs and Jackson (1981); Sonnino (1968)

ATTRIBUTE DEGREE OF QUALITY

Task

To incorporate a specific interpretation.

Description

To attribute a quality to a thing and to name the degree to which it has the quality, as in

Ex. 1 The machine is efficient.
   The machine is efficient enough.
   The machine is efficient enough at wordprocessing.

where the last example is much more specific than the first.

Degrees of attribution can be marked by enough, as in Ex. 1, or by 'so
. . . that,' 'very,' 'too,' etc. Some terms, like 'completely,' 'totally,' mark
an extreme degree, as in 'absolutely bald'; some indicate a slightly reduced
degree, for example, 'nearly,' 'virtually,' as in 'almost bald'; some mark a
moderate degree, like 'considerably,' as in 'fairly bald'; and yet others
mark a slight degree, like 'rather,' 'slightly,' as in 'a little bit bald.'

Persuasive value

1 The selection of one attribute rather than another can indicate C.'s
positive or negative attitude to something, as in the choice between 'He's
bald' and 'He's got blue eyes' when both are true of the same person. But
in addition to this, C. can also indicate attitude by naming a degree of
attribution. For example, C. can indicate approval for someone he or she
describes as 'absolutely loyal,' and less approval for someone described as
'pretty loyal.'
2 If C. and A. have a disagreement over a degree of attribution, for
example if C. states 'Mary is extremely prompt' and A. replies 'Well, she's
fairly prompt,' they are arguing about Mary's promptness. But since there
is so much vagueness about degrees of attribution, and they are correspondingly hard to argue about, their disagreement may well be about
something more concealed, and Mary's promptness is simply a false focus.
Such falsely focused debates help people avoid confrontation over the real
issues that concern them.

Further reading   Leech and Svartvik (1975); Quirk, Greenbaum, Leech,
and Svartvik (1985)

AVOID RESPONSIBILITY

Tasks

To avoid commitment to a view being expressed.
To avoid blame for a view being expressed.
To notice when others try to avoid commitment or blame.

Description

Some phrases show clearly whether C. is or is not willing to take personal
responsibility for whatever view, attitude, or opinion he or she is
expressing.

Persuasive value

Signs that C.s lack a sense of responsibility, either in general or for what
they say, should concern A.s, particularly where C. and A. must cooper-

ate, as colleagues, or team or family members; and indeed anywhere where they depend on each other for mutual support and joint effort. Such people are not to be trusted to perform as members of the community or to recognize the communal good. C.s should take care not to offer such signs inadvertently, and should avoid A.s who use them. The signs are illustrated in the following examples.

1 C.s can show no attachment to an opinion they offer, as in

Ex. 1 It's an interesting report you've done.

Contrast that version with the following more responsible versions:

Ex. 2 I am interested in the report you've done.

Ex. 3 The report you've done interests me.

2 C. can also evade responsibility, as in

Ex. 4 It annoys me when they talk like that.

which suggests that something vague, simply called 'it' and 'that,' annoys C., rather than that C. is annoyed; and externalizing the annoyance as though C. has no responsibility for feeling annoyed.

3 In the following example,

Ex. 5 We need to examine the case closely.

rather than

Ex. 6 I need to examine the case.

C. can hide behind an unspecified group's need when it is in fact a need that only he or she feels.

4 C. uses his or her low status to avoid a firm personal declaration, as in

Ex. 7 Though I am only a lowly member of the company I feel we should go.

(This should be contrasted with the very different and strong declarative power in 'As a longstanding member, I feel . . .')

5 C. can remove him or herself entirely from the act, as in

Ex. 8 You have to wonder what people will think of this.

Further reading   Sonnino (1968)

BALANCED REPRESENTATION

Tasks

To admit a fault in one's argument, but neutralize its effect by balancing it with a virtue.

To criticize someone or something and neutralize its effect with some praise.
To give a balanced assessment of something.

Description

If C.s, either of their own free will, or because it is demanded of them by others, admit to a flaw in what they are communicating, then its effect can be neutralized by simultaneously adding justification for the flaw, or some self-praise. Equally, if they need to offer criticism of another person or thing, the negative effect of doing this could be balanced by adding some positive compliment.

Persuasive value

When aware of a flaw in one's own communication, one should first consider whether there is any need to correct it, or whether it may be better to hope that it passes unnoticed. This will depend on one's estimate of A.'s attention at that point, his or her interest in the matter, etc.
1 If the fault is a relatively superficial one which just needs a slight adjustment of word choice, as in

Ex. 1 A: The only way to get students to work hard is to motivate them to do so, or rather to get them to motivate themselves to do so. They tell me I can manage to do this quite effectively.

So one can simply use a sign like 'or rather' to show that a correction is about to be given, and then give the revision, with little fuss. But just in case there is any adverse effect from the slight error, one could add a self-compliment like 'They tell me I can manage to do this quite effectively.'
2 If the criticism is of another, and is mild, as in

Ex. 2 A: If you go to the opticians to get your eyes checked they often put drops in so they can see—
B: Don't you mean the ophthalmologists?
A: I thought you were just asking about getting your prescription checked: if you need a proper examination then of course you need a proper eye expert.
B: Of course, that's right.

where the fault is one of word misuse only, it should be couched in mild terms like 'Don't you mean [the ophthalmologists]?' or 'Shouldn't that be [the . . .]' rather than 'Idiot, you mean [. . .]' or 'You must mean [. . .]' In the example, B takes the next opportunity of speech to pay A a compliment 'Of course, that's right.'
3 However, if the criticism of another is more serious, as in

Ex. 3 A: [writes] This report is a thorough and comprehensive analytic survey of the advertising needs of the company over the next two years.

B: [writes in reply] Thank you for your very useful notes, they will serve us very well as a preliminary set of observations.

where A has done a bad job of analytically surveying, B begins with a compliment, and then goes on to reasonable oblique criticism: the 'comprehensive analysis' is taken as just 'a preliminary set of observations.' At this point A may well look back to the compliment 'notes' and consider that this is a quite inappropriate term for a report, and a further sign of criticism.

N.B.   In a debate or argument where there are clearly two opposed views, those involved will expect that criticism and accusations of blame and faults will be bandied about. In this situation, then, to add even a modicum of praise for a minor matter can make the praiser sound like a genuinely balanced, honest arguer, and could affect some of those present to support his or her view.

One further effect of a little judiciously applied praise in the midst of criticism might be to surprise others into an awareness of their own negativity, and they could be brought to feel that they should reciprocate by praise of C.

See also **Impartiality: present**

Further reading   Sonnino (1968)

BEGGING THE QUESTION

Tasks

To notice when others use the fallacy called 'begging the question.'
To avoid using the fallacy 'begging the question.'

Description

People can reason badly by arguing in a circular fashion, that is, by assuming at the start the conclusion they are trying to prove, as in 'Students would not damage trees because they care for the environment.' This begins with the assumption that students care for the environment and then argues from this premise that because of this they would not damage the environment. This argument leaves untested that students care for the environment.

Persuasive value

1 The fallacy is not only a poor way to argue since it proves nothing, but it also gives a misleading impression of logicality which may persuade people that the arguer is being rational and so worth attending to.
2 Begging the question can lie concealed in a communication, particularly when it is in the form of an attribute given to something or somebody. For example, 'This lunatic politician should be fired,' where the question of his lunacy is begged, is assumed rather than proved, and so a decision to fire him rests on nothing more than an asserted opinion. It is important to be alert to the lack of real argument in such so-called logical statements.

Further reading   Corbett (1977, 1990)

BLUNTNESS: CHOOSE

Task

To communicate directly, without politeness.

Description

To use bluntness is to be direct and concise, and to take no explicit account of A.'s self-image.

Persuasive value

Using bluntness with strangers would seem a good tactic, since so little is known about them that it is hard to select the right politeness tactic. Yet, paradoxically, bluntness is less used with strangers, and is less well received by them than a moderate show of politeness. For example, people offer elaborate (and formulaic) apologies to strangers for brushing against them in the street, where they would say little or nothing to a member of their family or a colleague at work. The excess of politeness may be caused by a sense that the only bond between two strangers is what they say and do in that one meeting, and so any face threats are greater in social value, and the need for politeness is more important than between friends, where each single act is offset by the many thousands they share during the friendship. Except on the few occasions when bluntness is acceptable, it will be noticed as strikingly unusual, and will be noted by those present as important knowledge in their interpretation of the bluntness user. And they will often interpret the blunt person as socially inadequate in some way.

   The only value that bluntness may have as a usefully persuasive tactic is that those who use it are often judged not to be manipulative. This is a positive judgment which might work to the blunt person's advantage in persuasion. It comes about by the association of bluntness with directness and honesty, but of course this need not be a true or sensible association, and if a particular blunt communicator is found out to be neither direct nor honest just once, then the association will break down and cease to work persuasively.

It is possible also that blunt people who demand something without politeness or tact will get what they want. This could happen because by being so determined about the matter that they are prepared to risk both the face of others and the bond between themselves and others, the others will recognize how much the matter means to them, may predict that there could be a lengthy or angry argument about it, and assess whether they could tolerate this. They might ask themselves how strongly they them-selves care about the matter, and so how far they would go to resist the bluntness, and on weighing up all this could decide to give in. However, such an episode will make the others wary, and determined to ensure that no repetition of the blunt persuasion be allowed to happen. That is, while bluntness may work on the odd occasion, it is a short-term tactic only, and could have long-term adverse consequences.

See also **Politeness: absence of**; **Politeness: use blunt tactics**

Further reading   Brown and Levinson (1987)

BOAST

Tasks

To state something good about oneself.
To praise oneself.

Description

To boast is to say something in one's own praise in order to have others impressed by it.

Persuasive value

Just as it is difficult to **confess** to a fault without making others think poorly of one, so too it is hard to boast without offending others. Since boasting inevitably involves self-praise it can cause damage to the self-esteem of those who receive it.
1 If the boast is about something not possessed by A.s—something they cannot do or something they do not have—then they may feel inferior.

2 If the boast is about something which A.s themselves can do or about a possession they too own, etc., then they will feel C. has been arrogantly out of place in assuming he or she was the only one to be praised for it.

In the first case they might feel admiration and respect for C. as the possessor of something worth boasting about and so give credence to C. as one worth listening to. But they may also feel envy and a measure of dislike, both for C. as the possessor and as one who boasts about it.

In the second case they are likely to retort in their own self-praise, as in

Ex. 1 A: I've just been given an A for my essay.
       B: That's nothing, so did I and there were about six of us in grade twelve who got As.

This retort is typical in that it totally dismisses matter of the boast—'That's nothing'—so that C. ends in a less-respected position than before the act of boasting.

If a boast is accepted well, the boaster is likely to repeat the same act, even in the same words to the same people. This may be to draw again from them the support and admiration they evinced the first time, just for the pleasure of it. But it may also be done at times when C.s feel their self-confidence needs a boost. So when boasts occur they can be, though they are not always, a sign of weakness worth noting.

Further reading   Wierzbicka (1987)

BODY LANGUAGE

Tasks

To support what is verbally represented.
To act as representation of meaning.
To maintain bonding.

Description

Body language can be used alone or in partnership with verbal language to represent or reinforce meaning. So, a shrug can mean uncertainty on its own, or with a verbal expression like 'Who knows?'

N.B.   If the body language and verbal expression conflict in meaning, A. will be confused by the difference in signals or will postulate that a very complex act is being offered. Problems of this kind can arise particularly in cross-cultural communications. Body language includes eye contact, facial expressions, bodily distance, body stance, and gesture, etc. The most important from a persuasive point of view are: eye contact, bodily distance, and gesture.

Persuasive value

1 Eye contact: it is very important to look into the other's eyes at some time while interacting. However, a fixed, staring, gaze will be interpreted as intimidating and overbearing; this is because its 'dominance' does not allow the other to establish his or her own gaze preference. At the other extreme, a near-complete absence of eye contact is an equally bad tactic since it will be interpreted as avoidance, and reasons for the avoidance will be deduced (e.g. lying, abject submission, boredom, or personal dislike). The most neutral eye contact is one which varies from gaze to non-gaze and back again.

N.B. Eye contact has some particularly important tasks to perform as one speaker gives way to another (*see* **Turntaking**).

2 Bodily distance: in Western cultures the most-accepted bodily distance between participants in an interaction varies from one yard for informal gatherings to a maximum of three yards for formal meetings. Any variation (particularly excessive closeness) can cause discomfort, and if this becomes extreme it causes people to mishear or to resist what they hear.
    Currently bodily distance can be the cause of trouble between the sexes within Western culture, since close proximity, and particularly touching, could be perceived as sexual harassment by women who find it unsettling and disturbing.
3 Gesture: using the head, arms, hands, and shoulders to signal meanings can be used to add subtleties to verbal representations. For example, a vigorous nod adds positive strength to the word 'yes,' while a hand-waving from side to side could add a provisional quality to the words 'fine, yeah,' making them less absolute and the total meaning more like 'so-so'. Obviously, cross-cultural communications will prove difficult unless each participant understands not only the words but also the bodily language of the other. For example, problems have arisen with cultures which treat eye contact as too intrusively rude and so find Westerners arrogant, while they themselves are perceived by Westerners to be 'shifty' because they make too little eye contact. Middle Eastern cultures prefer a very close bodily distance when interacting, and perceive Westerners to be 'standoffish', while they themselves are perceived by Westerners as 'encroaching.' As a general guide, anyone dealing with another cultural group should note carefully its body language preferences and seek to match them. It would be useful to consult a text on the body language of any cultural group a C. might have frequent dealings with.

Further reading   Argyle (1975); Atkinson and Heritage (1984); Beattie (1983); Wiemann and Harrison (1983)

BRING CONTRARIES TOGETHER

Tasks

To put together two contrary ideas in such a way that their opposition is reduced.

Description

Where C.s wish to suggest there is no real opposition between two contrary ideas, and so to bring their opponents' ideas to the support of their own, they can design sentence structures to show this. For example, there is a debate about English studies at university, about whether the students should be taught basic communication skills, or whether they should be taught great literature. The debate usually presents the two views as if only one or the other could be done. In this context, if C. wanted to bring the two views together and suggest that they are not opposed, then it could be done as in

Ex. 1 Peter: The university must teach students practical skills so they can get jobs.

Bill: If the goal of a university is to teach the students to make a practical contribution to the life of the nation, then we must teach them the literary heritage of the nation which is its life, and that means teaching the great texts of the past and present.

The 'if . . . then' construction used here acts as a reminder of logical argument, and so gives an aura of reason to the text. In addition, Bill has represented Peter's view partly in Peter's terms—'teach,' 'students,' and 'practical'—and so seems to be accepting some of Peter's argument (and Peter may welcome this as face support), and yet he also represents Peter's views partly in his own terms—substituting the phrase 'life of the nation' for Peter's 'get jobs' because it suits both sides of the debate, by making a link between 'jobs' and 'life' and 'life' and 'literature.' So he hopes to make it possible to see both teaching skills and teaching great texts as one and the same thing, and bring over Peter's views to support his own.

See also **Face: sustain**

Further reading   Corbett (1977, 1990); Sonnino (1968)

'BY THE WAY'

Tasks

To introduce a socially difficult matter.
To notice another's social difficulties in introducing a matter.

Description

The phrase 'By the way' suggests that the topic of what follows is only peripherally related to what has gone before, and there is some assumption that it may be a relatively unimportant matter. Other similar phrases do function in this way, as 'That reminds me' and 'Oh, and while I think of it, I must say.' These are both tactful ways of introducing new topics which C. feels may be problematic either at that point, or at all. The first suggests that the next topic is not new, but linked with what has gone before; and the second gives a warning signal of a problem, 'Oh,' and two excuses, 'while I think of it' (i.e. I could forget it if I left it till the proper time) and 'I must say' (i.e. There is a need to say what I am about to say). However, 'By the way' is an exception.

Persuasive value

'By the way' seems related to these tactful topic introducers, but uses that apparent relationship to conceal that its new topic is important, and difficult, for C. to deal with. It is used, for example, when C. fears the consequences of introducing the topic, either because it is a difficult topic to communicate, like death or bad breath, or because it will cause dissension, or will attract blame to C., etc. It is a useful tactic to use in two different cases. First, where A. is known to be a poor communicator, it may work to persuade A. that it is really a side issue while being of more importance than that. Second, where A. is known to be a very skilled communicator, it will then function to show that C. finds the topic difficult to introduce, and this extra knowledge can help A. handle it satisfactorily. The obverse is obviously useful too, C. should note when it occurs in others' communications and act accordingly.

The most noted examples of 'By the way' are found in medical consultations, where patients frequently present with a problem, have it dealt with, and then, just as the interaction is about to end, they offer 'By the way,' and present a new problem. Doctors maintain that what follows is always the real reason for the patient coming to see them, and they take what is said next very seriously.

Further reading   Quirk, Greenbaum, Leech, and Svartvik (1985)

CASUAL CHAT: CHOOSE

Tasks

To have sociable interaction.
To build, maintain, or repair a social bond.

Description

Casual chat can happen at any time, in any place, and between any people, and can be brief or long. It is social interaction without any work-related goals, though it may take work, or indeed any other topic, as its focus. It is likeliest to occur at the beginnings of interactions, and when strangers meet.

Persuasive value

Casual chatter is often called 'small talk,' with the implication that it is of little significance. This is not true.

It may involve very casual language and be less coherent and organized than other genres, but it serves a number of important social functions, and acts as important tactic in many difficult interactional moments.

1 While chatting on apparently trivial topics, people can be jockeying for positions of influence in the encounter, can be establishing the social distance between the participants, and setting the tones and moods which are to be used in the more 'serious' part of the interaction. And they are able to do this important social work without mention of the main purposes for which they have met.

2 At moments of crisis in relations between the participants a move into small talk can allow tempers to calm and reason to be reasserted.

3 Where casual chat occurs in the middle of a 'serious' part of the inter-action, its presence can signal that a **phase change** is needed, either because the serious topic has just come to an end or someone wishes to stop it continuing. People may be covertly using it to fight for the right to nominate the next phase.

4 Someone who is a stranger amid those who know each other well should let the others decide on the degree and kind of casual chat, where their familiarity with one another will be a strong influence; it is usually agreed that the odd one out should not be the one to dictate the terms of any interaction, and that includes deciding the aspects of the casual chat.

5 It would be worth noting whether any notice has been taken of the stranger's presence in the amount or kind of chat offered: if there is very little, it could mean the others are unwilling to make allowances for the

difference between the stranger and themselves, and unwilling to make the stranger feel more comfortable by creating a friendly atmosphere.

Further reading   Argyle (1975); Freadman and Macdonald (1992) Nofsinger (1991)

CLAIM NECESSITY

Task

To justify oneself by claiming that what one is doing is necessary.

Description

To claim as a justification that necessity was or is the cause of one's action or, more broadly, was or is the cause of one's general demeanor and behavior.

Persuasive value

1 To claim necessity as justification means that one is confessing to some fault which needs this justification. If it is at all possible, it may be more sensible to deny any wrongdoing, so that the need for justification does not arise. C.s should consider well whether the others would know of the fault, and if not, then remain silent about it. If, however, the others are aware of the fault, then C. can choose whether to acknowledge it, and if so, whether to claim necessity as justification for it.

Where a fault is mentioned only obliquely, it can seem as if C. is all too conscious of the fault by immediately rushing to justify it. There is a standard folk saying, 'If the cap fits, wear it,' which shows the foolishness of allowing oneself to be caught accepting oblique criticism, as in B's response.

Ex. 1 A: This office is a real muddle, papers everywhere, files not put in their proper places . . .
    B: Well, I've been busy lately, but I'll get it tidied up soon.

It may well be possible to assume it is not addressed to B at all, and reply instead:

Ex. 2 B: Yes isn't it, but then it is one of the busiest offices in the building.

(This tactic will only work if it is possible to see the mess as not just B's responsibility—if it is entirely B's role to keep the office tidy, the response in Ex. 2 could be taken as rude evasion. Note that laying the blame on others is often taken as a poor defensive tactic and a weak excuse, and is therefore not likely to persuade people of its truth, even if others are really responsible. It always sounds like passing the buck.)

2 If justification is really required, then one of the best ways of doing this is to claim necessity in some form. It can be by:

(a) showing that the fault was something inevitable and not to be blamed on anyone in particular, as in

Ex. 3 B: The office is bound to be in a mess when there are so many people passing through each day.

(b) showing that the fault is a gradually accumulating one, and one which will continue, as in

Ex. 4 B: It used to be quite tidy, but with the increase in staff employed here, and company's growth to be dealt with, it will probably continue, and become even messier.

(c) showing that the fault arises from a situation which is not only necessary but also a positive thing, as in

Ex. 5 B: It was tidier once, but as the company has grown and its dealings diversified it has had to grow too, and let us hope that it continues to do so. A messy office may be a sign of growth and potential for further growth.

In this last example, B takes the opportunity, while claiming necessity, to move the agenda onto another topic, and away from any perceived fault in having a messy office. By the time this has happened, A may find it difficult to return to any criticism of B, since this would seem to dismiss the positive praise of the company that B offers.

Further reading   Sonnino (1968)

CLICHÉS

Tasks

To put A. at ease.
To put a matter into familiar terms.

Description

It is surprisingly hard to define clichés because the community has at least three senses of what clichés are and do, though they all agree in being negative. One definition is that they are familiar language; another that they are too familiar language, that is, they are trite, and hackneyed; and a third is that they are tired words masquerading as lively ones. People are likely to call any or all of the following 'clichés': 'at this point in time'; 'cool, calm and collected'; 'toe the line'; 'lay the foundations'; 'a hotbed of trouble'; 'a moment of truth'; 'it leaves much to be desired', and 'the bottom line'. Some apply the term to occasions when they feel they have spent too much time interpreting a word or phrase only to find that there was nothing of new information about it.

Persuasive value

There are serious problems in criticizing language as 'clichés,' and they bear upon its use in persuasion.
1 Familiar language is friendly language, and is therefore a useful tactic if C.s need to make A.s feel comfortable, for example where they are being asked to absorb quite new information.
2 To have a correctly adjusted **information flow** new information needs to be leavened with old, or with old language (i.e. clichés).
3 Communication has social goals other than the exchange of information, and the familiarity of clichés makes them suitable for sociability, or for building or maintaining bonds, etc.
4 As a particular aspect of this last, clichés can be used to repair trouble during an interaction, by changing the tone from quarrelsome to sociable.
5 Clichés are particularly helpful as ways of ending a topic in geniality or agreement, and are often used in this way as preclosure to the whole interaction. The most useful clichés here are those which are aphoristic, such as 'That's life,' or 'There's always someone worse off than yourself,' or simpler ones like 'I know what you mean,' 'It is the same with me,' etc. Once such clichés have been offered it is quite difficult for someone to continue with the topic, and, provided they are said with strongly marked 'terminal' intonation even to prolong the interaction.
6 Clichés can be badly used. They can be too frequent, or too bland, so that A.s feel there is nothing to keep their interest. They can be used with vague words, or with too many abstractions, and result in total lack of clarity.

Further reading   Chiaro (1992); Lakoff and Johnson (1980)

CLIMAX: CREATE

Tasks

To rank matters in priority.
To order matters in an incremental series.
To show relationship between matters.
To have one matter accepted as the climactic one of a series.

Description

C. can amplify and expand matters in the text so that they are taken as a series with one forming the climax, as in

Ex. 1 I don't mind your being rude about my house, because that's a matter of taste, and I can live with your criticism of my style of clothes because it is of little importance to me, but I resent it very much when you criticize my work, because I put a lot of effort into it, and have done so for many years.

Ex. 2 Some women spend their days doing housework, while others spend it doing menial work in factories and sweatshops, but some few are lucky enough to be able to spend their days in reading and writing about literature.

Persuasive value

The series seeks to persuade people to accept a comparison of a series of different things, and to accept that one of them is the best. This will always be a value judgment, so may be unacceptable to anyone but the C.; or it may be only partially true. In Ex. 1, C. seeks to persuade others to accept the relative importance of three things, home, clothes, and work, with work as the most important and home as the least. Anyone hearing it would know what C.'s priorities are, and, if he or she raised no objection to the ranking of the three things, would seem to accept it as a possible order of priority.

While this might only be a superficial acceptance, and one which saw the priority as just one way of ranking the three things, the absence of apparent resistance to the ranking could suggest to others present that it was accepted. And the more this happened the more this specific prioritizing would become acceptable in communication, and in the world which is represented in communication. If disagreement is not articulated it cannot be taken account of, and this expressed priority will win by default. The silent majority must speak even if it takes great effort to do so. Ex. 1 may seem a relatively uncontentious matter, and its acceptability to be of little consequence, yet it may be inappropriate for even this ordering to remain a cultural view, and unwise in the current state of world recession and unemployment to prioritize work as the means of sustaining one's self-esteem. Ex. 2 is more obviously contentious, and it is likely that more people would wish to resist it. However, the use of the series, and all its detail at each stage makes it hard to articulate a disagreement to one part of it, particularly in speech, for example, because there is no one phrase which could be picked up and repeated as a way of quickly interrupting the speaker. If someone just responds with some blanket phrase like 'What garbage!' it is not clear what is being resisted—the description of any one matter, or the whole series, or the ranking of the items.

Further reading Sonnino (1968)

CODESWITCHING: ROLE-PLAYING IN DIFFICULT TASKS

Tasks

To ease the performance of a socially difficult act.
To enhance group solidarity.

Description

Within most language communities there is (a) a standardly accepted, neutral code of communication, both words and grammar, which is used by most users of the language, and (b) several sub-languages or 'codes.' Some are dialects, (i.e. have a regional or social-class source); some are 'pidgins,' (i.e. amalgamations of different languages used in places where one language has been strongly influenced by another); and some are used by professional groups such as clergy, lawyers, or economists, and contain routine words and structures ('jargon') recognized as belonging to the work or social status the group is associated with. Codeswitching takes place when a C. temporarily adopts an inappropriate code.

Persuasive value

C. may switch to a markedly inappropriate code to perform some action which promises to be socially awkward, for example, if he or she has to reject a colleague's work as poor quality. By switching to, say, the code of a police officer, the difficult task can be done by creating a social distance from what is said by acting a social part; and, because this will be recognized, it allows the other to respond with less embarrassment and loss of face. For example:

Ex. 1 A: Hey, buddy, what's all this, this [report is not up to scratch].
    B: Sorry officer, you've caught me redhanded on this. [I'll have another look at it.]

Such codeswitching often invokes humor to lessen awkwardness as both participants recognize the source of the code and enjoy its inappropriate use.

N.B. The presence of codeswitching will reveal to A. that C. finds the task difficult. In such instances as criticizing a colleague's work, not much is revealed since most people would know that that is difficult, but in other instances it might reveal that C. has a problem, which A. might not otherwise have known.

Further reading   Mulholland (1991)

COMMAND/REQUEST

Task

To seek to have someone do something or to cause something to be done.

Description

To require someone to do something can be put bluntly as a command or politely and tentatively as a request, or as anything in between. But however the act is performed it is always face threatening. It may require someone to do something which is inconvenient and involves a good deal of effort, or it may request something be done which the other person is quite willing to do, and indeed may have been about to do of his or her own free will.

Persuasive value

To be successful as a face-threatening act, the command/request has two aims: it must not only achieve what is commanded or requested, but it also should do this with as little disruption as possible to the spirit of cooperation and bonding between C. and A. Achieving this will depend on the following main factors:

(a) the relative social status of C. and A.;
(b) the closeness or otherwise of the relationship between C. and A.;
(c) the intrusiveness of the imposition required by the act of commanding or requesting;
(d) the task commanded or requested of A.

1 If there is a social-rank difference between the two, then C. should be the superior if the act is to work: no one likes being commanded, or even requested, by someone much junior. There are, however, some temporary situations in which the usual social status is reversed; for example, when a child is ill, as an invalid it can demand things of senior members of the family and expect these demands will be met.
2 In a close relationship, for example family or long-time friends or colleagues, it is possible for C. to command or request without risking the

bond, unless of course it is done too frequently, or the acts required are serious impositions.

3 Any command or request needs careful representation if it is to work. (*See* **Politeness** tactics).

4 If the act required is of little difficulty, at the time and in the situation it is offered, it should achieve its aim. So, for example, requesting one's mother to pass the salt at the family dinner table can be little imposition if she is next to the salt, but if she is at that moment serving the food, or trying to eat a forkful of food, or deep in earnest conversation with someone, etc., the request will be badly received.

See also **Face threats: recognize; Questioning; State**

Further reading   Clark (1980); Davidson (1984); Ervin-Tripp (1976); Wierzbicka (1987)

COMMUNICATION CONTEXT

Task

To use the context to improve the communication.

Description

The communication context of any writing or speech consists of all those previous communications which reside in the memory of the C. and A. It is impossible to produce an absolutely new text, or a wholly individual or unique representation of the world. And even if it were possible, no one would understand it: it would be like reading a text in a wholly foreign language.

For both C. and A. the words, phrases, and grammatical patterns used in a current interaction must spark memories of other words, phrases, etc., in order that they can understand what the words mean, and how they represent the world. Also, the ideas represented should remind the participants of previous ones. This is not to say that communications are full of empty **clichés** but rather that words and ideas are very rarely new.

Persuasive value

If C. knows that texts arise from, and are dependent for their meaning upon, the communication context, he or she can increase the chances of persuasive success because this knowledge will enable C. to avoid some problems.

1 Care can be taken to avoid using terms and attitudes and ideas which have previously caused trouble with a specific A.

2 C. can try to strike a balance between the familiar and the new when deciding what information to supply.

3 If C. needs to increase the originality of the text the need to do so could be explained explicitly, and justified, in an early part of the communication so that A. can be persuaded to put the extra effort required into reading it. As in:

Ex. 1 The classic argument that we should proceed logically on this matter is no longer functioning well enough, and we must adapt some new formula.

4 If C. knows that the new idea will meet resistance just because it is new, then he or she could avert trouble by building in some links with the old familiar ideas, to guide A. on the path from the old to the new. As in:

Ex. 2 We have always done X, and it has always worked except in the case of Y. What I'd like to suggest is an adaptation, that we try . . .

or

Ex. 3 We built this company on good workmanship, and we must keep to our standards, but times change and we must change too.

Further reading Downes (1983); Fairclough (1989); Halliday (1978); Kress and Hodge (1993); Lakoff (1990); Lyons (1981)

COMMUNICATION CONVENTIONS: THE RIGHT TO COMMUNICATE

Task

To obey the social language conventions about who can and cannot communicate.

Description

Society has several conventions about excluding certain people from communicating, based on their status, and the time, place, and mode of the communication. Although the conventions are occasionally broken, this has social repercussions.

Low-status people are conventionally excluded from speech (and even to some degree writing) with those of very high status. So, for example, it would be very rare for someone to exchange speech with the President or the Queen. And if such an occasion did occur, it is conventional that any initiating should be done by the higher-status person. This convention is broken by those licensed to do so (e.g. the staffs of such dignitaries, and also by the press).

Low-status people are virtually excluded from the mass-media modes of communication also, just as children are excluded from 'grown-up' talk; and customers will find it hard to communicate with the chief executives of the companies who sell them their goods. In formal meetings and debates, there is a strict set of rules for who can speak, when, and how often.

Persuasive value

More importantly, from a persuasive point of view, although some of these low-status people may be able to reach higher-status people, what they communicate to them will be taken less seriously because of their difference in status. This is because their use of language, their ideas, and their values, could all be so different from what is expected, that little of what they wish to communicate will be understood, and is very unlikely to be accepted. This is why ordinary people sometimes wonder what kind of world journalists or politicians live in since its priorities, goals, ideas and values are so different from their own. This is why women sometimes wonder whether men belong to a different species from themselves.

There are less important but equally strong exclusions from communication on an everyday basis, as in the following examples. And where these occur, the one excluded is likely to feel isolated and unfriendly towards those who do the excluding.

1 Since there is a convention that without eye contact it is very difficult to begin a communication with someone, those who deliberately avoid eye contact can prevent interaction.

2 When a person comes upon a group engaged in talk it may be difficult to join in and share the communication, unless the group invites it.

3 By sheer speed and quantity of utterance, one person can exclude another from saying anything in an encounter.

See also the other **Communication conventions**

Further reading   Cicourel (1972); Leech (1983); Lyons (1981)

COMMUNICATION CONVENTIONS: THE RIGHT TO PERFORM AN ACT

Task

To obey the social conventions which restrict the performance of certain communicative acts to certain people.

Description

There are social conventions which govern who can perform what act in communication. Although these conventions are occasionally flouted, there are always bad social repercussions.

In general terms, there are some specific acts which society only permits to be performed by certain people – for example, marriages may only be performed by registered celebrants and medical prescriptions may only be issued by medical personnel.

Some acts are thought proper to one or other of the modes of communication, so, for instance, speech allows greater license in what acts are permitted than does writing. So the personal joke which is offered in a formal meeting is slightly more acceptable than one which is offered in a formal report of that meeting. Some acts must be performed in writing to constitute the act at all—the marriages and prescriptions mentioned above are two of these; it is the case that the couple who are marrying are not fully married until they sign the register (i.e. make a written act of marriage).

Persuasive value

1 In specific terms, there are also acts which society frowns on, whoever performs them—like boasting, which is only permitted in employment interviews or among very close friends (who are given a chance to boast in their turn). Performing any of these acts will cause C. to get a poor reputation, with adverse effect on his or her persuasiveness.

Others are usually to be performed by people designated for the task, so for example, social counselors, and (it would appear) those who serve drinks in bars, are 'licensed' to hear of people's troubles, so if others are forced to listen they may object, and C.'s persuasive intent in speaking will fail.

2 Certain acts are precluded by certain situations, so that personal remarks and jokes in serious formal encounters are thought extremely inappropriate, and those who perpetrate them will be badly perceived and not attended to.

When someone performs an act which he or she knows is one of the socially restricted kind, this recognition usually results in politeness tactics being used. A.s can interpret from the quantity and kind of tactics offered just how serious a transgression C. thinks it is.

See also the other **Communication conventions; Politeness** tactics

Further reading   Cicourel (1972); Leech (1983); Lyons (1981)

COMMUNICATION CONVENTIONS: THE RIGHT TO TOPIC

Task

To obey the social conventions in selecting a topic for communication.

Description

There are unwritten social conventions which concern the choice of topic, and constrain it to what is conventionally thought suitable for particular occasions and with specific people. They are conventions which are often broken, but always with repercussions.

Persuasive value

1 Generally a society has some topics which are judged quite unsuitable for most occasions. So, for example, to mention someone's bad body odor to that person is to cause social discomfort, and it would be increased if it were mentioned in the presence of others. It would be possible, of course, for a doctor to mention it, but very few others could do so without risking social trouble of some kind, antagonism from the person, and severe embarrassment from others present. Such general topic constraints change with time.

2 Specific topic restrictions exist in particular circumstances. So, for example, in the world of work there is a range of matters declared 'confidential'—details of tax and income, details of illnesses, letters of reference, business projections, details of new inventions, etc.—though these might be quite acceptable within a family, or among close friends.

3 Other topics which can cause difficulty are socially negotiated; that is, those who wish to raise them usually test the water first, and check that it is acceptable to do so. Some topics come to acceptability as participants sense a growing closeness, and use it to mention more and more intimate topics.

If these conventions are broken they cause damage to the perception of C., and to the relationship between C. and A. If C. is perceived as someone who does not know the social rules about topic, or deliberately breaks them, then this could be counterpersuasive in any later matter C. wishes to raise. If C. is perceived as someone who misreads the relationship and assumes it is more intimate or distant than it is, this is seen as encroachment or arrogance, and A. will probably respond by refusing C.'s persuasiveness for a while.

See also the other **Communication conventions**

Further reading   Cicourel (1972); Leech (1983); Lyons (1981)

COMPARISON

Task

To explain a matter.
To control A.'s interpretation of a matter.

Description

Comparison is the bringing together of two or more things by suggesting they have qualities in common.

Persuasive value

1 By comparing a new matter with one already known, C. can persuade A. that the new thing has particular qualities and should be evaluated in a particular way. So, for example, an A. who has never known a student deputation, or never thought that it might negotiate to have student workloads altered, could be influenced by a comparison with striking plant workers to see it as a very negative event.

2 The two matters could be compared absolutely ('this is good, and so is this'), or on a scale of degrees of likeness. So, for example, one book could be said to be longer, as long as or less long than another.

   Persuasion could be exerted through the selection of a particular quality to be used for the comparison, so that choosing 'long' in the case of the books could focus A.'s attention onto this feature, and away from others by leaving unsaid anything about the books' interest, stories, styles, moral values, etc.

3 Comparisons are more likely to be accepted if they are not too extreme, as in (in order of least acceptable to most)

Ex. 1 That car is the least efficient in the world.

Ex. 2 That car is the least efficient I've ever known.

Ex. 3 That car is the least efficient of the ones for sale.

Ex. 4 That car is the less efficient of the two.

Ex. 1 is so extreme it would probably be treated as **sociable language** and its referential meaning disregarded; Ex. 2 still sounds too sweeping but it does allow A. to consider what C.'s knowledge of cars is; Ex. 3 makes the comparison relevant to a discussion about the purchase of a car, and if this is the agreed topic of the interaction it could be highly influential; while Ex. 4 with its narrow scope might incline A. to accept the comparison as fairly judged.

Danger   The use of a comparison may draw A's attention to any contrasts involved, and this may be counter-productive. Also, if the comparison has been poorly chosen, and there are more differences than similarities between the two things it will not work at all.

Further reading   Corbett (1977, 1990); Sonnino (1968)

COMPENSATION

Tasks

To create or consolidate a bond.
To balance speaking styles to achieve the happy medium.

Description

It is said that informal talk obeys a social convention which requires that speakers aim to avoid the extremes of voice quality, pace, volume, pitch movement, and between simplicity and elaboration of style. (This view fits well with the **cooperative principle** and fair shares in **turntaking**.) Good evidence exists to show that where one speaker becomes louder and faster the other will become quieter and slower to compensate. And that the opposite also holds true: the quieter one speaker becomes, the louder the other becomes.

N.B. The convention does not apply to formalized interactions like interviews or meetings, where non-compensation appears to hold sway.

Persuasive value

1 If C. wants quietness or loudness from A. then he or she could produce the opposite kind of speech and hope for some likelihood of success.
2 If C. wants brevity or simplicity in style from A. then he or she could produce the opposite.
3 If C. meets with any extremism from A. then he or she could consider carefully whether it is aimed to make C. compensate, and should ask whether this suits his or her goals in the communication.
4 If in general the interaction seems to be becoming unbalanced in these ways, C. may find that restoring the balance in whatever way possible will rebound to C.'s credit as a good person to talk to. C. might say, as noise and speed build up,

Ex. 1 I think things are getting out of hand a bit; let's just stop a minute and see where we have got to.

or where things are slowing down and losing momentum,

Ex. 2 Well, let's see what else we have to do today.

Further reading　Giles and Smith (1979)

COMPLAIN

Tasks

To express unease, dissatisfaction, or censure.
To find fault in A.

Definition

A serious act of complaint must indicate what caused C.'s wish to complain; what the matter is about which the complaint is made; and who is thought responsible for the fault.

Persuasive value

1 Some complaints are merely generalized expressions of unease, as in

Ex. 1 We really need to get on faster than this.

where C.'s aim may simply be to have the complaint registered, primarily in order to have A.s know how negatively C. is currently feeling.
2 Other complaints focus on exactly what was done wrongly:

Ex. 2 It is far too late; the report is finished, this research should have been done earlier.

(Note that no one is specifically blamed for this fault.)
3 Others both declare an exact fault and apportion blame to someone. These three types of complaints need different responses.
4 The complaint may be very minor, as when it occurs in the **sociable language** parts of the interaction and is not directly addressed to anyone, as in

Ex. 3 The traffic today is impossible.

which can be just a call for sympathetic acknowledgment of C.'s hardship. On the other hand, a sociable complaint may be meant to establish common ground between C. and A., as in:

Ex. 4 It is just impossible to rely on suppliers these days, isn't it?

5 A speaker who offers too many complaints, of whatever kind, will be perceived as unpleasant because even if the acts are non-specific and not directed at A., A. is invited to agree with them, and to accept that they form common ground between C. and A., and A. may not like this kind of 'common ground.'

Generally speaking, in Western cultures, there is little positive value in making a complaint unless it is one of those for which A. can supply a practical remedy. But in cross-cultural negotiation the expression of an emotional or personal complaint may be an acceptable or even a required element. In some cultures a speaker who does not volunteer or share something about his or her feelings, both good and, as here, bad, may be considered to be hiding them for some possibly underhand purpose.

See also **Respond to complaint**

Further reading   Mulholland (1991); Wierzbicka (1987)

CONCESSION

Tasks

To concede points that cannot be won.
To concede good points of others.

Description

A speaker can concede a weak point in his or her argument:

Ex. 1 I am aware that our delivery date was not met, but the delay was a relatively minor one.

or can concede a strong point in another's argument, as in

Ex. 2 I grant you the report was good in some respects, but it did not cover all the issues.

(Both of these are examples of a **reflexive comment**.)

Persuasive value

1 If aware that there are weak points in one's own case, there are three choices.

(a) Omission, hoping that A. does not notice.
(b) Concede the weak point, present it in the best light and, if possible, suggest it is of little significance, as in Ex. 1. This concession presents C. as able to be critical about his or her own work, and so a fair judge, to be trusted.

   It may be possible to balance the concession with praise for the same point, as in

   Ex. 3 It may be a costly suggestion, but it would enormously assist our prime goal of efficiency.

   It would be tactless of A. to press the 'cost' aspect in face of C.'s comment about 'prime goal;' it would also be cognitively hard to do because A. would have to switch the relative importance of the two factors as well as find reasons for disagreement.

(c) Allow A. to raise it and have a good answer ready. One virtue in this tactic is that it allows A. a speaking turn. If C. has been holding the floor for some time, a chance to intervene may satisfy A.'s sense of proper turntaking, and so prevent an intervention at a less opportune moment.

However the conceded point is raised, it should not be given more attention than it deserves, certainly less than the stronger points. If a lengthy exchange of words about the weak point takes place, C. should increase the words used to represent any good points in order to restore their value.
2 When C. concedes a good point in another's views, C. should either weaken it, as in Ex. 2, or as in

Ex. 4 Certainly your recommendation fits our policy requirements, but so does Bill's suggestion and Susan's too.

(i.e. it is just one of three suitable proposals.)

N.B.   It is crucial that C.s make absolutely clear that the final verdict is rejection of A.'s views and support for their own.

Further reading   Corbett (1977, 1990); Sonnino (1968)

CONCORD

Task

To clarify references in the text.

Description

Concord is:
1 The grammatical agreement of subject and verb, so that a singular or plural subject will take a singular or plural form of the verb, as in:

   Ex. 1 They see the desk.

   Ex. 2 She sees the desk.

2 The agreement in number and gender between a noun and any pronouns which substitute for it in the text, as in

   Ex. 3 The girl liked her breakfast early, while the boy liked his late.

Persuasive value

1 Mistakes in concord will irritate those with a strong interest in language, and put them into an antagonistic frame of mind.

2 Concord rules can be used to influence interpretation, as for example when the pronoun 'they' is used for a 'company,' as in 'The B.H.T. company need to get their act together,' thereby indicating that it is a multiple entity, and that there are various groups within it. In contrast, the singular pronoun could be used, 'The University is pleased to announce . . .' where it is seen as a single entity speaking with one voice. The first shows a diversity, the second shows a monolith; interpretations which may influence response to the entities.

3 If control of concord is lost, as could occur during a lengthy sentence or paragraph in writing, or a long turn at talk, as in

Ex. 4 The content of the lecture on both dinosaurs and pterodactyls that all the students made such copious notes on are going to be written up and published.

A. could lose the sense of what is being communicated. Moreover, A.s feel uncomfortable putting themselves under the guidance of someone who is losing control of their material.

Further reading   Leech and Svartvik (1975); Quirk, Greenbaum, Leech, and Svartvik (1985)

CONFESS

Task

To communicate something bad about oneself without loss of face.

Description

To confess is to reveal some bad action or opinion or thought, etc., about oneself. Though C. may be reluctant to confess, either some inner need or compulsion, or A.'s insistence that the matter be brought into the open, forces the expression of guilt.

Persuasive value

Confession can clearly be damaging to C.'s self-esteem in two ways: first in the revelation of a fault, and second in the public act of confessing to that fault.

1 The first can be less damaging if C. anticipates the need to confess and performs the act before it is dragged from him or her. The second can cause less face loss to C. if the act of confessing reduces C.'s fault in some way. This could be done by:

(a) describing the fault as minor in itself, as in

Ex. 1 I confess I lost the report, but we had a copy on disk.

(b) describing the fault as almost inadvertent as in:

Ex. 2 I confess that I missed the class but it was because I got the time wrong.

2 The public act of confessing can be less face threatening if it is performed in a distanced way, as in:

Ex. 3 I gather I must confess to you about the report. I'm afraid it got lost for a while, though we have now found it again.

Here the formality of 'I gather' and 'must confess' appear to reduce C.'s involvement in the loss of the report, and they certainly omit any signs of the personal expression of guilt. The phrase 'I'm afraid' is the nearest C. comes to an expression of regret, but again it is a very formulaic and distanced one. The comments 'for a while' and 'though we have now found it again' minimize the fault, so that by the end C. has hardly confessed to much at all.

See also **Accuse**; **Face threats: recognize**

Further reading   Wierzbicka (1987)

COOPERATIVE PRINCIPLE

Tasks

To understand how social acts can be performed through language.
To interpret the communications of others.

Description

Interactions are not random outpourings of language but cooperative enterprises which can achieve social purposes. This is true at every level from the **exchange of speech** to a whole interaction. To understand what social purposes exist in an event there are some underlying principles, beyond the rules of grammar and vocabulary, which help an A. interpret what social act C. is performing. The principles show how it is that communication can produce more than the meanings of its individual words and grammar. (As children beginning communicative life we have to learn both the language and these principles, and so for a time can take literally an example like 'I feel like a coffee,' not recognizing that the speaker wants a coffee, and perhaps replying 'Well, you don't look like a coffee.')

One major principle is called 'cooperation.' It states that it is useful to assume that every communication is an offer of information, and that for this to be successful the amount and kind of information should be just right for A.s to grasp it. But, most importantly, the principle declares that communication is not often aimed solely at being informative but has many other goals, which are not easy to work out. But by assuming that information is the basis for communication, anything which does not fit this purpose can be seen as being there for some other, interactionally centered, purpose. And further, by measuring how much or how little information is given and how well or badly it is presented, A. can make an informed guess at what C. is trying to do interactionally.

The principle helps A.s to work out the meaning by clarifying just what good information techniques are; it offers them as a set of maxims to be followed:
1 Quantity—C.'s contribution should be as informative as needed for that stage of the interaction, and not more informative;
2 Quality—C.s should not say what they believe to be false, nor for which they lack evidence;
3 Relation—they should be relevant;
4 Manner—they should avoid obscurity, ambiguity, excessive length, and be orderly.
(The maxims are explained under the **Social convention** tactics.)

Persuasive value

Such a principle can give a good deal of help in the difficult task of interpreting communication acts. C.s have to know how to manipulate the basic principles on which interaction is based to achieve their ends. In addition, as A.s, they have to know how best to interpret the implications of the act being presented to them.

See also **Politeness: principle and tactics**

Further reading   Brown and Levinson (1987); Leech (1983); Lyons (1981)

CRITICIZE

Tasks

To criticize other people.
To criticize ideas, opinions, etc.

Description

Criticism can be of a person, including the one actually addressed, or it can be offered more generally of some idea, opinion, or happening in the world.

Persuasive value

The major difficulties involved in the act of criticism arise from the possibility of its being face-threatening act (F.T.A.).

1 To criticize is to seek power or influence, whatever is being criticized. Criticism is offered with the intention of making known the critic's personally held views, and more, to have some situation rectified. This has two aspects. It reveals the personally held views, which may not be to C.'s advantage. Though it may be constructive, and meant to help alter something for the better (as the critic sees it), it can also be destructive and seek only to have people understand that something is wrong and have it stopped. C.s should be aware how powerfully they are seeking to influence others when they criticize, and consider whether (a) they can actually effect any change, (b) whether others will resent their power, and (c) whether (a) and (b) in combination are worth the social risk to their relationship with A.

It follows that criticism is most worthwhile when it can effect some change, but even when it cannot, it may be worth doing as a way of indicating a strong feeling about the matter being criticized.

2 Critics must be careful to criticize the right person; if they are not sure who is responsible for a bad situation then the criticism should be kept general, as in

Ex. 1 This report has been badly typed. Whoever did this typing made a mess of the index.

Note, however, that if the person responsible is present he or she would be face-threatened.

3 Critics should note that sometimes direct criticism of one person may turn out to be also indirect criticism of another: and both could feel threatened by it. So for example:

Ex. 2 A: That new legal officer is difficult to deal with.
B: Oh, do you think so, I think he's good, but then I appointed him.

Ignorance of B's connection with the officer could have led A into offending someone senior, and might have repercussions.

4 Criticism which is carelessly thought out, as in

Ex. 3 Why do some job advertisements say that the job is for women only. I thought discrimination was against the law. Why are women being treated so much better than men?

marks the person who offers it as angry but also as illogical, and there could be repercussions from this.

Further reading   Belsey (1980); Wierzbicka (1987)

DEFINITE ARTICLE 'THE'

Tasks

To indicate known information.
To indicate alliance with A.
To create/enforce a sense of shared knowledge.

Description

The first reference to an object will usually use the indefinite article, 'a' or 'an,' but a second and later references to it will use 'the,' as in

Ex. 1 We saw a duck and a swan on the lake; the duck ate our bread.

'The' in such cases means 'the thing known' and this means known to both C. and A.

Persuasive value

1 'The' can be used as if an object is known, when in fact it is not, as in the first reference to 'book.'

Ex. 2 The book has come back at last.

If A. either cannot recall or has never heard of the book, it can be embarrassingly hard to say so. This is because either it seems to be such a minor matter to take issue with, and so not worth correcting C. about, or it would show C. that the bond between them is weaker than C. thinks (because C. appears to think A. shares some memory of discussing the book and A. did not do so). It could be an unfriendly use, and not in the least persuasive, in order to mark a bond weakness, particularly if C. is an important figure in A.'s life.
2 If C. uses 'the' more strongly, as in

Ex. 3 The book has come at last; it was definitely the postage that was the problem, as you said.

the assumption of shared experience may be so great that if A. pointed out the mistake, not only would it show their bond to be weak, but also C. would lose face as one who cannot remember who he or she has actually communicated with on the subject. There could be an added loss for A.: C. remembers A. as offering an idea 'that the postage was the problem' and this has turned out to be correct. A. then has (falsely) gained a good reputation with C.which may be worth keeping.
3 Frequent use of 'the' to signal shared experiences is a sign of **restricted code**, as in the following, which is the first reference to 'man'

Ex. 4   A: The man's just come in again.
         B: Already! That was quick.

Here both A and B seem comfortable with the use of 'the'; B knows which man, and knows of his previous actions. An outsider would have difficulty following this: a sure sign of restricted code.

Further reading   Halliday and Hasan (1976); Leech and Svartvik (1975); Quirk, Greenbaum, Leech, and Svartvik (1985)

DEFINITION

Tasks

To explain a matter.
To control A.'s understanding of a matter.

Description

A definition tells what makes a thing what it is, and shows how it differs from or is like other things. To be understood it should be carefully worded, and detailed enough to be clear. Definitions differ: they can name the class of the thing and relate it to others of similar type; they can use synonyms to explain their meaning, or provide a descriptive account, or examples of their use. They can be presented positively as: 'The concept is . . .' or negatively as 'The concept is not . . .'

Persuasive value

1 C.s can use definitions for new things or for things already known to A. In the first case, because of A.'s ignorance they can exert more influence; in the second, they must take into account A.'s own definition of the thing and if necessary seek to adjust it to what suits their goals. This can often be done quite easily because people rarely articulate their definitions of the matters that concern them and A.s may be happy to accept C.'s version as saving them work.
2 C.s can use definitions persuasively by careful selection of word associations as well as literal meanings when they define. So if, for example, C. defines good student behavior as 'attending lectures and tutorials and completing assignments on time,' the words 'attending' and 'completing' bring their associations of meaning (i.e. formal duties) with them and so the definition presents student behavior as a matter of meeting formal requirements. In contrast it could have been defined as 'studying what is said in lectures and playing an active part in tutorials,' where 'studying' and 'playing an active part' give quite a different meaning to being a student.

3 Because definitions can provide meanings for very fundamental concepts, their scope for influencing large numbers of interpretations is great. So if C. can convince A. of a definition's validity he or she can have a strong influence. For example, if C. persuades A. that the definition of a philanthropist is 'someone who gets pleasure and a strong feeling of self-pride from giving things to others' (instead of 'someone who enjoys giving things to others'), then A.'s mind can be influenced to see philanthropy as an exercise in ego-boosting, and perhaps reject the whole concept and those things associated with it—love, caring for others, selflessness, and a whole set of religious beliefs.

N.B.   Using a definition in a communication can act to halt discussion in its tracks, since for some people definitions are the end of thought not the start of them.

Further reading   Antaki (1988); Dillon (1981); Wierzbicka (1987)

DENY

Tasks

To claim that something that someone else has said is not true.
To claim that something bad attributed to oneself is not true.
To prevent people believing something bad about one is true.

Description

To deny something is to affirm positively that something negative is not true.

Persuasive value

The value of a denial depends to some extent on how public the knowledge is of the statement C. wishes to refute. It may be something known to the general public, or just to A. and others, or be private to C. A public perception about C. needs to be publicly denied: one which is known to some people should be denied to all those C. thinks have the knowledge; while one which is known only to C. should not be denied at all, since the denial would not only bring the matter into the public domain, but, in accord with the folk perception that there is no smoke without fire, some people could reject the denial and believe the negative.

Making a denial shows others that C. cares about the matter: one does not bother to deny something that does not matter. The more energetically C. performs the denial, the more he or she is seen to care. This can be so persuasive a sense of what a denial means, that if C. were to deny something which does not appear to be personally related, or a matter on which he or she could not possibly be concerned, then many will assume it must be of some personal relevance to C. or it would not be occurring at all. Not many people get agitated enough to deny something in which they are quite disinterested.

Denial may be a necessary act to perform: one cannot leave unanswered a damaging accusation about oneself or things that one holds dear, but since it can easily sound weakly defensive it should be produced with a calm firmness if it is to have the intended effect. So not 'I didn't, I didn't, that's not fair,' but

Ex. 1   That is simply not true, I was at no time on the committee involved in that trouble, and it is unfair of you to claim that.

The informal language, the repetition (as if one cannot think of anything else to say), and the exclamation sound weak; where Ex. 1 is much stronger because it uses formality, a firm negative statement, and a statement about fairness rather than an emotional exclamation.

N.B.   There is a different kind of denial: one which arises from a wish to keep something secret. So one can say 'I deny that I've ever been a member of the Communist Party,' but if this is meant simply to keep one's membership to oneself it will not be at all appropriate: it would be better to retort 'Mind your own business,' but that, unfortunately, is what some people cannot do. Since to offer anything other than a denial could be taken as an inability to deny (i.e. that the accusation is true), an accusation is an extremely powerful speech act because it locks the person responding to it into a no-win situation.

See also **Accuse**

Further reading   Wierzbicka (1987)

DESCRIBE SUBJECTIVELY

Task

To show attitude to something covertly through apparently factual description.

Description

Opinion and attitude can be offered in such a way that A.s hardly notice it, as in

Ex. 1 Face-to-face with Bill Smith, the new President of the Students'
Union, his permanent costume of tattered jeans and baggy T-shirt
with its 1980s' slogan seems even grubbier than it does when he is on
the political platform, and the man himself seems much shorter. His
dull and matted brownish hair falls untidily over one eye, and he
continually brushes it back with a nervous hand. His jerky and swift
gestures distract the attention as he rapidly mouths his political
slogans. His cigarette is always held oddly between the index and
middle fingers of his right hand, where its ash, growing longer by the
minute, eventually falls into the palm of his hand, and is flicked in
the general direction of the ashtray.

Persuasive value

There are many phrases in this example which offer a covertly adverse
response to Bill Smith; they do not work by giving an emotional response
to the man; they mainly work by assuming a community standard, and
saying that he does not fit it. Some people find it hard to notice a value
judgment unless it is represented in emotionally loaded terms, and so may
miss this criticism, and think that it is 'just a description' (i.e. to some
degree objective). The signs used for criticism, however, are there in
quantity:

(a) permanent costume—representing his clothes as never changing
    (never washed?) and a costume, that is, part of playacting;
(b) tattered and baggy—to the older generation this would be a sign of
    lack of smartness (i.e. not obeying the social rule that clothes should
    be worn to indicate to others how the wearer cares for him- or herself
    and cares to represent him- or herself to others);
(c) 1980s' slogan—out of date in the 1990s, and a sign that he is also out of
    date in his ideas;
(d) grubby—society expects people to be clean, and to have learnt this in
    childhood, so Bill Smith is breaking with society and perhaps even with
    his family's sense of priorities;
(e) shorter—society praises tallness over shortness, at least in men as in
    the phrase 'tall, dark, and handsome,' so Bill Smith is not up to one of
    the standards of society;
(f) the fact that he appears shorter than on the platform is strangely
    something to blame him for, as if he has been cheating people about
    his height;
(g) dull, matted hair—that is, not clean, not healthy, not good;
(h) brownish—an indeterminate color, as if suggesting he is an indetermi-
    nate person;
(i) the hair, moreover, falls untidily—still not fitting society standards of

tidiness, and his continually having to brush it back shows that he is aware that brushed-back hair would be better, and yet he does nothing about it;

(j) he is nervous—where society prefers serenity;

(k) he mouths his slogans—as if they come only from the mouth and not from the heart or mind (and anyway, slogans are second-hand thoughts rather than personal ones);

(l) he smokes—antisocial behavior;

(m) he uses an odd hold for his cigarette—so he does not even fit the socially accepted behavior of smokers;

(n) he does not notice the ash—is careless;

(o) he misses the ashtray—is careless again.

If A. shares any of these aspects of society's standards with C. then the attitude will be accepted, and A. will disapprove of Bill Smith. If, however, A. does not share this standard, perhaps because he or she is of another age group, race, religion, or gender, the persuasion will not work. It may well be that Bill Smith is entirely appropriately presenting himself for his student constituency.

The covert judgment C. is offering will not always be obvious to A. and so A. may not understand the strength of the difference between him- or herself and C., indeed may not notice that C. disapproves of Bill Smith at all: the fact that the account is 'description,' which A. expects to be objective, and the fact that it is full of details, may cause the covert quality of the judgment to escape A.

Further reading   Dillon (1981)

DESCRIPTIVE PHRASES

Task

To summarize some person or thing.

Description

It is possible to indicate a good deal of meaning and attach it to some person or thing, by using not that person's or thing's own name but substituting for it a well-known phrase.

Ex. 1 He's no Arnold Schwarzenegger, but he's O.K.

Ex. 2 She is the Imelda Marcos of the Department.

Ex. 3 He's the Australian Dan Quayle.

Ex. 4 There is something very Pollyanna-like about her.

Persuasive value

The substitution will only work if the descriptive phrase is well-enough known, and if it is clear what its essential meaning is. So, in Ex. 1, to understand what is being said, A. must know that Schwarzenegger is a muscled hero, though not more than that. All the other things that are true of the man, the films he has made, his private life, his political views, etc., are not being used here. So, if A. were not a film fan, then the message would be quite confused and the tactic would not work.

In the case of Ex. 2, it may well be difficult for A. to know what about Imelda Marcos is meant—since she is notorious for several things. In this instance, the substitution was intended to refer to her devouring passion for shoes, and describes a fellow shoe enthusiast. This might not be understood.

In Ex. 3, there would seem less likelihood of mistaking the focus of the substitution and its meaning. Dan Quayle's overriding fame is as a distorter of language and poor communicator, and it would be clear that this was meant here.

In Ex. 4, the substitution is not a real person but a fictional character, and in this case the meaning will only be correctly interpreted if A. is literate enough to recognize what constitutes Pollyanna's character. There is no need for A. to have read the book: it is just enough to have acquired through general knowledge this recognition of what Pollyanna stands for.

See also **Codeswitching: role playing in difficult tasks**

Further reading   Sonnino (1968)

DIRECT ADDRESS

Tasks

To speak directly to one's audience and appear to be conferring with them. To speak directly to one's opponents and appear to invite them to offer their views.

Description

C.s can incorporate into their texts a measure of direct address to their audience in several ways.
1 They can ask direct questions.
2 They can issue commands or requests.
3 They can represent a dialog with their A.s
4 They can switch to or from direct to oblique address, as in codeswitching.

Persuasive value

1 If C.s wish only to give the appearance that they are asking questions, then they will need to signal that the questions are not real, or they will get real responses and they may not be the responses they want.

If C.s want a specific response they should guide A.s to it by the form of the question used. Lawyers usually say that one should never ask a question, or even appear to ask a question, unless one knows in advance the answer one will get, as in the following example from a political rally:

Ex. 1 Are we ready for a change of government? [Shout of 'Yes.'] Are we ready for a better government? [Shout of 'Yes.'] Are we ready for a Smith government? [Loud and sustained shout of 'Yes.']

(*See* **Triplets**.) Here the wanted response is a simple one, 'Yes,' and it is the same one wanted for the second and third questions. A political orator who asked his or her questions so as to require 'Yes' for the first, 'No' for the second, and 'Yes' for the third could find the audience at the rally becoming confused.

2 C.s can directly command or request their audience to do something. If the act required of the audience is to happen outside the communication, and out of sight of C., it may not happen, no matter what is suggested in the interaction, and no matter what influence C. has over A.: for example, patients' compliance with doctors' instructions is very low. But in spite of this, the act of direct command or request serves an important communicative function that makes it a worthwhile exercise. It stirs the audience into attention as they decide whether to obey or not, and it suggests there is a practical value in what they are experiencing: it is related to action and could give rise to it.

3 C.s can invent a dialog with A.s within their texts, and so again stir audience interest as they listen to the role their imagined selves are playing, and decide how fitting it is, or whether they would wish to play a different part. An audience which is doing this is not only attending to what is being said, but is sorting out the information into what is acceptable and what is not, and though they may disagree with C.'s estimate of their reactions, that is incomparably better than them not paying any attention at all.

If the role given to the imagined A.s is interesting enough, the real A.s may accept it, and take it as a guide to their real response to the text.

4 C.s can use the switch from indirect to direct address, or back again, to indicate a change in relationship with their audience, with the direct form showing a degree of friendliness, while indirect address increases the social distance, as in

Ex. 2 You should think about this possibility, there are lots of ways in which it could be useful to your assignments: I'd like you to try to practice the first and second examples for next week's class. May I remind you all, students who do not submit their essays on time will be penalized.

Here the change in address from 'you' to 'students' shows the teacher increasing the distance between him- or herself and the students at the moment when the activity changes from cooperative interaction to issuing instructions. Any change of this kind should be noted for its implications.

See also **Codeswitching: role-playing in difficult tasks**

Further reading   Leith and Myerson (1989)

DIVISION OF MATERIAL: CREATE

Task

To present the material as if it naturally divides into certain parts, and have A.s accept this.

Description

To divide material is to split it into component parts and to use this as an organizing principle for a discussion of the matter, as in

Ex. 1 There are three things to consider about our recent loss of the Smith account: first there is . . . , second there is . . . , and finally, there is . . .

Ex. 2 The three most important things for us to learn from the meeting of the Board are . . .

Persuasive value

1 The first kind of division of material, as in Ex. 1, presents itself as objective and may be accepted as such without question. This is because most people understand that complex matters have to be divided in some way if they are to be examined carefully, and so are prepared to accept some division; and since there is no emotional language present in the example, just the simplest marking of the division in the terms 'firstly' 'secondly' and 'thirdly,' the division appears to be done with no self-interest by C. and so is accepted as inevitable. But no division of material is performed without some self-interest, or without some ideological slant. There can be either distortion of the material through the division, or there

can be complete omission of some aspect of it. No division should be accepted without close scrutiny.

2 The second kind of division, as in Ex. 2, is in one sense harder to object to, since C.'s judgment is declared openly in the words 'most important,' and most people accept that matters are subject to opinion. But at least this declaration of judgment makes it much easier to see that there is opinion behind the division, and acts as a reminder that since judgment is occurring, counterjudgments could be possible, and people can therefore be alerted to think about it far more than they were in Ex. 1.

N.B.   One of the divisions of material with the most serious implications is division into two opposed alternatives, which presents it as if it poses a dilemma, as in

Ex. 3 If the Honors program is a good one we will increase our student numbers, but if it is a bad program we will not.

A.s should ask of any dilemma, 'Is it the only possible division? Is it an either–or situation, or something different?' In this example, it is easy to note that student numbers increase for a variety of reasons which have nothing to do with the quality of programs—like easier entrance requirements, better job prospects, etc.

Further reading   Sonnino (1968)

'EITHER–OR' FALLACY

Tasks

To notice when others use the fallacy of 'either–or.'
To avoid using the fallacy of 'either–or.'

Description

A matter can be stated as consisting of two and only two possibilities, that is, it is an 'either–or' situation.

Persuasive value

Many of those who spend a lot of time in argument do so because they see the world in black and white terms: 'You are either for us or against us,' 'It's always a matter of them and us.' They always seek to find the extremes of differences in some concept, and, moreover to show how these differences can clash. As they persistently argue, they present a world without a middle ground, and are inclined to ask 'Whose side are you on?' and refuse to accept an answer which indicates a moderate position.

Some of the situations they see in this way are quite properly divided, because they present two and only two opposed positions, as in 'You either voted for Smith or you did not,' but about many other situations they are wrong, as when they fallaciously argue that you must have voted either for Smith or for Brown, when there was a third candidate standing for election, and the possibility that no vote was cast at all. Other fallacious statements of this kind include 'Teenage violence is due either to the parents' failures or the education system's,' and 'Defoe was either the greatest journalist of his time, or the worst.'

To test the validity of such arguments the question to ask is, 'Is there a third option or are the two choices the only ones possible?'

Not only is the use of this fallacy likely to result in unnecessarily polarized arguments, but its frequent use can persuade both those who use it and those who have it used to them that the world is about difference and division with little possibility of consensus.

Further reading   Corbett (1977, 1990)

ELABORATED CODE

Tasks

To show common ground with A.
To show there is no common ground with A.
To prevent offense to A.'s ego.
To give offense to A.'s ego.
To use clearly understood language.

Description

There are two important ways of using language within English: using a **restricted code**, which uses a small vocabulary and a narrow range of grammar, or an elaborated code which has a large vocabulary and uses the full grammar. The elaborated code is used whenever:

(a) C.s need to represent complex matters, abstractions, or supply specific details, etc.; or
(b) when C.s assume that A. does not share their experience of life with respect to any matter.

Persuasive value

1 The elaborated code is given high status, and is seen as the proper code for educated, professional communicators who deal in the more genera-

lized aspects of life, so an ability to use it will mark the user as socially and communicatively educated.

2 If someone responds with the elaborated code after others have used the restricted code it could persuade them that the person is someone who is of higher status, as in such an exchange as

Ex. 1 C: I thought it was great last night, didn't you.
       A: Are you referring to the Haydn concert?

whereas if he or she responded in restricted code when the others had used elaborated code, it would heighten the difference between that person and the others, whether it was done intentionally or not. It might even be taken as a sign of rebellion from their ideas and assumptions, and they could see him or her as someone who gives value to being 'down to earth' and hence is intending implicitly to criticize their 'highflown' view of the world, as in

Ex. 2 C: I think the company should consider its options very carefully on
        the merger.
       A: That's great, I'm with you on that one.

(An elaborated version might be 'I certainly agree that the options are important.')

Further reading   O'Sullivan, Hartley, Saunders, and Fiske (1983)

EMPHASIS

Tasks

To emphasize a matter.
To show strong feeling.
To insert a forbidden matter.

Persuasive value

1 At times the language seems so hackneyed and cliché-ridden that it has no way of representing in a fresh and exciting way something C. feels strongly about. It may seem too difficult to find suitable words to express an important matter. If C. feels this, and the matter needs freshness and vitality in order to have it received with due attention, the best tactic may be an overtly declared refusal to put it into words at all. The refusal must be strongly signalled so that A. recognizes that the refusal is a deliberate choice. This is usually done by use of a **reflexive comment**, as in:

Ex. 1 What can one say . . .

Ex. 2 And when it comes to how we have been treated by our employers lately, well, words fail me . . .

2 In another kind of situation, a matter may be being avoided (e.g. because it is shocking, or annoying). If C. feels that it must be dealt with, he or she will need to recognize the difficulty others will have with its shocking qualities. One tactic for doing this is in stating that the matter has been forbidden (by unspecified people); yet in spite of this C. will put the matter into words, as in

Ex. 3 And not to mention that shocking subject . . .

Ex. 4 I have been told not to mention X because it is a troublesome topic, but I think it needs attention . . .

In so doing C. shows how strongly he or she feels about it. And does so without depending on word choice to make the strength of the point. The matter acquires its emphasis in that A. understands it is forbidden and therefore realizes how important it must be to C. Thereby, A. may be persuaded to take it seriously, or to share C.'s evaluation of it.

See also **Foregrounding**

Further reading   Sonnino (1968)

EUPHEMISM

Tasks

To avoid embarrassing or taboo words.
To prevent offense to others.
To disguise a biassed view.

Description

A euphemism is a mild word substituted for a harsh one.

Persuasive value

1 The very existence of euphemisms in communication indicates society values mildness, and the avoidance of embarrassment. It is probably the social norm in writing and in formal speech, though not in casual talk. It follows then that the use of euphemisms could go unnoticed, but that their absence, and the consequent bluntness, could disconcert and distract A.s and cause them to resist accepting a text's views. Casual talk can absorb bluntness with less fuss, though it may still disturb some A.s

and prevent them from concentrating on and agreeing with what is being said.

2 Euphemisms should be used not only for the culturally defined embarrassing topics—death, sexual activity, excretion—but also where a topic's use could cause an awkwardness in a specific situation. On some occasions it could be difficult to mention A.'s personal failures, or C.'s personal successes unless euphemisms are used, as in:

Ex. 1 A: How did you do in the exam?
　　　　B: Oh, not too bad.

where A uses the mild phrase 'How did you do?' rather than the bald question 'Did you pass?'

Euphemisms work in three ways:

(a)　They allow an offensive topic to be represented and discussed without offense.
(b)　They show A. that C. is deliberately choosing not to offend, not to harm the joint bond.
(c)　They can also disguise matters so that they do not attract notice which would, in blunter terms, have caused debate and resistance (e.g. 'ethnic relocation,' 'the final solution'. Here their function is to prevent thought, not to avoid embarrassment. They are clearly a usable persuasive tactic.

Further reading   Corbett (1977, 1990); Sonnino (1968)

'EVEN'

Task

To be wary of expressing offensive value judgments.

Description

The word 'even' can be used to indicate that it is surprising that a certain matter resembles others, or could be included with others, as in

Ex. 1 They stole everything, even the laundry on the clothesline.

Ex. 2 He writes textbooks, scholarly articles, and even movie reviews for the local paper.

Persuasive value

The word 'even' should be used with caution in such cases, lest the surprise expressed reveals a value judgment which might cause offense, as in

Ex. 3 Women academics, women lawyers, even office typists, have read the book.

Ex. 4 The majority of women students and even some men have seen the video on sexual harassment.

Ex. 3 expresses surprise that office typists read books that academics and lawyers do—which is an arrogant attitude to reveal, and could cause those present to dislike the person who says it.

Ex. 4 expresses surprise that men should be interested in learning about sexual harassment, and this too is a negative judgment which could rebound to C.'s discredit.

In each case C. may think that what is represented is true and may be hurt by the accusation of negativity or snobbishness, but it remains true that such usages can be so interpreted, and would be unlikely to help C. achieve his or her persuasive aims.

Further reading   Quirk, Greenbaum, Leech, and Svartvik (1985)

EXCEPTION: ALLOW

Task

To improve the chance of a generalization being accepted by acknowledging some exceptions.

Description

It is a commonly understood ground rule of debate that generalizations should be avoided, and if they occur, they should be examined very carefully. So any generalization or sweeping statement will alert thoughtful A.s to the possibility of exceptions or flaws of some kind, and create resistance to it. This can happen simply because it covers too much ground, and those who oppose it need not have any clear knowledge of any specific exception to it. To prevent this danger, C.s who need to make a generalization can offer along with it some recognition of the exceptions that test it, as in

Ex. 1 The situation for business is as bad as in the 1930s, with no sign of improvement in world trade for many years and at home no sign of political initiatives to assist recovery, and no hint of awareness in the community that the good times of the 1980s are at an end. The outlook would be wholly grim were it not for the knowledge that it is bad times which often bring out the best in people: personal initiative seems to thrive on adversity.

Persuasive value

If C.s need to present a general view as part of an argument, it should not be placed in initial position, or else the argument could be halted at that point while the generality is debated. If it occurs after some detail it may be more easily tolerated by A.s.

If, however, C.s need to place the general comment early in their argument, then it would be useful to offer some exceptions along with it, to show that the presenter is well aware of the dangers of generalizing, but needs to do so for some purpose. If A.s feel that the ground rule has been understood, and would be followed were it not for some purpose, they may therefore hold their fire to see whether the purpose is good enough to justify breaking the rule.

If C.s can present themselves in this way as sharing the same unspoken rules of argument as A.s, they may be given the benefit of the doubt about the generalization just long enough for it to work.

Further reading   Sonnino (1968)

EXCHANGE OF SPEECH

Tasks

To interact with another through talk.
To initiate some action.
To impose an action on another person.
To respond to an action.

Description

Almost every utterance is assumed to be addressed to someone, and more, to require a response from that person. These together form an exchange of speech. Talk proceeds by a series of such exchanges.

A speech exchange consists of an **initiating move** and an immediately following **response**. The first part must be a conventionally recognized initiator (i.e. be an utterance that can stand without prior speech). The second part must be dependent on the first (i.e. be relevant in topic), be a suitably related speech act, and indicate that the responder has paid attention to the first part. Standard speech exchanges include question and answer, invitation and acceptance, greeting and greeting. Although there exist many instances of initiating moves without corresponding responses, these are usually held to flout convention, and are usually conspicuous, and often cause interactional problems.

Speech exchanges can be on any topic, or begin with any act, but once the initiating act is performed, the second part is constrained by it, and must be one of the set of appropriate responses.

Persuasive value

1 Every speech exchange is a microcosm of interaction, and even though it might take only seconds to perform it can have a strong effect, for good or ill, on the talkers' sense of the world, on their experience, and on their interaction. It can therefore either set the framework for persuasion, or ruin its chances.

2 A speech exchange can and does contain persuasion, since what the initiator says constrains what the responder can say in return. So it can force an answer to a question, or can limit the options of the responder.

3 Whatever the responder produces as the second part of the exchange will be taken as a response, whatever form it takes, however odd it seems, and however unrelated to the first part. On hearing it, the first speaker will search it for signs of connection to the first part, and will interpret it in whatever way he or she can. If it is difficult to find any link, it might be taken as a sign of the other's dislike, or of difference in outlook. If it seems very disconnected, it might be taken as due to inattention, or as an avoidance strategy. Only if totally baffled might the first speaker ask 'What has that got to do with what I said?' Even silence will not make the responder free. Silence as the second part of a speech exchange will be interpreted and given some meaning.

4 Once a speaker has spoken, whether as initiator or responder in a speech exchange, the words become a commitment, and he or she can and will be held to them.

Further reading   Coulthard (1985); Goodwin (1981); McLaughlin (1984); Nofsinger (1991)

EXCLAIM

Tasks

To express strong feeling directly.

Description

The emotion can be straightforwardly expressed, as in

Ex. 1 How fantastic! I am delighted for you.

or it can be expressed through a **reflexive comment**, at one remove from directness, as in

Ex. 2 I must say, that is good news.

Persuasive value

The first appears the more emotional of the two, because of its greater directness, but it is also a very informal way of expressing emotion, and could be less appropriate in a formal context than the second version. In an extremely formal context such an exclamation as Ex. 1 would be entirely out of place, and would make people uncomfortable as an uncontrolled display of feeling; any expression of emotion is more likely to occur in formulaic form, such as

Ex. 3 I think we would all like to congratulate Bill on his good news [applause].

While, if it occurred in a serious and dignified meeting, even such a mild form of enthusiastic exclamation as

Ex. 4 I think Mary has just come up with a tremendously useful idea.

could cause others to be resistant to the speaker. They could do this because the word 'tremendously' is very exaggerated, and overexcitement is taken to be a sign of lack of thought. They might think the speaker should calm down into rationality before they will listen to anything further from him or her. Formal events require that strong feelings be translated into strong reasons before they are attended to properly.

It follows then, that the placement of any exclamation is important: if it occurs early it can cause dismissal of the speaker's ideas for a major amount of the interaction, while if it occurs at the end it has less effect. It may be possible to make use of a (not too exaggerated) exclamation in the middle section of an event, to highlight some issue and call attention to the speaker's commitment to it, as in

Ex. 5 Chairman: And now we come to the matter of the office xerox machine.
       Bill: Ah, that's an absolutely crucial one; if we don't do something about that soon I shall blow my top.

It also matters what the exclamation is about. If it is about the others present, as in 'You idiots,' or 'Marvellous, that's a great idea, Mary,' it obviously depends whether it is negative or positive as to how it will be received. But even if it is positive, it may be problematic: for example, Mary might not want this degree of emotional support from Bill, since the emotional quality might suggest that it is a response to her as a person and not to her ideas.

If the exclamation is about something outside the event, something general in the world, as in 'I really hate it when the westerly wind starts up, it's just awful,' people could share the emotion and so find the exclamation appropriate, or, in the wrong context, could see it as a foolish protest about something that cannot be changed.

Further reading   Wierzbicka (1987)

EXEMPLIFICATION

Tasks

To make clear a difficult point.
To prove a point has important implications.
To covertly indicate an attitude.

Description

To incorporate into the text some examples of a matter which is being treated, in order to explain or elaborate on it so that it becomes more acceptable.

Persuasive value

Good examples can make difficult abstractions concrete, easier to realize, and in so doing make them clearer to A. They can show how valid an idea is by indicating how practicable it would be in real life. They can also be used to act as detailed explanations of how C. sees a matter as fitting his or her purposes.

Before using an example, however, it is important to consider whether the idea really needs support in this way: it may not be a hard idea to grasp, or A. might be willing to accept it without examples. To use examples in this case is not only a waste of time but it can also lead to trouble if anything in the examples provokes A. to resist the idea (or acts to distract A. from the main point).

If using examples seems worthwhile, they should be well chosen; that is, they should be vivid, specific, be understandable without having to supply extra context, they should make the idea seem plausible, or valuable, so that A. can see that the idea is worth accepting. To have A. adopt an idea, the examples should be ones that show the best side of the idea; while if the purpose is to have A. reject an idea, the examples should give the worst-case outcomes that would follow.

Examples should be introduced carefully, so that A. knows they are illustrations and not just the next point to be made. The standard signs are, of course, 'e.g.,' 'for instance,' 'as a case in point.' It is also important that A. is given some clue as to exactly what they are to illustrate; that is, which detail of the matter they will throw light on.

Some examples may need explanation, either because they do not fit exactly with what they are supposed to illustrate, or because they are complex in themselves, and this should be provided *before* the detailed example is given.

Danger The main danger with exemplifications is that they can take over the whole account; to prevent this they should be controlled, and kept subordinate to the points they are supposed to illustrate. A good rule of thumb is to make sure that the idea is given the same number of words as the example which is supposed to illustrate it.

Further reading Corbett (1990); Sonnino (1968)

EXPLAIN

Tasks

To make clear a complex concept.
To have one interpretation of an idea accepted.

Description

The following is a typical explanation:

Ex. 1 Let me explain. There are three different sections of the community involved in this exercise—the unemployed, the employed, and the Government. All want the same goal: lowering the unemployment rates to a manageable level, to about 6 percent.

Persuasive value

Such an explanation works to persuade A.s by its neatness and tidiness of expression, and because it sounds impressively thoughtful in the sweep of its coverage. It shows C. in command of the whole picture and of its details, and in its use of categorization presents C. as clear-thinking, and logical. It appears to be an unassailable truth. And, incidentally, should A. wish to object to any part of it, for example, the '6 percent,' he or she would be shown to be destructive of an elegant account of the world, and this could be unattractive to others who witness it.

Also, explanation persuades by showing some relevance to A.'s life. For example, a good garage mechanic could adjust his or her whole knowledge of the combustion engine and communicate only that part of it which matters to a customer as he or she wishes to know how some feature of his or her car is malfunctioning. Such partial explanations are easier to grasp and this makes them likelier to be accepted.

N.B.   The relevance need not be real, it can be manufactured deliberately by the explainer to enhance its acceptance.

Explaining sometimes meets with opposition when it seeks to change a firmly fixed meaning which is held by A. If this becomes apparent only after the explanation has begun, it may be possible to retain something of its power. One way is to note any term which meets with strong opposition and argue that it is not a major element in the explanation's meaning, or that it has a different meaning from the one A. attributes to it, and re-explain the term. It is unwise overtly to attack A.'s own terms or views because this can turn an explanation into an argument, and the revelatory and other powers which lie covertly behind explanation will be forced into the open and be less effective.

See also **Explanation: choose**

Further reading   Antaki (1988); Chaffee (1991); Wierzbicka (1987)

EXPLANATION: CHOOSE

Tasks

To make clear a complex concept.
To have one interpretation of an idea accepted.

Description

Many of the concepts of life are difficult to understand, and in communication they remain difficult. An explanation is an attempt to render such ideas easier to follow. It is a focussed endeavor to reduce the complexity particularly of any socially significant ideas, so that they are understandable. It usually works by assigning a single meaning to the complexity, and in this it differs greatly from **definition**. A definition lists all possible meanings which a word might have, and aims for general coverage, but explanations reduce the possible meanings to just one, and one which others can grasp.

Persuasive value

Explanations are a very important persuasive device, working in simple talk as well as in the mass media, to have people accept a particular interpretation of the world, which affects their everyday behaviors and their general philosophy.

The main source of power comes from the way they can attribute causes to things, or show where responsibility lies, or blame some adverse happening on people, a specific set of people, the environment, etc., and so uphold some ideological view or another, as in

Ex. 1 So the reason unemployment is so high is that people are not prepared to work hard, or indeed to work at all.

1 In selecting one meaning for an idea or concept or some other aspect of the world, explanations omit the others and A.s may not notice this distortion.
2 They claim to reveal what is hidden, and this is attractively persuasive for A.s who see themselves as learning something which others do not know.
3 If the explanation offers not only to be a revelation, but also one which presents a new angle on A.'s previous thinking (provided it does not reverse it or damage it in any way), then the intellectual excitement it presents could make it very persuasive.
4 If C.'s reputation is high, then this, as well as the logicality of his or her explanatory methods, will make the interpretation offered likely to be accepted.

Explanations do not come only from others, people also offer them to themselves. Every day explanations are found for matters people come across, and for things that happen to them, and these have important social power. For example, on hearing a noise in the night a person could explain it as 'just the cat' and go back to sleep, perhaps unwisely; or someone explains an examination failure as the unfairness of the questions, and so forgives him- or herself, and works no harder in future, feeling there is little point since the world is unfair.

See also **Explain**

Further reading   Antaki (1988); Chaffee (1991)

EXPRESS EMOTION

Tasks

To hint at one's emotional attitude to something.
To recognize from hints what others' emotional attitudes are.

Description

There are many important emotional attitudes that can be represented in communication, among them are:

1 pleasure;
2 worry or concern;
3 disappointment;
4 surprise;
5 disapproval.

Persuasive value

It is important to be able to hint at one's emotional attitudes to matters and have these understood, without having to go into detail about them. It is also crucial to be able to interpret hints from others and assess from these their attitudes, so that one makes as few mistakes in communication as possible.

1 Pleasure can be easily recognized from such words as 'marvellous,' 'wonderful,' 'exciting,' 'fun,' etc., but it is also less obviously expressed in such ways as

Ex. 1 We look forward to the pleasure of your company.

Ex. 2 It was a most interesting evening.

These examples are formally expressed, and their overt emotionalism is less obvious, but it is nonetheless there.

2 Worry can be informally expressed through words like 'perturbed,' 'anxious,' 'uneasy,' 'afraid,' and through the formal versions, as in

Ex. 3 The university finances are cause for some apprehension.

3 Disappointment can be informally expressed through such words as 'if only,' 'it is a pity that,' 'I am sorry that,' and more formally, as in

Ex. 4 Unfortunately we are unable to supply the goods today.

4 Surprise can be informally expressed through such words as 'strange,' 'unusual,' 'amazing,' 'incredible,' and more formally, as in

Ex. 5 The extraordinary events of the last week are now over.

5 Disapproval can be informally expressed through such words as 'awful,' 'dreadful,' 'poor quality,' 'naughty,' 'wicked,' and more formally, as in

Ex. 6 It would have been more useful if you had given us notice of this.

Further reading   Sonnino (1968)

EXPRESS PERSONAL DETACHMENT

Task

To choose how and to what extent to represent one's commitment to what is being offered within the text.

Description

For all communicators there is a choice between a strong representation of the self in the text, which is called 'involvement,' or a limited representation, which is called 'detachment.' When producing a written text C.s are more likely to present their material in a detached way; in speech they often choose the involved mode. Of these examples the first is involved, while the second is detached:

Ex. 1 I think the case will turn out to be . . .

Ex. 2 The case is this: . . .

Detachment can be shown by using all those tactics which present material as if depersonalized:

(a) not just the absence of 'I' but also all the other personal pronouns which name the members of the interaction;
(b) omitting C. as agent, as in 'It has been found' instead of 'I have found;'
(c) using nominalization, as in 'There was a decision' rather than 'We decided,' or 'A meeting was held' rather than 'We met';
(d) omitting strongly attitudinal words like 'amazingly,' 'fantastically,' whose only value is the expression of C.'s involvement with the matter;
(e) omitting exclamations, as in 'So at last the case was won!'

Persuasive value

1 By using the signs of detachment, C. can suggest that what is represented needs no personal endorsement but is communally accepted and generally true (i.e. its own authority is enough to make it powerfully persuasive).
2 Detachment signs will suggest C. wants to keep at a distance socially from A., or from what he or she is saying, as for example when acting as a spokesperson rather than in his or her own voice, or when saying something required by C.'s role rather than by C. as an individual.
3 Detachment signs may be used for a temporary purpose: for example, C. can switch to detachment, intending A. to notice this and see it as a sign of annoyance or offense, without anything explicitly being said.

See also **Express personal involvement**; **Naming**; **Omit agent**

Further reading   Chafe (1985); Tannen (1985)

EXPRESS PERSONAL INVOLVEMENT

Task

To choose how and to what extent to represent one's commitment to what is being offered within the text.

Description

For all communicators there is a choice about how they represent themselves in the text. They can use a strong representation of the self and their commitment in the text, which is called 'involvement,' or use a more limited representation, which is called 'detachment.' In written texts C.s are more likely to present their material in a detached way; in speech they often choose the involved mode. Of these examples the first is involved, while the second is detached:

Ex. 1 I think the case will turn out to be . . .

Ex. 2 The case is this: . . .

In the first example C. is directly presented in the text, and his or her relationship to the material is also indicated, in the phrase 'I think' which means 'I am fairly certain of what I am representing.' In the second example C. and C.'s commitment to what is communicated is absent.

Involvement tactics are those which make explicit how C. has constructed the text, and how he or she relates to the material, to A. and to the whole interaction. They include the following:

(a) the presence of the first person pronoun;
(b) the explicit naming of the speech acts being performed, as in 'This is a warning to us all that we should go carefully,' where C. is the person construing something as a warning and actually delivering it to A.;
(c) offering a strong opinion or attitude about the material: 'This is an excellent book';
(d) incorporating personal anecdotes;
(e) referring directly or indirectly to A., the interaction, or its immediate context.

Persuasive value

1 Involvement tactics are used when C. needs personally to vouch for the material presented and show a strong commitment to it. It may be in addition to other tactics, to support them; for example if C. were saying that something is true, and moreover he or she firmly believes it; or it could be used alone, for example if C. were saying that something is not universally accepted as true but that he or she firmly believes it. If the latter is the case, the persuasiveness of the matter will rest on C.'s personal authority and commitment, and nothing else.

2 The kind of involvement expressed can show whether C. is speaking as a single person or on behalf of others (or pretending so to do), as when C. uses 'I,' 'my,' or 'we,' 'our.'

3 C. can also reveal how he or she sees the relationship with A., for example in the choice between addressing A. as 'you' or by name, or profession, or social group—'you academics' or 'you students.' A marked absence of terms for A. when coupled with an overuse of terms for the self would mark C. as egotistical.

4 C. can ignore A.'s reactions to the material or call on A.'s support, as in 'know what I mean?' 'you know?' or 'O.K.?' In the latter case C. signals that his or her involvement with both the material and with A. are of more concern than the content of the communication.

N.B.   Involvement in the sense used here need not only mean agreement with the material: C. can be involved as an opponent of the material he or she is offering. C. can also show commitment to other aspects of the communication, for example to A., or to their interaction. So C. could offer the following, involved, utterance:

Ex. 3 I must mention the idea that one of our team has put forward. Though it hardly solves all the problems you have mentioned, it solves the ones we are most concerned about.

Here C. indicates an opposition to the team idea, while showing involve-:ment with A. A detached version of the same thing might be

Ex. 4 There is one idea which has been put forward by Personnel, and though it hardly solves all the problems it solves the major ones.

By noting such differences A.s can gauge the degree of commitment of C. to what is being presented.

See also **Express personal detachment**

Further reading   Chafe (1985); Tannen (1985)

FACE: SUSTAIN

Tasks

To preserve one's self-image.
To support others in their self-images.

Description

'Face' is the generally recognized self-image people have, a sense of their own importance, which makes them dislike being treated without respect by others. This is what is described in such phrases as 'She really lost face over that mistake,' or 'I made a mess of the report and ended up with egg all over my face.' For many people their face is bolstered by their material possessions, but a major face support occurs when people use complimentary words, or behave in some respectful way.

People should assume that others also have self-images they wish to preserve; and that it is in everyone's mutual interest as they enter interactions to maintain the others' face, in the trust that others will reciprocate.

Persuasive value

Face cannot be sustained without the support of others; it is never enough to say to oneself 'I am important.' So people need each other, and they are vulnerable as far as face is concerned, to the support or attacks of others. Or even to being ignored by others, which can be very damaging. The persuasive value of face recognition and support is that people feel gratefully inclined to the one supporting them, and may feel more willing to be persuaded to respond well to what C. wants. Equally, people are disinclined to agree to persuasion from someone who is tactless or bruising to their egos, and there are many folk-sayings which record this: 'She treats us like dirt, so I've just stopped listening.'

No one can entirely satisfy another's desire to receive face recognition, because some people have enormous egos, and because there are many occasions on which ego needs clash. But society accepts that there is value in the very attempt at ego support, in the signs of trying to give recognition to others' egos, and most people acknowledge them as an indication of goodwill. Though the attempt at face support may not work to persuade A. of the matter at issue on one occasion, A. may be more inclined to be persuaded at a later date.

N.B.   One of the most powerful sources of self-esteem is to succeed in persuading others, since this brings them into line with one's wishes, makes them share one's values, and imposes one's ego needs on them.

See also **Face threats: recognize; Politeness** tactics.

Further reading   Brown and Levinson (1987); Davidson (1984); Goffman (1959)

FACE THREATS: RECOGNIZE

Tasks

To assess the chances of success when performing an F.T.A.
To note one's own response when an F.T.A. is addressed to oneself.

Description

Many social acts involve a threat to the 'face,' self-esteem or ego of others. For example, it is obvious that any request makes an imposition on the time or energy of another, but so too do most other communicative acts, like 'Ask a question,' or 'Tell a story.' To be successful they must be performed with some recognition that this is so.

The degree of face threat of any act by C. can be measured by (a) the relative social position of C. and A., (b) the social distance between them, and the degree of liking, and (c) the degree of imposition involved in the specific act. So, where C. is lower in social position than A. (e.g. it is a child–parent or client–professional encounter), the threat to A.'s face is great. Where C. and A. are socially distant (e.g. rarely meet, and only on formal occasions), or in adversarial roles, the threat to A.'s face is great. And where the social assessment of the act recognizes it as a strong imposition (e.g. where it requires much effort from A., or takes up a good deal of A.'s time, or the circumstances are adverse for A., as when he or she is ill or busy), the threat to A.'s face is great.

These measures are social perceptions, rather than observable facts, since people differ in how they perceive these things. And their threat to face can vary even between the same two participants during the same communication, as for example when a degree of liking suddenly emerges, and the following face threats are reduced by that.

Some threats are to C.'s own face, as in apologizing; some are to A.'s face, as in **advise** or command; and some are to both, as in offer.

Persuasive value

Success in performing an F.T.A. is first dependent on C.'s recognition that every utterance or piece of writing can pose a face threat to A. Once that is recognized, success is a product of three things: (a) achieving the act so that it is understood by A. and produces the required result; (b) ensuring that no damage is done to the bonding of C. and A. which might jeopardize future F.T.A.s; and (c) safeguarding the face of both C. and A. Finally, it should be noted that A. will probably recognize the tactics used, and this is an important element in their success—that A. should see C. trying to avoid damage to A.'s self-esteem.

To do these things successfully there are a large number of tactics, called the 'Politeness tactics,' from which C.s should choose the ones best addressed to the problems of a particular F.T.A.

See also **Apologize; Command/request; Cooperative principle; Face: sustain; Politeness** tactics

Further reading   Brown and Levinson (1987); Davidson (1984); Goffman (1959)

FORBID

Task

To require someone not to do something.

Description

The act of forbidding seeks to prevent something happening. To be successful it must have certain features:

(a) C. must have some authority over A., because it is a very authoritarian act and severely restricts A.'s freedom of action;
(b) the situation between C. and A. must be such that A. would be afraid of some (usually unspecified) sanction if the forbidden act was in fact done.

The act can be performed in several forms, for example in speech:

Ex. 1 Don't do that.

Ex. 2 I do not want to see you doing that again.

or in writing:

Ex. 3 Members are forbidden to use the library after 9 P.M.

Ex. 4 Do not even think of parking here.

Persuasive value

1 If C. has insufficient authority to forbid that act to that person at that time, the act could fail, with consequent loss of face for C. Authority could be a matter of superior social status, institutional power (e.g. teachers, doctors), or interpersonal influence (e.g. as hostess or parent). If none of these is present, C. could create an authority by providing good and acceptable reasons, as when one roommate forbids another to go out with the argument that dinner is just ready.

Another possibility is to call upon community standards of morality or ethics, and let them provide the authority.

2 C.s should consider the consequences of failure (i.e. if A. goes ahead and commits the forbidden act). If C. has no sanctions to apply, then the end result of performing the act will be to leave C. in a weaker position than before doing it, and not only suffering severe loss of face but also being seen as one intent on forbidding others—a non-cooperative stance and one unlikely to attract support for anything else C. might do.

3 Since forbidding someone to do something is a risky act to perform, C.s should ask themselves whether A. is at all likely to do the act they wish to

forbid. If not, there is nothing to be gained from the risk, and indeed mentioning the possibility could put it into A.'s mind and cause the unwanted act to be tried.

Further reading   Wierzbicka (1987)

FOREGROUNDING

Task

To highlight or focus attention on a topic.

Description

Foregrounding can be achieved by: (a) placement within the text; (b) using a **reflexive comment**; (c) doing the unexpected in word use, sentence structure, voice quality, or speech acts; or (d) imposing a striking patterning (e.g. rhythm or repetition) on the matter.

Persuasive value

1 It is often assumed that the first matter in a text is the most important, and so initial position automatically gives emphasis; so too does last position, particularly when accompanied by a suitable signal, such as, 'And so, finally, and most importantly, there is the matter of . . .'
2 Any matter, at any point in the text, can be emphasized by using a reflexive comment, such as, 'The main point I want to make is . . .,' or 'Ultimately the matter is one of . . .'
3 C. can break with any personal or genre expectations, and so highlight some matter for special attention, as in

(a) choosing an unusual word for it: that is, one not usual for C., or for that genre, or for that kind of interaction;
(b) by using alliteration or a **metaphor**;
(c) by varying sentence length, particularly by using the odd very brief sentence where most others are long—the brief ones, and their content, will stand out well;
(d) in speech, by raising voice pitch or volume, or by increasing speed.

N.B.   However, there is danger in varying too much from A.'s expectations in order to highlight a topic. There are 'standard' variations which work well, where non-standard ones would only confuse. So, for example, in a letter from lawyer to client, it could be good to foreground a matter by using wit or clever word-play, but a jocular tone would be risky. Wit could work because the client expects to pay close attention to the wording of the text, and so could easily spot the wit, and get the desired highlight.

4 C. could create a strongly marked grammatical structure to highlight the matter. For instance, grammatical repetition could be used, as in 'This marketing campaign is not what we need; it is not what we asked for; and it is not what we paid for.' Or repetition and climax could be used, as in 'Our policy needs to be given a fair trial; more, it needs to be given an absolutely impartial hearing.'

N.B.   It is unsubtle to highlight by using underlining, capital letters, or italics, except in such genres as reports, or very casual memos or letters. But social judgments of such things change rapidly: for example, 'bullet points' are currently tolerated in many professional and business communications where some years ago they would not have been.

See also **Genre: choose; Idea arrangement; Triplets**

Further reading   Atkinson (1984); Sonnino (1968)

'FROM . . . TO'

Task

To be wary of expressing offensive value judgments.

Description

The use of the contrastive phrase 'from . . . to . . .' as in:

Ex. 1 From the East to the West the word had gone out.

Ex. 2 From the College Principal to the newest student in the Bachelor of Nursing course everyone reads the University newspaper.

presents the two ends of a continuum, and is used to show it as all-embracing.

Persuasive value

1 The phrase should be used with caution because it can inadvertently offend. By characterizing what is presented at one end as high status it automatically makes what is presented at the other as low status, and this could be contentious.

In Ex. 1 there seems little to be concerned about in designating the extremes as 'East' and 'West;' but in Ex. 2, although most people would acknowledge that there are real differences between the Principal and the newest student, in terms of age, experience, qualifications, and so on, it is the naming of the Bachelor of Nursing course as the other extreme from the Principal which could offend all those involved in that course.

The following example is also likely to be offensive to many:

Ex. 3 This is true from the most senior woman business executive to the housewife at home wiping the kids' noses.

Here the sense that the second group, the housewives, are being treated as low in status is reinforced by dropping the formal language which is used to represent the executives in favor of such casual language as 'kids' and 'wiping noses.'

2 The continuum can also cause trouble if it excludes a group who might feel they should have been included, as in

Ex. 4 From the most senior professor to the most junior faculty member, the staff join together to make the university great.

The administrative and support staff might well feel unfairly excluded and resent this representation.

Further reading   Quirk, Greenbaum, Leech, and Svartvik (1985)

GENERIC 'THE'

Task

To present a matter as important.

Description

As well as referring to some object as if it is known to the participants, 'the' (*see* **Definite article 'the'**), or its absence in certain cases, can be used to mark something as the name of a whole class or species, and thus to indicate its importance. For example, it can be used to make generic a single thing, as in

Ex. 1 The lion in Africa . . .

contrasted with the non-generic

Ex. 2 The lion we saw in the zoo . . .

N.B.   The **indefinite article 'a'/'an'** can also signify the generic nature of some things, but only in the one kind of case illustrated by:

Ex. 3 A lion is a beautiful animal.

The absence of 'the' can also act as a generic signifier, when used of more than one thing, as in

Ex. 4 Lions are beautiful.

contrasted with the non-generic

Ex. 5 The lions in the zoo look sad.

Persuasive value

To indicate that a thing is a generic, a whole class or species, is to say that it is an important factor in experience, and that it has subclasses and a variety of subcategories. So those things that are represented as generics should be carefully observed. It can be a strategy to have people hold them to be more important than they are. For example, when 'the television' began to be represented without the definite article, as 'television,' it showed that T.V. had become a major factor in social life. Compare:

Ex. 6 Television is an important medium.

and

Ex. 7 The television has a place in our lives.

In the second version there remains a sense of it as a specific object, associating it with the physical T.V. set, which gets lost as the article disappears and it becomes a generic entity.

Further reading   Halliday and Hasan (1976); Quirk, Greenbaum, Leech, and Svartvik (1985)

GENRE: CHOOSE

Task

To put A.s into a suitable reading or hearing role to have them accept the communication's message.

Description

Genres are sets of texts which share properties. For example, the following are standardly recognized genres: soap operas, personal letters, news broadcasts, small talk, letters of complaint, memos, reports, detective stories. Although it is not easy to say what properties each set shares, the sets are nonetheless accepted as being homogeneous groups, and people know what they mean when they call a specific film text a Western, and can even distinguish it from a spaghetti Western.

Persuasive value

The important thing to note about classifying texts into genres is what it does to readers or hearers to have these generic perceptions.

1 On noting the first sign of what genre a text is, experienced A.s have expectations of what is to come; so they know for example, that a written text headed 'Memo' will be about work matters, will be short, probably not even in grammatical sentences, it will be a reminder or a request, or some other means of getting A.s to do some act. If it does not meet these expectations, A.s will first try to make it fit what they anticipate, and only when that fails will they begin to work it out in its own right—but by then A.s will be slightly irritated by the earlier wasted efforts. If the memo matches expectations, it will be read only superficially, because A. can anticipate its message, and so any delicacies or complexities of meaning may get lost.

2 Once A.s note what genre a text is, they settle into the appropriate pattern of reading or listening behavior, playing the role that their experience of the genre suggests. So, for example, if they recognize the signs of 'argument' in a text, they move into the role of 'reader of argument' and this means thinking carefully about what is said, taking sides, asking questions about the validity of evidence, etc.; while if the generic signs indicate that it is an 'explanation' text, they know the role 'reader of explanation' is a more passive one, and requires them only to think 'Do I understand' or 'Has C. given enough detail to be useful?' etc. C.s should therefore choose the genre to put A.s into the roles that suit their persuasive purposes.

N.B.   The prevalence of genres means that communications are often seen as routines, and the more this is so, the less able people will be to accept what is strange or new as a view of the world. People often comment adversely on a text which does not fit the genres they know, object to its difficulty, or get angry with those who made it, as in 'I don't understand what that program was supposed to be doing: was it supposed to be a documentary or what?' Even when the subject matter and the language are plain enough, readers can be resistant to a text until they know its genre. So C.s should take care to match generic expectations.

Further reading   Freadman and Macdonald (1992)

GRAMMATICAL 'ERRORS'

Tasks

To avoid distracting others from the content.
To avoid offending others.

Description

There are three grammatical 'errors' which meet frequent criticism: (a) the split infinitive, (b) the dangling participle, and (c) the use of a preposition to end a sentence as in:

(a) The infinitive is the form of the verb which consists of 'to' + the verb, as in 'to be,' 'to forgive.' Some people, who were perhaps taught at school to do so, find it intolerable when a C. splits the infinitive by inserting a word between 'to' and the verb, as in 'to gradually understand,' 'to substantially increase.' Other people have no such resistance to the form as such, though they may think in a particular instance the inserted word would have been better after the verb, as in 'to increase substantially.' Others never notice such things.

(b) A dangling participle is a form like 'Being a Nobel Prizewinner in literature, I find Hemingway's work fascinating.' The problem here is that the participle 'being' is not attached to the sentence closely enough. The rule is that if no subject is present in such participle clauses as 'Being a Nobel Prizewinner in literature,' the missing subject is supplied by the subject of the immediately following clause, in this case 'I,' so the sentence reads 'I am a Nobel Prizewinner in literature and I find . . .' This is not what was intended.

(c) Instances of the use of a preposition to end a sentence are 'This is something I have never heard of,' 'This crisis is one we are unprepared for.' While sometimes it may be suitable to put the preposition elsewhere, in many cases it is quite unnecessary and produces overly complex forms, as in the classic example, 'This is something up with which I will not put' (rather than 'This is something I will not put up with').

Persuasive value

Such 'errors' may antagonize particular A.s, and cause them to be distracted from the content of the communication and even to be contemptuous of C. Where there is any likelihood of this occurring, as with an older, formally educated A., such 'errors' should be carefully removed from the text.

Further reading   Fowler (1983)

GREETING

Tasks

To set good mood.
To establish or maintain bonding.

Description

There are powerful conventions for greetings, of which the main ones are that people are required to greet each other on meeting, and that greetings should occur whenever meetings happen (with some modifications and exceptions). The kind of greeting depends on the quality of the bonding that exists between those meeting, and on the medium of communication, and on whether the interaction is cross-gender or cross-cultural.

Persuasive value

In face-to-face interactions, the basic convention in British and American society is that people should greet each other on meeting each new day. (Note: 'meet' in these cases means coming into eye contact with each other.)

If later meetings in the same setting during that day occur, they can have minimal greetings, but if people meet in a new environment in different roles, for examples if on a family outing to the theater one met there a work colleague, full greetings should be exchanged. So strong is the convention about the need for greetings in different environments, that even a minor difference can require a strong greeting. If colleagues share an office, and leave and enter it frequently, they will not greet with each new eye contact, but if they are both out of the office and meet on the stairs or in the elevator, they will greet, and if they meet accidentally in an unusual place, like the library, the greeting will be stronger—'Fancy meeting you here' is a typical greeting in such circumstances.

The correct greeting to use varies according to the degree of bonding, social roles, time factors, etc. It can range from faint gesture or slight facial expression between those of slight acquaintance who are in hurry, or where meetings occur with great frequency during the day, through the use of formulaic phrases like 'Hello,' 'Hi,' 'How're things?' to such emphasized greetings as embraces where the bond is close and the meetings infrequent.

Greetings will hardly be noticed if performed suitably, their value is mainly as an indication of bond maintenance, against which background persuasion tactics can work. If, however, C. magnifies the greeting (e.g. by exaggerated expressions of pleasure), A. could be made to feel in a particularly friendly relationship, and so be more easily persuaded. On the other hand, if the greeting is omitted, this will be of significance to the bonding, its absence will be marked, and the person concerned would see it as unfriendliness or arrogance, as a dismissal of his or her personal worth, and so be likely to respond badly to any persuasion. There are many indications of the powerful response that the absence of greeting can cause: for example, in such common phrases as 'He stared straight through me,' 'He never has the time even to say hi,' or 'Did you see that? He cut me dead, snubbed me!' Reasonably enough, it can anger and hurt people that they are ignored. It may happen unintentionally, but it will still have a bad effect on the relationship. If C. later learns that this has happened—if A. says 'I saw you in town the other day, but you didn't see me'—C. will need to apologize to repair the damage to the bond. This is so whether the whole greeting was omitted, or C. produced less of one than the other expected.

Problems arise whenever people differ in their sense of the appropriate greeting. To generalize, older people may expect more formality and greater length than younger people do; women may expect fuller greetings and more body language and closer proximity than men do; and across cultures there could be different perceptions about who performs the first greeting, what formulas are used, what topics can be used, etc.

See also **Greeting: by phone**

GREETING: BY PHONE

Tasks

To establish that the interaction is between the right people.
To enable each participant to recognize the other's voice.
To set a good mood.
To establish or maintain bonding.

Description

Phone greetings are complicated by the need to establish that connection has been achieved between the necessary two participants. Unlike face-to-face greetings, which can begin to establish a bond, phone greetings should be delayed until:

(a) the caller is sure the right number has been dialled;
(b) the person he or she wishes to talk to is available to come to the phone;
(c) any intermediaries—switchboard operators, members of the callee's family, etc.—have been dealt with.

Persuasive value

Greetings which begin too soon, before (a), (b), and (c) have been covered, will miss their mark. Once the right persons are at each end of the phone connection, greetings can commence. They usually last longer than face-to-face greetings because they have an extra goal: to enable the two people to adjust their auditory senses to the voice set of the other, to any distortions on the line, any background noises, and so on. So more **sociable language** is necessary, before the 'business' of the call is begun. Without this preparation, some features of the communication may not have their proper effect.

Phone greetings should incorporate a question from the caller which recognises that the call may be an intrusion:

Ex. 1 Have you a moment to talk now?

Ex. 2 Are you busy at the moment?

Ex. 3 Is this a convenient moment to ring?

and should allow the callee to reject the call in favor of restarting it later. No call can make its points very effectively if the recipient is busy, just out of the shower, in the middle of an embarrassing argument, and so on.

There is a convention among some people in British and American societies that the caller has the right to initiate the main topic on the agenda of the call, since it can be assumed that he or she had some goal in calling, and this should be addressed. They would, therefore, expect to be the one to end the greeting part of the encounter. However, some members of British and American societies, and indeed people from some other cultures, do not necessarily accept this. This clash of conventions can cause irritation in some callers, who feel that they have been denied their rights.

Some people obey the convention which requires that greetings should be offered to any intermediaries who help to get the right callee to the phone, and such people will have a few words of greeting for switchboard operators, for colleagues who pass a message about the call to someone who is out of the office, etc. If a caller does not follow this convention, any intermediaries may feel angry that they are being required to put themselves out for someone they see as impolite. They may, in future, make less effort to get messages to the right people.

Further reading   Clark and French (1981)

HANDLE A DIFFICULT TOPIC

Tasks

To represent a matter which could be badly received, in such a way as to prevent trouble.
To perform a communication act which is likely to cause trouble, so as to prevent the trouble.

Description

C.s may anticipate trouble of various different kinds:

(a) legal, because of the laws of slander and libel;
(b) personal offense taken by a person attacked; or
(c) personal revelation by C. of the commission of a social sin, for example, admitting to having had an affair, or of a crime, such as having violated a traffic rule.

Persuasive value

Where C.s can anticipate trouble from mention of a certain matter or from doing a certain communication act, they can seek to prevent trouble in various ways.

1 They can state that they know there will be trouble, but have compelling reasons to speak, in the hope that the compulsion will appear strong enough to A. to accept the communication without causing trouble.

2 They can declare that any trouble which arises from their speech would be unfair or unjust. These are two of the most important social measures of behavior; and to be caught being either one or the other of them is to attract social opprobrium: so C. hopes that A. will not take the risk.

3 They can state that there is value for A. in what they are doing, so any troubling aspects to it should be weighed against its helpfulness, and be dismissed.

4 They can call on the relevant general principles, of free speech, of the right of anyone to offer fair criticism, and of the right of everyone not to be punished for holding their social or political views.

Further reading   Brown and Levinson (1987); Davidson (1984)

HUMOR

Tasks

To lighten the mood of an interaction.
To enhance the social relationship with A.
To form a group from those present.
To present oneself well.

Description

A touch of humor generally affects the interaction in three ways: it is noticed as a language skill, it creates a social experience of enjoyment or laughter, and it reminds A.s of familiar behaviors and routines. It can also be used to dismiss an opponent or his or her case.

Persuasive value

Humor is a difficult tactic to handle well, and if handled badly can have a very adverse impact on the interaction.

1 If used well it can show C. to be entertaining, intelligent, and skilled with language. These attributes can suggest C. is generally worth attending to,

beyond listening to his or her humor, as a sensitive interpreter whose pronouncements are likely to be important and true. This will only happen, however, if the humor does not distract people from their goals.

C. will only be seen as entertaining if the humor uses the specifics of the occasion to make its point, as in witty comments which are closely tied to something in the communication and not just remembered jokes with no connection with the present topic, mood, etc. The humor needs to appear spontaneous and improvised, and be C.'s own individual work, not copied from another. So it is humorous to respond as happened in a recent discussion about a forthcoming salary raise: when the question was asked whether it would be backdated, the answer was 'No, retrospectivity is a thing of the past.' It is less humorous to say, quite out of place, 'That reminds me, did you hear that joke on T.V. last night? There were these two men . . .' The former proves C. is attending to A.'s question, and can quickly design a suitable and wittily formed answer; while all the latter shows is that C. is paying little attention to the interaction, but has a good memory for an irrelevant joke.

C.'s intelligence will be particularly manifest if the humor is not only relevant and witty but also illuminating (i.e. if it is a way of presenting an idea which makes an important contribution to the communication).

C.'s language skills will be shown if the humor involves wit, as in punning, or if there is a complexity about it which C. handles well. It should not just be word-play, it should also be idea-play, that is, not just verbal skill but more deeply cognitively skillful. But even as word-skill, it is certainly true that those who cannot tell a joke or comic story well, with crucial details omitted or the punchline mangled, are judged as bad communicators, and so their other communications may be rejected as unlikely to be accurate or well ordered.

2 Humor is powerfully persuasive if it generates shared amusement or laughter, particularly if it can remind A.s of things shared with C., and so suggest that C. and A. have common ground, that they are likely to share views, and hence that C.'s present communication should be agreed to. It can also be used to divide a group into an elite who share the laughter and the common ground, and those who do not. In this way it can be used to set up alliances and oppositions, and can act as pre-persuasion even before the central topic of a communication is begun.

It can also be persuasive by relaxing A.s, and preventing them noticing some detail which they might oppose. It is wise to note when humor occurs, and what in the immediate context it might be intended to hide.

3 Humor can be used to destroy the credibility of an opponent or an opposing view. Laughing at them suggests that the opposition are not worth serious attention, and while it will not work if A.s take the matter very seriously, it can often serve to reduce the power of an opponent's case. Humor has been used as one (among many other tactics) to disparage

tyrants or oppressive laws. Where confrontation exalts the enemy, humor reduces his or her significance.

4 However, humor can be dangerous as a tactic, for the following reasons.

(a) If it is a person's only contribution to the interaction, then it can suggest he or she is uncomfortable with what is going on, or has nothing else to say. If one person uses it a good deal, it may be interpreted as a sign of isolation, nervousness, or even desperation about being unable to join in in any other way. It may also be a sign of egotism in one who is feeling out of things and wants to be noticed.

(b) If the humor is of poor quality, is only weakly funny, or worse, is personally vindictive, dismissive of others, or racist, or sexist, it can reveal C.'s attitudes and opinions, and these may be held against C. long after the event. A politician recently made a 'humorous' aside to the effect that his opponent was not a true, red-blooded, Australian because he did not drive a car and had no children. Many people have seen this as an indication of a red-necked dislike of others who have a different lifestyle, and have been angered or concerned about what it revealed of an important political figure.

(c) C.s should be careful not to laugh at A., or a third party liked by A., or at things that A. cares deeply about. So to be effective humor requires knowledge about A.

(d) Sometimes humor is seen as avoidance of a difficult task in the communication, and this will put the humorist in a poor light: joking about being late with an assignment or being unprepared for a meeting is rarely received well.

(e) Written humor is always problematic because C. has no way of telling what mood the recipient will be in when it arrives, and can take no account of this or other features of A.'s situation.

Humor is also problematic in cross-cultural communications, since it depends so much on shared cultural experience, and on sensitivity to language implications and associations of meaning. And it can also, though to a lesser degree, cause problems when used in cross-gender encounters, because there are some differences in humor types between men and women.

See also **Jokes; Jokes: types; Puns**

Further reading   Jefferson (1978); Nash (1985)

HYPOTHESIZE

Task

To communicate a matter and have it discussed without penalty.

Description

To hypothesize is to set up a non-existent, non-real topic, in the form of a proposition, and to do so in order to explore its meaning, free of any connections with specific people or real-life events.

The hypothesis can be either totally conjectural or a highly probable possibility. It can be presented as a presumption and not spelt out, or it can be developed in some detail.

Persuasive value

The value of a hypothesis is that it allows a reasonably objective analysis because it is detached from real-life matters. But, of course, it is not really detached: what hypotheses can be formed depends very much on current interpretations and understandings of the world and the matters in it. But the idea of a hypothesis is to allow discussion in the abstract, without penalty or any other consequences. It can be a very useful way of exploring and anticipating the world's happenings, trying to predict the future, and preparing to handle what events it might bring. A discussion of this kind is intended to proceed without people taking up their routine positions, or uttering their routine comments. It can be unreal and new enough to draw original thought and expression from those taking part, and this could be fruitful for all concerned.

Hypotheses run into trouble, however, on two counts. First, not everyone is able to argue in the abstract, and many people cannot prevent their feelings and their routine responses from entering the discussion so that it loses its non-real aspect. Second, people may question whether it is really hypothetical, and why that particular hypothesis was chosen. If, for example, a senior executive of a company said 'Let's hypothesize that we had to fire 100 employees,' many of those present might begin to worry about their jobs.

Further reading   Chaffee (1991)

IDEA ARRANGEMENT

Task

To arrange ideas in good positions in the text.

Description

There are established conventions which indicate the best way to arrange points to be argued so that they are most likely to be understood and accepted.

Persuasive value

1 By convention, ideas known to A. should be given early, and newer ideas later, and any link between them should be stressed. Using this order frames A.'s thinking by first sparking off memories of some already known ideas, and then suggesting that any new ideas coming next can be aligned with that set. If used where there really is an alignment, then A.s may accept the new idea because it seems to be a simple or even a necessary outcome of their already accepted ideas.

Ex. 1   You know that the policy is . . . (a) and (b) . . . Our latest report shows that adjustments need to be made to our plans—therefore, one aspect of (a) should be revised by the company . . ., and as a corollary we should . . . Further, Mary suggests that we should . . .

If the first idea, 'that A. knows the policy is . . .,' is agreed, it follows that he or she could accept something of the adjustments, provided only that the links are emphasized.

2 Even if there is no real alignment between what C. offers as a known idea and the new idea C. offers next, C. might still manage to persuade A. that there is a link, and so to accept the new. This is more likely if A. strongly agrees with the known idea, and is persuaded that the new is 'just the same kind of thing.'

3 By convention, the first place in a textual section (i.e. the first paragraph, the first sentence in a paragraph), should be occupied by the strongest idea C. can produce. It will receive most attention, and will be used as a guide to the kinds of ideas that will follow, and how they connect. The conventions of placement ensure that this happens.

4 The last place in a section, and most certainly in the last place in the communication as a whole, is also assumed to contain one of C.'s strongest points. It creates the last memory that A. has as the communication ends, and this has impact.

5 It follows that any weaker ideas should be placed in the middle sections of the text, where they are less emphasized, and, if bad, may be forgotten, and so not act to prevent A. from being persuaded by the stronger ideas.

See also **Analogy; Foregrounding; Link material** tactics

Further reading   Corbett (1977, 1990); Dillon (1981); Sonnino (1968)

IMPARTIALITY: PRESENT

Tasks

To present oneself as impartial.

To present oneself as trustworthy.

To have the communication treated seriously.

Description

There are communicative signs that indicate C. is not biassed in raising and dealing with his or her topics. The signs are

(a) that a range of opinions and attitudes are supplied;
(b) that proper acknowledgment is given to the opposing view;
(c) that C. is relatively conservative in what he or she puts forward; and
(d) that C. shows signs of willingness to adapt his or her views if the others show that this would be right to do so.

Persuasive value

Since most people have some degree of opinion about most things, real impartiality of view is likely to be infrequently found. Yet this has never stopped people from regarding impartiality highly and treating any degree of bias as a sign that the point of view of C. is to be treated with caution or even resisted. (Apparently it is not taken as a possibility that a bias has been arrived at rationally and so could be deservedly supported.)

To avoid perceptions and even accusations of bias, the following signs could be used.

1 Mention of the two sides of any matter, or of opposed opinions on it, could be made in frequent and close juxtaposition (though these would, of course, support the one and reject the other).

2 Acknowledge the problematic nature of the view being put forward.

3 To display a bias but do so in a moderate way, use positive words for one's own position and negative ones for the opposition. For example, the following are positive terms:

Ex. 1 create, increase, (re)build, implement, do, introduce, endorse, provide, support, move, announce, start;

while these are negative:

Ex. 2 reject, destroy, lose, avoid, deny, argue, attempt, obstruct, fail, hinder, prevent, hint.

4 Present an appearance of having come to a judgment after the discussion rather than before it. So present the view tentatively at the start, and only consolidate its strength and rightness as the communication proceeds.

Ex. 1 [at start] I have been thinking, what if the policy we introduced last
year is not as useful as we thought . . . ?
[at end] So I think the policy is failing to serve its purpose.

Further reading   Chafe (1985); Corbett (1977, 1990); Sonnino (1968);
Tannen (1985)

INDEFINITE ARTICLE 'A'/'AN'

Task

To indicate that information is new.

Description

The use of the indefinite article 'a' or 'an' before a word indicates that the
information is presumed to be new to A.

Persuasive value

1 The use of the indefinite article with a representation of something
indicates that C. assumes, deliberately or not, that A. does not know of the
thing. It is often used with the first mention of a thing in an interaction,
where A. is certainly unlikely to know of the matter, as in

Ex. 1 I saw a new computer today.

where it can mean either that C. thinks A. would not know which computer is being referred to, or more broadly, that A. would not know of the
experience C. had in seeing a computer that day.
2 It can also be used as a tactic to exclude A. from shared experiences,
when used of something that A. does in fact know.

Ex. 2 There's a new typist in the office. She started on Monday.

If said towards the end of the week, and when A. is as likely to visit the
office as C., it seems to exclude A. from sharing C.'s knowledge. It seems
to be a sign that C. does not perceive A. to belong to the same group—
those who use the office—and could be seen, even if A. knows it to be
wrongly addressed to him or her, as a covert way of isolating A. (Equally
though, it may strike A. as a sign that C. is at fault in only just noticing
what everyone else noticed on Monday.) It is unlikely that a single instance
or two of this kind of usage would be noted, but if used in quantity it could
persuade A. into difference or even antagonism with C.
    There is a different kind of isolating that can also be achieved by using
the indefinite article, as in

Ex. 3 I saw a new computer today. It was a real beauty, and an absolute snip. A real value buy.

Here the quantity of indefinites, allied with the vagueness of the words used—'real,' 'beauty,' 'absolute,' 'snip,' 'value,' 'buy'—acts to exclude A. from knowledge of what the computer was like. It shows C.'s feelings, but not any information which A. could use in thinking about computers, and little that would be a guide to purchasing the one mentioned. There is simply nothing specific by way of detail that is supplied. A. would have to ask questions if he or she needed real information about it. Such communications seem to forget that A. has needs too, and needs more than just hearing C.'s feelings. These cannot be shared, which would create a bond, because there is nothing definite supplied to enable A. to have the feelings about.

3 It can act in quite a different way, as in

Ex. 4 I must see a doctor about this pain.
     I must pay a visit to Aunt Ethel soon.

where it communicates about a doctor or Aunt Ethel without implying relationship or involvement with them, as would occur in

Ex. 5 I must see my doctor about this pain.
     I must visit my Aunt Ethel soon.

Frequent use of the indefinite form for personal experiences of this kind suggest that C. isolates him- or herself from events and people. This may be useful information for a persuader to know.

See also **Definite article 'the'; Generic 'the'**

Further reading   Halliday and Hasan (1976)

INDIRECT CRITICISM

Tasks

To influence others indirectly to be critical of something by contrasting it with an ideal.
To influence others indirectly to be critical of something by suggesting it has the wrong priorities.

Description

1 Criticism of a matter can be made by showing how far it falls short of an ideal, as in

Ex. 1 Your report on the marketing plan is very good, as far as it goes.

Ex. 2 Your report on the marketing plan is very good, as far as it goes, but it needs some ideas for future marketing strategies.

Ex. 3 Your report on the marketing plan is very good. Did you think of any other alternatives for marketing strategies?

2 Criticism can be shown by representing that its priorities are wrong, as in

Ex. 4 I was glad that you mentioned in your letter on future plans the idea of radio advertising, and I think we could usefully discuss this.

Persuasive value

1 In Ex. 1 not only is a measure of praise offered, but also some criticism, although the fault is not made specific, while in Ex. 2 the fault in the report is spelt out in detail. In Ex. 3, on the other hand, while the communication also begins as praise, it then asks a question which indirectly implies that the report was faulty in omitting the alternatives, but it could equally be interpreted as praise for the report, and then, as a quite separate matter, an extension of the report's subject into alternatives. The third example is much less face-threatening than the other two.

2 An alternative form of indirect criticism is to hint that the priorities are wrong, as in Ex. 4. This would be a strong, if indirect, criticism if the radio advertising were only a tiny part of the letter, and here C. is ignoring the bulk of what it contained. C. is, in effect, trying to change the agenda from that set by the letter, to one which happens to suit his or her aims better.

See also **Describe subjectively; Face threats: recognize**

Further reading   Sonnino (1968)

INFORMATION: ADD

Task

To pack complexity of information, opinion and self-presentation into the written sentence form.

Description

Where the things to be represented in a communication need to be so closely linked that they should be incorporated into a single sentence, there are some general grammatical tactics that can be employed to extend each of the basic sentence elements to enable this to happen. For example, in a declarative sentence which has as its basis a subject, verb and (on most occasions) an object or complement, each of these can be expanded. So, for example, the simple sentence 'The woman gave the book to Peter' can be expanded in various ways:

1 The subject can be supplied with adjectives or participial phrases. These can be placed before or after the subject's headword, (here 'woman') as in:

Ex. 1 The intelligent and serious young woman doing the secretarial work gave the book to Peter.

2 Prepositional phrases can be added, either singly or in strings, after the headword.

Ex. 2 The intelligent and serious young woman doing the secretarial work for the firm of lawyers in the city gave the book to Peter.

3 Relative clauses, both the restrictive and non-restrictive kinds, can be added after the headword.

Ex. 3 The intelligent and serious young woman who came through the door, the one who was carrying the books, who is doing the secretarial work for the firm of lawyers in the city, gave the book to Peter.

4 The subject can be given in two or more forms by using **apposition**:

Ex. 4 The intelligent and serious young woman, my new colleague, a qualified real-estate manager, gave the book to Peter.

5 The subject can be added to by coordinating it with others,

Ex. 5 The intelligent and serious young woman and my new legal assistant came in together and gave the book to Peter.

6 The verbs in sentences can be made more complex by the addition of tense or mood signs:

Ex. 6 The intelligent and serious young woman was about to give/could have given the book to Peter.

7 The whole sentence could be expanded by adding new clauses (each of which can be simple or extended):

Ex. 7 The intelligent and serious young woman gave the book to Peter, and then gave the pen to Paul, and finally gave the pile of papers to Susan.

This density of information is only appropriate to written texts; spoken texts should be much less packed with information.

See also **Elaborated code; Written communication** tactics

Further reading   Quirk, Greenbaum, Leech, and Svartvik (1985)

INFORMATION: ASSESS

Task

To judge the value of information being offered.

Description

On being offered a piece of information, people need to assess its likely truth, its accuracy, and the interpretation that C. has given it.

Persuasive value

Unless the information can be evaluated for its true worth it can deceive A., whether C. means to do this or it happens inadvertently, and could lead A. to base his or her knowledge of the matter on a faulty foundation.

Assessing the information requires the following steps:

(a) The information should be checked against any memories of related or similar matters.
(b) The trustworthiness of C. should be considered. Is C. slapdash about details, or an accurate person? Is C. speaking from his or her own experience or from another source? Is C. or the other source a good or bad witness? Or a good or bad interpreter? What kinds of detail are given? Is anything obviously missing?
(c) Check the information either by asking C. to clarify it, or seek another source of information and compare the two accounts.
(d) Reinterpret the information in the light of previous experience of C. as an information provider. Discount any known biasses that C. has.

N.B. It is important that it is A.'s own interpretation of C.'s information that is stored in memory and not just C.'s version swallowed whole. So it is crucial that A. begin the process of reinterpretation as soon as possible after C. has finished communicating. For example, after listening to a lecture, a good student is one who subjects the information from it to thought, assessment, and to rewriting as soon as possible.

N.B. In assessing the value of C.'s information it is also worth thinking about how C. sees his or her relationship with A. Does C. see his or her role to be 'setting A. right about life' or is C. more tentative about giving information to A., acting as if 'asking A. to agree.' In the latter case it is more likely that A. can feel the information is right, because C. is prepared for A. to consider his or her own interpretation of it. Whereas when C. is setting A. right, he or she feels some strong compulsion that A. should accept it—it may be for the very good reason that it is something very much to A.'s advantage, but it may also be being offered for less helpful motives. A.s should always ask themselves why is C. telling this information to me, at this time and place.

See also **Information: choose; Informing**

Further reading   Ritchie (1991)

INFORMATION: CHOOSE

Tasks

To ensure that information is well received.
To have ideas accepted.

Description

There are general cultural expectations about what useful information is and what makes it useful and interesting. People first expect that what is told to them will be useful, and will be pleased if in addition it is made interesting.

Persuasive value

The criteria to follow to ensure that what is communicated has both qualities are as follows:

(a) A. will want the information to be clear, that is, the content should be understandable with enough detail to be useful, not vague or ambiguous, and be clearly expressed.
(b) A. will expect the information to fit in with his or her commonsense view of how the world works. For example, A. will expect standard effects to arise from standard causes, but will also be prepared to accept information about inexplicable accidents, disasters, etc. He or she will expect that accounts of specific people will be consistent with his or her own knowledge of their character and life stories. Information about unusual or inconsistent behaviors by people can also be expected occasionally, but the unusual must be believably attributable to the person (e.g. it would be good and interesting information to tell of a mean person suddenly spending wildly, but not perhaps suddenly dyeing his hair). This is because in the first case an old habit can always be broken but in the second it could be too completely out of character to be believed.
(c) A. will expect the information to be of some importance in the grand scheme of things: 'I fell in the shower and hurt my wrist' is more likely

to be seen as important than 'I've just had a shower' (though there are times when this too could be important—e.g. as a sign that the shower is now free).
(d) A. will expect incoming information to be tailored to fit his or her interests: friends can be more informative than strangers because they know of our interests.
(e) A. will expect the information to be of topical interest. And will want its currency stressed. Those who begin their informing acts with long accounts of the history of some event before stressing its currency will be seen as boring (i.e. just interested in information for its own sake).
(f) A.s will prefer information which supports their accepted views, but will accept material which contrasts sharply with it, if explained and made clear enough, because no A.s want to have inaccurate or useless knowledge. But A.s will appreciate it if C. can help by showing in what ways to adjust their knowledge of the matter to fit this addition.

The more C.s can tailor their information to these criteria the more likely A. is to recognize communality with C. and be inclined to accept other things offered in the future.

See also **Information: control**

Further reading   Ritchie (1991)

INFORMATION: CONTROL

Task

To present oneself as an important holder of information.

Description

Since the world is full of matters, and each one is complex, it will be a difficult and very important task to select what to communicate and give as information to others. Selection is necessary however since otherwise C.s would swamp A.s with information, which they would be unable to digest, let alone use to create knowledge and wisdom.

By this selection process, everyone who communicates acts as a 'gate-keeper,' excluding some things and allowing other things through the 'gate' to be heard by A.s. (The term originated as a description of the role of editors in the mass media as they decide what shall and what shall not be published, but it is equally applicable to any person who supplies any kind of information to another.) So people choose to allow through the 'gate' some information about an event at work, or decide whether or not to pass on a compliment, and so on.

In choosing what to impart, people decide also on how to present it (e.g. in good light or bad); how to develop it; how to connect it to other things known to A. (e.g. 'X happened yesterday' or 'X happened yesterday, just as you said it would'); or whether to give it in a very detailed way or just make a general point. And each such choice has an impact on how A. will interpret and understand it.

Persuasive value

All communicators should understand that when they select what information to impart and how to present it, they are exerting power over others.
1 If a C. gives all the information he or she has about a matter, in all its detail, while this may be useful to A., equally, its quantity could cause A. to be unable to absorb it, and hence to understand or use it. So although C. appears to be helpful, A. is worse off in the end, because he or she 'knows too much to really know anything.'
2 C.s have power as they choose who to give the information to. Not only can they make A.s more informed by telling them what they need to know, but by selecting one A. and denying information to another they can create groups among A.s, of those who know something and those who do not. For example, if C. has insider information about an up-coming job interview, by giving it to one A. he or she could greatly enhance that person's chances of interviewing well, and at the same time could make it harder for someone else who was left in ignorance. C.s can create cliques and elites who 'know,' and outer groups who do not.

The consequences of such actions will always be to produce enemies among those who know they have been excluded, but it will not always produce allies among the elite who know: some people may be grateful for information which helps them, but others dislike having to feel in another's debt.

Further reading   Shoemaker (1991)

INFORMATION FLOW

Task

To ensure that others receive the communicated information in the best way possible.

Description

The efficient transmission of information requires that there be a suitable quantity of information for each unit of communication (utterance, sentence, paragraph, etc.) and that this should be offered at a suitable pace, if (a) the material is to be understood, and (b) the readership is to be persuaded to accept it.

Persuasive value

1 The flow rates for writing and for speech differ, but in each case there is an appropriate pace for ease of reception. If the rate of information is too fast, A.s will be unable to receive much of the message at all, let alone understand or accept it. Contrarily, if the rate is too slow, and the message is almost without content, they will either cease to attend, or will have too much time to study, and resist, the material.

Determining the right rate for understanding depends on (a) perceiving the degree of difficulty, and particularly the predictability or lack of it, in the material, and (b) assessing the reader's skill at information reception. A communicator should use whatever sources are available to assess his or her A.'s preferred rates.

2 For information to be accepted, information flow rates should vary as the difficulties of the text require; however, this variation should never be too extreme for A.s to adjust to:

(a) At the start the information quantity should be fairly minimal, but as the communication proceeds the rate can be gradually built up, and then kept moderately steady.
(b) If at any point A.s need to make a marked adjustment to their whole approach to the text, perhaps changing from being listeners to an account of facts to actively taking up a stance in an argument about something to do with the facts (i.e. if there is a genre alteration), at this point the flow should be reduced, while the adjustments are made.
(c) If the text presents too many ideas at any point without preparing the ground for them, or if it ends with too many ideas in close proximity, it can cause misunderstanding, because of the way it requires A.s to reassess and revise their input rate.

See also **Genre: choose; Information flow: adjustments; Informing**

Further reading   Mulholland (1991)

INFORMATION FLOW: ADJUSTMENTS

Task

To handle adjustments to information flow without causing misunderstanding.

Description

Information should be provided at a rate which makes it easy for A.s to assimilate and understand it. C.s should note when the **information flow** needs adjustment, and then use one of the following tactics.

Persuasive value

1 Reductions in the rate of information flow can be achieved by various methods:

(a) By insertions—these could be in the form of elaborations, examples, analogies, details of supporting evidence, relevant side issues, or propositions.

(b) C.s could provide repetitions where the representation of content seems to be problematic.

(c) Additions can be particularly useful when they are addressed to showing how the next idea in the text fits in with the already treated ones, and how each one fits in with the overall theme or argument: for example, **reflexive comments** which show how each part of the information is meant to relate to others, or show how it is to be categorized, as in

Ex. 1 And this is the most crucial point (= consider this well) . . .

(d) also useful in steadying information flow are those **sociable language** tokens which are aimed at maintaining the social bonds among those present; or indicate how the communicator sees the current stage of the interaction, as in

Ex. 2 So, as I am sure we all agree on this, I shall go on . . .

2 Speeding up the rate of information can be done by:

(a) Packing more information into each noun phrase, each clause, and each sentence, as in this noun phrase:

Ex. 3 the special grade aluminum book casing [*rather than* the book casing was made of aluminum which had been specially graded].

(b) Reducing the sociable language component (if a large 'dose' of this is supplied at the start and end of the encounter it can be omitted from the middle).

(c) Using any specialized language that would be known to A.s, or, where unsure that a specialized term is known, defining it at the start, and then using it.

See also **Analogy; Informing**

Further reading   Mulholland (1991)

INFORMING

Tasks

To reduce A.'s uncertainty.
To increase A.'s uncertainty.

Description

C.s share things they know with another person; if they do so in such a way as to make their knowledge of some value to A.'s life, they are imparting information. If, however, they simply offer some facts or opinions with no relevance to anything in A.'s life, they are just imparting data and confusion. For example, it would be just supplying data to say 'There are 20,000 people in New York with red hair' to someone with no interest in such a fact, who could make no use of it, and who might reply 'So? Why tell me?' If however it had some significance for A., or C. was able to show that it had, then that would change it from 'data' to 'information.'

The social value of useful information is that it reduces A.'s uncertainty about some matter, or if A.s are already fairly sure about a matter it can consolidate their certainty.

Persuasive value

Before deciding whether to inform A., C. should ask the following questions:

(a) Does A. really want to know more about the matter? Some people are happier without detailed information on some matters (e.g. the gory details of a surgical operation). If C. supplies them with unwanted information they will dislike C. for it.
(b) Does C. know enough about the person to be sure what will be relevant information?

Giving any information at all to another inevitably discloses what C. thinks is important and hence how C.'s mind works. For example, if C. speaks of nothing but money, and the cost of things, C. will stand revealed as a person obsessed with money. This could either help form a bond with A. if the obsession is mutual, or break a bond if it is not. To avoid this latter possibility C. should not give too much information to anyone until there is some feedback to show whether A. shares this view.

Since information is received best when A.s see it as relevant, if C. has any doubt whether A. will recognize its relevance, he or she should wherever possible provide the relevance alongside the information.

Ex. 1 C: Your comments in your last letter about rewarding teaching
excellence suggest that you might find the following of some
interest, since it shows how excellence might be assessed.'

In this example C. might be producing information of real significance to
A. if it relates closely to A.'s expressed interest, but on the other hand if A.
finds it of only peripheral interest, he or she could see C. as trying to create
a false bond, and not one based on A.'s real interests.

See also **Information: choose; Information: control**

Further reading   Ritchie (1991); Wierzbicka (1987)

INITIATING MOVE

Tasks

To initiate a speech action.
To influence others to respond.

Description

This is an act of utterance which is isolable from any speech preceding it,
and is therefore seen as being an initial move. It is addressed to any or
all of the people present, and it requires that someone respond
immediately.

Ex. 1 A: What time is it?
   B: Three o'clock.

Persuasive value

Whenever an initiating move occurs it is an opportunity for a C. to
influence any or every aspect of the interaction—to set a mood, perform
an act, to bring some topic onto the agenda—with little pressure from the
immediately preceding utterance. It is therefore a very powerful role to
be an initiator, especially the first initiator in an encounter. C. can then
affect all that occurs from that moment on, though he or she cannot
control it. Anyone who wishes to resist C.'s influence and introduce their
own agenda has to persuade the others to divert the course of the event,
and to change its nature. People do not always welcome such changes, so
once the topic and mood have become established such change may be
very difficult.
   So important is the initiating role that anyone who has had few chances

to initiate during an interaction will feel thwarted. And, correspondingly, anyone who persists in the initiating role without serious justification will be criticized for being greedy. The convention that speaking turns should rotate among those present (*see* **Turntaking**) applies also to the rotation of initiating role.

Once the initiating move has been made it exerts strong pressure on those present to produce a response. If it is a question they must answer, if it is a statement they must support, amend, or resist it, etc.

However, while producing a response it is possible for the responder to add an initiating move of his or her own and so exert a pressure on others, including the first speaker:

Ex. 1 A: What time is it?
      B: Three o'clock. Why?
      A: Oh. I need to go at 3:30.

Initiating moves vary in the pressure they put on A. to respond, and in the degree of imposition this causes. So although a greeting move puts irresistible pressure on A. to return a greeting, the imposition is negligible. Questions can exert different pressures according to whether they are open or closed; and statements, which may appear to wield little influence, require some form of tolerance, agreement, or emendation.

See also **Exchange of speech; Questions: closed; Questions: open; Sentence structure** tactics; **State**

Further reading   Coulthard (1985); Goodwin (1981); McLaughlin (1984); Nofsinger (1991)

INSERTED SEQUENCES

Task

To clarify a matter before it proceeds further.

Description

An inserted sequence is one which occurs within an **exchange of speech**, and halts it, but does not constitute part of it. It can occur at any point, and is unpredictable. Its usual function is to clarify something in the preceding speech move before an adequate response can be given, as in

Ex. 1 A: How do you get to Main Street?
      B: Where from?

A: Sorry, from the University.

B: O.K. then, you take Schonell Drive and . . .

Here B feels unable to answer sensibly without further information, so suspends a response until this has been sought and received. This example shows A acknowledging that he or she has supplied insufficient information, in 'sorry,' and B signalling the return to the suspended exchange, in 'O.K. then.' Such acknowledgements are frequent but not inevitable.

Inserted sequences can also occur where the intending respondent is unsure of the meaning, is unsure that he or she has heard correctly, etc.

Persuasive value

1 Where it is important to get the response right, it is better to use an inserted sequence than to assume C.'s initiating move has been understood.

2 Since the insertion implies some criticism of C. for not being detailed or clear enough (or even for not being audible), such sequences should be carefully done to avoid setting up an antagonism.

3 Asking for clarification can rebound on A. if it shows that he or she has not been listening carefully, or is ignorant of some word's meaning, or does not share the world-view and experience of the other person. This can involve a good deal of face loss by A., especially if there are others present who understood fully what was said. If no one else looks puzzled it may be better to try to work the matter out without raising it.

4 Too many insertion sequences would mark the person doing them as quite out of step with the other speaker, and show up a severe difficulty in communication. It is more likely that the other person would blame the inserter for this than take the blame him or herself. It would produce a bad impression of the inserter, which might last well beyond any particular encounter.

Further reading   Coulthard (1985); Goodwin (1981); McLaughlin (1984); Nofsinger (1991)

INSINUATE

Tasks

To get someone to think something bad about a matter, without noticing how this has happened.

To be critical without others noticing.

Description

In an insinuation C. suggests something of a critical nature about something, but does it in such a way that afterwards it may be hard to think back to the source of the criticism. It is rather like the act of hinting, but with one major difference: insinuations are much more hidden. There is no compulsion on C. to believe any insinuations he or she makes.

Persuasive value

The tactic is a very anti-social one, stating a view, and a negative view, while hoping to avoid responsibility for the statement. It is unfair on both those who receive it and, more particularly, on those it is critical of.

Insinuations make very clear the negative aspects of the matter they represent, and are usually understood quite clearly. They differ in this from hints, which leave A.s with some thinking to do to understand them. So, for example,

Ex. 1 A: We need someone to organize the party, and it must be someone who knows all about parties. Bill?
B: . . . Alright, I'll do it. Hey, do you mean I go to too many parties?

where the hint 'someone who knows about parties' is put in the context of 'organizing' and is heard first as a request, and only after that as a criticism of B's lifestyle. The hint merely suggests a knowledge of parties, and B has to work out that certain consequence must follow if this is true (i.e. that B has been to a lot of parties), and that this does not just mean knowledge of parties but too much play and too little work, and so B eventually arrives at this understanding of the meaning.

An insinuation, on the other hand, is like the following:

Ex. 2 A: Some of the older staff find it difficult to teach well, just because they are so far removed from the students' interests and way of life: it's not really their fault, but it can be a problem. I know the Head of Department is very concerned about it; he said to me only the other day that there were one or two people who could take early retirement and if they did it would certainly be a good thing for the Department. . . . Have you ever thought of early retirement?
B: No, I haven't.

It is quite clear what A is saying: some older staff are past it and should retire. There is also a possible insinuation that B is being categorized as past it, and may have been one of the ones the Head feels should retire. There is no way of knowing this though, except by direct question, and it is entirely possible that A could deny there was any reference to B intended, and B could not prove there was. It is a nasty tactic and people should be on guard against it.

Further reading   Wierzbicka (1987)

INTERACTION: BEGIN

Task

To start the interaction well.

Description

Preparatory thought and effort must be given to any interaction, however trivial it seems, that involves people of significance to a person's life. While it is obvious that written communications need research and exploration of the topic, and predictions of A.'s response, it may be less obvious that so too do spoken communications. Here again it is obvious that formal meetings require research, but so too does small talk. It requires the same care (e.g. recalling evidence of the others' attitudes, opinions, moods, etc.) in order to produce the most favorable response from them.

Persuasive value

1 Written communications need to begin by offering signals of what would seem likely to persuade A. to respond well. The quality of paper, page layout, and printing styles all have a recognized influence on readers. And, in letters, so do such things as matching salutations and endings (e.g. 'Dear Sir' and 'Yours faithfully,' or 'Dear Mr./Ms. Smith' and 'Yours sincerely'), while reports should have clear headings giving enough information for the reader to know what to expect after each of them. Within the body of the text, C. should begin with material which can stand alone, without any preliminaries, as a starting point. Further, the first matter raised, and the way it is dealt with, should obey the rules of the genre being employed.
2 Many speech interactions begin with introductory chat, and this should be considered an important part of the event, not an insignificant ancillary to it. In it roles are set, social nearness and distance are set, alliances are arranged, and social positions are fought for. Participants should therefore use the time to talk with those who are important for their goals, should notice who is talking to whom and making or breaking alliances, establish the right distance (social and even physical) from those with whom they wish to be disassociated, etc. They could even look for a chance to

influence the agenda, by raising issues informally, or to take a prominent part in the event (e.g. by being the first to indicate that the business part of the event should begin). It may annoy the chairperson if done tactlessly, but it can present C. as earnest, hardworking, and, if the others agree to the shift in activity, as one who is prepared to take a lead.

See also **Genre: choose**

Further reading Mulholland (1991)

INTERACTION CLOSURE: SPOKEN

Tasks

To maintain the bond between participants beyond the event.
To influence others' memories of one's contribution.

Description

In spoken communication, good closure requires that the withdrawal of the participants be made as least destructive of their social bonding as possible. It should imply that the end of the interaction is regrettable, and that the friendliness generated by it will be sustained.

Persuasive value

In speech, closure requires that **sociable language** should be employed. There is a crucial convention about speech closure that should be obeyed or there will be adverse consequences. This is the convention of 'mutually agreed closure.' All parties must signal their agreement to the closure, and if one does not, the others will be forced to stay in interaction until he or she finally does. This is why sometimes people have to loiter in a colleague's doorway, unable to leave, even though there may be good reason to hurry away, until the other agrees to 'release' them. A clear instance of good closure is:

Ex. 1 A. So that is the last of them.
       B. Good. [pause] [end of business part of interaction]
       A. So, I'd better be off then. [preclosure begun]
       B. O.K. then. [preclosure agreed]
       A. O.K., see you Monday. [closure begun]
       B. Right, see you. [closure accepted] [exit A.]

One convention seems to be that the more formal the interaction, the more signalling of closure is needed. So in committees there is a set of closure actions after the formal agenda is concluded: first the chairperson calls for 'any other business,' then he or she may give the date of the next meeting, and then he or she declares the meeting closed.

Another convention seems to be that the greater the foreseeable gap between interactions, the more signalling is needed: as, for example, in family gatherings where the group meets only very infrequently, it may take hours of family farewells to produce the proper closure. And if someone does not manage to 'say goodbye' it is felt as socially damaging and something to be repaired.

The need for adequate closure arises from the perception that absence weakens the social bond, and this must be prevented by taking a large dose of cooperation at the point of closure. Typically the cooperation takes the form of:

(a) regretting the end of the current interaction;
(b) referring to the next meeting, as in 'See you';
(c) implying that something external is causing the end of the interaction, as in 'I must go now, I've got a lecture.'

See also **Interaction closure: written**

Further reading   Button (1987); Schegloff, Jefferson, and Sacks (1977)

INTERACTION CLOSURE: WRITTEN

Tasks

To maintain the bond between participants beyond the event.
To influence others' memories of one's contribution.

Description

In written communication, good closure requires that the last idea be one which clearly ends some matter, and which can stand alone as doing so. It should also be a strong idea, though of what kind depends on the genre used; for example, in a reasoned account the last point should never be the weakest, since its location means that it will be remembered, while in a narrative a coda offering a moral or ethical lesson to be learnt from the story can end it, following the grand climax, without appearing weak. Social bonding also requires a proper closure to any interaction.

Persuasive value

It is often useful in a complex account to end with a summary of points made, or with a statement of action needed as a result of what has been communicated, or with a set of recommendations that arise from the matters dealt with, and so on. Also, if C. can produce a pithy version of the whole it would be both persuasive and memorable; if C. can suggest that the whole account is in line with some basic assumption which is held not just by A. but by the whole community (e.g. can suggest that it has proverbial or mythic support), then though the matter may not be remembered well, it will be agreed, and will form the foundation of future action because it is 'taken for granted.'

There is a need for adequate closure that arises from the perception that silence or absence weakens the social bond, and this must be prevented by taking a large dose of friendly cooperation at the point of closure, otherwise the event is said to be ending 'on a sour note.' Typically the cooperation takes the form of:

(a) regretting the end of the current interaction;
(b) referring to the next communication, as in 'We must keep in touch on this';
(c) implying that something external is causing the end of the interaction, and it is not because of the writer's wishes, as in

Ex. 1 I must finish this letter now; people are waiting for me.

See also **Genre: choose; Interaction closure: spoken; Myth; Proverbs**

Further reading   Button (1987); Schegloff and Sacks (1974)

INTERRUPTION OF OTHER

Tasks

To halt a poor communication with least damage.
To insert an intervention urgently.

Description

A good interruption can halt a poor communication, and so improve its efficiency, but a bad one can prolong the communication because the person being interrupted may be thrown off balance, lose the train of thought, etc. A good interruption can make others think well of the interrupter, but a bad one can attract opprobrium. To avoid trouble, both the timing and the form of interruption need care.

Persuasive value

1 Timing an interruption:

(a) Early interruption is damaging. Let C. articulate at least his or her reason for the utterance, or make one substantive point.
(b) It should coincide with a pause in speech rather than overlap with it. If there are no suitable pauses, begin in overlap but use a supportive

token before the substance of the interruption (e.g. 'O.K./I know what you mean/I agree up to a point. But what about . . . . ?

(c) Note where C. becomes irrelevant, or provides known information, has too much or too little content, is speaking too slowly or too fast. Each problem can, tactfully, be used to justify an interruption (e.g. 'That's right, but we have that in the report in front of us,' or 'Hang on a second, let me see if I can follow you.'

(d) Beware—if it is the *tone* C. is using that seems unsuitable, perhaps too personal, it may be caused by some strong emotion, and an interruption may cause damage, or may stir more emotion or disturb the speaker's thoughts, and so ultimately be inefficient.

2 Forming an interruption—the best interruption is the least noticeable. Communicators should rehearse the best tactic they can manage so that they can perform it quickly when required. The following tactics are in order from best to worst;

(a) Signs should be given of active listening, implying that it is because the interrupter is attending that he or she needs to have something explained: 'Do the figures you are presenting include this week's results?' or that he or she not does need as much information as the speaker is supplying, 'Yes exactly, the report was, as you say, very clear, I saw that myself'.

(b) Use some mitigation phrases such as 'If I may . . ./Could I just . . ./Can I jump in here a moment. . .'

(c) **Apologize**, but note that this draws attention to the interruptive act, which otherwise might pass unnoticed.

(d) Use a **reflexive comment**; for example, 'May I interrupt you?' However, since this is the most noticeable form it may create trouble and waste time by prompting the person interrupted to consider how to react to the act of interruption itself as well as the substance contained in it.

Further reading   Bennett (1981); Mulholland (1991)

INTERVIEW: CONDUCT

Tasks

To communicate well when interviewing someone.
To understand the significance of a candidate's spoken communication.

Description

To design an interpersonal business or professional interview to test a person's suitability for employment or promotion, for example, needs an awareness of the way spoken (and written) communication works. While part of the preparation for interviewing must involve decisions about what qualities are wanted, another part must be about the kind of speech acts which would test these qualities in the candidate.

Persuasive value

1 The interview should be planned, and controlled, but it should also allow for some flexibility as matters develop in it. Interviewers should be aware that such planning and control will be most unusual phenomena for many candidates, and quite outside their normal communication experience. Unless they are well experienced at work, or at being interviewed, this control could throw them off balance. It may be useful to make as little fuss as possible about the control mechanisms, so as to make candidates feel more at ease, and hence produce a fair account of themselves.

2 Candidates may expect some sociability at the start of the interview, since this is the norm for most of their speech experience. However, to use some is fraught with difficulties since it may be perceived as a time for lazy talk, and the candidates reveal poor aspects of themselves. To be fair, then, it should be used (or not used) in equal amounts for each candidate.

3 In assessing the candidate's suitability as a communicator, such things as the following need to be considered: turn skills, which can reveal whether candidates listen well, respond relevantly, get the formality of tone right, do not interrupt, etc.; and use **politeness** tactics. If candidates appear to pause to a greater extent than the interviewers think normal, it may be just a sign of care, and arise from the candidate's awareness that every word counts in an interview. It need not be a sign of unfriendliness, or an inability to talk.

4 In assessing the candidates' responses to questions, interviewers need to consider what type of question is being asked: if they have produced a poor question they will undoubtedly get a poor response, and it is hardly the candidate's fault. Questions should be open wherever possible, so that candidates have a free choice of response: this will produce variation between candidates and be helpful in making choices between them.

5 If the interviewer wishes to have the candidate make a statement, care should be taken with the formulation of the invitation to state: candidates will naturally respond with different statements if invited to 'Tell us about yourself,' or 'Tell us the story of your life,' or 'Is there a statement you would like to make to the committee?' The first is likely to produce personal details, 'yourself' being usually understood as the whole of oneself, feelings, and attitudes as well as experiences. The second is likely to produce a narrative. The third is likely to produce a very formal, written-style statement, perhaps even a political or ideological one, as this is what many people understand 'making a statement' to mean.

6 An interview is a double-mode communication, consisting of a written submission and application, and then a spoken interview. Interviewers should think how candidates are likely to view this. Many candidates think that they do not need to mention anything that has already been submitted in writing, which they assume the interviewer to have read.

7 If the interview is conducted not face-to-face but via the telephone, interviewers should be careful in making judgments about candidates, since any interaction will be very influenced by this mode. It can make comparative judgments between candidates very difficult if some are interviewed in this way and some face-to-face.

See also **Greeting: by phone; Interview: respond to; Narrative: choose; Questions: open; Sociable language**

Further reading   Mulholland (1991)

INTERVIEW: RESPOND TO

Task

To communicate in the best way possible at an interview.

Description

The goal of an interview, is to assess someone's suitability, for example for employment or promotion. The goal of the candidate must be, therefore, to be found suitable.

Persuasive value

1 Note carefully any information about the position that has been supplied, and do research if necessary to discover what qualities the interviewers would consider suitable. Examine carefully how best to put one's qualifications, etc., so as to meet the qualities wanted.

2 Estimate what questions might be asked, and what subjects might be raised, and prepare brief responses to them. To be sure of being brief it could be useful to rehearse and time one's responses.

3 Most interviews last from ten to twenty minutes only, and so there is little time to waste. Interviewers will therefore use every minute, even the apparently 'small' talk which may begin the interaction, to investigate the candidate.

4 Each element of spoken communication plays a part in interviews and should be considered carefully. Candidates will have to perform well at **turntaking**, at responding to the initiations of others (they may not be allowed to make initiations themselves), be wary of interrupting others, be

prepared to be interrupted. They need to be prepared with appropriate **politeness** tactics. One of the most powerful traps for unwary candidates is the question which sets up a **preferred response**, which may not be what the candidate wishes to use; for example,

Ex. 1 A: I suppose like most women today you have strong views on feminism?

C.s should always pause for a brief time whenever a question is asked, so as to have time to think.
5 During an interview there may be an unusual sharpness about the exchanges, quite different from the candidate's experience. Candidates should avoid becoming agitated by this, and try not to be thrown off balance by it. Take it as a useful reminder that one is not among friends, and so say nothing trivial nor anything to one's detriment.
6 In interviews there may be sudden changes of topic, and they may not be signalled. Again candidates should try not to be startled by this. They should also be aware that, unlike more informal interactions, topics are carefully planned and controlled, and should not be changed by the candidate.

N.B.   After an interview, whatever its outcome, it could be useful to write down as much of it as can be remembered in close detail. By studying this account, candidates can see behaviors which caused trouble, and can begin to monitor themselves, so that the next time they are interviewed they handle things better.

N.B.   If during the interview it is necessary to confess to some failing, perhaps lack of experience or poor exam results, think carefully about how best to present this in the best light. For example, the first of the following pair seems a better way of putting it than the second:

Ex. 2 I am afraid I have so far been unable to get any experience, but I intend to keep trying.

Ex. 3 No, I haven't got any experience, but it is very difficult to get any. I've tried at least twice.

See also **Interview: conduct**

Further reading   Mulholland (1991)

INTONATION

Tasks

To assist a listener's understanding.
To add extra information to words and grammar.

To express attitude.
To assist turntaking.

Description

Intonation is the way that something is said, 'vocal expression,' the patterning of tone of voice, rhythm, cadence, and stress which happen as people speak, and which can change the meanings of words by the way they are said. People often show a strong sense of the influence of intonation, when they say 'It's not so much what she said as the way she said it,' or 'You had to be there [to know how it sounded].'

The major features of intonation are tone unit signals, pause, pitch of the voice, and stress or emphasis: these are treated as separate **intonation** tactics.

Persuasive value

Intonation changes provide interest for the listener and also helps A. to separate C.'s units of thought from one another, so that he or she can manage to take it in, understand, and absorb it. It adds a clue to C.'s attitudes to the matter spoken about, and also his or her feelings about A. and about the interaction itself. It also acts as spoken punctuation, indicating degrees of importance among the matters dealt with, by passing quickly over lesser ones, and emphasizing more central ones. It provides many of the signals of **turntaking**.

Intonation is usually present in some form or another; it would be extremely rare to hear someone speak in a monotone at an even pace and with no pitch movement. If it did happen, it would be difficult to follow what the speaker is saying. So rare is it that an example is seen as a caricature of some kind, as in jokes about the monotone of a police officer reading aloud the report of crime, with nothing in the voice to show how startling the report is: 'I was proceeding in an orderly fashion in the course of my duty when I stumbled across a corpse.'

See also **Emphasis;** the other **Intonation** tactics

Further reading   Beattie (1983); Crystal and Davy (1969)

INTONATION: PAUSE

Tasks

To note hidden aspects of another's communication.
To assist turntaking.

Description

Pauses can occur at any point in the stream of utterance, both within and outside a speaker's turn at talk. Their location is important for discovering their meanings.

1 Within an utterance a pause can occur just before the start of a grammatical item (word, phrase, clause), and when it does it can show that the speaker is hesitating: perhaps about how best to formulate the item as a representation of some matter, or how to manage to be tactful about it, or indeed whether to say the thing at all because it appears likely to cause trouble. Pauses can also happen just after a complex piece of information or awkward social act, as a sign that C. wants some indication that it has been well received.

2 At the start of a response utterance it can indicate that the responder is having trouble producing the **preferred response**.

3 At the end of a turn, where it is usually understood to be the speaker's pause rather than the hearer's (and it is usually not too difficult to make this distinction), it is a sign of turn completeness, and often the language supports this (e.g. when a speaker's words tail away into pause).

What length a pause must be to be a recognizable pause is a relative matter, not an absolute one: that is, it is to be measured according to its difference from the speaker's norm of taking breaths as he or she speaks. Pauses take recognizably longer than this. Since however speakers have different speeds, the pauses of a slow speaker could be much longer than those of a fast speaker: this should be ignored, but the difference between a long pause and a short pause by the same speaker could prove to have quite different meanings.

Persuasive value

1 Pauses allow A.s to guess that the C. has some difficulty about the next thing to be said. They can consider what this might be by noting whether the next act will be socially awkward, like a request or apology.

2 Any pause at the start of a response means that A. does not want to use the preferred response, and even if the preferred response does then follow, the pause has shown that A. is uncomfortable about doing it.

3 If a pause occurs at the end of a turn it can show that C. has run out of ideas, or is feeling uneasy about continuing to hold the floor. If it seems to be the former, it could be a sign of the weakness of C.'s argument; if it is the latter, it could be a sign of modesty or unwillingness to be assertive. Both pieces of information could be used persuasively.

See also **Turntaking**

Further reading   Beattie (1983); Crystal and Davy (1969)

INTONATION: PITCH CHOICE

Tasks

To assist a listener's understanding.
To add extra information to words and grammar.
To express attitude.
To assist turntaking.

Description

Voice pitch is voice movement, the rise and fall of the voice as it moves from the beginning to the end of each stretch of speech. There are five main pitch movements, as in:

Ex. 1 'I've got a new pen' — as in a normal statement.

Ex. 2 'Have you seen my pen?' — as in a question.

Ex. 3 'I. said. be. quiet' — as in quiet anger.

Ex. 4 'I've got a good mark, I think' — where the statement ends up as a question.

Ex. 5 'Have you seen my pen, it's a red one' — where the question ends up as a statement.

Persuasive value

The normal pitch movement in English where the C. is sure of what is being said, or is making a statement, is a falling one, and its role is mainly to show when a 'sentence' has ended, and it does this by falling at the end, and then starting up the next 'sentence' at a higher pitch and slowly falling throughout it. It can also indicate that a turn is ending.

A rising pitch is used where the speaker is uncertain about what he or she is saying or is asking a question. It is not always clear from the words that the speaker is uncertain about something, but pitch provides a useful clue that this is so. And of course it is useful information to know that C. feels tentative about what he or she is saying.

A monotone is where every word is said at the same pitch level, and is used where every word is to be stressed equally, or to be equally unstressed. It is meant to fix A.'s attention on each word, rather than just on the meaning of the whole 'sentence.'

Sometimes C. can begin confidently but end with uncertainty, as in Ex. 4, and this is obviously useful for A. to notice, particularly if it is possible to tell just where the uncertainty began (and therefore what may have caused it) as the pitch movement changes from falling to rising. C.s can also use the same pitch movement where they notice at some point that A. is looking puzzled or as if disagreeing, and wish to respond to this.

The rise—fall pitch movement of Ex. 5 can show that C. realizes that A. needs to be given more information in order to answer the question, and provides it in an added ministatement.

No matter what the grammar and words indicate, pitch choice should be noted; it can change a grammatical statement into a question, or a grammatical question into a statement, or a statement into a greeting, etc., and is the most important clue to show that this is being done. It enables A. to produce the right response.

Further reading   Beattie (1983); Crystal and Davy (1969)

INTONATION: TONE UNITS

Tasks

To assist a listener's understanding.
To add extra information to words and grammar.
To express attitude.
To assist turntaking.

Description

A tone unit is, very roughly, the equivalent in speech of a clause in writing; that is, it is a relatively discrete unit of thought. It may be grammatically like or quite unlike a written clause. It can consist of one word or many. It is held together by having only one pitch movement. (To test what this sounds like, the radio news headlines could be listened to with the volume turned down so that the words are not clear. The pitch movement can then be heard as what signals the change from one headline to another.)

Persuasive value

Tone units can match words and grammar, and reinforce them, or they can provide a counter-meaning. For example, the strongly marked end of a tone unit could occur at a point where the grammar of a clause is incomplete and the listener could understand that the speaker has in one sense finished what he or she wants to say, and yet has left the grammatical aspect incomplete. There will be something to be deduced from this confusion of signals—perhaps that the speaker has some difficulty in thinking of how best to represent something at that point, or has suddenly become aware that the topic is going to become an embarrassing one if it continues, etc.

Tone units, like sentences in writing, are ways of showing that all the ideas that are to be most closely connected are together, in one unit, and the end of it tells A. that that part of the topic is complete, and another part is about to begin. They help A. know how to categorize the incoming information in blocks of meaning (i.e. in units).

Noting the height of the pitch that begins a tone unit is also useful, because it tells A. how long the unit will be. A very high start suggests that the unit will be long, a lowish start that it will be relatively brief. This can help A. manage the amount of incoming information in the best way to ensure understanding.

The end of a tone unit is a sign to A. that C. wants some evidence that A. has been listening attentively, and that the information in the utterance is in the right-sized units to be understood.

N.B. Speakers who do not signal clearly the ends of their tone units are most probably indicating that they do not wish A. to recognize the end of a unit, and therefore be able to take a turn at speaking. It is one way to hold onto the speaking turn.

Further reading Beattie (1983); Crystal and Davy (1969)

INTONATION: VOICE STRESS

Tasks

To assist a listener's understanding.
To add extra information to words and grammar.
To express attitude.

Description

Voice stress is the use of emphasis on particular words or syllables. It is, for instance, what distinguishes the verb 'record' from the noun 'record,' as in 'She recorded "Cheers" last night,' and 'I've bought the latest Springsteen record.'

Persuasive value

When stress is employed it can provide useful information about the meaning of something being communicated, and can alter meanings according to where it is placed, as in the following response to the question 'What assignments do you have?'

Ex. 1 'Three for history.'

If it is said with equal stress on 'three' and 'history' it means that my three assignments are for my history subject. If it is said with stress on 'three' only, it means that the most important thing the speaker wants to say is that he or she has got three assignments, and they happen to be for history. If it is said with stress on 'history' only, it means that the speaker focusses on the fact they are for history, and their number does not matter so much.

When words which are very rarely stressed, like the article 'the,' or when the prepositions 'on,' 'under,' or 'of' are given emphasis, it is usually to make some strong point, as in:

Ex. 2 I have been *of* the group but not *in* it.

Ex. 3 He was *the* most interesting person there.

Ex. 4 It is *under* the bed, idiot!

In Ex. 2 the stress makes a contrast in meanings between 'of' and 'in.' In Ex. 3 the speaker uses stress to make an absolute statement of the interest felt in a person, and does so without showing what he or she finds interesting; that is, no specific qualities are attributed to the man. In Ex. 4 the stress also points to a contrast, this time with something not spoken— perhaps the idiot is looking on top of the bed—but it is also acting as an expression of feeling (further illustrated by the use of the word 'idiot'), and when stress does this it is not so significant which word carries it, just that it occurs at all.

Further reading   Beattie (1983); Crystal and Davy (1969)

IRONIC UNDERSTATEMENT/OVERSTATEMENT

Tasks

To use shared knowledge to create a bond.
To infuse some originality into language use.

Description

Ironic under- or overstatement is deliberately to represent a matter as less than it is or more than it is.

Ex. 1 Michelangelo was a pretty good painter.

Ex. 2 Somehow I have done no work at all today.

Persuasive value

All ironic representations fail if they are taken at face value, so to use **irony** is to assume enough shared knowledge with A. for A. to succeed in understanding it. If it works it forms a closeness between A. and C.

In Examples 1 and 2, for the under- or overstatement to work A. needs to know the inappropriateness of the term 'pretty good' for the great Michelangelo, or the untruth involved in C.'s claim to have 'done no work.' The first example bonds C. and A. as members of the same culture while the second makes a much closer bond because it relies on specific knowledge, that C. works hard, that A. knows it, and shares an understanding of how therefore it could make any sense to state 'I have done no work.'

The tactic is used also to add interest to the communication, by making an 'odd' statement (i.e. one that A. must pause to decipher, and get pleasure out of the activity, rather like the enjoyment people get from crossword puzzles).

Ironic understatement/overstatement is frequently used for **humor**, a most important bonding device, which works by producing a discrepancy between the 'truth,' of Michelangelo's genius and C.'s work habits, on the one hand, and their representation on the other. The wider the gap, and therefore the greater the under- or overstatement, the funnier it will be. Contrast the humorous example (Ex. 3) with the less amusing one (Ex. 4):

Ex. 3 I've suddenly got a million spots on my face.

Ex. 4 I've suddenly got dozens of spots on my face.

(where the actuality is three, large, spots).

Further reading   Corbett (1990); Sonnino (1968)

IRONY

Tasks

To communicate obliquely as a test of bonding.
To communicate ironically.
To give emphasis to a matter.

Description

One of the hardest tactics to describe, and to use, is irony. Essentially, as it is used in the kind of interpersonal interaction which is the focus of this book, irony is a representation of something which contradicts either the rest of the text, and/or the generally understood and socially agreed view of the world, as in

Ex. 1 [in a soaking downpour of rain]
    A: What splendid weather!

Ex. 2 [as the speaker drops a plate]
    A: Damn, I just love it when things go well, don't you?

Ex. 3 We achieved the most successful outcome to the negotiations that we could have anticipated:

both the vendor and the purchaser are at this moment each cursing each other.

Ex. 4 [written in response to bad news about the company's future]
    Thank you for your letter. It was just what I wanted to hear.

Persuasive value

For the receiver of irony, the major problem is how to interpret it correctly; for the producer of it, the major problem is why and when to use it. 1 To understand Ex. 1, A. needs to undertake the following cognitive process (which happens in life at such speed that it seems to be just a flash of intuition):

(a) understand that C. is saying the weather is splendid;
(b) hear that there is a clash of words and tone which suggests it is not meant in a straightforward way;
(c) note the context—that C. is soaked;
(d) work out that being soaked is not splendid;
(e) test whether this is a general social view (i.e. likely to be shared by C.) or just personal to oneself;
(f) ask oneself if C. has gone crazy and no longer holds to general social views;
(g) infer that C. means to say something crazy-like without being crazy;
(h) know from general social awareness that being 'crazy-like' is humorous;
(i) check whether C. has done this kind of thing before in this way;
(j) finally understand that C. is being obliquely humorous, and offering the exclamation ironically.
The next question for A. is why would C. do this. It could be to test whether A. shares the same standard social awareness, and shares the same perception of the ironic. It has been said that one of the closest bonds, closer even than a shared sense of humor, is when

people share an instant recognition of irony. If A. feels this could be its intent, then it needs to be acknowledged with some sign of recognition of the irony, or even an ironic response, for which C. is patiently waiting, such as:

Ex. 5 It's marvellous: my outfit just needed a good soaking.

2 C.s must carefully consider when, where, with whom, and why to use irony. As should be obvious from the account above it is a difficult tactic.

(a) It is an excellent means of creating or affirming a bond, if it works, but it must be predicated on a good knowledge of A. If it fails it damages any bond because of the awkwardness it generates.
(b) It must be in an appropriate place and occasion, one where humor is allowable.
(c) It should have a simple topic, so that the irony is not buried in the complexities of a difficult or abstract or new topic.
(d) Is A. likely to welcome a bond based on word skills? Some A.s hold these in high regard and would appreciate shared ironies; others, less skilled in wordplay, or less familiar with it, could find it unsettling, and could take it literally and be annoyed if this caused laughter or mockery.
(e) Irony often presupposes a cynical view of the world—the weather, accidental breakages, etc—and that some people are clever enough to recognize the folly of the world and others are not, and some A.s would not share this view, and not welcome being assumed to share this view.
(f) Some uses of irony set up one group, those who understand and share its wit, and oppose this group to those who cannot understand it.
(g) In Ex. 4, C. both sets up the irony as a bonding mechanism, but at the same time is obliquely critical of A. and the letter A. sent. To say 'It was just what I wanted to hear' is to accuse A. of doing something C. did not like.

N.B. The power of irony to be a means of criticism can be adapted for good purposes, as in

Ex. 6 [wife to husband as it pours with rain]
    You said it would be a good day to go to the beach!

Here the wife manages to be critical, but chooses a subject for her irony 'the weather' to blame the husband for, when it is obvious he is not responsible for the rain. In doing this, she is able to be critical, but not about anything which is closer to the husband's self-esteem, or about anything that is a significant part of their marital bonding.

N.B. Irony can produce pleasure and entertainment in those who recognize it as well as those who use it, provided it does not address topics which affect face.

See also **Face: sustain; Face threats: recognize**

Further reading   Corbett (1977, 1990); Schiffrin (1991)

JOKES

Tasks

To lighten the mood of a communication.
To enhance the social relationship with A.
To form a group from those present.

Description

Joking is a particular form of humor which uses set patterns of words, grammar and social routines to make some social point. It is often begun with a **reflexive comment** which signals that a joke is about to happen, and it often ends with a specially funny punch line.

Persuasive value

Like humor in general, a joke can lighten the mood of an interaction, or defuse a socially awkward moment, or fill a damaging silence. It is meant to create sociability, and to make people feel good. A joke does not always evoke laughter, but can amuse or cause pleasure by its playfulness. It will be well received if it appears relevant to the event, and to the specific moment at which it occurs. It will be less well received if it is too long — telling 'shaggy-dog' jokes makes an assumption that the teller is entitled to usurp others' rights to speak by holding the floor for that long. It will also fare badly if it is inadequately told, or if it is unconnected with the focus of the communication that precedes it.

Jokes seek to persuade A.s to accept C.'s version of the world; that is, to accept the presuppositions of the joke, and to be complicit in its implications, to forget the world of seriousness, and to escape from social responsibility for a while. Many jokes, for example, depend on **stereotypes** for their point (e.g. that the Irish are stupid, that scientists are crazy, that children are rebellious, etc.), and while people continue to laugh at these, they are giving cognizance to those stereotypes.

Joking needs to be signalled, otherwise its words might be taken literally. There are standard openings to jokes, such as 'Did you hear the one about,' or 'I say, I say, I say,' while some jokes make themselves known by

their opening lines, such as the limerick 'There was an old man of Brent.'
In speech C. can employ a change of voice, perhaps adopt an accent, and
so signal a joke is coming. C.s can also speak in a way which is hard to fit in
with the maxims of **social convention**, and this causes A. to wonder what is
happening, and C. can then do the joke. For example,

Ex. 1   A: Hello, you are looking great today.
       B: Thanks. [joke signal] Hey, hey, what's all this? You have cut the
          legs off your pants!
       A: [laughs] No, they are the new business-style shorts.

Here C. breaks the maxim of quantity in saying 'Hey' and 'hey' and
'What's all this?' and so warns A. that the next part of the utterance needs
special attention, in this case because it is a joke. If this does not work as a
signal, then A. could be insulted.

There are many jokes which could be taken as insults, or other negative
acts. Since joking often uses inversions and exaggerations of ideas to make
its point, a literal interpretation could be very damaging, as for example, in
the well-known two-part graffito:

Ex. 2   A: My mother made me a homosexual.
       B: If I gave her the wool would she make me one?

Here the serious statement of the first line could be taken as a committed
and intimate communication by C., and the second line could therefore be
seen as a frivolous and rude reduction of that personal statement, unless
the speaker prefaced the lines and signalled the joke with 'Did you see that
thing written on the toilet wall?' Even with this preface, he or she should
be prepared to find it badly received, and stand ready to justify telling it. If
those present are to accept it as a joke, then they have to allow it to be free
of social consequences, they have to suspend their sympathy with those the
joke is about. There are jokes about many serious topics— money, mother-
hood, death, sex, and religion—and C.s must judge well whether a particular joke about one of these would work at that particular time with that
particular audience.

Jokes which run counter to the focus of the communication can also be
badly received. For example, jokes which pick on lesser details rather than
major points, as in

Ex. 3   A: Bella Smith sent in this report.
       B: And is she a beauty? [laughs]
       A: What?
       B: You said 'Bella,' you know, 'beautiful,' and I asked if she
          was—oh never mind.

Each community has a reservoir of socially acceptable jokes, and the use of
one of these can remind people of their communality, and perhaps cause

them to agree to the joker's views, since he or she appears to share common ground with them. This reservoir is continually added to, with jokes arising from new experiences all the time. This does not mean, however, that the latest joke is always the best to use, since the latest ones tend to be overused for a while and lose their excitement and interest. Sometimes an old one can be resuscitated in a new context, as in

Ex. 4   A: Did you hear that new secretary has been assigned to work with Bill?
B: There's always someone worse off than yourself.

See also **Humor; Jokes: types; Puns**

Further reading   Chiaro (1992); Sacks (1974)

JOKES: TYPES

Tasks

To lighten the mood of a communication.
To enhance the social relationship with A.
To form a group from those present.
To give A. a specific role to play in the interaction.

Description

Some jokes are solo performances while others are dialogs.

Persuasive value

Solo jokes require A. to play the part of audience, that is, to laugh or show some other response of enjoyment. If the joke fails, this can be an awkward social role, and they can feel angry or embarrassed about performing it.

Dialogic jokes exert a more specific pressure on A.s, requiring them to perform the role of straight man, as in a vaudeville comic turn, with C. as the comedian having all the best lines. A.s may not like this strong control, and the way it dictates the very words they must use, as in

Ex. 1   A: I say, I say, I say. Why did the chicken cross the road?
B: I don't know. Why did the chicken cross the road?
A: To get to the other side.

The main types of solo jokes are 'one-line' jokes, for example:
1 Slogans or definitions, as in

Ex. 2 If you think education is expensive try ignorance.

Ex. 3 Eskimos are God's frozen people.

Of these the first example could be highly relevant and illuminating, while the second is just clever word-play with little cognitive value as a contribution to a communication.
2 Maxims or proverbs, as in

Ex. 4 He who remains calm in the face of all the circumstances probably doesn't understand them.
Ex. 5 Those who can, teach,
Those who can't, teach teachers,
Those who can't teach teachers, do education research.

Again the first example can be useful, as a jocular summary of previous talk, while the second is clever word-play but (perhaps) little more.
3 Provocative questions, as in

Ex. 6 Why do teachers of education never know how to teach?

These can be useful if they contribute to ordering or clarifying the discussion, as here, where the joke sets up an opposition between the study of education and teaching.
4 Straight statements, followed by a joking gloss, or a phrase that reduces the statement to a punch line, as in

Ex. 7 The days of graffiti are over—the writing's on the wall.
She hasn't a leg to stand on, as the surgeon said to the nurse.

The first is clever word-play but does not move the discussion forward. In the second, C. begins with a strong opinion that some woman has no argument, then turns the opinion into a joke. This might be done as a way of withdrawing the opinion, perhaps if the others look angry about it, or as C. realizes that it sounds rather rude and balances this with a little sociable joking.
5 There are a number of instantly recognized solo joke forms or routines, such as the limerick, or such triplet patterns as 'There was an Englishman, an Irishman and a Scotsman . . .,' or (referring to the novel *Watership Down*, this example seen on a meat-shop window) 'You've read the book, you've seen the movie, now eat the cast.' On hearing any of these begin, A.s can get ready for their role as respondent to the joke. There are also many dialog jokes with a strongly marked pattern; this is absolutely necessary if A.s are to recognize their part and join in at the proper moment. For example: such as those beginning

Ex. 8 How many . . . does it take to change a lightbulb?
How many (e.g. elephants) can you get into a (e.g. car)?

What is X, Y, and Z (three apparently incompatible qualities, as in 'What is yellow, thick, and can kill you?,' to which the answer comes 'Shark-infested custard').

To all these A. is expected to respond with 'I don't know' to set up C. with the punch line. It is not a very ego-satisfying role for A. The best jokes, and the ones most likely to entertain A, are those in which the two cooperate to produce a joint joke, while the worst make a fool of A. In the former case they can make A.s respond well to what C. says elsewhere in the communication, but in the latter they can antagonize A.s and put them into the opposing camp.

See also **Humor; Jokes; Puns; Triplets**

Further reading   Chiaro (1992); Sacks (1974)

LEAVE MATTER INCOMPLETE

Tasks

To strengthen the representation of a matter.
To have a representation completed by another.

Description

To stop short before completing a representation, doing so quite noticeably.

Ex. 1 So I thought we could just . . .

Persuasive value

1 If the rest of the matter can be predicted by A. it can save time.
2 If predictable it could also cause A. to fill in the words—perhaps where C. finds it difficult to do so. This may be because, for instance, the matter is complex, or it is embarrassing to put into words, or it requires a good deal of tact. C. is saved the effort if A. either produces what is missing, or accepts it unsaid.
3 However, if the absent representation cannot be predicted by A., this will prove C. is bad at estimating what A. knows or is prepared to accept. In this circumstance A. will require C. to complete it, as in

Ex. 2 A: So perhaps we should leave this to . . .
      B: To what?

This could make the completion a more difficult task, because A. now knows C. finds it difficult, and will be paying more than normal attention to it. Some C.s are flustered by this. Further, if A. feels particularly unfriendly towards C. he or she could be provoking enough to insist that C. spell out every tiny . . .

Further reading   Sonnino (1968)

LECTURE: CHOOSE

Tasks

To produce a lecture or presentation successfully.
To judge a lecture or presentation by another.

Description

A lecture is a hybrid communication which consists of a written basis and spoken delivery, so it can incorporate more material than informal speech, but not as much as in written texts which are read aloud.

People who attend lectures or listen to presentations expect that the following features will be present:

(a) the lecturer will speak with either personal or institutional authority;
(b) the lecture will contain serious information of high social value;
(c) it will fill the allotted time;
(d) it will be addressed to its specific audience but also be of more general relevance;
(e) its delivery will be good;
(f) it will be designed as a text to be spoken.

Persuasive value

1 A lecture is, in effect, a very long speaking 'turn', and it therefore needs to be justified as a social imposition, and its listeners, who are denied their turn, need to be pacified. The lecturer can do this by presenting him or herself as one with authority, either personal expertise or reputation, or institutional, as when a lecturer speaks on behalf of a profession or organization. He or she also needs to sound like a knowledgeable communicator with whom the listeners can feel secure as they put their attention into his or her hands for some appreciable time.
2 Because A.s expect valuable information they will attend carefully to the text—unless or until they feel cheated. Lecturers should not waste this goodwill.

3 A.s usually have some knowledge of how long the lecture will last, and will plan their attention accordingly. They can be disconcerted by a lecture which is too short and annoyed by one that is too long. They can be made uncomfortable (and therefore unreceptive) if the design of the lecture structure is difficult to follow or if it seems not to fit the timescale: for example, if a lecturer promises four sections in fifty minutes but is still on the first section after half an hour.

4 A lecture should make such specific reference to its listeners to enable them to understand that it is planned to be of relevance to their circumstances and so is worth attending to. Equally it should show that there are useful general implications to be drawn from its material.

5 Lectures must be spoken and not just read aloud. Attention should be given to volume, speed, **intonation** and **voice quality**, and particularly to varying these over the period of the lecture so that listeners are kept alert. Since it is a very long speech turn it could be useful to allow listeners some opportunities to 'take their turn,' perhaps by allowing questions, or using dialog within the lecture to simulate the audience's turns, or even to joke and allow them to laugh.

6 In the planning stages a lecturer should decide how best to design the speech so that it is both a written text, with something of the complexity of thought and representation that belongs to writing, and yet is also a spoken text, with simpler material and representation. Listeners cannot easily handle lectures that are just written texts read aloud and respond badly to them.

See also **Lecture: design**; **Turn** tactics

Further reading   Freadman and Macdonald (1992); Goffman (1981)

LECTURE: DESIGN

Tasks

To design a lecture to achieve the best representation of material.
To design a lecture to be listened to well.

Description

Lectures usually begin with a preamble, with some **sociable language**, then with an introduction to the subject matter. Once the main body of the material is being dealt with it needs to be broken into manageable sections for listeners to digest. Lectures usually close with summaries of their main points, a gathering together of the threads of the material, or a striking or memorable idea.

Persuasive value

A lecture is a difficult communication for listeners to attend to for the whole of its duration, and for them to absorb the material that is represented. To assist them, both the material and the spoken delivery need to be carefully planned.

1 The material should be divided into sections, of roughly equal proportions if possible. These sections should be numbered and the numbers indicated to the listeners, as in 'I shall make three main points, one . . ., two . . ., three . . .' Each separate section should be planned to present a point, highlight it, and then to provide repetition and development of it, through examples, quotations, analogies, etc. There should be a similarity of pattern obvious to the listeners so that they can anticipate and predict as well as hear what is currently being said. This gives them some contextual form into which to put the words as they hear them, so they can digest the material as it appears.

The beginning and end of each section should be clearly signalled, so that listeners can take good notes, with headings and subheadings. It can help if lecturers provide simple guides to such headings: for example, single words to be copied down, or by using audio-visual aids, or written guides to the lecture. Any change in approach to the material should be signalled, for example if the lecturer moves from approving what is being offered to warning of the dangers of something—he or she might notify listeners of such a change by a dramatic use of voice and the words 'But be warned, there are serious problems . . .'

2 Since the attention span of listeners is fairly small, devices to maintain it are needed. Every ten minutes or so lecturers should provide a spur to attention—a touch of humor, a startling way of expressing the material, an unusual example or quotation, a marked voice shift or body movement, a direct address, an audio-visual aid, etc.

Students indicate that they listen more judiciously to lecturers who make the material appear linked to everyday life, and so it is worth using examples of this kind whenever suitable. Students also maintain that they prefer lecturers who are courteous: that is, who begin by introducing themselves, make some reference to the students present, and who close the lecture's with a 'thank you for listening' and a reference to the next meeting—students, and perhaps others too, like some sociability in the lecture's opening and closing phases. It can serve another useful purpose as well. Since the last words of any lecture are often lost as listeners stir themselves to leave the lecture room, it is foolish to leave any major point to the last, and it may be best to use some sociability during this time.

See also **Lecture: choose**; **Listening: use**

Further reading   Goffman (1981)

LINK MATERIAL

Tasks

To present the material distributed through the text in the way most likely to prove persuasive.
To show the relations between the various parts of the content of the text.

Description

For A.s to understand how to categorize and store in their memories the matters presented in the text, and to do so in the way that C. wishes, the matters must be placed carefully with respect to one another, and any important connections should be overtly demonstrated, as in

Ex. 1 The most important matters for us to consider today are 1 . . . 2 . . . and 3 . . . Taking these together it is obvious, at least to me, that they lead to only one conclusion . . ., with one proviso, that in the event of . . . we would need to do . . . and . . .

Matters can be linked with one another as expansions, examples, developments, reformulations, additions, as they rank against one another, as they are subordinates or coordinates, as they are causes or effects, as they can be compared and contrasted, or set up as alternatives, or **appositions** or substitutions, and so on.

Persuasive value

There is value in using linkage, of whatsoever kind, because it is almost impossible to understand or remember facts or ideas which are presented randomly. If C.s wish to have the matters understood, they must therefore control the distribution of the content of their text, and thereby guide A.s' understanding of it. Good linkage of material sets a cognitive plan for A.s to follow as they consider the ideas presented; so for example, in Ex. 1, A.s hear that there are to be three matters presented which the C. takes as important. So when they hear the first they know to ask themselves whether it is important, they know the extent of the first matter —everything that is said after '1' and before '2'—and that the three matters 1, 2, and 3 are roughly equivalent in importance. Then from the next signal, 'taking these together . . . they lead to the conclusion,' they know that they are to think about all three matters 'together' and see them as leading to a conclusion, which is what C. then presents. And so on.

Control of linkage like this can prevent A. from asking if there any other reasons that would lead to the same conclusion, or if has C. omitted any matter, at least until the end (in case C. is going to cover it as part of the plan—it is impolite to anticipate omissions until a presentation is finished). This will not necessarily cause A. to agree with it, but unless it is done A. will not understand it enough to judge whether to agree or disagree with it. And what it can do, if the control of linkage is strongly enough displayed, is influence A.s not to search their own minds for linkages with their own ideas and to categorize the materials in their own ways, any of which could mean a failure of C.'s plan to influence or persuade. Intelligible ordering of textual material also enhances the authority of C., as it is thereby made clear that he or she knows the material well.

Further reading   Beaman (1984); Dillon (1981); Gleitman (1965)

LINK MATERIAL: ADDITION

Task

To present material as separate items linked into a set.

Description

When C.s have more than one item of material to present they can do so by adding the items together, using 'and,' 'both . . . and also,' 'as well as,' 'first . . . second,' 'to start with . . .' and 'finally.'

Ex. 1   The architect's plans for the new building and the costing details are in your folders, as well as the photographs of the site.

Persuasive value

Addition seems such a straightforward way to link matters that its persuasive impact may be missed. Using these simple signs of addition means that C. wants the matters which are joined to be taken as of equivalent value, with no one item more important than any other. It is however possible that the last item in the list is to be understood as the most important because it is placed where climaxes are usually put.

1 If C. wants the matters to be seen as of unequal value, then another kind of link must be used, or the items must be more separated, perhaps put into different sentences, as in

Ex. 2   The plans for the new building are in your folders. You will also find there the costing details. At the front of the folder are the latest photographs of the site, to which I would particularly draw your attention.

In speech it is possible to give extra emphasis to one item by using **voice quality**, but not in writing.

2 If C. uses a lot of simple linking signs, particularly 'and,' the communication becomes boring, and in fact sounds like a child's narrative: '. . . and we went out, and we met Bill, and we played ball, and we ran down the road, and then we came home.' Alternatively, when faced with such simple linkage A.s are likely to form their own, more complex, relationships between the items, and these may not be what C. would want. So, C.s need to be more sophisticated in their linkage of material, both in order to appear as skilled communicators, and to control the thinking processes of A.s about the material they present.

3 Using addition to bring materials together can imply that together they share some quality, as in

Ex. 3 The reports, and the committees that produced them, have failed to address the issues.

Ex. 4 The books broaden the scope of the course, and the lectures narrow its focus, and each one is useful to the student.

N.B.   When adding items together C.s often end the set with 'etc.' or 'and so on.' When these terms are used it means that C. will accept additions beyond those mentioned, so is not being exclusive or thinking that the set is concluded. But if C. uses 'just X and Y' or 'X and also Y' or 'and even X,' then these signs indicate that C. means that the list is closed. In this latter case A.s should watch out for any omissions before they accept the set is complete.

See also the other **Link material** tactics

Further reading   Leech and Svartvik (1975); Quirk, Greenbaum, Leech, and Svartvik (1985)

LINK MATERIAL: ALTERNATIVES

Task

To present some matter as two or more alternatives.

Description

It is possible to present a matter as being two or more alternatives. To do so involves using one of the following expressions:

(a) or;
(b) either . . . or;
(c) otherwise/or else;
(d) alternatively.

As in:

Ex. 1 We have three options or (in other words) alternatives.

Ex. 2 We can either decide on the textbooks now or leave it till early next year.

Ex. 3 We need to manage this well, otherwise/or else there will be a loss of employment in the industry.

Ex. 4 We could settle the matter now. Alternatively, we could leave it till after the exams.

Persuasive value

The problem with alternatives is twofold: are the alternatives really different from one another, and do they cover all alternative possibilities of choice?

In the following example, the alternatives could be seen as very similar:

Ex. 5 We could either get the video of *The Sound of Music*, or we could rent some other musical.

where the similarity lies in renting and videos and musicals, and the only difference, the only element of choice, is between a specified and an unspecified musical. Such an alternative is more noticeable for what it leaves out than for what it allows.

In the following example the alternatives do not seem to be comprehensive and all inclusive:

Ex. 6 There are two ways of tackling this problem: we could get Mary to do the party catering for us, or we could employ an outside company.

Mary may easily be able to come up with a third alternative:

Ex. 7 Or we could get one of the male staff to do the catering.

In any set of alternatives, people should consider whether some other alternative is being excluded from the agenda.

It is not always easy to notice exclusions, or even that matters are being presented as alternatives. In the list of expressions given above it is possible to rank those which exert more persuasive power and those which exert less. The criterion is whether they do or do not suggest that a choice has been made, or could be made.

1 The use of 'or' alone makes it hard to notice that alternative options are being listed. The signal is an ambiguous one, since it is also used to mark two versions of one thing without implying that there must be a choice between things, as in Ex. 1.

2 The use of 'either . . . or' is usually noticeable enough to warn people that a set of alternatives is coming, so they can prepare to analyze it carefully.

3 The use of 'otherwise,' or 'or else,' also signals alternatives, but these are not necessarily equivalent options, as in Ex. 3. They are not two courses of action to choose from, but one action, 'manage this well,' and a result from an unspecified action which must be 'not manage it well'; that is, it could have been 'We need to manage this well, otherwise/or else if we do not manage it well there will be a loss of employment in the industry.'

4 The use of 'alternatively' makes it clearest of all that a set of options is being presented.

N.B.   Some alternatives are presented as free choices but in fact are less free than they look. For example,

Ex. 8 Students must write on this topic or see their tutor if they wish to use another topic.

This might imply that there is a free topic choice, but the presence of 'must' in the first part strongly suggests that the tutor wants the first topic to be chosen.

See also the other **Link material** tactics

Further reading   Antaki (1988); Argyle (1975); Leech and Svartvik (1975); Quirk, Greenbaum, Leech, and Svartvik (1985)

LINK MATERIAL: RANK MATTERS AS THEY ARE ADDED

Task

To present a set of matters with the items ranked in importance.

Description

C.s can add items to a set of matters and in so doing show A.s in what order of importance they are to be understood. So for example, they could be in ascending or descending order, as in

Ex. 1 Students are concerned about their fees, are worried about their marks, and about their job prospects they are extremely alarmed.

Ex. 2 He set out by plane, travelling swiftly through the air, covering thousands of miles in a few hours, and continued by fast train, managing rather fewer miles in rather more hours, and ended up by doing the last few miles by bus.

Persuasive value

1 In Ex. 1, C. has shown the importance of each item by using a stronger word each time for 'concern/worry/alarm.' He or she has also inverted the last clause's structure to give extra value to the last item.
2 In Ex. 2, it is the number of words used that is the signal of importance, with the most important item, the first, having the most words, and the last having fewest.
3 Another tactic for showing rank is to mention one matter only, when everyone receiving the communication knows there are others that should be mentioned.
4 Another tactic, in the same situation, is to make explicit a judgement of one matter as 'important,' 'significant,' 'decisive,' or 'crucial,' and only mention the others with no judgment offered.

See also the other **Link material** tactics

Further reading   Beaman (1984); Leech and Svartvik (1975); Quirk, Greenbaum, Leech, and Svartvik (1985)

LINK MATERIAL: SUBJECT AND EXPLANATION

Task

To present a matter and add an explanation as a second version.

Description

This addition can be made as an expansion or clarification of the matter or some part of it. In many cases, the tactic is used where the first version is a generalization of some sort, and explanation is then added in the form of details to give specific information. There are also instances where details are given first, and as explanation C. presents a generalization drawn from them.

Persuasive value

1 It can be useful persuasively to present two versions of a matter, if the C. has some strong feeling about it that is to be expressed, as in:

Ex. 1 The classics professor, that is, the one who really knows these Latin terms, said that 'et cetera' means 'and all the rest,' so that must be right.

This explanation is in one sense unnecessary, since one could presume that A. would know that classics professors know Latin terms, but C. presumably wishes to produce a clinching opinion in a debate about the meaning of 'et cetera,' and so doubles the presentation of the reason to show how much it matters to C. that this view should be taken as right.

2 C.s can give first a generalization and then explain its meaning (as they interpret it), as in:

Ex. 2 The philosophy of literary Marxism is that the context in which a text is produced strongly influences what kind of text it will be.

The explanation can be useful in instances like this where the terms used in the first version—'philosophy,' and 'literary Marxism'—are so broad that they need to be narrowed in meaning or the discussion could go badly astray. (However, C.s should take care to judge how necessary such an explanation is for a specific audience—it would seem quite out of place at a philosophy conference, and could be seen there as assuming A.'s ignorance, and be rejected for that reason.)

3 C.s can proceed in the opposite order, giving details first and then forming a generalization out of them. This can influence A.s to accept either the generalization as the proper outcome of the details or, if C.s so plan it, to accept some one detail as part of a list adding up to a generalization when in fact they would not normally do so, as in

Ex. 3 Our salaries, our teaching and research obligations, our right to promotion, our career prospects, in short, our whole working conditions, are at risk under this proposal.

C. may just be giving a set of details and then explaining them as 'our working conditions' to help A. remember what is being discussed, but it may be that C. is inserting an item in the list and hoping to have it included in the generalization and accepted as part of it. In this example, 'our right to promotion' does not belong in the list, and for truth's sake should have been presented as 'our opportunities for promotion.' Such details should be carefully studied along with the explanations offered for them for any discrepancies.

See also the other **Link material** tactics

Further reading   Leech and Svartvik (1975); Quirk, Greenbaum, Leech, and Svartvik (1985)

LINK MATERIAL: SUBSTITUTION

Task

To present a matter in two or more versions in order that it is properly understood.

Description

A matter can be presented and then some other form of words for it can be given, as a substitution or reformulation, where C. thinks it would help A. to understand or accept it.

There is a set of terms used to signal substitution: 'or,' 'or rather,' '(or) in other words,' 'namely,' 'i.e.,' 'sorry,' 'well,' 'or at any rate,' 'or to put it more exactly/bluntly/usefully,' etc.

Persuasive value

In speech, the need for substitution may arise if one sees an adverse reaction to one/s first version, and seeks to accommodate to it. Also, if one finds that some presentation sounds wrong as it is being delivered, one can try to clarify it by giving a substitute version. This is quite acceptable in speech, but it is not so in writing, where the process of drafting should remove the need for such reformulations in the communication.

It follows, therefore, that if substitution occurs in a final written presentation which otherwise appears to be well drafted, the double-version form may well be intended, and readers should ask what advantage the writer saw in it. For example, the existence side-by-side of two representations of the same thing could be a way of emphasizing it and focussing A.'s attention on it. On the other hand, it could be that the two versions have an interplay of meaning that is what C. intended. Some possibilities are given in the following examples.

Ex. 1 They borrowed my pen and haven't returned it; i.e. they've stolen it.

Ex. 2 The Director has given permission for staff to close the office from 1–3 on Tuesday; in other words we can have our Melbourne Cup Party.

Ex. 3 The Government is planning to revise the Gambling (Racetrack and Lotto) Bill in the drafting stage; to put it bluntly, they've at last noticed their mistakes.

Ex. 4 Mary is always grumbling about people, or at any rate whenever I meet her she is always grumbling, but of course I don't often see her these days.

In Ex. 1, the substitution shows an increased intensity in C.'s response to the borrowing. If, however, one asks why C. did not just say 'they've stolen my pen' as the only version, the answer may be that it is too strong an accusation, so C. first explains it then shows a depth of feeling about it.

In Ex. 2, the substitution is a significant change in meaning for the same thing—closing the office is very different from having a party. One might ask why the Director did not directly give permission for the party, if he or she knew that was why the office was to be closed. Perhaps authority cannot give formal permission for a party, but accepts one will occur. By juxtaposing the two C. can show this complexity, and people can enjoy the Director's permission perhaps being naughtily misused (though in Australia most offices close for the race, and he or she would not be fooled for a minute).

In Ex. 3 C. appears to be reporting the matter in the first version, while in the second he or she is offering a personal interpretation of it. This is not directly stated anywhere, but the difference between the formality of language in the first version and the personal informality of the second would help A.s to interpret it correctly. In reporting the obliqueness of the form of words in which the Government acknowledges its error (i.e. 'is planning to revise') and showing it in contrast with the personal feeling represented in the second version, C. manages to make this apparently simple message carry a lot of meaning.

In softening the criticism of Mary in Ex. 4, C. may be responding to signs of rejection by A.

See also the other **Link material** tactics

Further reading   Leech and Svartvik (1975); Quirk, Greenbaum, Leech, and Svartvik (1985)

LISTENING: ACTIVE

Tasks

To show that attention is being paid to the speaker.
To show that the listener agrees with the speaker.

Description

Listening is not a passive occupation; when a speaker holds the floor listeners are required to give signs that they are actively listening. These signs may consist of body language, for example nodding the head for mild attention, or note-taking; however the most frequently used signs are such noises as 'mhm' or 'aha', or words like 'yeah', 'right', or 'exactly,' called 'support noises'. Another set more positively encourages the speaker to continue, for example, 'go on,' and 'what then?' Every listener favors a particular noise; and establishes a personal rhythm and rate of occurrence for its use. Some listeners repeat the other's words to indicate a high degree of understanding, but this may irritate the speaker by disturbing his or her right to complete the speaking turn.

Persuasive value

When present, such noises are not consciously noted: but any variation from them has a persuasive effect.

1 An occasional absence or just a perceived insufficiency of support noise indicates to C. that listeners are (a) not listening at that point, or (b) disagreeing with the content, or even (c) denying the speaker's right to speak. This can make speakers uncomfortable, uncertain about listener response, or angry at the lack of agreement.

2 An extended absence of such noises can be very damaging, and can disrupt C.'s ability to communicate. For example: on hearing no support noise and thinking it means disagreement, speakers may become hesitant, or slow down, or falter. On the other hand if they can guess at the reasons for disagreement they may be able to 'rewrite' their content to be more persuasive.

3 The placement of one's support noise in the other's speech flow is important. It must fit the content, and should occur, for example, not in mid-thought but rather at a relevant thought end, or else the speaker may think that either the listener is anticipating too well (and therefore that the **information flow** is wrong) or that the listener is not attending properly. Busy parents often misplace their support noises when children speak, and they get the response 'Mommy/Daddy, you aren't listening to me.'

4 Support noise which occurs too frequently can be taken as a sign of impatience.

5 When it noticeably increases in frequency it is a sign that the listener urgently wishes to speak.

See also **Turn: request**; **Turntaking**

Further reading   Antaki (1988); Sacks, Schegloff, and Jefferson (1978)

LISTENING: USE

Tasks

To understand how the listening process works.
To prepare a text to be easily listened to.

Description

Listeners attend to the text in two ways: as 'readers' attending to what is represented, and as potential speakers preparing to take their turn.

As readers their ability to comprehend the text is at the mercy of the speaker since he or she sets the pace that they must inevitably follow. They cannot scan other parts of the text, nor easily stop the speaker in mid-flow while they digest a difficult idea. It is therefore important that speech contains relatively easy material, neat ordering, familiar language, and a reduced proportion of new or difficult concepts.

Listeners can, however, provide feedback to speakers, if given the opportunity, and so can state their difficulties, hint at their oppositions, and, with a sensitive and responsive speaker, actually affect the very way the text is produced. In this sense they act together with the speaker to produce a joint text.

Listeners use the spoken word more as a trigger to set off their own thinking than as C.'s version of the world to be carefully stored in memory. So what a speaker says is often less remembered than what he or she caused the listener to think about.

Listening proceeds in bursts of active thought, alternating with more passive moments when listeners feel that nothing of personal interest is being said. In the active moments they search their experience for material to augment what the speaker is saying, filling in any gaps with their own knowledge, and supplying meaning for the vague terms of the **restricted code** if it is being used. It follows that spoken texts whose meanings depend on very careful attention to the form or structure of the speech, or which use precise words and grammar for some effect, may lose their audience, or be thoroughly misheard.

As potential speakers, listeners are also putting in mental effort, searching the text for the signs that they can take their speaking turn, and begin to prepare what they will say if they get the chance. If no opportunity arises, or someone else beats them to a turn, they may discard their preparation, and adjust themselves to the new situation, and start preparing for the next chance. While they are doing this, it is obvious that their total attention is not on what the current speaker is saying.

While listening, and as mutual participants with C. in the interaction, people are also expected to offer signs of active listening and they must expend effort judging how and when to do this best.

Persuasive value

Speakers should design their speech aware that this lack of attention is inevitable, and so reduce the complexity of topic and language that they use, making fewer points than in writing, and reinforcing the ones they do make through repetition, examples, analogies, and by the use of **intonation**, **voice quality**, etc.

See also **Listening: active**

Further reading   Chafe (1985); McGregor and White (1986)

METAPHOR

Tasks

To set an agenda.
To discover the agenda of others.

Description

Metaphors act to represent one thing, X, called the 'tenor,' in terms of another thing, Y, called the 'vehicle,' and in so doing can direct a reader's perception of X by aligning its meaning with that of Y. This can involve a fair comparison, or the exclusion of some aspect of it, or a distortion, as these suit the C.'s goals.

Persuasive value

Metaphors, therefore, provide clues to the understanding of two importantly persuasive aspects of discourse: (a) C.'s attitudes to the subject matter of the communication, and (b) C.'s sense of the nature of the current interaction. Conversely they enable a person to read such things from another's usage.

There are many quite familiar metaphors in constant use which are barely perceived because they are the **clichés** of discourse. But though they are so common, choosing to use one can demonstrate a particular attitude, and suit a particular goal. The influence of these cliché-metaphors can in fact be greater than more strikingly obvious ones, since they work in a more surreptitious manner.

Any metaphors, whether clichés or not, that occur frequently in communications can set hidden agendas which are influential because they are hard to spot and therefore hard to counter. For example, a metaphor can be used to insinuate a representation of the current activity, perhaps by representing it as an argument, using for it the metaphor 'war,' as in such phrases as 'defending one's view' or 'attacking other's speeches,' 'targetting opponents' weak points,' claiming they hold 'indefensible positions,' etc. If this metaphor is allowed to work, it will make the activity an oppositional one, and make it hard to find a compromise solution, because this does not fit with the 'war' metaphor.

Individuals may show a preference for the use of a particular metaphor at a significant moment in an interaction, and this can reveal much about their attitudes, as in

Ex. 1 I would say, let sleeping dogs lie.

Ex. 2 This is central to our case.

The use of the first suggests a preference for avoiding trouble, rather than resolving problems; the second involves a preference for making judgements about matters, ranking some as central and others as peripheral. In each case the user might hope that his or her version might prevail. To take another example in more detail:

Ex. 3 The bottom line.

This implies that the user thinks:

(a) the total is what matters (i.e. the end matters more than the means);
(b) the matter is one of profit versus loss (i.e. is an opposition with no gray area in the middle);
(c) material considerations should prevail over values or attitudes;
(d) a conclusion of a particular kind should be reached (i.e. there should be a result rather than a summation, a climax, or a finalization).

See also **Metaphor: extended**; **Metaphor markers**

Further reading   Corbett (1977, 1990); Lakoff and Johnson (1980); Sonnino (1968)

METAPHOR: EXTENDED

Tasks

To help people understand a complex matter.
To make coherent a matter which has many different strands.
To add an imaginative dimension to interest people.

Description

An extended metaphor is a comparison of some matter with something different, which C. considers shares certain characteristics with the main matter to be represented. It can take the form of a simile, and be signalled by 'like' or 'as,' as in Ex. 1, or it can be verbally unsignalled but recognizable as a metaphor because of its difference from the matter.

Ex. 1 Using figurative language in an essay is like diving in the Olympics. If you do without it and produce straightforward prose, you perform a simple pike as your dive, and it needs to be absolutely perfect to win. But if you train hard so that you can try a double back twist rolling pike and use figurative language, it will not only entertain the crowd but it will give the judges more to award marks for, and even if it is less than perfect it would win points for effort.

The two ideas, 'using figurative language' and 'diving,' are each developed and the connection between them is maintained: so A.s could understand that using no figurative language is writing very simply, and so unlikely to attract high marks unless perfect, while using figurative language, though it requires more work and training, means a chance of a higher mark.

Persuasive value

Just as a brief **metaphor** can help A. understand a matter, and can usefully reveal something of C.'s attitude to it, so too can an extended metaphor; and its greater development provides more material to be useful to A.'s understanding, and to the revelation of C.

Extended metaphors are more noticeable than brief ones, and so do not so easily persuade subconsciously, but they substitute for this a power to influence by giving pleasure through the exercise of wit, and they create a bond between C. and A. because they jointly recognize that an extended metaphor is being used.

Extended metaphors take great skill, because of the need to keep the parallel going between the two ideas, but if they work they can provide a coherence for the text, and may be a very persuasive way of doing this; this is especially so where the matter has complex details which are not easily linked, where it would otherwise be hard for A. to sense the whole picture and how its details fit. One student recently produced this as an account of what it was like to be a first-year student at university:

Ex. 2 Being a first-year student at university is like being a mouse in an experiment designed for rats. Dealing with the administration is like going round and round inside a wheel as one is passed from one section to another; and finding one's way round the library stacks is like being lost in a maze with no way out. And the cruelest experiment of all is when you hand in your assignments and, without ever knowing why, sometimes get a reward and sometimes an electric shock.

Further reading   Lakoff and Johnson (1980)

METAPHOR MARKERS

Tasks

To distinguish metaphorical from literal language.
To signal that extra attention to the language is needed.

Description

Because a **metaphor**, saying one thing in terms of a quite different thing, requires A. to concentrate on interpretation in a special way, it must be clearly marked as distinct from literal language. The markers used are:

(a) a word such as 'like' or 'as';
(b) juxtaposition of literal and metaphorical words for the same referent, as in 'the black bat night is flown';
(c) close grammatical connection, such as adjective and noun, or adverb and verb, as in 'dancing kettle' or 'verbally attacked';
(d) omission of the literal and substitution of the metaphorical, as 'measuring life in coffeespoons.'

Persuasive value

The most powerful metaphors are the ones which are not marked at all. They can do their work without A. noticing them, or being able to prepare a defense against their power, so when marked, they allow A. a degree of freedom of response.

1 When 'like' or 'as' are used, C. warns A. that the next words refer to the preceding idea, and are metaphorical, and meant to enrich it. A.s then understand (a) that unusual cognitive exertion is required, and (b) that the two things, literal and metaphorical versions of the same referent, should be viewed as connected. A.s also know which is literal and which is not. One effect of the marker is to stop A.s in the process of absorbing the text, and make them concentrate. This will only be received badly if the stopping and concentrating is not worth doing (e.g. if the literal matter does not need enhancing), or if the metaphor is a **cliché** and does not enrich the meaning.

2 Juxtaposition as a mark of metaphor suggests a very close linkage or overlap in meaning, even fusion. Since both the literal and the metaphorical are present, A.s can see how valid the link is, and can be brought to work out what similarities and differences exist. If the effort to do this enhances the meaning, then the A.s will enjoy the experience, and perhaps accept the point.

3 Where adjectives or adverbs are non-literally applied to objects or actions, they work to describe the object or action in the usual way, but they cause an extra stir in A.s thinking as the two disparates are brought together and C. tries to control the scope of A.'s thought to the linkage.

4 Where no mark is supplied, a metaphor may either work extremely well or it may fail entirely in being taken literally or in not becoming the object of A.'s thought.

Further reading   Lakoff and Johnson (1980)

METAQUESTIONS

Tasks

To make sure of understanding something recently communicated.
To be precise.

Description

Metaquestions ask for information like some other questions, but are addressed to a previous communication and involve direct mention of the word or phrase about which they seek information, as in

Ex. 1 A: We have got the grant!
     B: What do you mean by 'got'?

Ex. 2 In your letter of the 15th you mention a 'printer' but give no specifications for it; could you please inform us. . . .

Persuasive value

1 The metaquestion is a very precise question since it pinpoints the source of the difficulty to a word or phrase.
2 It reveals that the questioner is a serious respondent, a careful reader, and is finicky about words as representations.

   This might suggest to others that they should give more care to the words they use. If they do not do so their views will be unlikely to achieve acceptance from the questioner.
3 Since such questions halt the communication flow, they reveal that the questioner is more interested in accuracy than the speedy use of language. They may indicate that the information flow is too fast for the questioner to absorb it.
4 If the questions occur in quantity, either every few paragraphs or utterances, or as a series at one moment, they can cause severe damage to the speaker's concentration as he or she is halted over and over again, and they can cause the topic to be aborted. They also anger those to whom they are addressed, particularly where the substance does not seem to warrant such questioning, or where the event is a sociable one and not a time for accuracy and criticism. The following example, like many sustained meta-questionings, suggests that the questioner is more interested in the surface than in the essence of what is being said.

Ex. 3 A: So I thought we could do the article jointly.
     B: What do you mean 'jointly'?
     A: Well, I could do . . . and you could do the other.
     B: What do you mean 'the other'?
     A: Have you got a problem with this?

B: What do you mean by 'problem'?
A: Oh, forget it, forget I ever spoke.

Further reading   Quirk, Greenbaum, Leech, and Svartvik (1985)

METONYMY

Task

To guide interpretation of a matter.

Description

Metonymy is the selection of a part of something to represent the whole. For example, in 'All hands on deck,' 'hand' is selected to stand for the whole body. The selection here is probably because the hands of the sailors were the parts most used in the work of the ship, but the choice is not always so reasonable.

Persuasive value

A C. can select any part that suits his or her goals to stand for the whole, and in so doing may persuade A. to accept it as a fair representation. So, for example, the metonymic use of a few words from a political leader snatched as he or she rushes from one appointment to another can appear to stand for the whole of the leader's policy on some matter. So also, an account of an hour-long meeting might be metonymically represented by a focus on a five-minute clash of personalities which occurred at it, ignoring the rest of the quiet and well-conducted interaction. As a result, a report of the event could suggest that it was 'a personal argument,' which would be untrue to the event.

Metonymy is a useful tool and is almost necessary as a shorthand way of communicating accounts of events and people, etc. (and so is stereotyping); no one has time or energy enough to present, or listen to, every matter given in full detail. It is important, therefore, when using or interpreting metonymy to realize that it is just a part, and not the whole, that it has involved selection by C. and that it may therefore be biassed.

It is, however, hard to notice when metonyms are used, because they do not draw attention to themselves as metaphors do. And so they can work covertly and very persuasively. They work by presenting, as it were, a minipicture of something, and A. builds on this to construct the rest. A clever choice of metonym can cause a very distorted picture to be accepted, as in

Ex. 1 A: How did Ken take the fact that you all opposed him?
       B: He looked furious.

where the 'furious' look may have lasted only a short time and Ken showed
many other responses not mentioned. It suits B., however, to metonymize
a 'furious' moment—perhaps to suggest his or her own success in
opposition.

See also **Stereotypes**

Further reading   Antaki (1988); Corbett (1990); Sonnino (1968)

MINIMALISM

Task

To avoid being antisocial.

Description

To be minimal in speech and especially in response is in many cases poor
communication. Exceptions are in formal interrogations, or form-filling, or
in emergencies where time is at a premium. So the following responses are
unsatisfactory:

Ex. 1 Ann: We went to San Francisco for our holiday this year. Have
              you ever been?
       Bill: No.

Ex. 2 Mary: Our legal department seems to be meeting some difficulties
              over this issue and we need to talk; would you agree?
       Peter: Yeah.

Ex. 3 John: Have you seen Fred anywhere?
       Susan: Yeah.

Persuasive value

In most cases to offer only a minimal response is to be less than cooperative, or even to be actively unhelpful. It is perceived very negatively.

In Ex. 1, Ann and Bill are engaged in informal sociability, so when Bill is
invited to respond to the question about San Francisco, although he has to
be truthful and say that he has never been, and so appear negative, he
makes what he says offensive by being minimal. However true they are,
negative responses are dispreferred (*see* **Preferred response**), and so
should be given some positive quality to offset the negative; in this case Bill
supplies nothing, though he could have said 'No, but I keep meaning to
though,' or 'No, but they say it is very nice.' Even a doubling of the

negative would have been better, becauseit is less minimal, so he could have said (in an even monotone) 'No, no, never.' Strangely enough, two or more negatives can be perceived as less negative than just one. His minimality will be seen as lack of interest and of cooperation.

In Ex. 2, Peter ignores the signs that Mary gives that she wants to talk about the issues. And though he responds with a positive, by being so minimal in doing so he displays a high degree of non-cooperation.

In Ex. 3, Susan's positive answer is also quite uncooperative; she answers the surface meaning of the words, and ignores the real meaning of the question which must be 'Where is Fred?'

A minimal utterance is hard to respond to; for example in Ex. 3 John might find it difficult to think what next to say. Should he ask the underlying question 'Where is Fred?' knowing that Susan probably understood that this was his intention in his first version and yet refused to answer it. Would he fare any better if he tried again? And if Susan is being so uncooperative is there any point in saying anything at all?

In Ex. 4, the minimalism makes it even harder for the first speaker.

Ex. 4 Alan: Have you considered the consequences of making this decision, that it will make it difficult for these students to fund their studies?
    Ken: No, I haven't.

Alan's problem is should he continue, perhaps with 'Well, why not?' when Ken is clearly being unsupportive of the view Alan has expressed. If he does he could be perceived as irritatingly persistent, and is therefore unlikely to achieve a great deal, except perhaps a discussion of reasons and argument, but no change in the decision. Minimalism in communication is a major social rebuff.

See also **Sociable language**

Further reading   McLaughlin and Cody (1982); Mulholland (1991)

MODERATION: DISPLAY

Tasks

To take up a middle ground position.
To counter extremism in others.

Description

There are two ways to demonstrate moderation:

(a) by avoiding the two extremes of a polar opposition;
(b) by showing that the two extremes amount to the same thing, and are both bad.

Persuasive value

Moderation is not an easy view to represent, since it lacks the excitement and strength of expression of extremism. The problem is compounded since a moderate person may also need to change ground to counter different versions of extremism as the communication proceeds: as one extreme appears to be winning, a moderate needs to oppose it but soon after may need to express a very different opinion as the other extreme begins to win support. Moderates are therefore often accused of being turncoats, and also of sitting on the fence, of not knowing which side to take, and so on.

One form of moderation is to present the middle view as in opposition to both extremes, and so change the discussion from a debate about one or the other extreme to a debate about moderation versus extremism. The other form is to seek to defeat both extremes and leave the moderate view as the only viable view to accept.

To achieve a reasonable success as a moderate, a person needs not only to defeat the extremists but also to state the moderate view so strongly that it attracts consent in its own right. So, for example, if there were an extremist argument opposing gluttony and dieting, a moderate could show first that both extremes lead to death, and then that a reasonable food intake of a specified kind would produce excellent effects. That is, a successful moderate would take the argument right away from the extremes, and so change the agenda.

Since moderation is less exciting than extremism, moderates need to use powerful words to represent the middle position; for example, it may be better not to call it 'moderate' or 'middle' but refer to it as the 'central' or 'pivotal' position, as these are stronger terms. If it is possible to give it a name this could also be useful. For example, in faculty appointments, the requirements are that applicants should be good at both research and teaching, but this is usually offered as an opposition, with the result that those applicants who do both, or perhaps do research into teaching, may be perceived as doing neither research nor teaching properly, and so not be appointed. Such an applicant may need to settle on a positive term for his or her work, perhaps 'synthesizer,' or 'coordinator,' and in cricketing countries at least, it may be possible to use the positive term 'all-rounder.'

See also **Naming**

Further reading   Sonnino (1968)

MOVE: FOLLOW-UP

Tasks

To close off an exchange of speech.
To show oneself as powerful.

Description

Most **exchanges of speech** consist of two parts, initiating and response moves, but some have a third part, called a follow-up move, as in

Ex. 1 A: Did you get that book for me?
       B: Yes, it's on your desk.
       A: Good.

The follow-up move is made by the person who initiated the speech exchange and signals that it is complete, either satisfactorily, as in Ex. 1, or not, as in Ex. 2:

Ex. 2 A: Did you get that book for me?
       B: No, I forgot.
       A: Oh dear, what a nuisance.

The form is much used by teachers in classrooms.

Persuasive value

Follow-up moves can make explicit how the initiator of the exchange feels about its success or failure as a mini-interaction. This brings his or her feelings to the surface and records them for all to hear. If the exchange has failed, as in Ex. 2, it is often the case that the next move is an apology by the second speaker with loss of face, and social embarrassment.

Equally, the initiator can set up as a judge, and either offer praise for correct answers, or blame for incorrect ones—both of which are tactics that put C. into a dominant position, like that of a teacher in a class of students. In addition, by using the follow-up move, C. has retaken the floor, and hence grabbed another turn at initiating. (*See* the **Turn** tactics.)

Using the follow-up move enables the initiator to close off the exchange very dominantly, much more strongly than the way, for example, an answer closes off a question-and-answer exchange.

Sometimes the follow-up move is not made where it is expected, as in both Examples 1 and 2, it would be noticeable by its absence. In such cases its absence would tell A.s that their responses have been inadequate in some way. On the other hand, sometimes its absence will reflect badly on C., as in

Ex. 3 A: Did you manage to get those books for me?
       B: Yes, here they are.
       A: [Silence]
       B: Aren't you going to say thanks?

See also **Initiating move; Responses**

Further reading   Coulthard (1985); Goodwin (1981); McLaughlin (1984); Nofsinger (1991)

MYTH

Tasks

To reinforce a specific idea by appeal to the general beliefs of the community.
To incorporate a community belief into one's communication to assist one's persuasion.

Description

Myth in the sense used here is not a falsehood or fantasy, but rather is a particular social and cultural understanding of some aspect of the world. So, for example, Western society for many years has believed in the myth of 'progress;' that is, that things can be and should be explored and investigated, because then new ideas, discoveries, policies, and results will be obtained and these will be good. Believing in this myth, society expects that life will get better or should get better. It is acknowledged that for many people in the world life is becoming worse, but because the myth is believed, this is seen as just an aberration, and can be rectified by some new progress. A counter-myth would be to see any such bad situation more fatalistically, as God's will, or just that the world is a bad place.

A myth of a quite different type is the Western one of the 'nuclear family seen as an ideal.' This myth presents a picture of society in which the best way to live is as a member of a nuclear-family group—mother, father, and (a few) children. Other groups or family units are judged negatively against this model, although in 1993 many Western societies have a higher preponderance of people in other types of group. The ideal still remains the nuclear-family one, and all groups are held in higher regard than solo livers. This myth, like the progress one, and the many others which affect how we interpret the world, gains impact by being promulgated in personal communications, in all parts of the mass media, and especially entertainment, and in political and religious debates.

Persuasive value

So prevalent are its manifestations that they are used to measure the desirability of ideas, arguments, and in general to assess the 'rightminded-ness' of the content of any text. So that, if C. wishes to have a text's content accepted, it should be shown to fit the prevailing myths. So, for example, in making out a case for a new computer, C. could argue that it will improve work capacity (the 'progress' myth), while an opponent could retort that it would isolate each worker from others, and therefore prevent them from forming a group of colleagues, which is a bad thing, against the myth of shared living.

Myths can be very broad, as in these examples, or they can be quite narrow in focus. One narrowly focussed myth is that people are attracted to each other by good looks, and must be attracted in this visual way if they are to be what society would accept as 'truly in love.' So strong are the forces of such myths that someone who falls in love with one who is not good looking will become defensive about it: 'I know others don't think so but I like the way he looks,' 'She may not be beautiful on the outside, . . .' or may make excuses like 'I fell for looks with my first wife, this time I'm trying compatibility.' These defenses occur without any criticism from others: they simply reflect the power of myth.

See also **Word combinations**

Further reading   O'Sullivan, Hartley, Saunders, and Fiske (1983)

NAME: CALL

Tasks

To have someone respond.
To set the topic agenda.

Description

If C. wishes to have someone respond while not in eye contact, the quickest and most certain method is to call the person's name.

Persuasive value

1 If one hears someone call one's name, it is conventionally impossible to resist, especially if known to be within hearing distance, without rousing the caller to anger and requiring an apology for not answering. An angry caller is unlikely to listen to any persuasion by the other or to be willing to recognize the other's goals.
2 Of further persuasive value is the conventional routine which often develops from the name call, which can be the means of setting up the first topic to be treated when the interaction begins. This consists of the following:

Ex. 1 A: Mary? Are you there?
      B: What?

The response 'What (do you want)?' sets up a question to the name caller, and requires him or her to answer. In giving this answer the name caller is able to set the first topic. This gameplaying frequently occurs, and it does so because of the conventions around the notion of **turntaking** in spoken communication. It is an important convention that no one person should be too dominant in taking the floor. However, by virtue of the name-call game A. does not actually 'take' the floor, but rather sets it up that B. 'gives' A. the floor. B. does this by saying 'What?' and so asking A. to expand on the reasons for the name call. On occasions the name calling takes place where it seems patently set up to do just this. If a C. does it too much it will eventually be non-productive, and non-persuasive.

Further reading   Nofsinger (1991)

NAMING

Tasks

To influence others' perceptions.
To have an interpretation accepted.

Description

The world of experience is a complex mass of events, people, ideas, etc., all interlocked. When a matter from the world is put into communication it must be isolated from the interlocked complexity, and given a name. The name records a perception about the matter, and it may not be the only perception possible.

Persuasive value

1 The act of naming causes the thing named to acquire a tangibility, or 'reality,' in communication, and hence a validity in people's experience, which it might otherwise not have. So the complex notions involved in ecological interrelations can be named 'ecosystem,' and so characterized as a system (which may not be yet strictly true), and be widely accepted. So also chatting in a corridor at work can be named 'discussion took place' and acquire extra significance and value.
2 The choice of name brings with it word associations, and these attach to the matter named. It can therefore be a highly significant act to name something, particularly if the name is accepted. The nursing profession is currently seeking to rename patients 'clients,' because it fits with their sense of their professionalism, aligning themselves with others who have clients, like lawyers. The Queensland Police Force has just renamed itself the Police Service. Feminists know the power of naming, as they seek to have such masculinist names as 'Chairman' and 'policeman' changed to

'President' and 'police officer.' Changes in naming can either illustrate changes in social perceptions, or may be deliberately employed to bring such changes about.

3 When something has a set of possible names, as an interaction could be named 'discussion,' 'chat,' 'talk-fest,' 'informal meeting,' or just 'work,' the choice of one, and its reiterated use, can influence others to interpret the thing in that and only that way. The choice has interpretive value, as in the following which are different names for the same event.

Ex. 1 He OD'd. (i.e. overdosed on a drug)

and

Ex. 2 He succumbed to his fatal addiction to heroin.

The first is blunt and somewhat derogatory, the second gives a higher social cachet to the event, by using 'literary' words.

4 Naming is a relatively unobtrusive attempt to guide interpretations and may be successful as persuasion precisely because it passes unnoticed that it is only an opinion or partial judgment.

See also the other **Naming** tactics; **Title choice**; **Word combinations**

Further reading   Mulholland (1991)

NAMING: ONESELF

Task

To explicitly present oneself in the most suitable way.

Description

When introducing oneself to strangers, it is usual to name oneself. This can involve using one's full name, or a part of it, giving one's marital status (a problem for women only), social position, or specified role in the encounter.

Persuasive value

All self-namings can cause social difficulty for C.s and A.s.

1 To name oneself in too detailed a way can suggest that A.s are ignorant of who one is or what position one holds, and A.s may resent this if in fact they know this information.

2 How one names oneself will indicate the social distance that one finds suitable. For example, to name oneself by surname only, 'Smith,' or as 'Dr. Smith,' suggests a distant connection is wanted, while using 'Mary,' 'Smithy,' or 'Mary Smith' suggests a much closer one.

3 Some namings are more appropriate to one kind of interaction than

another. Formal meetings take formal namings for granted just as informal ones take more friendly names as normal. It follows, then, that using an unusual naming for the interaction type will have a major impact. A guest visiting in a family home who named himself 'Dr. John Smith' would be interpreted as anti-social in some way.

4 C.s of high social position, say in the top ranks of a company, can either insist on naming their rank, 'I'm Vice Pres. Marketing,' or understate it 'I'm John Smith from Marketing,' and the choice will have persuasive influence. A.s could read insistence on rank as meaning that such people want the trappings of social rank to be granted to them in the interaction —authority, floorholding rights, etc. If C.s of low social position make a fuss of naming themselves by their position, it can often be a sign of resentment, sometimes a sign of humility, and sometimes just a plain statement of fact—to decide which is meant, other aspects of the person's behavior would need to be studied. For many people the middle way is the preferable one, and to do this they can name themselves with a mixture of declared rank and due modesty, as in 'As you probably know, I'm Mary Smith. I'm in charge of P.R. in the Company.' This allows for the problem stated in 1 above; suggests a moderate distance; and states her position not through her title 'Vice Pres.' but through the phrase 'in charge of.'

N.B.   It is crucial that usefully informative naming be done; most people want to know who the people are that they are communicating with. It saves such embarrassments as telling someone how to market goods, and later learning that he or she is V.P. Marketing for some company: such happenings can be difficult for both people to handle.

N.B.   Many cultures differ in their preferences for self-naming: some like detailed specification, others like no detail at all.

See also the other **Naming** tactics

Further reading   Mulholland (1991)

NAMING: PEOPLE

Tasks

To influence judgments of a person.
To consolidate or weaken social bonding.

Description

How the people who are associated with the participants in interaction are named in communications can affect how those texts are accepted. People can be given their first name, their family name, their first and family name together. Their marital status or professional qualification could be used, or their official position or role at work, or a friendly nickname.

Persuasive value

1 The choice of name reveals something of C.'s attitude towards the person named, or his or her own status relative to the named person, etc. It may indicate the tone C. wants to prevail in the interaction: formal names used when a formal tone is needed, casual names for small talk. A.s will note this, and respond accordingly.

2 Where one person is referred to by the participants by very different names, choosing which name to use is complicated. For example, if there is a need to conciliate A.s, and to seem to share attitudes with them, using the same name establishes a bond of similarity, while using a different name focusses on difference, sometimes to great effect, as in:

Ex. 1 A: Is Mr. Smith here yet?
       B: Oh, Bill's always late.

where B's reply shows close familiarity with a person A apparently does not know, and so gives him- or herself status over A.

   Sometimes, however, other factors might make it unsuitable for the name to be shared: for example, one person might be a family member with the named one, while the other is not. It would be taking a liberty for C. to call A.'s brother 'Fatty,' though of course A. can.

N.B.   Something of the same problem of name choice can arise where differences in name (or other word) pronunciation are exhibited. Should C. echo A.'s pronunciation where it differs from his or her own, or stick to their own version? A difference in pronunciation can often be taken badly, and seen as criticism by those with little self-esteem, while it will be seen as wrong by those who are supremely confident of their own speech.

See also the other **Naming** tactics; **Title choice**

Further reading   Sonnino (1968)

NAMING: SUBSTITUTE PHRASE

Tasks

To characterize something or someone by using a descriptive phrase rather than a proper name to focus attention on some aspect of the matter.
To refer to something or someone without mentioning names.

Description

One can use a characterizing descriptive phrase to designate something or someone specific, as in

Ex. 1 the Old Man
       Her Indoors
       the anti-personnel officer
       the Departmental scrounger
       old Mr. Holier-than-thou

Ex. 2 the office junior
       the xerox monster

Ex. 3 some highbrows
       the brandy and cigar boys
       the Establishment

Persuasive value

The phrase can be used for a specific person, as in Ex. 1, or a specific social position whoever occupies it, like 'the office junior' in Ex. 2, or some object, no matter which specific instance of it, as in 'the xerox monster,' or it can be used without individually specifying at all, as in Ex. 3 where the C. characterizes a whole group.

The people referred to by the phrases in Ex. 1 may or may not know the description that is given of them. If they know of it, they may dislike or like it; this decision rests more on their personalities than on the quality of the name: some people enjoy being spoken about even in an insulting phrase, preferring it to not being spoken about at all. If it is not known to the person, others can derive a mean but enjoyable pleasure in using it even in the person's presence. The use of the phrase forms a solidarity among its users. The phrase can also act as a group indicator for those who share knowledge of it, by excluding those who do not. It is often a mark of achieving a particular rank that one is allowed officially to use some naming device that new colleagues use.

Since the Ex. 3 instances can be used without explicitly referring to any one person or group, they allow criticism to occur without face loss to any members of the group being attacked since no one need admit to being one of the 'brandy and cigar boys'; and they allow people to criticize without naming names.

N.B.   The use of 'highbrows' as an agreed term of criticism in society means that whenever it occurs society is endorsing a judgment that intellectuality is regarded poorly. It seems an odd social judgment.

N.B.   The use of such descriptive phrases as 'The Establishment' and 'The Government' (and of course 'They') is also a sign of an important social judgment. The terms are used in such sentences as 'They shouldn't allow it,' 'The Government should put things right,' etc., and by being so vague and non-specific they make it harder to realize what the user is communi-cating—that he or she wants the world putting right by a collection of ordinary, specific, and nameable men and women who have gained elected office or work at bureaucratic jobs. The vaguer the name the harder it is to recognize what one is asking for.

See also the other **Naming** tactics

Further reading Sonnino (1968)

NAMING: TEXT

Tasks

To influence the interpretation of a text.
To change the nature of some interactive acts.

Description

By giving a text a name C.s can give it a particular social valuation. For example, by naming a piece of writing a 'document,' or a 'scribble,' or indeed 'a piece of writing,' C.s can influence how seriously others will take it.

Persuasive value

Whatever name is chosen for a text needs to be to some degree appro-priate—it would not be acceptable to any A. to have a ten-page report called a 'brief memo,' but they may accept it being named 'a preliminary account,' or even 'John has gathered his thoughts on the matter and has provided us with some useful ideas.' John, incidentally, might find it difficult to object and insist his report is a report since this would involve sounding defensive (often poorly received by others) or aggressively assert-ing his work's value (also often poorly received).

1 Naming allows C.s to indicate that a text is 'serious,' 'valid,' or 'irrel-evant,' etc., and to do so in a covert way, and to have others accept this interpretation. Compare the direct criticism in:

Ex. 1 This is a very poor report, it only briefly touches on the issues.

or with the more covert criticism in

Ex. 2 This draft report could form a starting point for our discussion, and having helped us get the minor issues out of the way, we could move on from it, and proceed to deal with the main issues.

The mixture of praise and yet dismissal of the importance of the report would make it difficult to object to, and so this may become the accepted version.

2 The first person to name a text has the best chance of having that interpretation accepted and used. And the more the name is used, both in the interaction and beyond it, the more it will harden as the natural, inevitable name for the text, and the more difficult it will become to remember what it was first called.

See also the other **Naming** tactics

Further reading   Mulholland (1991)

NARRATIVE: BEGIN

Tasks

To guide A.s as they follow the communication.
To warn A. that a new genre is starting.
To encourage A. to accept the interpretation.

Description

Narratives can begin with whatever can be isolated as the first event in a series or the first idea in a set, etc. They can also begin with a preamble before the story proper begins. This could justify the creating of a narrative or show its appropriateness to the present circumstances, if C. feels it necessary, as in

Ex. 1 This matter is becoming very difficult to follow, perhaps I could try to tidy it up . . . [starts story]. We began our association with the Smith company in 1990 . . .

Or it could provide clues that a narrative is to follow, as in

Ex. 2 I think that at this point it would be useful to look back to when we first . . . and see if we can get the whole story.

Or it could bridge the gap between the kind of interaction it has been to this point and the new narrative interaction that is about to begin, as in

Ex. 3 This discussion [present interaction] has been interesting, but what I think might finish the meeting off productively would be an account . . . [begins story]

If it suits C. to do so, the action could be told from the start of the events, or in flashback, from the last event or idea, and show how it came about, or could begin with some item in the middle of the events if C. wishes to emphasize it and have it form the focus of the account. However the story begins, it should be planned to hold A.'s interest.

One of C.'s main tasks at the start of a narrative is to present what is being communicated as a naturally linked series of matters that result in an inevitable conclusion. Narratives make what is told in them seem unavoidably true, and C.s should try to work towards this aim from the moment they start the story.

Danger   If the start fails to set the main thread of the story, or to begin from the first point that could be seen to lead to the conclusion, or even describes the actors carelessly or in insufficient detail, the failure will not only result in A.s not listening to the story, but they are also likely to find the narrator poor value as a colleague or friend.

See also the other **Narrative** tactics

Further reading   Goodwin (1982); Jefferson (1978); Mandelbaum (1989)

NARRATIVE: CHOOSE

Tasks

To disguise the complexities of an event.
To make an account easy to read and accept.

Description

Narratives represent their material, whether it is a concrete series of events, or a set of thoughts or ideas, in such a way that there is a clear viewpoint, a plot, a set of actors and events, and correlations of cause and effect, etc.

Persuasive value

Narratives play a major role in our communicative experience, whether they are the fairy tales and moral fables of childhood, or family anecdotes, or the novels of adulthood. Narrators use the story form to offer an understanding of the world; and through it they supply social and cultural meanings for what happens in life. People become habituated to learning to evaluate life through narratives, and to accepting the lessons they offer. There are two major persuasive consequences of this. First, people are disposed to find a 'story' (that is, a sense-making explanatory pattern) in any new experience. C.s can utilize this disposition, by heightening whatever is story-like in their material, and encouraging A.s to search for the viewpoint, the plot, the actors, and events, etc., in what they read or hear. Having done so, they can be almost certain that A.s will, out of habit, go further and accept the viewpoint and meaning expressed. Second, the attractive simplicity of narrative can be used to disguise complexities and ambiguities in the material, and strongly subjective elements in the way the material is communicated.

The persuasion partly works by setting up a resemblance of pattern between the new communication and the stories of the past; A.s assume that this guarantees a similarity of meaning, so the new account therefore finds support from previous experience, and is finally accepted as 'true.' A.s are also inclined to regard good narrators highly, as people who can produce clear accounts from the confusions of life.

A.s' familiarity with narrative structuring is such that from the moment they recognize that they are receiving a narrative they can fall into the well-established behavior for such occasions, which is to be carried along with the story line. The predictability of the narrative form can distract them from noticing, let alone criticizing, any awkward details, or implications of the meanings presented, and if they do notice, it can create a willingness in them to suspend their disbelief at least temporarily. It is difficult to resist the meanings that a narrative imposes on its material, because it requires A. to restructure the whole of the material into some other version of meaning, and this requires a good deal of cognitive effort; A. would need to be well motivated to feel the effort was worthwhile.

See also the other **Narrative** tactics

Further reading   Goodwin (1982); Jefferson (1979); Mandelbaum (1989)

NARRATIVE: DESIGN

Tasks

To disguise the complexities of an event.
To make an account easy to read and accept.

Description

Any material, however apparently unrelated to a 'story', can be made story-like if the following conditions can be met.
1 C.s can find a steady-state point in the material to begin the narrative, and present matters as moving through conflict and confusion to a resolution. The departure point should be well defined, and the material isolated from what surrounds it; and the narrative should end strongly with a climax and an explanation of the story's relevance to A.
2 C.s can express the theme of the material in terms of actors, actions, and those who are affected by the agents and actions, and make any abstractions concrete.
3 C.s can separate the aspects of the material into central and peripheral ones.

4 C.s can provide early evidence that they are trustworthy narrators, producing a well-structured and predictable account, for example, by giving hints of what the end will be so that readers can settle themselves into their routine of narrative reading.

In addition it may be useful to make analogies with familiar narratives (perhaps ones in the immediate context which readers have already accepted); this link could cause readers to remember material which could support the meanings being offered in the current communication.

Chronology or some other device for shaping the material can be used, with clear signals given of the start and finish, and of any important stages within it. The following is a typical example of a narrative, in this case used as a way of producing a report:

Ex. 1 This account *must begin* (= sign of structure) with a consideration (= action) . . . *As a result of this* (= cause and effect) *we* (= actors) must discuss our future management policy (= action) so that the campaign can start on time (= effect) . . . *However, it is important to note at this point* (= structure) what the history of that aspect of policy has been (= background story) . . . *Three examples should make clear what I mean* (= structure) . . . a (= story), b (=story), c (= story) . . . *Therefore, taking all this into account* (= sign of approaching climax) I consider that unless *we* (= actors) *do this soon* (= action) *we will lose the opportunity* (= climax, of consequence to readers).

Persuasive value

Narratives are most useful when communicating unusual or complex material, or an opinion which is likely to be resisted. By using the familiar form, the complexities appear to be sorted out, and the unwelcome opinion can lie hidden as the story sweeps along.

See also the other **Narrative** tactics

Further reading   Goodwin (1982); Jefferson (1979); Mandelbaum (1989)

NARRATIVE: ELEMENTS

Tasks

To disguise the complexities of an event.
To make an account easy to read and accept.

Description

The basic elements of a narrative are:

(a) the isolation of one matter from all that surrounds it;

(b) the structuring of events into a 'plot,' from a stable beginning through crisis to resolution;

(c) the material should be separated into actors, actions and resultant effects, and also into foregrounded matters and background ones;

(d) any inherent repetitions in the material should be emphasized;

(e) the ending should be clearly climactic and tie up all the loose ends;

(f) the narrator has some role to play either in the story or by the way he or she tells it. As in:

> Ex. 1 What seems to have happened so far is that John began by saying . . . Susan agreed but added . . . Peter made his usual witty comment, then the discussion got down to business with everyone taking sides. The problem [crisis] as I see it is that we must decide . . . or we will have wasted two hours of hard talking [moral lesson to be drawn].

Persuasive value

There is a value for the potential narrator in searching material for its narrative qualities. It sets up a good analytic method, and a very familiar one, for C.s to use to clarify their understanding of some aspect of their lives. In particular it is useful because it draws attention to the structural aspects of the material; that is, how matters relate to one another, and cumulatively come to have a final meaning. Without a clear sense of this it is hard for anyone to communicate anything. Equally, seeking to find narrative qualities in something can show C.s how to reduce some of the complexities of real life into a single coherent meaning.

Narratives are also valuable for their readers. They present something of the world in an easily mastered way, along with a familiar mode of reading it. They are especially powerful influences on A.s because of the way they present the world as if it can be easily understood if only someone looks closely at it. This goes some way to satisfy the basic need in people to believe there is a basic design behind the apparent chaos of the world, and to feel that by recognizing the design they are in some way controlling it, and the world.

C.s can obviously use narrative to incorporate their own prejudices and biasses into their account, as they create the actors as good and bad, the actions as useful or foolish, etc. C.s can choose a narrator's position to suit their goals: for example, they can act as a witness to the events of the story, or an actor within it (one good role is that of the magic helper to the hero), or an omniscient observer. Each role can enhance C.'s status in real life.

See also the other **Narrative** tactics

Further reading   Goodwin (1982); Jefferson (1979); Mandelbaum (1989)

NARRATIVE: END

Tasks

To round off an account to produce the best meaning.
To present oneself as in control—of language and the world.

Description

Most narratives give clear termination signals. These are usually either a recognizable resolution of the crisis, or an additional section or 'coda' in which the narrator provides a moral or social lesson to be learnt from the story.

Persuasive value

1 By providing a clear ending, which rounds off the events of the story and pulls all of its threads together to make a united conclusion, the narrator can exert a strong influence on A. This is because of the major difference between narrated and real-life events, which is that in real life there is no clear rounding off to happenings, often many loose ends remain, or perhaps there is no sign at all that an end of any kind has occurred. In imposing an ending on the complexities (and indeed relating their beginnings to the ending, and by structuring the whole story from the disorder of real events) the narrator takes on a god-like role. This will to some degree be recognized by the others as they admire the skill with which C. has found a pattern in events and communicated it to them. It is also possible that they will accept what the ending, and hence the whole narrative, means as an interpretation of life just because it is so clearly explicable as C. puts it.
2 Many traditional stories, and particularly fables, end not with the resolution but with a 'coda' in which an interpretation of the whole story is offered. It is a summing up which is useful to A.s because it tells them what to think the story means, how to organize their thoughts about it. It is also easily memorable, and therefore can influence their future thought and actions.

Ex. 1 [As the narrative draws to a close] So, in short, after we had settled on the design of the course, and appointed staff to teach it, we were finally able to decide on the quota of students, the only possibility was 500. [coda begins] To take more would be to jeopardize the whole scheme, and waste all the hard work that has gone into organizing it.

Since the coda is offered in the narrator's own voice, and own person, the lesson will be associated directly with him or her, and not left unattributed, as just an aspect of the story. And since it can be offered in something resembling a proverbial saying, both its meaning and its proverbial quality would work together to make it very hard to reject.

See also the other **Narrative** tactics**; Sum up**

Further reading   Goodwin (1982); Jefferson (1979); Mandelbaum (1989)

'NEXT'

Task

To refer correctly to a specified time, using 'next.'

Description

The word 'next' when it is used in association with a time phrase, like 'next Friday' or 'next week,' is a socially hard word to interpret, particularly for those from outside that language community.

Persuasive value

1 For example,

Ex. 1 He will do it next Friday.

could mean in two days' time if the sentence were said on a Wednesday, but if said on a Thursday it must mean Friday of the following week; the next day Friday would be referred to as 'tomorrow.' The problem could be compounded if this communication were reported to someone else and the hearer had to adjust the term 'next,' remembering what day it was when the original communication was said, and taking into account what day the report is offered. The word should be excised if precision is needed, and a better version put in its place.
2 The word is also difficult to interpret where it is used to designate one part of a sequence of actions, as in

Ex. 2 I've got a couple of things to do at the moment, but I'll do your machine next.

This leaves quite unspecified and unclear when exactly 'next' is. There is no way of telling how long the 'couple of things' could take. It might, however, satisfy A. as an indication that some priority is being given to the matter, while C. can feel pleased to have escaped without having to mention the exact time the machine will be done.
   Such vaguenesses arise because the word is much used in informal,

socializing communication, and is generally regarded as rightly belonging there. Sociability places little value on specification and exactness, preferring geniality and casualness. It would be out of place to be too formally precise, as in C.'s response in the following:

Ex. 3 A: We just got back from our holiday last week. It's awful being home again.
B: Oh, do you think so? We came back a couple of weeks ago and I was glad to be back. What about you Fred?
C: We came back on Friday the 17th of May and it was good to be home.

Further reading   Quirk, Greenbaum, Leech, and Svartvik (1985)

OBJECTIONS: ANTICIPATE

Tasks

To reduce the chances of others objecting to one's material.
To anticipate and answer potential objections.

Description

There are various ways in which people can anticipate and block potential objections:
1 They can prevent any possibilities of objection.
2 They can answer potential objections in advance.
3 They can concede any points which might be objected to.
4 They can correct their points as they proceed.
5 They can require A.s to delay raising objections.

Persuasive value

No one can totally avoid objections from others: if people feel strongly enough about something they will raise objections. But some objections, the milder kind, can be avoided.
1 It may be possible to block all objections by declaring such narrow boundaries to the subject matter that many objections could be ruled irrelevant. Or, it may be possible to claim at the start that a comprehensive coverage will be given, and that all objections will be dealt with later.
2 It may be possible to prepare well enough to anticipate objections and answer them. If making a public presentation in writing or speech it may be possible to consult possible objectors in advance and design the presentation to forestall their criticisms.

3 C.s can present themselves as ready to concede any opposing views provided they do not destroy the main thrust of the argument, and so, although they receive objections, they can incorporate them without losing control of the discussion.

4 When speaking publicly, C.s can notice non-verbal signs of disagreement and respond to them, and so preempt the objections which are about to be formed.

5 If any objections occur, C.s can address the objectors by politely asking them to hold their objections until the end. It is entirely possible that by that time, even if their objections are valid, they will seem out of place and inappropriate, and will therefore be less threatening to C.'s argument.

Further reading   Corbett (1977, 1990); Sonnino (1968)

OBLIQUE REPRESENTATION

Task

To have someone understand and accept something without actually putting it into words.

Description

There are many forms of oblique representation:

(a) omission, which is the most oblique of all;
(b) indirection in its various aspects;
(c) hesitation about representation;
(d) state a part only, and so obliquely imply the rest.

Persuasive value

In a spoken interaction (d), a second speaker can take up what the first speaker has said, and in so doing can make oblique revelations, as in

Ex. 1 A: My husband and I had this terrible fight yesterday . . . but then we are always fighting about something but whenever we fight we always make up the same day.
        B: We always make up over a glass of wine.

In this example, B picks up on one part of A's story, the climax, and in so doing implies that the rest of the story is true also for her in her own relationship with her husband. If she had replied:

Ex. 2 B: We never have to make up at all.

by denying the result of the fighting, she denies the fighting as well.

Sometimes the response may be not just oblique but vague and hard to follow, as in

Ex. 3 A: I really worked hard this term so I was truly pleased with my high marks.
       B: I never really work hard.

It is not clear what exactly B is implying; perhaps it is just what is said, or perhaps it is implying that because he or she has not worked like A, he or she has not the same high marks as A: it avoids being specific.

See also **Omit** tactics; **Politeness indirection** tactics

Further reading   Corbett (1977, 1990), Sonnino (1968)

OFFER

Task

To present something for acceptance or rejection.

Description

An offer may be made because it is thought useful to another, or to the self, or to both, or in the general expectation that everyone will exchange offers, and that everyone will benefit. (Note: because it is better to make a weak offer than to offer nothing, some people even make 'rhetorical' offers to act, that is, ones they can be sure no one will take up.)

In order to offer something, C. must either own it or have discovered it or at least have worked it out in the mind. Also C. must be willing to share it or to have it taken up, or made the focus of attention by others. If the thing is a concrete object, C. could lose possession of it, though an idea or opinion will be retained, even if others use it.

Persuasive value

How C. registers ownership will influence the offer's persuasiveness. For example, the following choices entail different responses:

Ex. 1 My view is that we should . . . What do you think?

Ex. 2 In my view it needs a report. I am willing to do one if you like.

Ex. 3 I've just had an idea. Why don't we . . .?

Ex. 4 I heard this useful idea last week. Why don't we . . .?

Ex. 5 What do you think of the idea of doing . . .?

Ex. 1 makes the strongest declaration of ownership—'my view is that . . .' (which is interestingly stronger than Ex. 2 'in my view'); if taken up it would acknowledge the offerer's authority. Ex. 2 makes a double offer, and so requires two responses, and therefore extra effort from the recipients. In Ex. 3 the 'idea' offered is not 'mine,' it is 'an' idea, and I have 'just had' it (i.e. it is new), and so is less owned by C.; while Ex. 4 is in reported form, and therefore the possession is second-hand and so it is less rude to reject it. Ex. 5 makes no mention of ownership, and begins with the question form, thus reducing the whole to a tentative offer and allowing the freest range of actions to the recipients.

To avoid loss of face, from having offers rejected, C.s should:

(a) make only a reasonable number of offers: too many and it may appear as though they feel inferior and are trying too hard to be useful, or, strangely enough, the converse, that they feel superior and are being too domineering;
(b) be tentative, not about the quality of the idea, but about whether it will be accepted;
(c) separate themselves enough from ownership to ensure that rejection is not too painful.

Various general consequences arise from offers:

(a) C.s may be seen as having special knowledge, or good ideas.
(b) All offers will influence the event, for good or ill.
(c) The offerer may gain credit as the first to have the idea (however unfairly).

Further reading   Wierzbicka (1987)

'OH'

Tasks

To show a revision in the speaker's ideas.
To show different responses to the speaker's ideas.

Description

'Oh' is traditionally seen as an exclamation of emotion in speech, but its roles are more important than this suggests, and they mainly relate to the reception of information.

Persuasive value

1 A speaker can use 'Oh' to indicate that he or she is about to correct the preceding information, as in

Ex. 1   It came yesterday; oh, sorry, it was early today.

This is a **self-repair** tactic, useful when a mistake has been made, which can stop anyone else doing the correction with consequent loss of face for the speaker.

2   A hearer can use 'Oh' to signal the reception of very new information or a remembrance of something relevant. As in:

Ex. 2   A: It was Tom Cruise in *Rain Man*, not Tom Selleck.
       B: Oh, really? *or* Oh, that's right, Tom Cruise.

3   'Oh' can be used to link the current matter to something in the previous part of the discourse, however tenuously, as in

Ex. 3   Oh, that reminds me . . . *or* Oh, I forgot to say . . .

4   'Oh' can indicate that the hearer lacks some information and so cannot follow properly what the speaker is saying, as in

Ex. 4   A: I've just seen the new teacher.
       B: Oh? I didn't know there was one.

This is a sign that the speaker has mistaken the knowledge that the hearer has, and needs to redesign what is being said or it will not be understood, let alone accepted. This kind of 'Oh' may also mean that A. finds the rate of **information flow** needs adjustment.

   If too many 'Oh's are received, it could mean a serious lack of shared knowledge, or boredom, and C. should either rethink the subject matter completely, or drop it.

5   The point at which 'Oh' occurs can be important, as in

Ex. 5   A: We've just bought a new house. It is an old country-style one, with wide verandas and it's got a pool.
       B: Oh, a pool; that's good.

'Oh' marks a moment of interest, and so could be used to set up a dialog, or to focus the discussion on the pool, etc.

Further reading   Schegloff (1982); Schiffrin (1980, 1987)

OMIT AGENT

Tasks

To avoid problem issues.
To hide problem issues.
To avoid naming an agent.

Description

Actions can be represented without naming the cause or the process which produced them, or the agent who performed them. One way is to use the passive form, which is available for many English verbs. So one can not only say 'I ran over the cat' (= active) and so declare (oneself to be) the agent; but also 'the cat has been run over' (= passive) and so omit the agent ('by me').

Persuasive value

If the audience already knows the agent, the passive can simply be used to avoid redundancy, as in

Ex. 1 As you all know the report was submitted today.

but it can also be used deliberately to exclude mention of, and therefore possible discussion of, the agent it omits. So it can be used in advertising:

Ex. 2 Clinical tests have been conducted on the product.

This leaves unspecified what kind of people performed the tests, whether they were research chemists, members of a pharmaceutical company, let alone whether the tests were performed by an individual (Mr. F. Smith), or by a team (a university chemistry department), or an institution (National Center for Research in . . .). It seeks to persuade readers to accept the validity of the testing without them thinking about these important details.

Faced with a delegation from the factory floor, a works manager could end the meeting by saying:

Ex. 3 Thank you all for your opinions on this difficult matter, a decision will be made on it next week.

Here the passive avoids any specification of who will be responsible for the 'decision'-making, and so it obscures a powerful source of agency.

It could occur in a report:

Ex. 4 The meeting was organized efficiently.

Here the omission of the agent enables this particular writer to avoid giving praise to a rival who did the organizing, while in 'the meeting was very badly organized' a communicator could avoid attributing blame to a colleague. In such cases the communicator may be seeking to preclude certain activities (e.g. praising or blaming) from becoming topics of discussion.

Agent omission occurs with some 80 percent of passives in English. Its frequency of occurrence is what ensures that people rarely notice the omission; persuaders can take advantage of its frequency, and be sure that few readers will notice.

Contrary tactic　If, however, the more unusual form of passive with agent specified is used, strong attention will be focussed on the agency:

Ex. 5　The meeting was well planned, by Bob Smith of course.

A.s could then take up either the topic of 'well-planned meeting' or that of 'Bob Smith as good planner.'

Further reading　Mulholland (1991)

OMIT PROCESS

Task

To direct people's attention away from the process by which something has come about.

Description

It is possible to direct attention away from the process by which something comes about by presenting the process in verbal-adjective form (called 'gerund'), as in

Ex. 1　Recent falling world grain prices are affecting our farmers badly.

What is omitted in Ex. 1 is that 'falling' is a process with causes, and agents, as well as the consequence named. Some factors in this particular process—climatic conditions, political and trade agreements, and poor marketing strategies, etc.—have caused the fall, but are left unmentioned, and the brevity of the expression 'falling,' tucked away as it is in the noun phrase, also makes it hard to notice what is being spoken about. The consequence is that:

(a) In a given case, like Ex. 1, people may not think about the process at all, but see the fall in prices as 'just there,' not something actually caused by some factors, for which something or somebody is responsible.
(b) In general, after reading many similar phrases which conceal processes, people may come to an impression of the world as a place where things just happen—prices fall—and it is just a fact of life. So people can be persuaded to a fatalistic view of the world, and so no action will be taken to alter the bad situations or to maintain the good ones.

Luckily, in this case, enough people, mainly farmers, would differ, have a well-informed response, and be more fully aware of the forces which cause falling prices, so they could know what is being presented; they could 'read between the lines,' but they may have a hard time convincing others.

Further reading   Fairclough (1992); Quirk, Greenbaum, Leech, and Svartvik (1985)

OMIT RESULTS

Task

To leave unspecified the result of an action.

Description

English has a number of verbs which can be used without any need for an object, complement, or result to be supplied: they are called 'intransitives.'

Ex. 1 She spoke well at the meeting.

They leave unspecified any mention of the effects of the action (here, no results of her 'speaking' are given), in contrast with 'transitive' verbs, as in

Ex. 2 The report alters nothing.

where the effect is specified. There are many verbs which can be used in this way:

Ex. 3 Things are looking up.
     The contract fell through.
     Nothing new has cropped up lately.

Persuasive value

1 The presence of a named result, (in Ex. 2 the word 'nothing'), allows A. easily to object to C.'s view of the matter, since the mention of 'nothing' suggests to an A. who wishes to oppose C. how to do so, by just finding 'something' which was in fact 'altered' by the report. To prevent this, C. could have said 'the report doesn't matter,' which requires greater mental effort from A. to formulate a retort.
2 The absence of a named result allows C. to produce a very brief account of something, and in some circumstances this can be more appropriate than detailing the result. For example, C. could judge that A. needs less or more information, and so choose

Ex. 4 You can't see him now, he's working.

rather than

Ex. 5 You can't see him now, he's doing the books.

If A. needs to know more about his unavailability, Ex. 4 is too little and could provoke 'I assume he's working, but what's he working on?' In other circumstances Ex. 5 could be too detailed and lead to the response, 'I know that, I just want to know when he will be free.' The wrong choice could lead to an awareness of difference between C. and A. which might prove counterproductive.

3 The possibility of omitting the result allows C. a choice between showing a judgment or opinion of some matter or not. So to say 'John spoke,' is less judgmental than saying 'John made a statement' or 'gave an opinion,' 'offered a suggestion,' 'bored his listeners,' etc. The absence of a declared judgment means that C. can wait to see how others judged the event before giving his or her view. This may be useful in the presence of those holding power over C.'s life or work, etc.

4 Omitting the result can still allow C. to link matters, to show something of what occurred after an action, without being too specific about cause and effect. So C. could say 'John laughed and we were angry,' with the effect removed somewhat from the cause, in contrast with 'John's laughter made us angry.' The first version suggests that some of the responsibility for the anger is ours, rather than John's; whereas the second makes John the direct cause of the anger.

See also **Omit agent**

Further reading: Quirk, Greenbaum, Leech, and Svartvik (1985)

PARAGRAPH DESIGN

Tasks

To arrange matters in the best structure.
To order material to its best advantage.
To assist readers to follow ideas.

Description

Just as the whole communication text should be designed to suit its goals (e.g. as argument or explanation), so should each paragraph have an internal structure which arranges the material to suit its goals, and also assists the reader to follow its development. Although paragraphs have great flexibility in details, their design structures depend on only a few basic patterns, the main ones being 'chain,' 'journey,' 'stack,' and 'step.'

Persuasive value

Unless a paragraph is grasped as an entity, and its parts recognized in themselves and in their relations to each other, for whatever contribution they make to the representation of the material, no reader will easily follow the account, let alone accept the view put forward.

1 The design should find appropriate rates of **information flow** so that readers can handle the combination of old and new ideas, recognize familiar juxtapositions and accept unusual combinations of ideas, etc.

2 The design should help readers distinguish between ideas, and the examples which support them, and between main and subordinate points, so that they can estimate the interpretative value to be given to them.

3 It should make clear which matters are foregrounded and which are explanatory background to them.

4 It should indicate connections between ideas as the communication proceeds, so that readers know whether they are following a steady accumulation of support for a view, or a loose amassing of details about it.

5 It should provide signals about the amount of coverage each point is to receive so that readers can anticipate how long each idea will take to be developed, and when there is a move to a new one.

6 It should have a signalled beginning, differentiating its material from the preceding paragraphs, and a signalled end where the reader can pause to assimilate what has been offered to that point.

See also the other **Paragraph design** tactics

Further reading   Dillon (1981); Nash (1980)

PARAGRAPH DESIGN: CHAIN

Tasks

To arrange matters in the best structure.
To order material to its best advantage.
To assist readers to follow ideas.

Description

The 'chain' paragraph differs from the other design possibilities, in that its structure is not planned, but rather that the writer seeks to retain freedom of idea movement. The only restriction it uses is that of making a following idea form a 'chain,' through word echoes or repetitions of sentence patterns, with the one immediately preceding it, as in

Ex. 1 The office staff's workload needs to be *lightened*. Any *reductions* should take the form of reallocating administrative *staff needs*. At present they *need* X and Y, . . . and also *quickly* produced *typing*. It is essential there is a *fast* turnaround on *typing* because of *admin* needs. . . . *Administrators* need this because they have *obligations* to fill. They *must do* X and they *must* do Y.

So, 'lightening the load' is chained with 'reductions,' 'staff needs' with 'need,' 'typing' with 'typing,' 'quickly' with 'fast,' etc.

Persuasive value

Since this is the only 'ordering' in the paragraph, following the ideas will be difficult for readers, since its development will follow no predictive pattern that they can use to handle the inrush of ideas that the communication contains. It is the kind of paragraph which readers balk at, and they will only proceed if the writer shows that the uncertainties of idea handling will be worth encountering, perhaps by demonstrating an excitement, or a practical value, which will make readers feel that the end will justify the means. It may be the case, however, that the paragraph design comes in a fairly ordinary text, as in Ex. 1: here the construction is neither helpful nor unhelpful.

It is a useful design for those writers who do not know exactly where the writing will take them, and for readers who do not mind this exploratory quality in the writing. However, it is problematic for readers who prefer to feel that the writer is being a strong guide through the mazes of his or her ideas. A lack of control in the writer may make a reader less likely to accept the ideas and values on offer. It may cause them to argue, as it were, 'Well if the writer does not know where he or she is going, why should I follow?'

There is a linkage, of course, on offer, through the word and sentence echoes and repetitions, but it is recognizably a superficial linkage, and not one which arises from the nature of the ideas, their complexity, their implications, etc. That is to say, it does little for readers by way of making them agree or disagree with what is communicated. It is unlikely to make the ideas memorable, and it is unlikely to redound to the writer's credit that this design was used. At best the paragraph will not be remembered, while at worst the superficiality of its ordering may be used as evidence that the writer does not know what he or she is doing, or is unskilled at mounting a case.

See also the other **Paragraph design** tactics

Further reading   Dillon (1981); Nash (1980)

PARAGRAPH DESIGN: JOURNEY

Tasks

To interest readers to follow the ideas.
To order matters to their best advantage.

Description

The 'journey' paragraph design follows narrative patterning to some degree, beginning with a present state of flux and proceeding through adventure to a final state of steady calm. As in:

Ex. 1 At present we are faced with the following situation, . . . which I think is a real problem, and cannot continue because . . . We need to address this creatively, not just with a few amendments to our present practices. As one alternative we could try . . . or, secondly, even try . . . But both would have some bad effects as well as some good ones. We need a third way which would improve without any bad effects. This would be a test of our fortitude, but if we can do it, it would enable us to work better, with less effort in the future.

Persuasive value

The 'journey' paragraph begins with a provocative introduction which excites readers' interest, and entices them to continue by promising that this will be worthwhile. It may be a bold statement or a difficult question, as:

Ex. 2 If we are to remain a viable business our priorities must be rearranged.

Ex. 3 Why would anyone wish to become a university student?

Having enticed the reader to investigate this provocation, the paragraph continues by taking up aspects of the opening sentence in a way which opens up the ideas; at times perhaps seemingly randomly; at others in an orderly manner; at all events progressively; and so takes readers on a journey through the text, making it seem exciting and intriguing, and so encourages readers to continue.

The design distinguishes any agents or agencies involved in the material, and focusses on them, and is careful to relate how they cause what effects—so the overall effect is of action and related results, in line with its narrative template.

The provocation which roused readers' interest at the start can be gradually lessened, as the new ideas gradually become familiar, and perhaps more acceptable, until the final part of the paragraph is presented, comforting the readers and calming them down to an acceptance of the 'good' conclusion the writer supplies.

See also **Narrative** tactics; the other **Paragraph design** tactics

Further reading   Dillon (1981); Nash (1980)

PARAGRAPH DESIGN: STACK

Tasks

To arrange matters in the best structure.
To order material to its best advantage.
To assist readers to follow ideas.

Description

The 'stack' paragraph design works by providing an initially complex topic and then dealing one by one with the main features represented in the words of the topic. It moves from one to the other, without obvious connection, just until the writer feels enough has been given on each feature. It should cover all those features which are likely to be troublesome, i.e. which readers might resist. As in:

Ex. 1 Some policy decision must be made about voluntary redundancy. We can exempt *some* sections of the business perhaps, but for the rest we must *decide*. On the whole we need a *policy* on the issue in order to ensure we are principled and fair . . . We must act *decisively*, and soon, so that funds can be prepared . . . It should be a *voluntary* scheme because . . . rather than obligatory for any group because . . . It is a better *policy* than resorting to dismissals which cause . . . So in summary, we should *decide* . . .

Persuasive value

The power of this design rests in its apparent completeness of coverage of the elements of the topic. No aspect of its implications appears to be left undealt with. Also, it can persuade by the way it rushes the reader from point to point, making it hard to stem the tide of points, each of which raises a wholly different aspect of the issue, as in the example above where the writer talks of 'policy,' then 'exemptions,' 'decisions,' 'voluntariness,' and 'dismissals.' Readers must be quick to jump from point to unconnected point, and have no time to assess their response, or to prepare for resistance to any aspect of it; the writer has moved on by the time they do.

It makes for comfortable reading, once the amplication of points begins, because readers can predict the plan being followed: that is, they know that the terms in the topic sentence will be taken one by one in the order they were given in. (Note: it will cause confusion if the writer varies from that order: the reader will not predict this. For the same reason it will also cause trouble if one feature is omitted.)

A good 'stack' design is one which makes the amplications of each feature of the topic seem comprehensive.

Any connections between ideas that the writer wishes to make can be achieved by echoing words from one expansion of one feature to the next. It is not a logical link, but word-echoes function to suggest links, and this may prove convincing.

Since the focus in a 'stack' design is on developments from the topic sentence which begins the paragraph, it is often worthwhile to end the paragraph with a reiteration of it. This suggests that the matter has been fully dealt with, and that the conclusion is settled, inevitable, fixed, and final. This is suggested by the way the beginning and ending are 'the same.'

See also the other **Paragraph design** tactics

Further reading   Dillon (1981); Nash (1980)

PARAGRAPH DESIGN: STEP

Tasks

To enable readers to follow the ideas.
To order matters to their best advantage.

Description

The 'step' paragraph design follows the pattern of instruction manuals, taking the reader in a very controlled manner step by step through a logical sequence of ideas. As in:

Ex. 1 We have all seen the report. I think we should adopt its recommendations. This means, re recommendation 1, that we do . . . and this could provide for . . . Its second recommendation would enable us to do . . . and . . . The third is made optional. I would take the option up, because it would result in . . . In all, we would find ourselves able to do . . . much more thoroughly as a result, and could enhance our company's reputation.

Persuasive value

The design suggests, by association with the manual, that what C. is doing is just showing how something works. This can preempt any discussion of whether it is good to have the thing, or whether it will be really useful: it takes that for granted. And so it can persuade readers to ignore such questions.

By plotting a set of steps through the ideas, the design instructs readers to assimilate the ideas, one by one, and to see that they add up one by one to an inevitable conclusion. If done well, the pace of information can make it hard for readers to stop, think about, and perhaps resist what is being presented. For example, the movement step by step invites the belief that the next stage might solve any problems found in the present one.

The ideas are presented not in a cumulative way, with each one built on an understanding of the previous one, but as a set of separate units which by sheer weight of numbers is convincing. The absence of clearly delineated relationships between ideas leaves it to readers to work out the linkage, but again the pace of the ideas as they follow one another onto the page prevents readers from making judgments whether there are any links at all, and whether this affects the value of the ideas. Such work is difficult and would be avoided unless a reader was very determined; the rest would probably 'go along' with the writer.

The step design should not be disguised since it is its resemblance to manuals that persuades readers into unquestioning acceptance. It can even be enhanced by grammatical or word patterns. Regularities in sentence structures and word repetitions add to the sense of orderly progression and linkage between the ideas, as if those which are expressed in similar patterns must be similar in meaning.

Its narrowness of focus reduces the number of ideas raised, and this could exclude ideas which readers might see as worth resistance.

See also the other **Paragraph design** tactics

Further reading   Dillon (1981); Nash (1980)

PARENTHESIS

Task

To make a side issue of a matter.

Description

Parentheses are devices for presenting an extra item of information by inserting it into another item, without grammatical links, and in order to emphasize its nature as an addition.

Ex. 1 Bill said (and I think quite rightly), that we should . . .

In writing, a parenthesis can be indicated by bracketting, or by a pair of dashes or commas acting as brackets. Bracketting is best reserved for important additions which need heightened attention; dashes serve to emphasize that the addition is 'free-floating,' that it has no grammatical place in its surrounding sentence; while commas indicate that the parenthesized material is only just marginal.

In speech a parenthesis is indicated by changes in voice quality, usually a drop in volume and increased speed.

Parentheses will cause problems if they are too long, if there are too many of them within a communication, or if they contain other, embedded, parentheses. They will be very confusing if the grammar of the parenthesis and that of the main sentence are not kept separate; they will prove serious distractions if they bear no clear relation to the matters in the surrounding words and sentences, both of which are so in:

Ex. 2 We need to consider carefully (and we'd better make it off the record) and what our proposal is [*sic*].

Persuasive value

In using a parenthesis, C. presents some matter while simultaneously showing that it is not on a par with the surrounding matters. That is, C. makes it quite clear that the parenthesized matter will need to be processed differently by A. In Ex. 1, for instance, C. not only reports what Bill said, but also provides a different type of information, his or her opinion that Bill is right. So the example contains (a) a report and (b) an opinion about it, quite separately but in very close proximity, so that A. receives them together but also understands them to be separate, and has to work out the link between them. A contrasting method of offering the same two things would be:

Ex. 3 Bill made a good suggestion, that we should . . .

where C.'s opinion is presented only in the adjective 'good.' The important difference is that in a parenthesis the two matters are much more noticeably separate. So both of them are available for A. to take up, knowing that for C. they are of different value.

Using parentheses can have different effects:

(a) Since the two things are available as potential topics, C. should not use the tactic if it is unsuitable to have the matter in parenthesis brought into the discussion, and the matter would be better omitted.
(b) The parenthesis suggests that the matter was so urgent that C. could not wait for a suitable grammatical place to put it. If A. cannot understand the urgency, he or she may feel irritated by the tactic. It also suggests that the matter is an afterthought, and A. may feel that the matter should have been presented properly in its first version, not as what appears to be a first draft along with a revision.
(c) While parentheses are often used to insert a personal opinion, as in Ex. 1, they can also present some better version of a matter than the one first offered, as in

Ex. 4 The view we took of this matter, our opinion on the implications
of the offer, was that it was good.

Danger   Paradoxically, the parenthesized matter can be so highlighted by
the punctuation or voice quality that A. is quite likely to take it up instead
of the main topic. This is particularly likely if the parenthesized matter is
witty or provocative.

Further reading   Corbett (1990); Nash (1980); Sonnino (1968)

PEOPLE PRESENTED AS THINGS

Tasks

To downgrade the significance of a matter.
To understate the consequences of an act.

Description

People can be depersonalized (i.e. represented as objects rather than as
complex human beings): in a hospital a person could be characterized as a
medical case, as in 'The stomach ulcer in Ward 5'; or in law as a legal case,
as in 'We have three drink-driving cases waiting to see you.' Women and
men can also be seen as sex objects. Sometimes the tactic uses some part of
a person for the whole, as in 'Is that Susan, the lovely pair of legs by the
window?' It can also use the things people do, as in 'There's another late
assignment on the phone for you,' or the things that are done to them, as in
'This is a shampoo and set, if you are ready for her.' Overall the tactic
reduces the individuality of people by naming them as instances of some
general phenomenon.

Persuasive value

1 If C. is able to omit the human dimension when arguing for an idea, he
or she can press the view on A. without mentioning any effects on people
that might follow from it, as in 'My plan will work. All we need to do is just
change the holiday arrangements' (i.e. change the plans people have made
for their holidays).
2 C. can make part of his or her argument the suggestion that things just
happen in the world and that they owe nothing to human agency. So a
political newspaper article could be headed 'Planes bomb Beirut,' which
represents the bombs as being dropped by planes, not people flying the
planes, and certainly not by the people who commanded the planes to fly,
etc. By omitting agency, and responsibility, the situation just seems to have

come about of itself. If this tactic is used frequently people can be brought to believe that the events they worry about in the world cannot be altered, because they are not anyone's responsibility. If, however, people were given representations which show that the worrying acts are performed by human agents, they could seek to have the agents change their behavior, or to have them removed. This tactic is a very prevalent one, many persuaders have taken advantage of what it offers, and so it has been a great social influence on people's thinking for a long time.

Further reading   Corbett (1990); Sonnino (1968)

PERSONIFICATION

Tasks

To introduce an attitude or judgment covertly.
To find the covert attitudes of others.

Description

Personification is to give a human voice and human attributes to something that is not human. It can be quite obvious when applied to inanimate objects, or non-human animates, as in

Ex. 1 This powersaw is trying to kill me.

Ex. 2 The grass waits till I turn away, then it grows six inches.

Or it can be less obvious, as in representing ships as women, or pets as having human qualities, as in 'The cat is asking for its supper.'

Persuasive value

It is more covert, and more consequential when used of groups or nations, etc. Its main use is to persuade people that these entities have only one voice and one set of attributes, as in

Ex. 3 This country needs a good five-cent cigar.

Ex. 4 The University ignores student needs.

Here neither 'country' nor 'the University' can be sensibly characterized in this way, as a monolithic entity. Yet so frequent is this tactic that it is often unnoticed, with the result that a view of the world as full of monoliths is prevalent. This is a powerful persuasion, and one which has resulted, for example, in evoking pessimism about the ability of a single person to change things.

   Personification is also powerful, and in much the same way, when used of abstractions, and belief systems, as in

Ex. 5 Colonialism seeks to destroy cultural differences.

where the abstraction hides the fact that it is only some individuals who live by a belief in colonialism.

It is particularly useful to use, or to note others' use, when what is personified is given specific emotions or strong attitudes, as in

Ex. 6 The boat gave a long mournful whistle as we waved them off.

Ex. 7 These figures insist that we are right.

The mournfulness in Ex. 6 is not really the boat's but C.'s. Such clues to C.'s emotional state may be useful. Some of them are well concealed, as in Ex. 7, where it is C. who is 'insisting that we are right,' and using the figures as a surrogate. This may be a useful tactic where C. does not wish to appear as an 'insistent' person.

Further reading   Corbett (1977, 1990); Sonnino (1968)

PHASE CHANGE

Task

To cause a change in activity during an interaction.

Description

During an interaction participants perform **exchanges of speech**—like question and answer. These in turn form larger units of interaction, called phases. For example, a medical consultation could consist of five phases: sociability, discussing the problem, examination, discussing treatment, and closure. Each phase consists of a particular set of activities which change to another set when a phase ends: for example, the examination phase would consist of a series of 'instructing' acts, 'Breathe in, out, turn round,' which would change to 'discussing' acts when the next phase began. An inter-action consists of one or any number of phases.

Persuasive value

1 In each phase the participants will focus on one set of communicative activities. If one set causes problems for C. it could be worthwhile to try to terminate that phase and make another, more suitable one, start. This could be done by:

(a) saying something which declares the subject matter to be closed, such as making a summary, suggesting a pivotal point has been reached, or producing a proverbial saying, indicating that an end has been reached;

(b) saying something which declares the activity is ended, such as seeking to defer its continuance till another day;

(c) by doing (a) and/or (b), and also offering a phase change signal. These are 'O.K.,' 'right,' 'now then,' 'well,' and 'good,' when they are said with strong stress, heightened pitch, and followed by a pause:

Ex. 1 Well now! I think we've covered all the points.

Ex. 2 Now then! We'd better get on with . . .

The signals can be accompanied, as in these examples, by a **reflexive comment**. (There is also a phase signal that seems to be restricted to casual talk only—'Hey listen!')
2 Since changing a phase is a strong exercise of power, with an effect on everyone present, the others may object to it in itself—because they wish to continue the current activity—or because the persons trying to do it has no social right to do so. Doctors may change phases in consultations, and chairpersons, hosts at dinner parties, and leaders of street gangs have the power, but anyone else may not have sufficient status to be allowed to do it. It is advisable therefore to use a somewhat tentative reflexive comment after the phase signal, as in

Ex. 3 O.K. then! What d'you say we move on?

Ex. 4 Well! I wonder if we should now. . . .

3 If the others allow C. to change phases easily, this acknowledges that he or she has some personal or social power in that group.

See also **Proverbs**

Further reading   Craig and Tracy (1983); Halliday and Hasan (1976); Mullholland (1991)

POLITENESS: ABSENCE OF

Task

To preserve one's self-image.

Description

To use no politeness tactics at all is to perform a communicative act bluntly (i.e. to be direct and concise, and to take no explicit account of A.'s self-image). Examples of concise blunt acts are 'Lend me your pen,' 'There's a phone call for you,' or 'I got your memo.'

Persuasive value

1 To communicate bluntly is to run some risk of offending A., either damaging his or her positive sense of self-respect, or causing resentment at

an infringement of his or her liberty. So the decision to use no politeness tactics should not be undertaken lightly. Some of those who are blunt frequently declare with pride that they communicate straightforwardly, 'with no beating around the bush,' and this sounds quite reasonable, until one notes how little it considers the others involved in the interaction. Directness may mean no tact, as in 'You've failed your assignment,' rather than 'Your assignment wasn't quite up to standard,' or 'Your assignment should have been better.' Those who use bluntness seem not to recognize that people are very skilled in interpreting the meaning of such tactful acts, and so there is nothing vague or unstraightforward about the combination of politeness and meaning: what is present in such tactful acts, however, is not only the basic meaning, but also some explicit signs that C. respects the other person.

2 Some A.s express a preference for bluntness, using phrases like 'Give it to me straight.' If they really mean it, then C.s should oblige, in order to preserve A.'s rights to decide what they want.

3 Bluntness is, oddly, associated with honesty. So to use it may suit C.'s purposes and be the correct tactic to use. However, it is not always a sign of honesty, any more than tact is a sign of hypocrisy. Bluntness is certainly a tactic that should be in everyone's repertoire, though it should be used with caution.

See also **Bluntness: choose**; **Face: sustain**; **Face threats: recognize**; the other **Politeness** tactics

Further reading Brown and Levinson (1987)

POLITENESS: ADMIT DEBT TO OTHER PERSON

Tasks

To respect A.'s right not be imposed on.
To avoid damage to A.'s face.
To show one is aware of imposing on A. as a person.

Description

C.s can choose to reduce the imposition of an F.T.A. on the other person by explicitly admitting that they will be in the person's debt if he or she does what the act requires, as in:

Ex. 1 I'd be really grateful if you could lend me a couple of dollars till tomorrow.

Ex. 2 It would be most useful if you could check these figures for me.

Ex. 3 I'm in an awful mess with this essay. It would really help if you could let me have an extension.

Persuasive value

The admission of a debt does not lessen the imposition on the other person's freedom of action, but what it does is tell the person that C. will owe him or her a favor, and this can be an equal imposition on C., when it falls due.

The tactic will work best when C. names a reasonable degree of indebtedness, and will work least well when the debt is exaggerated, as in

Ex. 4 I'd be eternally grateful if you could see your way to lending me your newspaper.

The degree of debt is far too high for such a minor social act as a loan of a newspaper. The person addressed could feel that C. is not taking the request seriously, and so feel he or she is being imposed on by someone who cares little about what is being done as an F.T.A.

The presentation of too high a degree of indebtedness could also make the other person wonder whether the act is as minor as he or she would otherwise have thought. A literary scholar working on a minor novelist noticed one of her novels in a second-hand bookshop and exclaimed:

Ex. 5 How marvellous! Oh could I possibly buy this from you? I'd be forever grateful! I've been looking for this everywhere!

The bookseller responded that that particular book was not for sale—though this was disbelieved by the scholar. He probably did so because he thought the book must be monetarily valuable because the scholar was so keen on it, and said she would be in his debt to a far higher degree than he was used to from the normal book-buying public.

See also the other **Politeness** tactics

Further reading   Brown and Levinson (1987)

POLITENESS: AGREE WITH A.

Tasks

To show that C. and A. agree on some topics and so C. has common ground with A.
To have an F.T.A. accepted with least damage to bonding.

Description

By setting up their agreement on some topics, C. can claim he or she belongs to the same set of people as A., and therefore shares common ground with A. In doing so C. can imply that he or she understands or even shares A.'s wants and needs, and so in any F.T.A. addressed to A., A. can be sure that C. will not do anything that is against A.'s best interests.

Persuasive value

C. can initiate topics which can be predicted to cause agreement by A.: for example, the standard **sociable language** topics of the weather, T.V. programs, politicians, etc. However, since these are shared by most members of a culture they do not form a very personalized bond between C. and A. To create a distinctive bond, C. should guess at A.'s interests, opinions, and choose something which will create agreement out of them. For example, if A. is a keen golfer, or has six children, or collects postage stamps, or whatever, C. could use this knowledge to find a degree of mutual agreement—perhaps the stamps, or perhaps the collecting of anything. Having exchanged information and experiences on such a topic can make A. feel less threatened when C. then produces an F.T.A.

The rapport engendered by such discussions also reduces the emphasis on any F.T.A., almost loses it amid the small talk, and suggests that C. did not just have that in mind when entering into the interaction with A.

If A. him- or herself has introduced a topic which C. can use to create agreement, this makes it less obvious that C. is the one seeking rapport. C. can develop it and adjust it to suit his or her purposes, but there is a more powerful way to use A.'s topics, and that is just to repeat what A. has said, and so indicate not just a shared understanding, but unanimity. As in:

Ex. 1 A: I have three assignments to do for Monday.
       B: Three assignments! How awful, and for Monday!

See also **Listening: active**; the other **Politeness** tactics

Further reading Brown and Levinson (1987); Davidson (1984); Goffman (1959)

POLITENESS: ATTEND TO A.

Tasks

To use attention to A. to offset any threat to face.
To have an F.T.A. accepted with least damage to bonding.

Description

To show an explicit interest in A. It can occur within the F.T.A., or immediately precede it, as a form of pre-persuasion.

Persuasive value

C. can show an interest, which can be a general interest or one arising from a specific circumstance, in:

(a) A.'s wants, as in:

> Ex. 1 C: Let me have those parcels, they look heavy. . . . Remember we want a report by 5 P.M. today.
> Ex. 2 C: Here's your coffee. . . . We want you to take us to the movies tonight.

(b) A.'s needs, as in

> Ex. 3 C: You must be tired; here, sit down. . . . Your reports are due.

(c) A.'s interests, as in

> Ex. 4 C: Your plants are thriving! . . . I need my book back.

(d) A.'s status in life. This comprises those aspects of a person's life which symbolically represent his or her self-image. It can include the physical elements of life: cars, houses, furniture, clothing, food, modes of travel, children, pets; or the non-physical personal attributes of birth, rank, qualifications, manners, and customs. In short, all his or her possessions, habits, and behaviors.

> Ex. 5 C: How's the world's best doctor today? . . . Your patients are waiting.
> Ex. 6 C: Your car looks great. . . . We need a new computer.

N.B.   To use the tactic *after* the F.T.A. is not likely to be viewed as favorably as when it occurs before it. This is because in the postposed position C. will instantly recognize it for what it is, and moreover will judge it to be an afterthought—and no one likes receiving politeness just as an afterthought.

See also the other **Politeness** tactics

Further reading   Brown and Levinson (1987); Goffman (1959)

POLITENESS: AVOID DISAGREEMENT WITH A.

Tasks

To show that because C. and A. do not disagree, C. knows what is acceptable to A.
To have an F.T.A. accepted with least damage to bonding.

Description

By avoiding disagreement with A., C. can imply that he or she understands or even shares A.'s wants and needs, so in any ensuing F.T.A. addressed to A., C. will not do anything that is against A.'s best interests.

Persuasive value

After any initiating statement or request or question by A., though they must reject it, C.s can avoid the 'threat' of disagreement by using some form of 'token' agreement. It can be done in the following ways.

1 By echoing the words as far as possible before producing the disagreement, as in

Ex. 1 A: You live in Kenmore, don't you?
B: I used to live in Kenmore, now I'm in St. Lucia.

2 By delaying the disagreement or negative response, as in

Ex. 2 A: Are you coming for a coffee?
B: I've got to finish this, so I can't.

The matter inserted before the disagreement can be an excuse, as in Ex. 2, or a partial agreement as in

Ex. 3 A: Will you be on the bus tomorrow morning?
B: If I can, but I may be late, so don't wait for me.

3 By offering a social lie, as when invited to approve something of A.'s when C. wishes to avoid this, as in

Ex. 4 A: What do you think of the report?
B: It's fine . . . apart from the last section.

4 By using a tentative phrase, such as 'sort of,' 'in a way,' 'more or less,' before agreeing, in order to make the response weaker, as in

Ex. 5 A: Do you like my new office?
B: In a way, yes.

5 By suggesting that there has been an initiation by A. to which C. is responding, though what C. offers is itself the first thing said, as in

Ex. 6 A: [as she appears at the door of B's office] O.K. So I'll see you tomorrow then.

See also **Cooperative principle**; the other **Politeness** tactics; **Preferred response**

Further reading   Brown and Levinson (1987); Davidson (1984); Goffman (1959)

POLITENESS: AVOID PRESUMING ON OTHERS

Tasks

To respect A.'s right not to be imposed on.
To avoid damage to A.'s face.
To minimize any imposition on A. from a potential F.T.A.
To save one's face in case of a failure of an F.T.A.

Description

In performing a potential F.T.A., C.s should not presume:

1 that the other person wants to experience the F.T.A. itself;
2 that the other person wants to do whatever the F.T.A. requires of them.

Persuasive value

1 C.s should be aware that in addressing A. at all they are making some kind of intrusion into A.'s life. It is most noticeable when they startle or distract A. from some pursuit, or interfere with some pleasures (e.g. speaking when a favorite piece of music is playing, etc.), but it is also an intrusion even in more favorable circumstances, where, for example, C. and A. are talking together in a relaxed fashion over coffee. C. can always potentially disturb A., with some information, such as 'Did you know the assignment was due yesterday?,' or by some encroachment on the relationship, as in 'You look as if you've put on a lot of weight; what do you weigh now?' etc. They may affect A. accidentally, or purposefully, but it is always true that a speech act has an impact on those who hear or read it.

   C.s should take care to consider what may be happening to A. as they communicate if they are to perform the act well, and achieve what they want from it. It may be useful to state explicitly that they are aware of imposing on A. by communicating at all, as in

Ex. 1 Do you have a minute?

Ex. 2 Is this a bad time to catch you?

Ex. 3 I hope I didn't disturb your supper.

Such politenesses are very important when initiating a telephone call, since the caller has no way of telling just how intrusive the call is.
2 Requesting something of A. is obviously not only such an intrusion in its own right, but what the act requires A to do can also be an imposition, and so this should be minimized.

See also **Minimalism**; the other **Politeness** tactics

Further reading   Brown and Levinson (1987)

POLITENESS: BE APOLOGETIC

Tasks

To respect A.'s right not be imposed on.
To avoid damage to A.'s face.
To show one is aware of imposing on A. as a person.
To save one's face in case of a failure of an F.T.A.

Description

By apologizing at a moment when C. wishes to offer an F.T.A., he or she can use it as a tactic to give respect to the other person and so show an awareness that the F.T.A. is an imposition.

Persuasive value

Suitable apologies can address various aspects of the F.T.A.:

(a) that C. is impinging on the freedom of action of the other person;
(b) that C. knows that what is required by the F.T.A. will be a nuisance for the other to perform;
(c) that C. is performing the F.T.A. only reluctantly;
(d) that C. has very compelling reasons for requiring the threatening act be done by the other person.

1 The first possibility can be an explicit admission that C. is aware of the other person's freedom of action, as in

Ex. 1 I know that you are always busy, but could you look at this report for me?

Ex. 2 Can you do me a favor and lend me your car?

2 C. can explicitly state that he or she is conscious that the act required of the other person will not be a pleasure, will take up his or her precious time, or is beyond what can be expected of the person by a sense of duty, as in

Ex. 3 I know you hate parties, but could you come to this one? It is quite special.

Ex. 4 This may be a nuisance to you when you are so busy, but could you just have a look at this for me please?

3 C. can indicate a real or a false reluctance to perform the F.T.A., as in

Ex. 5 I hesitate to ask you this, but could you check this report?

Ex. 6 This is embarrassing, but have you the time to do a lecture for my course?

Ex. 7 I hate to be a nuisance, but have you any computer paper?

Ex. 8 I hope I've got the right person, but can you let me know about university enrollment?

4 C. can show that there are strong reasons for his or her performing the F.T.A., and that it is not just a whim or fancy that has caused this intrusion on the freedom of action of the other person, as in

Ex. 9 There seems to be nobody else around at the moment and I need to know today where can I get an enrollment form.

Ex. 10 It's absolutely essential that I get this assignment right. I made such a mess of the last one, so could you help me by looking at this draft?

Ex. 11 I'm lost. Where are the nearest toilets?

As part of the apology, C. may go further than showing a reluctance to perform an intrusive act, and may make an extra call upon the other person's time and effort. That is, C. can ask for a sign from the other person that the F.T.A. has not damaged the relationship. So C. could show this at the beginning or at the end of the F.T.A., as in the following:

Ex. 12 I hope you will forgive me if I ask you to have a look at this essay.

Ex. 13 Can you look at this essay, if it isn't too much of a nuisance?

and in so doing C. is imposing another burden by requiring the other person to do something as a verbal or non-verbal sign of forgiveness.

See also the other **Politeness** tactics

Further reading   Brown and Levinson (1987)

POLITENESS: BE DIRECT

Task

To avoid restricting the freedom of action, or negative face, of another.

Description

Since negative politeness is action directed at avoiding any restriction on the freedom of action of another, it follows that any aspect of any act which imposes on another should be avoided as far as possible. And if some imposition must occur, then it should be minimized in whatever way suggests itself.

Persuasive value

Negative politeness tactics are the set of very formalized behaviors which society has evolved to redress the face threat of imposition. One of the most used ones is directness. Directness preserves A.'s freedom by making the communication of an act as minimal as possible. No matter what is in the act by way of content, and irrespective of whether the content involves curtailing A.'s actions, the act itself should be performed speedily and efficiently to save A.'s time and patience. Rather than requiring A. to listen to a roundabout way of speaking, C. should come to the point quickly. So, for instance, when a junior colleague has to request a work matter from a more senior colleague, it is better to offer:

Ex. 1　Excuse me, could I borrow the files?

rather than:

Ex. 2　Excuse me, I was wondering if it would be possible for you to let me have the files? I am sorry to be a nuisance, only we need them to sort out the salaries for the month and our files are in the computer which is down at the moment.

Even the apologetic elements are more than is needed for efficiency of communication. However, even the first example did include an apology, 'excuse me,' and this is because it is not really socially acceptable to be absolutely minimal, except in emergencies. A direct act should usually contain one of the formulaic politeness phrases—'sorry,' 'excuse me,' 'please,' and 'thank you.'

See also the other **Politeness** tactics

Further reading　Brown and Levinson (1987)

POLITENESS: BE INDIRECT

Tasks

To save C.'s face.
To respect A.'s right not to be imposed on.
To avoid damage to A.'s face.

Description

One major way in which face can be saved by both participants in a communicative act is to perform the act so indirectly that its potential face threat is more or less hidden.

Persuasive value

By using indirection C. saves the other person's face by leaving it to him or her to choose whether to recognize that an F.T.A. has occurred. In performing the F.T.A. in such an oblique way, C.s also save their own face, by leaving themselves the option to deny that they meant the act, or even that the act was a face-threatening one.

To be indirect, the act must be represented in such a way that several interpretations of it are possible. For example,

Ex. 1 It is cold in here.

could be heard as a comment on the temperature, or as a request to do something about the temperature, perhaps closing the door. If A. chooses not to take it as a request, with its face-threatening implications, then he or she can do so, without the appearance of incivility. On the other hand, if A. takes it as a request, and responds badly to it:

Ex. 2 Am I supposed to do something about it? What's stopping *you* from closing the door?

C. could reply 'I was just making a comment.'

The art of managing indirection lies in presenting the act in such a way that it could achieve C.'s goal—in this example, getting the door closed—but could be withdrawn if it proved divisive. That is, in this example it must be clear enough that C. wants to perform a request if A. is to do as requested, yet it must also be oblique enough for C. to deny that it was meant to be face-threatening if A. responds badly.

Luckily there are established routines and tactics by which people can communicate indirectly and, in most cases, comprehend what lies hidden by the indirection. Children only slowly learn this as they progress through the process of socialization, and so indirection is a risky tactic to use with a child. It is also likely to fail if used with people from other cultures if they have not yet learnt the indirection techniques.

Indirection is recognized by a complex judgement which rests on two factors:

(a) that C. breaks one of the standard conventions of communication so that A. is invited to think why this has happened and to assume it may be that C. wishes to do some act indirectly;

(b) that C.'s act is considered in relation to some specific feature of its particular context or to some aspect of the background knowledge of the participants which will suggest its hidden meaning.

What A.s ask themselves is 'Why is C. saying or writing that to me in that way and in these circumstances?' Once this questioning process begins, A.s have to use the two factors to judge what C.'s underlying goal is. For example, C. could violate one of the maxims which are meant to ensure efficiency in communication, perhaps the **social convention of quantity**, and represent something in too great detail or at too great length, as in

Ex. 3 Gosh, it was really crowded along the Drive today! It took me hours to get a hundred yards, and then the idiot in front of me broke down at the lights. What a nightmare!

If this were said in a casual chat, in response to an utterance about how the traffic seems to be growing in volume, then it could be just a comment of a sociable kind. But if it was said to a supervisor on first coming into work for the day, and being late, then it could be an indirect excuse or apology. C. could be saving face by quickly offering the traffic as a reason for lateness before the supervisor could criticize, and C. could also save face by doing the excusing or apologizing act indirectly.

See also **Politeness indirection** tactics

Further reading   Brown and Levinson (1987); Clark (1979)

POLITENESS: BE PESSIMISTIC

Tasks

To respect A.'s right not to be imposed on.
To avoid damage to A.'s face.
To minimize any imposition on A. from a potential F.T.A.
To save one's face in case of a failure of an F.T.A.

Description

C.s can reduce the imposition of an F.T.A. or of the task it seeks to have A. perform, by explicitly being pessimistic about the chances of A. doing it, and hence, paradoxically, improving the chances of having it done.

Persuasive value

This can be done in several ways, each of which persuades differently.
1 C. can use phrases with negative probability in them.

Ex. 1 You couldn't possibly help me with this typing?

Ex. 2 There's no chance, I suppose, that you have a couple of dollars to spare?

2 C. can use the subjunctive form of the verb—'could,' 'would,' 'should,' or 'might'—which expects a more remote a chance of success than the other verbs—'can,' 'will,' 'shall,' and 'may,' as in

Ex. 3 Could you let me have an extension on the essay?

which is more pessimistic than

Ex. 4 Can I have an extension on the essay?

3 C. can use an if-clause, as in

Ex. 5 If you could help me, I'd be grateful.

Ex. 6 If I were to ask you nicely, would you . . .?

4 C. can use a negative statement with a positive tag question, as in

Ex. 7 You haven't today's newspaper, have you?

Ex. 8 You haven't seen the cat by any chance, have you?

5 Or C. can use other negative expressions like

Ex. 9 I don't suppose you could possibly lend me that book.

Ex. 10 There would be no possibility of your giving me a drive home, I suppose.

See also the other **Politeness** tactics; **Questions: tag**

Further reading   Brown and Levinson (1987)

POLITENESS: CLAIM GROUP IDENTITY WITH A.

Tasks

To show that because C. and A. belong to the same group C. knows what is acceptable to A.
To have an F.T.A. accepted with least damage to bonding.

Description

C. can show common ground and therefore common interest with A., and so imply that because he or she understands or even shares A.'s wants and needs, in any F.T.A. addressed to A., C. will not do anything that is against A.'s best interests.

Persuasive value

To show solidarity with A., C.s can use the terms of address that indicate closeness, or use a shared version of **restricted code**, or a shared technical language.
1 Address terms include: 'guys,' 'mate,' 'darling,' 'sweetheart,' 'pal,' 'buddy,' 'dear,' 'babe,' 'honey.' To these should be added the family terms: 'Mom,' 'Dad,' 'sis,' 'Aunt,' 'Pops,' etc. (Note: since they vary with

differences in age and region, these terms can cause trouble if unacceptably used, for example between the sexes.)

The terms suggest that there is not just common ground but also a peer relationship between C. and A. This may not be acceptable to A.s, who feel that their superiority should be acknowledged. The diminutive terms, like 'pet,' 'poppet,' 'sweetie pie,' are prone to cause trouble, since they both show closeness and also a mild reduction in importance of the person addressed. Teenagers let their parents know when they no longer find the diminutive effect of their nickname suitable for their adult dignity.

2 C.s can switch from formal language to restricted code when they wish to show a close bond with A. Both the code and the noticeable switch to it will signal to A. that C. wishes to establish closeness. And conversely, a switch out of restricted code into more formal language is a strong marker of damage to the relationship.

3 In-group specialized language can create closeness, and remind A.s of the collegial bonding that exists between themselves and C. It does this particularly when someone who does not belong to the group is present. However, some people feel uncomfortable about the rudeness in excluding others present from knowing what is taking place, and may resist C., and so be less receptive to C.'s F.T.A.

See also the other **Politeness** tactics

Further reading   Brown and Levinson (1987); Davidson (1984); Goffman (1959)

POLITENESS: EXAGGERATE INTEREST IN A.

Tasks

To exaggerate interest in A. to offset any threat to his or her face.
To have an F.T.A. accepted with least damage to bonding.

Description

To show an exaggerated interest in A. It can occur within the F.T.A., or immediately precede it, as a form of pre-persuasion.

Persuasive value

The interest can be just that, interest, as in

Ex. 1 C: How absolutely fascinating! Can I have another coffee?

(Note that the exclamation is a response to some communication by A.

Note also that the question form is another politeness tactic: *see* **Politeness: negative**.)

Or it can be an expression of approval, as in

Ex. 2 C: You have done brilliantly with your roses! They perfume your whole office . . . You are wanted in the Committee Room.

Or an expression of sympathy with A., as in

Ex. 3 C: What a horrible nuisance it must be with that arm still in a sling! . . . I need your report.

The above examples use exaggerated language, but C. could also use exaggerated paralanguage, (i.e. **intonation**, **voice quality**, pitch, etc.)

See the other **Politeness** tactics; **Sympathize**

Further reading   Brown and Levinson (1987); Davidson (1984); Goffman (1959)

POLITENESS: EXAGGERATE OWN MATERIAL

Tasks

To intensify the interesting qualities in what C. says to offset any threat to A.'s face.
To have an F.T.A. accepted with least damage to bonding.

Description

To pack one's communication with interest for A. in recognition of A.'s face-need to be kept interested. It can occur within the F.T.A., or immediately precede it, as a form of pre-persuasion.

Persuasive value

C.s should present their subject matter in as interesting a way as possible, not just to keep A.s attending to it, but also so that A.s know C. has recognized their right to be treated as people worth the exertion of making a good communication. A.s should be aware that C. knows it is important not to waste their time by giving them boring speech or writing. Most A.s appreciate a good story teller, or a wit, or someone who speaks or writes sharply to the point.
1 Interest can be added by dramatizing anything of action in the subject matter, as in

Ex. 1 C: So then I suddenly noticed that the whole room had gone quiet, and I was the only one singing. I felt an absolute fool. . . . Anyway, back to business. Your report is supposed to be ready today you know.

2 In casual conversation, and **restricted code**, anecdotes can be made interesting by switches from past to present tense, which keep A. alert to the happenings, as in

Ex. 2 C: The cat has injured himself again; he is a nuisance. There he lies one minute, looking as if butter wouldn't melt in his mouth, and the next he was out of the door and into a fight with a dog! Can I borrow the car to take him to the vet?

3 Some C.s use direct speech, or passages of dialog, during their communication, since these can make A. be like someone watching a drama.
4 Some C.s use extreme overstatements as they communicate, to give added interest. As in:

Ex. 3 C: I feel as if I have gone three rounds with a boxer.

Overstatements must, however, be so obviously untrue that they cannot be taken literally, or else misunderstanding can occur.

See also **Humor**; the other **Politeness** tactics

Further reading   Brown and Levinson (1987); Davidson (1984); Goffman (1959)

POLITENESS: GENERALIZE ONE'S ACT

Tasks

To respect A.'s right not to be imposed on.
To avoid damage to A.'s face.
To show one is aware of imposing on A. as a person.
To save one's face in case of a failure of an F.T.A.

Description

One tactic to reduce the imposition of an F.T.A. is to disassociate from it both the person offering the F.T.A. and the person to whom it is being addressed.

Persuasive value

In some circumstances C.s may be in a position to imply that what they are communicating is not being offered personally by C. to an A., but arises because of some general community obligation or social convention. If C.s want the other person to do something, this is not because of an F.T.A. but because it is a general social requirement, as in

Ex. 1 Gentlemen lift the seat.

Ex. 2 Here in the Physics Department staff always clean the board after a class, thank you.

Many of these generalizations are communicated as an institutional act, either by the institution of the family or some broader entity. C.s may therefore not be in a position to speak or write in this way, however, if they hold any official or semi-official position, even it is only treasurer of the local tennis team, they can perhaps use this to frame their F.T.A.s.

One implication of such generalized F.T.A.s is that because it is a generally accepted matter it happens to others: in effect it is just part of everyday life. And so it can be suggested that C. is just drawing attention to a rule and not imposing a face threat at all, as in

Ex. 3 Children should speak only when spoken to.

Ex. 4 That is rude, people don't ask questions like that.

But these are also restricted to those who have the social or institutional right to use them; for instance, it could be socially damaging if someone used the second examples with someone else's child.

See also the other **Politeness** tactics

Further reading   Brown and Levinson (1987)

POLITENESS: GIVE DEFERENCE

Tasks

To respect A.'s right not to be imposed on.
To avoid damage to A.'s face.
To give signs of respect to A. as a person.
To save one's face in case of a failure of an F.T.A.

Description

There are two possibilities of indicating deference in English: one is by giving recognition to the higher status of the other person, and the other is declaring one's own lower status. They can be used for some generally persuasive effect or can be specifically used on the occasion of some F.T.A. which C. fears may not prove successful.

Persuasive value

In Western cultures the preferred deference tactic is to acknowledge the higher status of another person; it is much less acceptable to humble oneself. Those who do so are understood to lack self-esteem, and will be judged accordingly. For example:

Ex. 1 I'm sorry I'm late. I must be going crazy! I thought the meeting was not till noon.

Ex. 2 The kitchen is in a mess, I'm afraid, but anyway, would you like a cup of coffee?

Ex. 3 Oh, it's you! And me in my old clothes! Still, you had better come in.

It is socially proper for people to behave as if they have more self-confidence than these examples show, and any variation into this kind of humility (or, of course, into its opposite, arrogance) will produce discomfort, embarrassment, or even rejection. All humility might persuade people to do is to feel pity. As a consequence of this social preference, people from other cultures where the correct form of deference is to appear humble can find themselves misunderstood and judged badly.

Modes of deference to the higher status of the other person which are acceptable tactics in English are as follows.

1 The use of titles, such as Mr. Smith or Ms. Smith, is more deferential than using first names. Where the person has a high-ranking professional title—Counselor, Doctor, Senator, Professor—or has a knighthood or is a member of the peerage in England, the use of this term gives deference. It is important to get such titles right, however, and to know whether a person is just a Deputy Sheriff or a Sheriff, and to know how to address the daughter of a Duke (as 'Lady Mary Smith') or the wife of an appointed Lord ('Lady Smith'), etc., otherwise the deference will fail, and even rebound on the user who will be judged as ignorant (and humble?).

2 The use of 'sir' and 'madam' are possible deferential signs, though they are used mainly by business and professional people whose work involves a relatively superficial deference to their clients.

3 It can be deferential deliberately to exclude a higher-status person from one's mistakes or folly, as in

Ex. 4 We all acted like idiots at the meeting. Did you hear about it?

where 'we all' and our foolishness are opposed to the other person, and he or she is allowed either to indicate common ground with us, and this would be done if he or she responded 'Yes, I did. I wish I'd been there to join in!' or to keep to a social distance, and say 'Yes, I did. Why did you do that?'

It follows that to include the other in one's group or activity, particularly when the group or activity is not quite proper in some way, is to refuse the other person any degree of higher status, as in:

Ex. 5 Oh, come on, you must have enjoyed it when the boss fell down. We all did.

N.B. Deference can also be conveyed by **body language**. People can perform actions which physically lower them, as in holding the head low, or lowering the gaze, and so humble themselves, or they can move back from the other person, as an image of the social distance they wish to allow to others.

See also the other **Politeness** tactics

Further reading   Brown and Levinson (1987)

POLITENESS: GIVE REASONS

Tasks

To supply reasons for the act, and so reduce the face threat involved in the F.T.A.
To ask A. for reasons why the F.T.A. should not be met.

Description

C. can offer his or her reasons for performing the F.T.A., and in so doing assume that A. is a rational being who will understand and accept them. Alternatively, C. can ask A. to supply reasons why what C. wants should not be agreed to, and in so doing assume again that A. is rational, and if he or she has no good reasons against the F.T.A., that it will be met.

Persuasive value

1 C. can give a reason for the F.T.A., and this can either be the real reason or one carefully chosen to appeal to A. This latter could be determined by analyzing C.'s experience of A.'s own reasons for behaviors, and also by a study of A.'s opinions on what justifies an F.T.A. Information can be gleaned from A. saying such things as 'He always has fifteen good reasons why he should be allowed to do what he wants, but there is never anything in it for me'; or 'She asked if she could borrow my books because she has an assignment, but she always returns them late and in a filthy condition.' In saying the first, the speaker shows a dislike of too many reasons, particularly where none of them show thought for his or her own advantage; while in the second, he or she shows a dislike for tardiness in returning books, and for dirt. After hearing such examples from A., a C. who wanted to borrow some wine glasses for a party would be advised to offer

few but good reasons, to include some reason why the act would benefit A. as well as him- or herself, and also to make clear that they would be returned on time and clean.

2 C. could present the F.T.A. in a way which asks A. to supply reasons why it should not be met, as in

Ex. 1 Would there be any reason why you couldn't lend me your bike?

The assumption is that if A. cannot think of any reasons, he or she would have to fulfil the request. This tactic makes it difficult for A. to refuse, not only because he or she is asked to exert thought to find reasons if the act is to be refused, but also because before communicating the reasons they will have to be judged for their politeness or lack of it. For example, A.'s reason for not lending C. the bike may be because C. was recently involved in an accident and A. fears that C. caused it, and might have another and therefore damage A.'s bike. To put this tactfully into words might be difficult in itself, and to say it at all might cause more damage to the bond between A. and C. than damage to A.'s bike would. In view of these difficulties, A.s may well decide, even against their own good sense, to agree to the act's request.

See also the other **Politeness** tactics; **Principle of least effort**

Further reading   Brown and Levinson (1987); Davidson (1984)

POLITENESS: GIVE SYMPATHY

Task

C. can give something to A. to offset the potential face loss if the F.T.A. is met.

Description

C. can offer something to A. as a pre-persuasion tactic, perhaps long before communicating the F.T.A., so as to increase the chances of A. offering to meet the F.T.A. when it occurs.

Persuasive value

There are several things which C. can offer to A., of which the most important is a general sympathy with A.

1 This can take the form of caring about A.'s work, family, or self. It can be a moderate sympathy, as when C. shows a willingness to listen to A. talk about work or family events, or to A. expressing a personal view about something. Or it could be a forceful sympathy, expressed in some act or

acts volunteered by C. which help A. So, for example, C. might remember that A.'s son wants to get onto a football team, and on reading in the paper of a local vacancy, contacts A. with the news. Or C., knowing that A.'s car has broken down, could volunteer to give A a drive to the garage to pick it up.

While both kinds of act should meet with appreciation, many people express a strong preference for and give a high value to those who offer a sympathetic ear. The gender of A. may make a difference here, since on the whole women have expressed a stronger liking than men have for the type of sympathy which consists of listening well. And the converse is usually also true, that women provide this kind of sympathy better than men do.

N.B. The giving of sympathy is at all times a complex act; *see also* **Sympathize**.

2 C. can also give cooperation to A., and so pre-persuade him or her. This could consist of making sure they work well together when their employment requires it, with as little expressed friction as possible, or it could be a passing offer of help, perhaps when C. sees A. struggling with a load and volunteers to help to carry it.

3 And C. can also give gifts to A.: tangible gifts on birthdays and at other celebrations, or just as minor friendly gifts during their meetings. Problems can arise over gift-giving though: for example, if the gift is too expensive or too many are offered to be just a friendly gesture, the act seems to put the receiver under an obligation. Some cultures do not like gift-giving precisely because of this obligation, and so may omit a gift where in Western culture it is expected. And, of course, since both C. and A. know that gifts are a matter of exchange, A. could be uncomfortable receiving a gift, knowing that it should be 'paid for' by some reciprocal gift or act at some time.

See also the other **Politeness** tactics

Further reading Brown and Levinson (1987); Davidson (1984)

POLITENESS: MAKE ACTION JOINT

Task

To indicate that the F.T.A. is not a threat because both C. and A. are involved jointly in it.

Description

By making a single agent out of both C. and A., C. can suggest that they are jointly acting in whatever the F.T.A. requires.

Persuasive value

1 C. can suggest close cooperation and can combine him- or herself with A. by using the word 'we,' in such an act as:

Ex. 1 We need a good holiday. I've booked us on a flight to New York for
        Friday.

The term 'we' can here really include A. with C., and so be for the common good of both, but it could also be used where only C. wants the holiday, and means 'I need a good holiday,' or where C. thinks only A. needs a holiday, is unlikely to agree to it, and so seeks to bring this about by suggesting that it is a joint need.
2 C. can also combine him or herself with A. by using the phrase 'Let's,' as in

Ex. 2 Let's have a coffee.

where again C. may judge it to be true and for the common good of both of them, or just for his or her benefit, or for A.'s benefit only.
   In both cases it is the possibility that it could be true for both participants that makes this use of the joint terms different from the 'we' or 'let's' used where it could only mean A., and so be condescending, as in

Ex. 3 Let's just run through your piano piece once more. [where only A.
        will play the piano]

or could only mean C. and so be selfish, as in

Ex. 4 Let's have one of your chocolates then, please.

See also **Politeness: point of view**; the other **Politeness** tactics

Further reading   Brown and Levinson (1987); Davidson (1984)

POLITENESS: MAKE THE ACT IMPERSONAL

Tasks

To respect A.'s right not to be imposed on.
To avoid damage to A.'s face.
To show one is aware of imposing on A. as a person.
To save one's face in case of a failure of an F.T.A.

Description

The threat to the other person's face can be reduced by communicating the act as if both the communicator and the person addressed are involved not as individuals but only in an impersonal way.

Persuasive value

Making the act impersonal could be done by various means.
1 The F.T.A. could be phrased as if C. is absent from the act; for example:

Ex. 1 It would be helpful if you got a new computer for this office. [i.e. I want a new computer]

C. presents the other person with two options here: by using the 'It' clause, C. allows the other person to refuse the request without involving the speaker; and C. also leaves an opportunity for the other to form a rejection easily, 'It might be helpful, but there is no money for new equipment.'
2 C. could phrase the F.T.A. as if it is being performed on behalf of others, as in

Ex. 2 The Chairman wants your report by tonight. We need to know what you are going to do about this.

This saves something of the other person's face by showing that C. is not whimsically intruding on his or her time, but at the same time, when the act suggests that the other person is in some way deficient, as in this example, it is a strong threat to A.'s face and could be resented, and so affect the relationship between the two.

N.B. C. uses the 'royal' version of the word 'we' to mean the single person performing the F.T.A. This is occasionally used as a way of hinting that C. is not alone in wanting the F.T.A., but it fails to be very persuasive as a polite tactic if the other person knows that C. is acting alone. Then it sounds like arrogance on C.'s part, making out that he or she has the right to speak as if a group when this is not the case.

3 C. could only indirectly refer to the people threatened by the act, for example by generalizing them as members of some group, as in

Ex. 3 You people haven't yet put in your report cards.

Ex. 4 The accounts section needs to put in its results soon. [where the person addressed is a member of the section]

This shows the threat to be not to the individual but more generally addressed. The implication for the person's face is that he or she is a member of a group and they will all perform what is required by the act—put in report cards or results—so the imposition on the single person is less. However, people do like to be addressed as individuals, and may somewhat resent being undifferentiated from their group. In Ex. 4 for instance, no specific group is in fact named, and the person is addressed as 'you people': this could be resented more than the second instance where the person could sensibly recognize that he or she is a member of the section and can be addressed as such.

4 C. can impersonalize the F.T.A. to such an extent that the other person is simply omitted, as in

Ex. 5 Someone needs to get these reports done soon.
Ex. 6 Someone needs to get her report done soon.

In Ex. 5 the other person is offered a set of refusal options, ranging from agreement, 'Yes, someone does (not me),' through a bland lack of understanding, 'Who do you mean?' to acceptance, 'Yes O.K.' This wide range is a reduction of the imposition on the person, and it both reduces the threat of the act of requesting because the person can really or can pretend not to recognize it, and the threat of the act required, doing the report, because the person can avoid taking responsibility for it.

Example 6 encroaches much more on the person's freedom, since the use of the word 'her' makes it clear that 'someone' is only a polite tactic to soften the F.T.A. by a touch of humor, and the person is being directly addressed, and threatened.

In written communications, because they are more formal than spoken ones, it is possible to use other tactics.
5 The passive form of the verb can be used, as in

Ex. 7 It would be appreciated if the lights are turned off after the last class at night.

Ex. 8 It is required that all enrollments are submitted by 10 May.

Here no individual is seeking to impose on another, but an institution is setting behaviors for all to follow. And no individual is being directly addressed. In Ex. 7 people can easily ignore the F.T.A., and do nothing about the lights, though in Ex. 8 they will face a sanction if they do not do the act required.

See also the other **Politeness** tactics

Further reading   Brown and Levinson (1987)

POLITENESS: MINIMIZE IMPOSITION ON OTHERS

Tasks

To respect A.'s right not to be imposed on.
To avoid damage to A.'s face.
To minimize any imposition on A. from a potential F.T.A.
To save one's face in case of a failure of an F.T.A.

Description

C.s can reduce the imposition of the task they are seeking to have A. perform, by suggesting that the imposition is a very minor one.

Persuasive value

This can be done in several ways, each of which persuades differently.
1 The word 'just' can be applied either to the communicative act as an imposition on A., as in

Ex. 1 I just wanted to say that we are meeting in three minutes.

or to what is required of A., as in

Ex. 2 I just want to use your pen.

2 The act required of A. can be reduced in importance, in the time it will take as in

Ex. 3 May I have your pen for a moment?

or in the amount of the request, as in

Ex. 4 May I have just a spoonful of sugar for my recipe?

or C. can cheat by using a verb of lesser imposition, as in

Ex. 5 May I just borrow a cup of coffee from you?

where 'borrow' really means 'be given.'

See also the other **Politeness** tactics

Further reading   Brown and Levinson (1987)

POLITENESS: NEGATIVE

Task

To avoid intruding on A.'s freedom of action.

Description

Negative politeness tactics are the set of tactics which acknowledge the need for people to have freedom of action, and to have it unimpeded by others. People need to be able to make their own decisions, not to be imposed on, for example, in their time or energy or their possessions. So negative politeness would be needed to offset such different impositions as 'Could I borrow your lecture notes?' or 'Could you give me a drive home?' or even the friendly invitation 'Would you like to come for coffee this evening?' Impositions can range from calling someone up on the phone and inadvertently interrupting their dinner, to telling long stories when people are in a hurry, to such heavy impositions as seeking a time extension for an assignment from a member of faculty.

Persuasive value

Negative politeness tactics are used to suggest that C. is trying as far as possible to avoid troubling A., and they could involve any of the following.

1 Explicitly recognize that A.s have their own rights, and that these are respected.

2 Show that the act being performed by C. will only require a minimal interference with A.'s life.

3 Show that C. is aware of taking liberties with A.'s life but that these have been reduced as far as possible.

4 Be indirect in the way the act is performed, that is, conceal the fact that C. is imposing on A. (though this may make it harder to use the possibilities in 1–3).

5 Maintain enough social distance so that A. feels less compelled to do what the act requires. There is much greater compulsion when friends seek to impose on us than when strangers do.

See also **Face**: **sustain**; **Face threats: recognize**; the other **Politeness** tactics

Further reading   Brown and Levinson (1987); Davidson (1984); Goffman (1959)

POLITENESS: POINT OF VIEW

Task

To makes others the center or focal point of what one says to support their face.

Description

It is usual for C.s when using referring terms to take as their focal point their own position as speaker or writer. So when they use the terms 'here' and 'there,' 'here' is where they see themselves as being, and 'there' refers to places away from them. Also the terms 'I' or 'we' refer to themselves as speakers, and 'you' refers to those they are addressing.

Persuasive value

1 One tactic is to use the referring terms 'I' and 'we' so as to make A.'s position the central one, as in

Ex. 1 [doctor to patient] We'll need to watch this arm.

Ex. 2 [teacher to pupils] Now, what we'll do next is write down the answers to the questions I shall give you.

Doctors and teachers use the tactic frequently, as do parents to young children, and it has therefore become associated with speakers who have power over A.s. Because of this, users who have a peer relation with other participants should use the tactic very carefully, otherwise it could be resented as a sign of wanting power where the speaker has no right to it. Even in such an ordinary event as walking up to a couple of friends who are talking together and saying 'Hello, what are we talking about then?' the tactic could be judged too intrusive, or too possessive, and would be counterproductive.

2 Another tactic is to use the directional verbs—'come' or 'go,' 'bring' or 'take'—to make A. the focus of attention, as in

Ex. 3 Shall I come and visit you in hospital?

Ex. 4 I'll bring you some grapes!

where the alternatives

Ex. 5 I'll go and visit you.

Ex. 6 I'll take you some grapes.

both sound rude, and both suggest a distancing of C. from A. and hence a weakness of bond between them.

Note, however, that unlike Ex. 5:

Ex. 7 I'll go with you to the hospital if you like.

is not rude. The difference between the two is that in Ex. 5, C. places him- or herself at the center of attention and A. at a distance, over there in hospital; whereas in Ex. 7 C. is saying that he or she will accompany A. as they both go to the hospital, which represents them as being together 'here,' and both going 'there.'

See also **Politeness: make action joint**; **Referring terms: external**

Further reading   Brown and Levinson (1987)

POLITENESS: PRESUME AGREEMENT

Task

To presume that A. could easily grant the F.T.A., as an offset to the face threat.

Description

In the way C. presents the F.T.A., he or she assumes that A. will agree to it. The assumption can rest on:

(a) the opinion that A. is rational and can see the value of the act;
(b) that A. is generous and would naturally accede to C.'s wishes;
(c) that the act will produce something of use to A.;
(d) that it is not a major imposition.

Persuasive value

Ex. 1 I have run out of money. You could lend me $5 till I get to the bank, couldn't you?

1 Here C. offers an explanation of need, one which A. could easily understand, and requests only a small amount of money, for a short time, and so presumes that A. must agree to the request.

Ex. 2 I'm sure you won't mind lending me your lecture notes. I know you lent Susan them last week.

2 Here C. speaks as if A. is generous 'I'm sure you won't mind,' and gives evidence of the generosity in the loan to Susan, and so presumes that A. must agree to the request. In fact, the reference to the Susan acts as a precedent and will make it hard for A. to refuse, so it is a strong persuader.

Ex. 3 Your jacket needs a good brushing before you wear it again.

3 Here C. 'commands' A. to brush his or her jacket, but since it is obviously to A.'s advantage to agree to this, the 'command' is likely to be obeyed. It is presumed that C. will also find advantage in the jacket-brushing, perhaps that A. will make a more neatly dressed companion as they go out together, but this is left quite unmentioned in the F.T.A.

Ex. 4 I need to borrow a pen.

4 C.'s lack of a major persuasive tactic, other than the mild phrase 'I need,' could be intended to show A. that no major persuasions are needed since the imposition is a very minor one. And if it is minor, then A. should have no difficulty in acceding to the request.

See also the other **Politeness** tactics

Further reading   Brown and Levinson (1987)

POLITENESS: PRINCIPLE AND TACTICS
Task

To avoid damaging A.'s self-esteem.

Description

Positive politeness tactics are the set of tactics which acknowledge the need for people to feel important, and to be addressed with respect. Such tactics should be employed whenever it is suspected that A.s are showing signs of anger or resentment at not being taken seriously, or where C. anticipates there could be a risk of this happening. And it will inevitably happen when C. performs one of the many communicative acts which threaten A.'s self-esteem.

N.B.   Though the name given to the tactics is 'politeness,' this should not be confused with such superficialities as etiquette, table manners, or formal protocols. In the context of communication with others it is a much deeper, essential, component of social interaction. While not everyone employs a high degree of politeness, everyone behaves as if he or she recognizes the value of it; everyone certainly notices, and usually reacts badly to, its absence. This can have a deleterious effect on persuasion, and on the very notion of cooperation.

Persuasive value

The principle of positive politeness assumes that if people are treated with respect they will be more likely to respond well in interactions, and may therefore be more inclined to help C. achieve his or her purposes. To show positive respect to others can be done by using tactics which suggest one or more of the following:

(a) Show them that they are perceived as friends, their personal qualities are liked, and that they belong to the same group as C.
(b) Show that what C. wants is the same as they want for themselves.

They should then perceive that any face-threatening act that ensues will not be intended to undervalue them or offer them disrespect, and so they can respond well to it. It is particularly important to do this when C. knows that he or she may at some time have to act in ways that will damage their self-respect, for example if C. is a supervisor and knows he or she may one day need to accuse them of work failure. A.s will not, of course, always respond well to acts of this kind, even when addressed with the utmost respect, because they have their own agendas and these may clash with C.'s.

See also **Face: sustain**; **Face threats: recognize**; the other **Politeness** tactics

Further reading   Brown and Levinson (1987); Davidson (1984); Goffman (1959)

POLITENESS: SHOW CONCERN FOR A.'S NEEDS

Tasks

To reduce the face threat of an impending act by showing concern for A.'s needs.
To show that C. and A. are cooperators with the same goals.

Description

C.s can demonstrate a recognition of and concern for A.s needs, and also can indicate that their own goals are similar to those of A.

Persuasive value

1 C.s can articulate their recognition of A.'s wishes and needs by way of preface to an F.T.A., as in

Ex. 1 I know you wanted to go to the theater this week, so I've booked tickets for *Cats*. I'm sure you will like it.

where C. has taken a general wish by A. and gone beyond it to choose a show, to select a day, and to purchase tickets all without consulting A. Also C. has presumed that A. wants to go to the theater with C. rather than someone else. C. knows that A.'s lack of participation in this decision-making would constitute an F.T.A. for A., so to offset it, C. has offered as an excuse that he or she knew of A.'s general wish.

The comment 'I'm sure you will like it' is also an F.T.A. in the way it presumes to know A.'s liking, and even if it turns out to be true that A. is happy to go to *Cats*, he or she might offer a qualification to C. such as 'Well, O.K., but next time check with me. I might have an engagement that night, or I might not like the play.'

2 C.s can show their knowledge of A.'s wants, wishes or views, in **sociable language** before making an F.T.A., by using the negative question form, which presumes a positive answer, as in:

Ex. 2 You'll be wanting the newspaper now, won't you?

Ex. 3 Won't this rain be splendid for the garden?

Ex. 4 You have seen this article I think.

This particular form, if C. has correctly presumed A.'s views, not only shows A. that C. has been attending to A.'s previous communications, and to A.'s general behavior, but it also allows A. to respond with the least effort, and A. could be appreciative of this.

See also the other **Politeness** tactics

Further reading   Brown and Levinson (1987); Davidson (1984)

POLITENESS: USE A PROMISE OR OFFER

Tasks

To offset a potential F.T.A. to A. by promising something to A.'s advantage.
To offset a potential F.T.A. to A. by offering something to A.'s advantage.

Description

C. may make a promise or produce an offer which is clearly to A.'s advantage in order to offset the potential for face threat in the near future.

Persuasive value

If a promise by C. is to be effective, and to have maximum impact as a counterbalance to the face threat A. will soon meet, it needs to occur just beside the F.T.A. Moreover, it should require of C. as much effort and inconvenience as the F.T.A. will cause for A. So for example, with a future request to A. in mind like

Ex. 1 May I borrow your car for an hour or so?

C. could promise to lend A. something of equivalent value, and for an equivalent time, as in 'And I promise I'll lend you my new bike on Sunday afternoon.' If C. chooses to make an offer rather than give a promise, the same equivalence is required for the face threat to be reduced, as in 'And I'll help you with your homework tonight, if you like.'

What A. really perceives as equivalence is not easy to assess: for example, in C.'s promise of a loan of the bike, A. may find no value at all, since he or she neither likes bike riding, nor would he or she want to spend Sunday doing that. If A. thinks C. must know A. doesn't go bike riding, then he or she would think of C. as ignorant of A.'s likes and dislikes, and therefore with no real bond to A. Or A. could judge C. as devious, promising something while knowing the promise will not be taken up. On the other hand, if A. knows C. could not know of the dislike of bikes, and indeed has evidence to think A. might like them, A. will recognize that the offer is meant to be an equivalence, shows good intentions, is socially correct, and in that spirit let it offset the face threat of the car request, as in 'Thanks for the offer, but I'm O.K. for Sunday. You can borrow the car.'

Equivalence should probably not be too obvious, as in 'Lend me your book and I'll lend you mine,' since that suggests that the relationship is not strong, but depends on commensurate effort on each person's part — 'You come to dinner and I'll expect you to invite me to dinner next week,' or

'She owes me a dinner since I invited her to my place last week.' Relationships of this kind are usually strained. To hint that the bond between C. and A. is of this kind is to damage it. (Though it is also true that relationships where one person does all the giving and the other does all the taking are equally strained.)

See also the other **Politeness** tactics

Further reading   Brown and Levinson (1987); Davidson (1984)

POLITENESS: USE BLUNT TACTICS

Task

To justify or excuse the lack of politeness.

Description

Bluntness is the absence of politeness tactics and it therefore neglects to incorporate into the communicative acts any recognition or consideration for others' face and the impositions caused by those acts.

Persuasive value

The absence of politeness tactics is accepted without question in the following cases.

1 Where urgency exists and is recognized by both interactants. Where only C. thinks there is urgency and A. does not, the tactic may cause damage.

2 Where the channel of communication is less than perfect: where C. and A. are far apart, as when people call out to others to attract their attention, or where there is a poor telephone line, or the telephone call is expensive, etc.

3 Where the interaction is agreed by both interactants to be solely task-related, as when engaged on some project together. At such times blunt instructions are perfectly acceptable 'Pass me the book. No, no, that one!'

4 Where the act C. is performing bluntly can be easily seen by A. to be solely in his or her best interests, and for his or her benefit, as in 'There's a smudge on your face,' or 'Have a cookie,' or 'Breathe in. Out. In again,' [said by doctor while examining a patient]. It follows therefore that it may be possible to have bluntness accepted, or to excuse a past bluntness by appealing to one of these reasons to justify its use. So C. could try:

(a) to have A. see that the matter is urgent, as in 'Hey listen, I must tell you . . .';

(b) to suggest that channel noise exists, as in, when answering the phone, 'I have someone with me at the moment';

(c) to pretend that the interaction is task-focussed, as in 'Lend me your pen. This is a really important letter';

(d) to suggest that the act is or was in A.'s best interest, as in 'Show me your essay, and I'll check the spelling.'

See also **Bluntness: choose**; **Face threats: recognize**; the other **Politeness** tactics

Further reading   Brown and Levinson (1987)

POLITENESS: USE FORMALITY

Tasks

To respect A.'s right not to be imposed on.
To avoid damage to A.'s face.

Description

One mode of politeness is to speak or write in an extremely formal language, and so to couch an F.T.A. in very stilted terms is to reduce it as an imposition, as in

Ex. 1 Your cooperation is earnestly requested.

Ex. 2 The University Library opening hours will be curtailed.

Ex. 3 The company's obligation is to commence legal proceedings.

Persuasive value

The formality of the language serves to remove personality or individuality from the text, and from the F.T.A. When this is done, the act does not appear to come from any single person seeking to impose on another, or to be addressed to a single person but the act exists, as it were, outside individuals, and outside the acts of people. It is, in other words, a socially derived and focussed event.

See also the other **Politeness** tactics

Further reading   Brown and Levinson (1987)

POLITENESS: USE INDIRECTION

Tasks

To respect A.'s right not to be imposed on.
To avoid damage to A.'s face.

To minimize any imposition on A. from a potential F.T.A.
To save one's face in case of a failure of an F.T.A.

Description

If C.s feel that some act, whether a request, question or other potential
F.T.A., could prove a problem, then they can choose to perform the act
indirectly. That is, they can choose a form of words that have a literal
meaning which seems unthreatening, but which in the specific context can
be recognized as a face threat by A., and if need be, if there is major
opposition to it which would cause face loss to C., it can be denied by C. It
is a very commonly used tactic, and one that is learnt early in childhood.

Persuasive value

For example,

Ex. 1 Can you make an omelet?

looks like a question, and as part of a discussion on cooking. But if it
occurs in specifically suitable circumstances it could be an indirect request
for A. actually to make an omelet. If it was said in a kitchen, where the
people are old friends, they are hungry, and there are only eggs in the
fridge, and C., the host, has broken his or her wrist, then A. would quite
clearly understand its intent. At the same time, A. would know that C.
had chosen a politeness tactic which allows A. to ignore the request if it
seems too much of an imposition: since it looks like a question, A. could
just answer 'Yes, I'm quite good at omelets.' If A. did this, C. would also
know what had happened, that A. has avoided the request, and knowing
that could decide whether to plough ahead and try again or to leave things
as they are.

The assessment of the context is a very specific one, with very delicate
shades of meaning. So if C. asks 'Isn't it hot in here?' hoping that
someone would open the door, it would make a difference to how the
question is interpreted and whether its function as a request is recognized,
if it is addressed to someone in the middle of the room or to someone by
the door: only the person by the door could easily see it as a request,
because for any of the others it would be too great an imposition, and
they would assume that this is not meant for them.

Because the tactic is to disguise to some degree the F.T.A. through the
use of indirection, the disguise may be too good, and it may not work.
There is always a possibility that A. would genuinely not understand the
act or its goal. However, another clue is provided by the question form,
used in Ex. 1 and in many other indirect F.T.A.s as a conventional
indirection tactic. There are many typical examples of this form:

Ex. 2 Can you pass the sugar?

Ex. 3 Have you seen my pen?

Ex. 3 Have you finished with that magazine?

Ex. 5 Have you got a light?

So when people hear a question addressed to them there is a strong possibility that it is a disguised request. So they spend time noting the literal message, assessing whether that is all that C. is trying to present, using the context for clues, using their own world knowledge (in the omelet example their knowledge of hunger and how to alleviate it, kitchens and their purposes, eggs and their connection with omelets, etc.). However, if A.s are distracted, half-asleep, or concentrating on something else, then the tactic may fail because they do not give it enough attention.

Indirection is primarily used for requests because they are major impositions on others, but it is also used for questions and statements and the other socially difficult F.T.A.s like a reprimand or a complaint.

See also the **Politeness indirection** tactics

Further reading   Brown and Levinson (1987); Clark (1979)

POLITENESS: USE SOCIABILITY

Tasks

To show that because C. and A. have a friendly relationship C. will not damage it by threats to A.'s face.
To have an F.T.A. accepted with least damage to bonding.

Description

Sociable language or small talk or gossip is talk about matters which are unrelated to any business or purposive interaction. It occurs also in written communications, most often in the opening and closing sections of letters, memos, etc.

Persuasive value

Such talk can be used as pre-persuasion, by representing the bonding that exists between A. and C., before that bond is tested by C. requiring something of A. which threatens A.'s face. It can work in several ways.
1 It can remind A. that they share mutual interests, that they are friends, and so C. is likely to act in ways that would be to A.'s interest.
2 It can remind A. that in the past A. has made requests of C. and that

since these were met, so A. should try to reciprocate and meet C.'s wishes on this occasion.

3 The degree of effort and time that C. puts into the sociability is a measure of the high regard C. has for A., and in the light of this A. could postulate that C. is unlikely to act gainst A.'s interests.

4 Specifically, the sociability can be directed towards showing that C. and A. share opinions, attitudes, and beliefs, even where they do not. C. may be able, with a little thought, to remember some opinion of A.'s which is germane to C.'s impending F.T.A., and so show how well it fits A.'s views, and hence it is not face-threatening at all. As in:

Ex. 1 I know you care about the environment, so I thought you would like to go to this meeting about tree preservation tonight—I've saved you a ticket.

5 Ex. 1 also uses another bonding tactic—**restricted code**, as represented by the word 'this.' The word assumes a shared knowledge of the meeting, and although that may be false, A. will understand C. is attempting to show they share it as a sign of their group identity, and shared interests.

Other examples are:

Ex. 2 That looks good, not your usual thing is it?

Ex. 3 You saw that program last night, didn't you? I hate the way he does that.

See also the other **Politeness** tactics; **Sociable language** tactics

Further reading   Brown and Levinson (1987); Davidson (1984)

POLITENESS INDIRECTION: AVOID ADDRESSING THE TARGET PERSON

Task

To perform an F.T.A. so as to save both C.'s and A.'s face by addressing it to someone other than the one for whom it is meant.

Description

One way to make an imposition on someone, without loss of face to either party, is to hint indirectly at it, by addressing it to someone other than the person for whom it is meant. This could cause the other person to recognize that the act may be an indirect one, with some other meaning than its surface suggests, and hence that it is an F.T.A. As in:

Ex. 1 [meant for John who is talking to Susan] Susan, could you help me with this heavy parcel?

Ex. 2 [meant for Alan] Mary, did you borrow my pen?

Ex. 3 [meant for Paula] Ann, did you make this lovely cake?

Persuasive value

By leaving unspecified who the target of the act is, and addressing it to someone else, C. can indirectly make an F.T.A. without face loss to the person addressed.

In Ex. 1, C. can indirectly request John to help carry the parcel, and by addressing it to Susan, can save John's freedom of action if he does not wish to oblige. It also saves him from having to refuse, since he need say nothing at all, pretending that he thought it was addressed to Susan. On the other hand, it does nothing for Susan's freedom of action, which is directly impeded.

In Ex. 2, C. can accuse Alan of borrowing a pen, and leave his face unthreatened, since he also can pretend that the accusation is not addressed to him.

In Ex. 3, another variant on indirectness is offered. Here the target person, Paula, is a child hoping for a compliment on her cakemaking. By asking if it was made by Ann, C. has deliciously delayed the glorious moment when Paula can claim the cake as hers. It can be made a strong compliment if Ann is a good cook, and C. implies that the cake is good enough to be hers.

See also **Face threats: recognize**; the other **Politeness indirection** tactics

Further reading   Brown and Levinson (1987); Clark (1979)

POLITENESS INDIRECTION: BE INCOMPLETE

Task

To perform an F.T.A. so as to save both C.'s and A.'s face by expressing it only partly, and leaving something incomplete.

Description

One way to make an imposition on someone, without loss of face to either party, is to hint indirectly at it, by expressing it only in part, leaving something incomplete. This could cause the other person to recognize that the act may be an indirect one, with some other meaning than its surface suggests, and hence that it is an F.T.A. As in:

Ex. 1 Well, if you will leave your assignments till the last minute . . .

Ex. 2 Too many cooks . . .

Persuasive value

By leaving the communication incomplete, C. violates the maxim of quantity, which requires that one says enough to be understood. A.s can then consider what C. means by this incompleteness.

In Ex. 1, there is some doubt about how C. might have finished the communication, but clearly it is meant as a criticism of A. for not managing his or her assignments better. Not knowing what is missing means that the act is less face threatening: it could have been completed with such bluntness as '. . . till the last minute. You are a fool.'

In Ex. 2, there is no doubt what C.'s communication leaves incomplete, because it is a well-known proverb. However, by not articulating it, not criticizing in so many words, C. manages to save at least some face for A.

See also **Face threats: recognize**; the other **Politeness indirection** tactics; **Social convention of quantity**

Further reading   Brown and Levinson (1987); Clark (1979)

POLITENESS INDIRECTION: CONTRADICT

Task

To perform an F.T.A. so as to save both C.'s and A.'s face by offering a contradiction in terms.

Description

One way to make an imposition on someone, without loss of face to either party, is to hint indirectly at it, by using a contradiction. This could cause the other person to recognize that the act may be an indirect one, with some other meaning than its surface suggests, and hence that it is an F.T.A. Contradictions in this case are communications which express contraries which cannot both be true at the same time. As in:

Ex. 1 Mary: I need the report for tomorrow. That's no problem, is it?
      Beth: Well, yes and no: it is and it isn't.

Persuasive value

In Ex. 1 Beth uses a statement which contains contraries, and thus breaks the maxim of quality and appears not to be telling the truth, and sounds insincere. When this occurs, Mary should note the convention has been broken and consider why this has happened. In her own speech she makes a command/request of Beth, and presumably expects that Beth will comply, though her question 'That's no problem, is it?' suggests that Mary is trying to be polite in allowing Beth an escape route, suggesting she can respond either positively or negatively. However, this may not be an accurate reflection of the power relation between the two. If Mary is the boss, then the politeness is not meant as a real opportunity to refuse the F.T.A., and certainly the question form shows that Mary expects Beth to agree that it is no problem. When Beth replies as she does with this contradictory statement, she must therefore be doing something that is unexpected, and hence probably an F.T.A. She appears to be trying to resist the assumption that it will be no problem for her, and may be trying to wriggle out of doing the report. But it is very indirect as she expresses it , and she leaves her options open so she can respond to Mary's next utterance as safely as possible.

See also **Face threats: recognize**; the other **Politeness indirection** tactics; **Social convention of quality**

Further reading   Brown and Levinson (1987); Clark (1979)

POLITENESS INDIRECTION: OVERSTATE

Task

To perform an F.T.A. so as to save both C.'s and A.'s face by using overstatement.

Description

One way to make an imposition on someone, without loss of face to either party, is to hint indirectly at it by using an overstatement. This could cause the other person to recognize that the act may be an indirect one, with some other meaning than its surface suggests, and hence that it is an F.T.A. as in

Ex. 1 I phoned you dozens of times yesterday but you weren't in.

Persuasive value

If C. violates the maxim of quantity, and says more than is necessary, in the case of Ex. 1 by offering the exaggeration of the 'dozens,' it should suggest to A. that the speaker means to do something more than make a statement about what he or she did yesterday, and it could therefore be deduced that an F.T.A. is being performed, in this case a criticism or complaint. If the speaker is addressing someone of superior status (e.g. if a student used it to a member of faculty), then it is an oblique way of saying that the faculty member has committed a fault by not being available. The member of faculty should appreciate that the complaint is being made obliquely, to save his or her face, and give the student credit for this.

However, such overstatements do not always save the face of the person offering them—it is fairly obvious that the student is complaining, and he or she could hardly claim to be just telling what was done the previous day.

Other examples of overstated acts which are F.T.A.s are:

Ex. 2 You never ever clean the car. [complaint and/or request]

Ex. 3 You are grotesquely fat. [command/request]

Ex. 4 This report is taking forever. [command/request]

Ex. 5 I woke with the most dreadful headache this morning. Couldn't raise my head from the pillow. [apology]

See also **Face threats: recognize**; **Ironic understatement/overstatement**; the other **Politeness indirection** tactics; **Social convention of quantity**

Further reading   Brown and Levinson (1987); Clark (1979)

POLITENESS INDIRECTION: PRESUPPOSE

Task

To perform an F.T.A. so as to save both C.'s and A.'s face by using presuppositions.

Description

One way to make an imposition on someone, without loss of face to either party, is to hint indirectly at it by using a presupposition which will cause the other person to recognize that the act may be an indirect one, with some other meaning than its surface suggests, and hence that it is an F.T.A., as in

Ex. 1 I washed the cat's bowl out again today.

Persuasive value

Here C. relies on A.'s understanding of what is presupposed so as to have A. know that this is a criticism of A. for not washing out the bowl. The process of thought A. needs to go through in order to understand correctly is to note that C. says this in some context and it may relate to that context. Perhaps A. has just said 'I had to tidy your papers away this morning,' meaning 'I have just had to do something for you which you should have done for yourself.' C. responds with Ex. 1, which would here mean that C.

too has done something which the other person is responsible for, so they are quits. If, however, C. just offered this out of the blue, with no apparent relevance to the context (i.e. it breaks the maxim of relevance), A. would have to know that (share the presupposition that) they have an agreement that they take turns each day washing the cat's bowl, and it was not C.'s turn, hence A. could understand the 'again today' is C. offering a criticism. And criticism is an F.T.A.

Other instances of criticism F.T.A.s which depend on shared suppositions are:

Ex. 2 At least I don't wear my clothes till they are in shreds.

Ex. 3 I hope you are going to change before we go to your grandmother's.

Ex. 4 I don't understand how some people can be so late with their essays.

See also **Face threats: recognize**; the other **Politeness indirection** tactics; **Social convention of relevance**

Further reading   Brown and Levinson (1987); Clark (1979)

POLITENESS INDIRECTION: UNDERSTATE

Task

To perform an F.T.A. so as to save both C.'s and A.'s face by using understatement.

Description

One way to make an imposition on someone, without loss of face to either party, is to hint indirectly at it by using an understatement which will cause the other person to recognize that the act may be an indirect one, with some other meaning than its surface suggests, and hence that it is some F.T.A., as in

Ex. 1 Alan: What did you think of that new man of Mary's?
       Beth: He's O.K.

Ex. 2 Alan: Was the new fantasy film as exciting as you hoped?
       Beth: It was pretty exciting, I suppose.

Ex. 3 That novel that won the prize isn't too bad.

Ex. 4 That theater ticket wasn't as expensive as I thought.

Persuasive value

Here the maxim of quantity is being apparently broken, because in Ex. 1 Beth says less than Alan was expecting. First, if Alan had asked the question feeling that Mary's man was nice, and conveyed this by tone of voice, he could therefore expect that Beth would respond with some agreement, as befits the **cooperative principle**. When she does not, Alan would understand that there must be some reason for this, and try to work out why. He could work out that it is not necessarily that Beth wishes to convey that she is less than pleased with Mary's man, but that she is being critical of something unsaid.

In Ex. 2 Beth is also less than enthusiastic, and while this could just be understood literally to be an understatement for dislike of the film, one must wonder why she is understating it rather than saying that it was awful. Alan could understand that she is being polite, and wishing not to offend his face by rejecting his view 'Was it exciting?' which expects the **preferred response** 'Yes.'

In Ex. 3, A. would understand that C. is being less than complimentary to a prize-winning novel, which one might expect to receive praise, and so A. could interpret the act to mean that C. is being critical, but does not wish to sound negative, which might offend A.'s face. And in Ex. 4, by being less critical than might have been expected, the speaker is being complimentary about the price of the theater ticket. Interpreting this last would depend on a shared understanding that theaters are costly venues.

See also **Face threats: recognize**; the other **Politeness indirection** tactics; **Social convention of quantity**

Further reading   Brown and Levinson (1987); Clark (1979)

POLITENESS INDIRECTION: USE IRONY

Task

To perform an F.T.A. so as to save both C.'s and A.'s face by offering an ironic communication.

Description

One way to make an imposition on someone, without loss of face to either party, is to hint indirectly at it, by using irony. This could cause the other person to recognize that the act may be an indirect one, with some other meaning than its surface suggests, and hence that it is an F.T.A., as in

Ex. 1 [after someone has made a mistake] That's brilliant!

Ex. 2 [when someone has put C. in an awful situation] This isn't my idea of heaven!

Ex. 3 [on receiving a student's grubby essay] What a beautifully presented assignment!

Persuasive value

Irony is a difficult communicative act, and depends for its recognition on the other person sharing the ideas, attitudes, etc., of the user. But if it is recognized, then it will be seen as violating the maxim of quality by not telling the truth but stating the opposite of the truth. In the preceding examples the irony is fairly obvious. On noting it, A.s should consider why it is being offered, and one possibility is that it is a disguised F.T.A.

In Ex. 1, it is a disguised criticism of the person who made the mistake. And by using an exclamation as the kind of expression, C. is able to let off steam and express feelings, all indirectly, and so in a face-saving way.

In Ex. 2, C. is also offering a disguised criticism, in this case disguising the attribution of responsibility for the awful situation; that is, C. leaves unexpressed that anyone might have caused the situation, and so does more to save the face of A., if in fact A. did set up the situation.

In Ex. 3, the disguised criticism could well fail, since it is likely that the faculty member who receives the assignment and the student who submits are very likely not to share standards of beautiful presentation. Irony here is likely to fail, unless the tone of voice was strongly ironic, and the student could well respond:

Ex. 4 Thank you.

See also; the other **Politeness indirection tactics**; **Social convention of quality**

Further reading   Brown and Levinson (1987); Clark (1979)

POLITENESS INDIRECTION: USE METAPHOR

Task

To perform an F.T.A. so as to save both C.'s and A.'s face by offering a metaphorical communication.

Description

One way to make an imposition on someone, without loss of face to either party, is to hint indirectly at it, by using a **metaphor**. This could cause the other person to recognize that the act may be an indirect one, with some other meaning than its surface suggests, and hence that it is an F.T.A., as in

Ex. 1 She's a real pig.

Ex. 2 He's an artist about his clothes.

Ex. 3 Bill is a virtuoso performer with women.

Ex. 4 That rings no bells with me.

Persuasive value

Using metaphors violates the maxim of quality in being not the literal truth. If A. notices this, and considers why the metaphor is being used, one reason could be that the act is a disguised, indirect, F.T.A.

In Ex. 1, the metaphor 'pig' is a word with negative associations, and A. could understand that what is being said here is a criticism. It is not hard to see it as a criticism, so it is not much of a disguise, but what is disguised is what exactly is being criticized. Is it the woman's eating habits, or some specific meanness, or her general nastiness? By leaving this unclear, the speaker has left him- or herself a face-saving escape route if the act meets with antagonism: if this occurred, C. could continue with 'But I just meant that she was unhelpful when I asked her to get me a coffee.'

In Ex. 2, by using the metaphor of the 'artist,' which could be either praise or criticism, depending on how C. and A. view a man's concern with his clothes, C. here too saves face if A. rejects it as criticism.

In Ex. 3, the metaphor of the musical performer leaves vague just what it is that Bill does with women, and so it leaves unclear just what act C. means to perform. If it is a criticism, it is well disguised.

In Ex. 4, C. is admitting that he or she cannot remember anything of what A. has just spoken about. But rather than just state this bluntly, the metaphor is used. It is useful as a way of avoiding stating a fault in oneself, a bad memory in this case, and as phrased here, suggests that it may be A.'s fault in saying something which does not 'ring any bells' in C.'s mind.

See also **Face threats: recognize**; the other **Politeness indirection** tactics; **Social convention of quality**

Further reading   Brown and Levinson (1987); Clark (1979)

POLITENESS INDIRECTION: USE RHETORICAL QUESTION

Task

To perform an F.T.A. so as to save both C.'s and A.'s face by offering a rhetorical question.

Description

One way to make an imposition on someone, without loss of face to either party, is to hint indirectly at it by using a rhetorical question. This could cause the other person to recognize that the act may be an indirect one, with some other meaning than its surface suggests, and hence that it is an F.T.A., as in

Ex. 1 How many times do I have to tell you to scrape the plates?

Ex. 2 How was I supposed to know you meant it for supper?

Ex. 3 Did she once offer to help with my exams?

Ex. 4 Now just why would I do that?

Persuasive value

Using rhetorical questions violates the maxim of quality which requires people to be sincere, and to say what they mean. When, therefore, someone asks a question with no intention that it should be answered, then it could be assumed that something else is happening, indirectly.

In Ex. 1, the speaker not only asks a rhetorical question, but uses one which contains the direct face-threatening act—telling A. to scrape the plates. There could be no mistaking that act, and A. should realize that the rhetorical form is there to indicate feelings of annoyance that this request has had to be repeated.

In Ex. 2, the speaker is responding to some attack on his or her behavior—probably eating something which was meant for supper. In order to save face, he or she defends the act by a disguised attack, asking this rhetorical question and so suggesting that it is A.'s fault for not making the situation clear.

In Ex. 3, the speaker is offering a criticism, and its indirectness, though slight, is meant to soften the bluntness of its meaning, which is 'She never offered to help with my exams.'

In Ex. 4, the words 'now just' are the only sign that shows this is a rhetorical rather than a real question, and that it is meant to be defensive in response to an F.T.A. They could, however, be missed, and the question taken literally, and answered, thus defeating the purpose.

Rhetorical questions are dangerous communications, because they can often be unrecognized, and responded to, thus taking control of the communication away from the speaker.

See also **Face threats: recognize**; the other **Politeness indirection** tactics; **Questions: rhetorical; Social convention of quality**

Further reading Brown and Levinson (1987); Clark (1979)

POLITENESS INDIRECTION: USE TAUTOLOGY

Task

To perform an F.T.A. so as to save both C.'s and A.'s face by using tautology.

Description

One way to make an imposition on someone, without loss of face to either party, is to hint indirectly at it by using a tautology. This could cause the other person to recognize that the act may be an indirect one, with some other meaning than its surface suggests, and hence that it is an F.T.A. Tautologies in this case are unnecessary repetitions of something, as in

Ex. 1 Your pyjamas belong in the drawer marked pyjamas.

Ex. 2 Alan: My son Peter has just bent the fender on my car again.
      John: Boys will be boys.

In Ex. 1 the statement is so obvious it is not worth saying, unless something else is intended by it, while in Ex. 2 the folk-saying is also too obvious.

Persuasive value

In saying such obvious things as these, and so breaking both the maxim of quantity by saying too little, and the convention that what is communicated must be tellable, C. must mean to do something else when offering Examples 1 and 2. A sensible guess would be that it is an F.T.A. being offered indirectly.

In working out what F.T.A. is meant by Ex. 1, A. could consider the options: is C. saying that he or she has just marked a drawer 'pyjamas' and is telling this information to A.? If A. knows that this could not be so because he or she knows that the drawer has long been so marked, and if A. considers that the person offering the statement is a mother, and knows from experience that mothers might be concerned with putting things away tidily, then it would not be far-fetched to interpret the statement as a **command/request**. Its obliqueness should be appreciated, when A. thinks of the range of blunt command/requests that could have been performed.

In working out what F.T.A. is meant by Ex. 2, Alan has a rather harder task because of the generality of John's statement, and could find it difficult to see that it is meant to be a reply. The folk-saying has a meaning, of course, which is something like 'That is the kind of things boys do and you need to expect it,' but people do not usually work out the meanings of such well-known sayings, and for Alan to interpret it could therefore be a problem. And he has then to think why John is offering such an obvious, tautological, statement at that point, and hence what F.T.A. is being indirectly offered. One possibility is that he might remember the use of such folk-sayings to round off a discussion, as also in

Ex. 3 A: . . . and so we found ourselves at last at home.
      B: That's life.

Ex. 4 A: . . . and they all lived happily ever after.
      B: It's the same the whole world over.

If this seems likely to be the meaning of John's act in Ex. 2, then John is performing a terminating act, which is certainly likely to be an F.T.A. if Alan wanted to continue telling about his son and the car. It also shows a lack of interest on John's part, and this too is an F.T.A.: showing boredom.

See also **Face threats: recognize**; the other **Politeness indirection** tactics; **Social convention of quantity**; **Tellable topic: choose**

Further reading   Brown and Levinson (1987); Clark (1979)

POLITENESS INDIRECTION: USE VAGUENESS

Task

To perform an F.T.A. so as to save both C.'s and A.'s face by offering a high degree of vagueness.

Description

One way to make an imposition on someone, without loss of face to either party, is to hint indirectly at it by using a high degree of vagueness. This could cause the other person to recognize that the act may be an indirect one, with some other meaning than its surface suggests, and hence that it is an F.T.A., as in

Ex. 1 Someone has left the door open again.

Ex. 2 Mary is very politically astute.

Ex. 3 John certainly knows how to use persuasion.

Ex. 4 People who live in glass houses should not throw stones.

Ex. 5 This grass needs to be cut.

Persuasive value

In being highly vague, C. leaves a good deal to be interpreted by A. In so doing, the maxim of manner, which states that one should be clear and precise, is broken. A. may just think that C. is being vague and a poor communicator, but may also try to see if there is any reason for the vagueness. One such reason is performing an indirect F.T.A.

In Ex. 1, C. is vague about who might have committed the fault of leaving the door open, and hence modifies the criticism and saves the face of the person concerned.

In Ex. 2, C. makes what could amount to a vague comment about Mary. It may be that its vagueness is not noticed, and it is just taken as a straightforward comment, but in fact it leaves unclear just whether being 'politically astute' is praise or criticism. If it were meant as criticism, it may be done deliberately vaguely in order to leave C.'s options open in case A. objected to it. This would save C.'s face.

In Ex. 3, exactly the same thing occurs; it is just mentioned here to remind readers of this book that while persuasion is a means of achieving one's purposes in communication, having a reputation for being good at it is regarded as a criticism. One could, of course, argue that anyone whose persuasiveness is as noticeable as John's is not in fact a good persuader.

In Ex. 4, C. offers one of the many **proverbs** which incorporate an attitude of criticism, and uses it as an indirect criticism. By using the proverb, with its aura of general community acceptance, C. implies that anyone in the community could make this criticism, and that it is not just C.'s individually.

In Ex. 5, C. makes an apparently general comment, and leaves it to others to decide if it is meant as a request.

See also **Face threats: recognize**; the other **Politeness indirection** tactics; **Social conventions of manner**

Further reading   Brown and Levinson (1987); Clark (1979)

POSTPONEMENT: EXTRA CLAUSE

Tasks

To indicate a degree of personal distance between C. and a text.
To give authority to an opinion.

Description

There are various grammatical ways in which C. can postpone mention of something by prefacing it with an extra clause. For example,

Ex. 1 It doesn't matter//how she does it.

Ex. 2 It's a good thing//that she is away.

This extra clause includes a word like 'it' to stand for the main clause, then follows the gist of what is to be said. Putting the gist so late is an alternative to, for example,

Ex. 3 How she does it doesn't matter.

Ex. 4 That she is away is a good thing.

Persuasive value

1 The effect of leaving the gist of the sentence's meaning until so late is to present it as less urgent than matters which come earlier. This happens

because of the general assumption that first things come first; A. will read with that in mind.

2 It appears to create more distance between the C. and the matters mentioned because C. takes the trouble to construct a form which delays them.

3 It also works to incorporate C.'s opinion of the matter before the matter itself is mentioned, as in

Ex. 5 It is a fact that our policy is working well.

contrasted with

Ex. 6 Our policy is working well.

This not only makes A. recognize that any resistance to the 'policy is working well' will involve opposing C.'s opinion 'that it is a fact,' but also gives time for that recognition to be absorbed before A. knows what the opinion is.

4 The extra-clause formulation usefully allows C. to issue covert commands, as in

Ex. 7 It is good practice to check your sources.

which means 'check your sources.'

5 Most importantly, in some cases, the extra clause can suggest that there is a generally agreed view of a matter, and hence that A. should agree to it, as in

Ex. 8 It has been said that all men of fortune are in search of a wife.

Ex. 9 It is unlikely that the meeting will run late.

Such constructions would be more likely to receive assent than just the statement 'All men of fortune are in search of a wife,' or 'The meeting will not run late.'

See also the other **Postponement** tactics

Further reading Leech and Svartvik (1975); Nash (1980); Quirk, Greenbaum, Leech, and Svartvik (1985)

POSTPONEMENT: SPLIT SENTENCES

Task

To emphasize a point in a sentence.

Description

There are various grammatical ways in which C. can postpone mention of something by splitting the sentence. One such way is to use the construction 'It' + some form of the verb to be + the main point to be emphasized, followed by a relative clause, as in 'It + is + the Smith Report + that makes it clear.'

Ex. 1 It is the Smith Report that makes it clear.

Ex. 2 It was the letter she found annoying.

A split in a sentence can be used to emphasize any part of sentence structure:

(a) the subject, as in 'It was Peter who saw it first.' (instead of 'Peter saw it first.');
(b) the object, as in 'It is the main letter we have here.' (instead of 'We have the main letter.');
(c) the complement, as in 'It was as a lawyer that she wrote.' (instead of 'She wrote as a lawyer.');
(d) adverbials, as in 'It is on the client's behalf that we must act.' (instead of 'We must act on the client's behalf.').

It is best used as a tactic at the revision stage of written communication.

Persuasive value

1 As the examples show, using a split-sentence construction means that C. can unambiguously emphasize any point in a sentence. Its particular value is that it does not require the use of a different word, or any additional words, both of which might introduce unwanted ideas into the communication, as in 'It is the excellent/long-awaited Smith Report that makes it clear,' or 'It is the latest instruction that makes it clear.' It emphasizes solely by arrangement of items.

2 Used in quantity split sentences impart an air of impersonality, coolness of attitude, and serious professionalism to a text, particularly when associated with relatively abstract word choices.

See also **Information: add**; the other **Postponement** tactics

Further reading Leech and Svartvik (1975); Nash (1980); Quirk, Greenbaum, Leech, and Svartvik (1985)

POSTPONEMENT: 'THERE'

Tasks

To emphasize a matter.
To show distance between C. and the matter.
To give authority to an opinion.

Description

There are various ways in which a C. can postpone mention of something. One such way is to use 'there,' as in 'There' + inverted order of the subject and verb of the main part of the sentence:

Ex. 1 There is a report still to be done.

instead of

Ex. 2 The report is still to be done.

It could be paraphrased as 'There exists a situation in which "the report is still to be done".' It contrasts with the second version, which could be paraphrased as 'C. is of the opinion that the report is still to be done.'

Persuasive value

The word 'there' is much used in **proverbs** and proverbial sayings, which record standard social beliefs, as in

Ex. 3 There's a time and a place for everything.

Ex. 4 There is good and bad in everyone.

Ex. 5 There is no peace for the wicked.

Its use for social platitudes gives the structure an aura of social authority, and this can be usefully transferred to any matter which is put into this form by anyone.

   The platitude form also works to distance C. from what he or she is uttering: it appears to stand alone, without author, as if C. is just a mouthpiece rather than the one who chose to insert the matter into the communication at that time. This may be a useful tactic if the matter is one which people will not want to hear, as in

Ex. 6 There is need for further discussion on this.

rather than

Ex. 7 I think we need further discussion on this.

or if there is a difficult social act to perform, like making an accusation, as in

Ex. 8 There is something wrong here.

rather than

Ex. 9 I think something is wrong here.

Further reading Leech and Svartvik (1975); Nash (1980); Quirk, Greenbaum, Leech, and Svartvik (1985)

PRAISE: USE

Tasks

To make another person feel good.
To present oneself as generous spirited.

Description

Praise is the expression of approval or admiration of someone or something which is thereby marked as exceptional or deserving of special attention.

Persuasive value

To praise others shows the self as generous in spirit, which suggests that one can be trusted. It can make those praised feel both pleased with themselves and pleased with C. for recognizing their good qualities. It creates a special bond, on which a persuader can build.

However, the act is not inevitably one with good effects.
1 The reason for which the praise is given should be one that the other agrees is praiseworthy. It should be 'Your assignment was very interesting,' not 'You were clever to avoid doing that awful job.' If the praiser knows the other person strongly believes in some quality, the best praise for that person would be to declare that he or she has shown that particular quality.
2 Praisers should not present themselves as superior when doing the act, not 'As someone who got an A myself, I think it is wonderful that you managed a B.'
3 Some praise is double-edged (i.e. it serves two goals): it praises and it notes an error at the same time, as in 'It was honest of you to admit to that mistake.'
4 Faint praise is no praise at all, it should be whole-hearted or not given at all. Not 'You did rather well' or 'You did rather well, considering it isn't a particular skill of yours,' but 'You did very well indeed there.'
5 Praise can be given as if from the giver, or can be reported as coming from others. Expressions of praise can differ in value quite markedly, as in:

Ex. 1 I think you were great today.

Ex. 2 People thought you were great today.

Ex. 3 Other people thought you were great today.

N.B.   If others are present while the praise takes place, it can make them uncomfortable, wondering whether to join in (and they might disagree with the praise). It can also make them feel they are being implicitly criticized for not being as good as the person praised. It may help to find a general praise for them all as well as the specific one for one of their number.

Further reading   Wierzbicka (1987)

PRAISING ANOTHER PERSON

Tasks

To give some praise to another person.
To make someone pleased with one, and with life.
To present oneself as generous natured.

Description

Praise can be addressed to the general nature of a person, or to his or her specific qualities. It can be given for actions, ideas, attitudes, personality, or character, etc. (i.e. for some matters which are within A.s control and some which are not). It may be given in public, before witnesses, or in private. Since praise is the articulation of something good about the person, it must be overt, and clearly recognizable as praise if it is to be effective.

Persuasive value

The usual intention when praising A. is to please that person, and so to make A. respond well to the praiser.
1 In order to do this, the praise should be about something A. holds to be important, and this can be judged from previous experience of A.'s likes and dislikes. If, for example, A. were a serious businessman, he might well not care about his good looks and not be pleased to be praised as handsome. Equally, an art student might not see it as praise that she has neat handwriting. Much so-called praise is about qualities that the praiser, and not the recipient of the praise, finds important, so it fails in its purpose.
2 It is usually true that general praise is held in lower regard than specific. So telling A. that she is a truly wonderful human being, or that she is the envy of her friends could have little impact on A. One reason for this is that such praise is easily given, so easily that the first example is a **cliché**. Most people have memories of ritualized and empty praise, thanking hosts for splendid evenings, thanking the outgoing treasurer of a society for all that heroic effort. Another problem with it is that it can be too fulsome—or at least for some groups or cultures it seems so (British and Australian societies tend to interpret mild praise as true, and high praise as untrue, where

American society takes high praise as the norm). If it seems too much of a compliment (and makes the recipient uncomfortable) or out of all proportion to the matter praised, as in

Ex. 1 I just love the way you pour out that water, straight into the glass, and not a drop spilt.

it fails in most of its intended effects.
3 Another problem with general praise is that it does not show any specific knowledge of A. and so arises from ignorance and can be dismissed. Contrast the power of such specific and appropriate praise as

Ex. 2 This photo is excellent, well up to your usual standard, and I tell you it is better than the ones I saw in that exhibition. I thought when I saw them, Ruth's photos are better than this. Your composition is better, and so is your light and shade thingamajig, you know, . . . I've forgotten the name.

The last part of this example, which shows the praiser as not too knowledgeable about photography, weakens part of the effect of the praise. While A. should appreciate that the praise is based on interest in A., and it intimates that C. thinks about A. when they are not together (it is always good for the ego to know this is happening), A. might worry about being valued as good when the valuer knows little about the matter. It would be a sign of poorly designed praise if the art student complimented on her handwriting replied:

Ex. 3 I don't care if you do like my writing or not, you know nothing about it.

4 The relative status of the praiser and person praised can also have an impact on the effectiveness of the praise. While it is proper for a higher-status person to praise one of lower status, and such praise is highly regarded, it is not so good to receive if the high status is too high: for example, for the President of a company at its annual meeting to praise the office juniors for their contribution can be taken as just a duty statement, and not really meant praise, mainly because it is built on ignorance. Conversely, it is also not proper for a much lower-status person to praise a much higher one; it can appear impertinent if the office junior thanked the President for his efforts. Praise needs a sensitive awareness of the roles of praiser and praise, if it is to have the pleasing effect intended.

Further reading   Antaki (1988); Argyle (1975)

PREFERRED RESPONSE

Task

To respond relevantly and with due recognition of the initiator's goals.

Description

The second part of an **exchange of speech** presents a restricted set of options for the second speaker. This set can be divided into preferred and dispreferred options. A preferred response is one which responds to the form and subject matter of the first part, and acknowledges the aim of the first speaker. So, for example, if the first speaker asks 'What time is it?' a preferred response should tell the time, or quickly show the listener cannot help. Note that a negative response offered neatly and efficiently is a preferred response, though it does not do what the initiator wants: it is perfectly acceptable because it responds relevantly and as closely to what the initiator wants as the responder can.

Preferred responses are relatively easy to produce, because they can use the assumptions and word formations of the initial move. Dispreferred responses are harder to produce since they require a new form, of both grammar and words, and they also need to create a link with the initial move since they are not echoing it. Moreover, since they will come as a surprise for the initiator, their unpredictability needs to be reduced so that they can be understood. And, of course, since they break the **cooperative principle** they may need justification.

Favorite devices for justifying a dispreferred response are:

(a) using hesitation, as a sign that the unexpected will follow;
(b) providing explanations for producing the dispreferred option;
(c) offering an apology;
(d) recognizing the worth of the initial move, even though the second speaker cannot respond well to it.

Persuasive value

1 Because preference is socially and cognitively powerful, those who initiate can exert strong influence on others to accept or agree with what they offer. Even though responders might have mental reservations about doing so, in giving the preferred option they commit themselves to what they say, and will have to stick by it.

See also **Preferred response: types**; **Presequences**

Further reading   Bilmes (1988); Pomerantz (1984); Sacks (1987)

PREFERRED RESPONSE: TYPES

Task

To measure a response as it fits the aims of the persons seeking it.

Description

The range of preferred response types is measured according to how much or how little they respond to the aim of the initial communicator.

Persuasive value

Most speakers know from experience how to rate responses from preferred to dispreferred, and so can determine how persuasive they have been as they invite, request, etc. In order from most successful (i.e. most preferred) to least, the following responses to Ex. 1 may be useful.

Ex. 1 Bill: Have you seen my pen anywhere?

1 The best response would be something like 'Borrow mine.' Its strength is that it goes beyond just responding to the question, to understanding the reason for it (Bill needs a pen), and responds by supplying the perceived need. (Note: it might be inappropriate: Bill might want his own pen for some reasons, but the response would be seen as very 'preferred'.)
2 The second-best response might be 'There is a spare pen over there.' This also goes beyond a simple response and helps Bill fulfill his need for a pen, but requires that he do something himself to get it.
3 A good response might be 'Mary has it,' which answers the question, though does not go behind it to Bill's aims in asking it. It is specified enough to enable Bill to take the next step in finding his pen. Contrast this with the following.
4 'Mary I think had it, though it might have been Fred.' This, while it supplies as much information as the speaker has, is too unspecific to be useful. If this is the best that one can do it might be more efficient to respond with just 'Sorry no, I haven't seen it.' It is too tantalizing to be what Bill wishes to hear.
5 'No, I haven't. Is it urgent?' This is efficiently negative, and the first part fits as a preferred response. The second part however is more debatably useful, since it does not affect in any way Bill's aim of finding his pen. It serves as sociability though, and as a way of sympathizing with Bill's loss may appeal to him as a friendly gesture.
6 'Yes, but I can't remember where.' This may begin with a positive sign, but the rest of the speech makes it clear that it is not at all positive as a help to Bill. It is annoying because it gives the appearance of being informative while being nothing of the kind, and like the instance in point 4 is tantalizing.
7 The worst response of all is silence. Provided that the initiator can be sure that the communication was heard, it will never be taken as no communication at all, but rather it will be recognized as a complete absence of sociability.

Further reading   Bilmes (1988); Pomerantz (1984); Sacks (1987)

PREPOSED ADJECTIVES

Task

To add qualities to the representation of a matter.

Description

Adjectives are words which firmly attribute qualities to a thing, as in 'the good book.' If produced in such forms as 'the book is good,' or 'the book is useless,' they make the attribution of the quality open for debate.

Persuasive value

Adjective placement before rather than after the word it applies to causes a significant difference in persuasive effect. For example,

Ex. 1 This tentative proposal suggests that we should . . .;

is contrasted with using an adjective placed in post position:

Ex. 2 This proposal is tentative; it states that we should . . .

Preposing the adjective can have two persuasive effects:
1 A.s pay less attention to the judgment 'tentative' because it is not grammatically emphasized.
2 In speech A.s who wish to object to the meaning expressed in a preposed adjective will have to do so by formulating an objection from scratch, without being able to copy the form used by C.
Compare the ease of response in the following response:

Ex. 3 A: This proposal is tentative.
      B: No, it isn't.

with the extra effort required for the response in

Ex. 4 A: This tentative proposal suggests that we should . . .
      B: But it isn't tentative.

Ex. 4 uses one clause to express two views ('that the proposal is tentative' and 'that it suggests something'), so forcing B to consider quickly whether he or she objects to either or both. If B wishes to object to the first, its early placement in the sentence could make B's objection an interruption, because there is no natural clause break after 'tentative.'

Further, objections to such adjectives sound serious because B must repeat the word and stress it. A potential objector may decide the point is not worth the extra attention this will attract.

Note that the more information there is in the noun phrase after the preposed adjective the harder it is both to formulate an objection to some single item within it, and to make an objection about it, and the more serious such an objection will appear. For example,

Ex. 5 A: This tentative proposal about the sales campaign that the marketing division has produced . . .
B: But the proposal isn't tentative.

In speech interaction timing is very important: if one misses the right time to say something it is difficult to turn back the interaction, and restore the right conditions for the speech act. Here B's objection is too late, will draw extra attention to itself, and attract social opprobrium, and this may inhibit others from accepting B's point.

Further reading Leech and Svartvik (1975); Quirk, Greenbaum, Leech, and Svartvik (1985)

PRESEQUENCES

Task

To prevent loss of face when offering an invitation, request, etc.

Description

Some speech acts, for example, requests, invitations, and offers, and even some questions, could meet with an adverse response. To prevent this, C.s often preface such acts with a presequence designed to establish whether the act is likely to meet with acceptance.

Ex. 1 A: Can I ask you a question?
B: Well I am rather busy right now.
A: That's O.K. It can wait.

Ex. 2 A: Are you doing anything tonight?
B: I'm going out to dinner, why?
A: Oh nothing; I just wondered if you were going to be at home.

Persuasive value

Receiving a refusal would present problems of face loss for the one performing such acts, and these are lessened if a presequence tests the water first. For example, if in Ex. 1 A had originally planned to ask B to go to the theater, by using this presequence that invitation can be left unsaid, and so no face loss is experienced over a refusal. A can, as here, downgrade the invitation to a query about what B would be doing.

However, presequences are usually recognized for what they are, so the other person usually knows that some potential invitation or request is in the offing, and that C. is fearful of face loss about it. If on hearing what C. says next A.s can guess what the missing act was, and if they themselves would not see this as a worrying matter of face loss, they will see C. as more diffident than necessary, and as very different from themselves.

Taking advantage of a presequence to avoid an unwelcome invitation or request may rebound to the inconvenience of the person doing so, as in

Ex. 3 A: Are you doing anything tomorrow night?
       B: Er, yes, I'm going to see Susan in the hospital.
       A: Oh, that's a pity. I have a spare ticket for the theater I thought
          you might like.

Unless B is a quick thinker and can ditch the visit to Susan without seeming callous, he or she would lose the opportunity of a good invitation. If B had any suspicion that the invitation or request might be good, he or she would be wise to use only the vaguest of excuses: not 'I'm going to see Susan in the hospital' but rather 'Well, I was thinking of doing some work.' This could easily be adjusted either way according to whether the invitation or request is good or bad.

Further reading   Brown and Levinson (1987); Davidson (1984)

PRINCIPLE OF LEAST EFFORT

Tasks

To save oneself energy as one produces a communication.
To save energy as one interprets a communication.

Description

A basic interactive principle is that all participants will take the route of least cognitive effort, if at all possible, as they communicate or interpret others' communications. What this means is that they will seek to reduce the cognitive exercise involved in the work of communicating—selecting words, grammatical patterns, choosing examples, ordering ideas, etc. So C.s will use any **clichés** or familiar grammatical routines that come to mind unless they seem very wrong, and will imitate what they remember of the style of others in performing the same communicative task.

The principle is equally important in the reception of communications, where it encourages people to lean on any interpretive guidance C. uses, and to be content to find only an approximate match in their experience for what C. seems to be saying, and hence only half absorb what C. has said. It also means they will be less receptive to new ideas, words, or grammar because these require extra cognitive effort to handle.

Persuasive value

1 It is this principle that produces the **preferred response** to **initiating moves**, as in

Ex. 1 A: It's a good company.
       B: Yes, it is . . . [but then] well, it's not bad. . . . I suppose it depends what you mean by 'good.'

2 If C. needs to make an original or provocative representation if it can appear to be familiar; by the use of familiar language and simple grammar it is quite likely to be accepted.

3 If in addition C. represents the opposed view in unfamiliar language and complex grammar, A.s will want to agree in rejecting this view because it is too hard to follow:

Ex. 2 There are only ten people whose jobs would be affected by my proposal; whereas the Accountancy Department in its most recently revised scheme suggests that some 0.65 percent of the workforce of 5,000 could face some degree of jeopardy in employment security under its 'Forward Management Plan.'

4 If C. provides the cognitive effort of describing or naming or explaining something that A.s need to articulate themselves, and does so in terms which A.s could themselves use quite comfortably, C.'s version is likely to be accepted, repeated, and become the standard rendering. (It is this approach to the principle that advertisers use in producing their slogans, so that they become adopted and widely used.)

Further reading   Bilmes (1988); Leech (1983); Sacks (1987)

PROMISE

Task

To declare a commitment to undertake some action.

Description

A promise is a commitment which encourages A. to believe that the thing promised will occur. It is important that the terms of the promise are made clear: a vague promise is no promise at all.

Persuasive value

1 Promising as an act assumes that the thing to be done is one A. would be pleased to have happen. This may be done deliberately, knowing it is a

completely false assumption. A mistaken promise is difficult to deal with because A. has to correct the false assumption and also thank C. for his or her good intentions. So this kind of promise can create a good deal of social awkwardness for A., which may be to C.'s advantage. As in:

Ex. 1 I promise that I shall go to the meeting on your behalf.

where A. does not want C. to go to the meeting. It may prove so difficult for A. to escape from this situation that it will be allowed to dictate the situation, and C. will end up at the meeting though A. is unhappy about it.
2 A promise assumes there is doubt that C. can or will do something, and at the same time it removes the doubt. But it may cause confusion if in fact there was no doubt, until the promise was made, as in

Ex. 2 A: I promise I'll be teaching my class as usual at 5 P.M.
      B: But, er, surely you were scheduled to do that anyway?

While this promise may arise because of something B does not know, perhaps that A has toothache, it might also be the case that A makes this promise solely in order to worry B, or to introduce the topic 'why I might not be able to teach tonight,' so that A can become the center of attention.
3 A promise assumes that what is promised is not to C.'s advantage, but meets some need of A.'s. 'I promise I'll bring those apples for you.' In so representing the thing to be done, C. can put A. (falsely?) under an obligation, and could make use of this later.
4 A promise can indicate that C. will personally do the thing, or that he or she will take steps to bring it about. In this latter case, a much weaker promise, A. is left not knowing precisely what C. is personally committed to, and what will depend on others. Confusion can arise about responsibility if the promise is not fulfilled. Promises of this kind should be clarified when they are first made.
5 Some promises are forced, after such pressures as compliments or reminders of mutual obligations. But even is this is so, if C. promises, then it is a commitment and must be fulfilled.

Further reading   Mulholland (1991); Wierzbicka (1987)

PROVERBS

Tasks

To close off discussion, have the last word, summarize.
To adduce general social support for an idea.
To set or change the agenda.

Description

Proverbs are sayings made authoritative by frequent use and acceptance by a culture, and thereby considered to be truths to be heeded.

Persuasive value

1 Using a proverb can act to close off a discussion, even if others wish to continue, if it appears neatly to encapsulate the gist of the discussion.

Ex. 1 This case, then, in effect, is an instance of putting the horse before the cart.

Ex. 2 Well that's just a matter of too many cooks spoiling the broth, isn't it?

2 The proverb's interpretation of the interaction, which is C.'s version of it, may become the generally accepted summary of the event, so this is a powerful way to influence the agenda.

Using a proverb supports an argument with the weight of its cultural authority, and so inclines people to accept the argument or else to face arguing against their own cultural conditioning.

3 There are proverb-like sayings, for example famous quotations and pithy epigrams, whose source is nameable (e.g. those by Shakespeare or La Rochefoucauld), which can be incorporated into an interaction. They are unlike true proverbs in that their power rests entirely either on their own merits as representations of cultural truths or on the reputation of the author. In the latter case they have a quite different effect when introduced into a communication.

(a) They present C. as a cultured person with a good memory, and this in itself may help his or her case.

(b) On the whole, however, they are not such weighty supports for an idea unless A. agrees about the authority of the proverb writer. But even then they have less power than general proverbs because they clearly derive from a single author's opinion. Even Shakespeare's quoted views can be questioned more easily than those of the whole culture.

Further reading   Lakoff and Johnson (1980)

PUNS

Tasks

To lighten the mood of a communication.
To enhance the social relationship with A.
To form a group from those present.

Description

A pun is a play on words, and is possible in any language which contains words which resemble one another in shape or sound, called 'homonyms,' as in 'bear' and 'bare,' and words of very different shape which resemble one another in meaning, called 'synonyms,' as in 'girl' and 'woman.' These differences in shape and meaning can be deliberately played with, or they can occur unconsciously in a text. That is, they may be used to some communicative purpose, or they may occur because memory has brought some words to the surface for possible use and they escape the C.'s control and are produced without due care.

Persuasive value

Many people dislike puns, whether consciously or unconsciously used, and two main reasons are usually given:

(a) They show the pun-maker to be attending only to the surface of what is being communicated and not to its substance.
(b) Importantly, they remind people that language is unstable, and is not an objective representation of the world, but a set of idiosyncratic ways of recording the world, and hence liable to error and bias. Puns remind people that they are at the mercy of word manipulators, and this can perturb or render them uncomfortable.

To notice and interpret puns needs close attention, and so they can require people to concentrate. They demand hard work, and if after working hard at the pun people find the meaning of the words involved was not worth the effort, they will be made antagonistic. On the other hand, puns which provide richness of meaning, or which provoke people to an unusual but helpful way of considering something will be praised.

Good puns are actually enjoyed, giving pleasure as people recognize the skill involved and the useful purpose to which it has been put. Their appreciation is rather like that of enjoying good music or art as skilled endeavors which can prove rewarding and enlightening.

See also **Humor**; **Jokes**; **Jokes: types**

Further reading Redfern (1984)

QUESTIONING

Task

To ask a question.

Description

Any question makes an intrusion into the life of another person. It raises some topic, and more, it requires the other person to produce a response on this topic. This may not be to their liking, it may be difficult, or too personal, etc. Questions can be asked as part of **sociable language**, or in any other part of an interaction. They can occur in speech or in writing.

Persuasive value

Even the standard inquiry made to a stranger, just to be sociable, 'And what do you do for a living?' is now, in a period of mass unemployment, potentially a social embarrassment.

One problem with questions for those who have to answer them is that there is a social expectation that A.s will respond in the way predicted by the form of the question, and by the apparent aim of the questioner. It is usually obvious what answer is wanted, and A.s feel some pull to provide it. If they do not wish to, or cannot, then they will feel they have done something less than socially desirable.

This compulsion can be made worse for the person addressed if the question is not of the open kind, as in 'Have you any children?' but is of the closed kind, either relatively closed, as in 'How many children do you have?' or the absolutely closed, as in 'Are your children at school?' People with no children would find it difficult to extract themselves from this last, and whatever their response it would draw attention to their lack of children, and in a way that makes it a negative rather than a positive thing. And questioning can be much more intrusive and difficult than this, at job interviews, medical consultations, etc.

Asking a question makes a presumption that the other person would not volunteer the material without being asked. This can be annoying to those who were just about to supply it anyway, and are unable to do so freely, or to appear to be volunteering it. The question makes it appear that they are having it brought out against their will.

Questioning places the persons questioned in such a position that whatever they do after the question will be presumed to be their answer: there is no avoiding this. Silence, or changing the subject, or joking, or leaving the room, etc., would all be taken as some form of answer, and interpreted accordingly.

In some circumstances it may be difficult to address a question to someone; for instance, it can be hard to ask a friend who has just had a hospital test for cancer what the result was: many people would feel it more tactful to wait until the information is volunteered. In other instances questioning is too difficult because it is left too 'late.' For example, a colleague assumes that one has some specific knowledge, and for various reasons one fails to question the assumption at the start, and after a time it is impossible to reveal one's basic ignorance and state, 'I'm sorry, I don't really know what you are referring to.'

In some cultures it is not acceptable to ask questions about certain matters at all, not just about such socially difficult subjects of death or religion, but even about relatively simple things like 'Where are you going?' which to a Tamil speaker is a rude inquiry about God's plans for his or her future.

See also; **Preferred response;** the other **Questions** tactics

Further reading Lakoff (1973); Larson (1968); Leech and Svartvik (1975); Schegloff (1980)

QUESTIONS: CLOSED

Task

To ask a question of A.

Description

There are two main kinds of direct questions: open or closed. Closed questions are offered in a form which constrains the answer to be 'yes' or 'no,' or 'maybe.' The form of the sentence is with the verb divided, with one part coming first, before the subject, and then the rest of the verb after the subject, as in

Ex. 1 Can you meet me on Friday?

Where the verb consists of only one word, as in the statements 'That is a good book,' or 'She swims in the summer,' they are converted into questions by putting the only verb before the subject, or adding the verb 'do,' as in:

Ex. 2 Is that a good book?

and

Ex. 3 Does she swim in the summer?

The form of these three questions expects the answer 'Yes.' The following versions all expect the answer 'No':

Ex. 4 Can't you meet me on Friday?

Ex. 5 Isn't that a good book?

Ex. 6 Doesn't she swim in the summer?

Persuasive value

The most obvious value is that closed questions appear to force A.s into one of only two positions, with a possible third if they can offer 'Maybe.'

A.s may not in fact answer 'Yes' or 'No,' or even 'Maybe,' but they know that they should, and so may feel compelled to apologize or explain if they produce another kind of answer. In some circumstances, as in law courts, any answer other than 'Yes' or 'No' will be seen as avoiding the question, and lawyers can be heard saying 'Just answer the question, yes or no.'

Closed questions assume that simple answers are possible, and this is sometimes not at all the case, yet just because it is assumed, people do answer simply, knowing all the time that what they have said is not the whole truth. They leave A. little opportunity to question one part of the question while accepting another, as in

Ex. 7 Do you say that you were responsible for introducing this new, and very inadequate, system into the company?

If A. wishes to object to the opinion that the system is inadequate, or to say that he or she introduced the system into a section but not into the whole company, or that others were involved in the decision to introduce the system, it is made very difficult to do so.

Closed questions make yet further impositions on A.s since they intro-duce topics which A. may not wish to have raised, yet is compelled to answer. So A. might find it uncomfortable to make any answer at all to Ex. 7 since the person who was actually responsible for the poor decision about the system is sitting opposite, and is A.'s boss.

As well as being impositions on A., closed questions also allow A.s to impose on C.s. C.s expect short answers to closed questions, and A.s can disconcert C.s by producing not only 'Yes' or 'No' but also a long expla-nation or excuse, etc.

See also **Questioning**; the other **Questions** tactics

Further reading   Lakoff (1973); Larson (1968); Leech and Svartvik (1975); Schegloff (1980)

QUESTIONS: NEGATIVE

Tasks

To guide A's response to a question.
To show an attitude of annoyance.

Description

There are various types of negative questions:
1 Where the verb is negated, as in

Ex. 1 Haven't you finished that essay yet?

2 Where the subject of the clause is negative, as in

Ex. 2 Does no-one want to go to the bar?

3 Where the object of the clause is negative, as in

Ex. 3 Is there nothing I can do about my grades?

4 Where an adverb phrase is negative, as in

Ex. 4 Are we never going to get our dinner?

There is also the closed question, one form of which predicts, and pressures A. to give, a negative answer, as in

Ex. 5 Does the mechanic have to charge so much for my car repairs?

Persuasive value

In each case, the question is asked with an assumption that the world is a negative sort of place, or that only bad things happen. So in Ex. 1, C. is grumbling about a situation in which things are not what he or she wants (that the essay writer is finished). In Ex. 2, C. is complaining about another bad situation, in which no one will go to the bar as he or she wishes. In Ex. 3, C. assumes that there is nothing that can be done about bad marks. In Ex. 4, C. thinks things are so bad he or she could starve. In Ex. 5, C. assumes that A. agrees in having a negative view of the world of car mechanics and their prices.

In a single instance of this kind, C. tries to set the agenda as negative, defeatist, even depressed; while by offering a series of instances of this kind, C. can succeed in making the whole interaction one of gloom.

Using negative questions of this kind also reveals that C. has strong feelings about something: negative questions can indicate attitudes of annoyance, anger, fear, etc. And this should be noted for persuasive purposes.

See also the other **Questions** tactics

Further reading   Leech and Svartvik (1975); Quirk, Greenbaum, Leech, and Svartvik (1985)

QUESTIONS: OPEN

Task

To ask a question of A.

Description

There are two main kinds of direct questions: open or closed. Some questions are completely open, and framed so broadly that they allow A.s to make any response they wish, as in

Ex. 1 Did you see the movie last night?

A.s could reply with a simple 'Yes' or 'No' or take up any of the topics raised—'seeing' as in 'I was listening to the radio,' or 'movie' as in 'Was it as good as they said?' or 'last night' as in 'We went out to dinner last night.'

Other open questions narrow the range of answers to some extent, for example those which begin with the 'wh' words—'who,' 'what,' 'when,' 'where,' and 'why.' These constrain the response to deal with at least one aspect of the topic, though the answerer can go on from there relatively freely, as in the exchange:

Ex. 2 A: Who were you with last night?
    B: Susan, but I wasn't really with her. We just met by accident at the theater.

Persuasive value

Although any act of questioning imposes constraints on A. to answer, open questions are the least constraining. They are worth using because it can be very illuminating to see what A. will produce when given a free choice. Closed questions get the answers they expect, but open questions get anything the listener wants to say. They therefore afford a glimpse into A.'s mind which might otherwise not be possible.

Closed questions often get brief answers, but open questions can produce lengthy accounts, in the course of which C.s can learn important things, things they could not have known otherwise. A closed question presupposes that C. already knows a good deal about some matter, and just wishes to have a detail clarified. On the other hand an open question can be asked in relative ignorance and be a valuable learning experience.

Open questions can be used to more than one listener, and can produce several answers from those present, and again C. may be pleasantly surprised by who answers and what is revealed.

See also **Questioning**; the other **Questions** tactics

Further reading Lakoff (1973); Larson (1968); Leech and Svartvik (1975); Schegloff (1980)

QUESTIONS: RHETORICAL

Task

To express strong feeling without specifying it.

Description

A rhetorical question is one apparently asked of another person, but neither expecting nor wanting an answer. It is distinguished from a real question in two ways: (a) by voice quality, in that its pitch range is usually wider (e.g. though it rises at the end of the question like other questions, it either starts from a lower point or rises to a greater height); and (b) by being a **cliché**, or a familiar routine given general recognition as the rhetorical variety of questions.

It mainly acts as a strong assertion, as in 'What do I care?' The forms it takes produce different results:

1 If it is positive in form, as in

Ex. 1 Is the government's failure something we should think about?

it should be understood as incorporating the answer 'no,' in this example, 'no, we should not think about . . .'
2 If it begins with a 'wh-' word, as in

Ex. 2 What can I do about it?

it incorporates a negative interpretation, as in 'I should do nothing about it.'
3 If it is negative in form, as in

Ex. 3 Surely it is no business of ours to pay this?

it should be understood as having the answer 'Yes, we should question whether it is our business.'

Persuasive value

1 Rhetorical questions affect A. as being indications of strong feelings, but do so without naming what the feeling is—whether anger, bitterness, irritation—and without focussing it on any specific person. They therefore allow C. some useful flexibility, leaving his or her options open, as in:

Ex. 4 A: The boss says we should not go home early today.
       B: Who cares?

which is a non-specific resistance, and does not commit B. to obedience or disobedience.
2 If the rhetorical nature of the question is not recognized, and A answers it, B will think A is either not listening, or not knowing the language, or joking. (The joke with a rhetorical question is to treat it as real, while simultaneously indicating that the joker knows it is not.)

See also **Questions: self-addressed**

Further reading   Corbett (1977, 1990); Sonnino (1968)

QUESTIONS: SELF-ADDRESSED

Tasks

To focus one's mind.
To check one's memory.
To have a dialog with oneself as a way of sharing oneself with another.

Description

These are questions which are not intended to be answered by others (*see also* **Questions: rhetorical**) but to receive an answer from oneself.

Ex. 1 Where was I?

Ex. 2 Let me think. Did I leave my glasses in the office?

Ex. 3 What will I do next?

Persuasive value

1 Self-addressed questions may be real questions, wanting real answers, as in Ex. 2, where it acts to get the mind to focus. Such questions work on the principle that putting things into words makes them more accessible to thought.
2 They may be used more as a prompt to memory, pulling some matter out from memory storage so it can be dealt with.
3 They act as a means of tidying up thoughts and focussing them, enabling the thinker to settle priorities, etc., and here they work on the principle that preparing lists of work to be done is a good way of creating order out of confusion, though it does not always get the work done.
4 When such questions are offered in the presence of others they allow an apparent glimpse into C.'s very thought processes, so that C. can be better 'known' to them. This deliberate 'insider view' shows that C. is prepared for closeness of bonding with them. However, it need not, and perhaps should not, be a real revelation of personal life, opinions, or beliefs; C. may find it of more persuasive use to keep these concealed. None of the examples above gives away any secrets.

Further reading   Sonnino (1968)

QUESTIONS: TAG

Tasks

To ask a question of A.
To ask A. for support.

Description

A tag question consists of a statement plus a brief question clause 'tagged' onto it. For example,

Ex. 1 That shirt has been sold, hasn't it?

Ex. 2 That shirt hasn't been sold, has it?

The form of the tag depends on the form of the statement. Where the statement is positive, the tag is usually negative, as in Ex. 1, but where the statement is negative, the tag is usually positive, as in Ex. 2. Occasionally there are examples with two positive clauses, as in

Ex. 3 You've seen the report, have you?

The choice of pronoun and verb in the tag should match those in the statement, as in the examples above. Other verbs used in tags are 'be,' 'can,' 'will,' and 'do.'

The tag asks A. to confirm what has been said in the statement. And it seeks to control how this is done quite strongly. If the tag is negative, as in Ex. 1, the speaker expects the answer 'Yes,' while if the tag is positive, as in Ex. 2, the speaker expects the answer 'No.'

Tag questions mainly occur in spoken communication.

Persuasive value

Tag questions have been much researched because they look like instances of a lack of self-assertion. It was thought that C.s produced a statement and then had second thoughts and watered down their certainty about what they had said by asking for A. to confirm it. And there are cases where this is a reasonable interpretation, as in formal debates or discussions where participants are expected to offer their opinions firmly, and tag questions seem to weaken them, and make them appear tentative. One way of judging this is to examine the importance of the view expressed in the statement part. If it states a belief of some intrinsic significance, then the tag does appear to be a weakening of its strength; but where the statement is of little intrinsic value, as in the examples above, then it hardly seems to be reduced by the use of the tag. And indeed there are instances where it is clear that the tag is a dominant act, constraining A. to agree with the speaker, as in

Ex. 4 Most people in the department think we should buy a new computer, don't you?

Ex. 5 It is clear that this is the only reasonable option for us in the present circumstances, wouldn't you think?

And there are other possible non-tentative interpretations.

1 Tag questions can be used during sociable exchanges as a means of allowing opportunities for A.s to join in the talk, and show solidarity, while C. maintains control of the topic, and also of A.'s response. By using either a positive or negative tag C. sets an expectation which A. knows should be met.

2 They can be used in exchanges directed only at a specific A., to create common ground between C. and A., perhaps in opposition to others present. That is, C. and A. could use tags to each other and so be heard by others as in alliance, confirming what each is saying.

3 They can be used to entice a hesitant person to speak: for example, they are used by teachers with weak students. Since they clearly indicate what response should be given, they pose no threat to timid speakers, who know they just have to make confirmatory noises.

See also **Questioning**; the other **Questions** tactics

Further reading Lakoff (1973); Larson (1968); Leech and Svartvik (1975); Schegloff (1980)

QUOTATION

Tasks

To provide authority to support judgment.
To improve status.
To present matter with wit.

Description

There are various types of quotation, with different persuasive values:

(a) sourced quotation from a respected authority;
(b) unsourced socially accepted epigram;
(c) use of a colleague's words;
(d) skilled variation of a well-known saying.

In all cases the quotation should be appropriate to the context, and in the cases of (a), (b), and (c) should be accurate or the user will lose face.

Persuasive value

1 In any oppositional interaction, C.s can supply support for any views expressed, either their own or others', by showing that a reputable auth-

ority figure also holds them (and thereby implying that any opposition to them should cease). To be persuasive the authority must be one the others will accept as having views worth hearing; so one could quote Einstein to physicists, or Chomsky to linguists. But authority waxes and wanes, and there would be not only no value in quoting Freud to psychologists who think his theories were wrong, but it would rebound onto the quoter that he or she does not know how out of date the authority is.

The others must also agree that the authority quoted has something of relevance to say about the issue at hand, so although Einstein may still be respected, he would be a poor choice to quote to architects as an authority on house design.

2 In interactions with no strong opposition of ideas, just differing views being expressed, it would be too heavy-handed and domineering to use an authority as in 1 above. Better support could be found by using a generally accepted social epigram. These could come from a reputable figure of the past, like Shakespeare or H.L. Mencken, or from any current favored author. But the choice of person to quote should take into account whether A. knows of the author and hence the quotation. There are two persuasive possibilities. If A. knows the quotation it will have influence both as coming from an authority, and as having good ideas in it. But even if A. only knows that the author is esteemed, and does not know the quotation, it can have influence because A. wishes to appear to be informed, and so accepts the view expressed.

Using an unsourcable social epigram or **proverb** can also be persuasive, by bringing to the support of a view the generally accepted perceptions of the community. Again this can be persuasive, even if A.s do not recognize it specifically, provided only that the forms of words are distinctively 'literary' enough for A.s to recognize that an epigram is being used.

3 If using the words of a colleague, the quoter must give credit to their source. Such a quotation can be used to lend authority if the colleague is an influential figure, but it can also be used in quite a different way, to insert an idea into the discussion while denying ownership of it, and so perhaps avoiding criticism or blame. It is a useful tactic if in doubt about the acceptability of the idea. It may backfire though if the idea receives praise, since this will go to the quoted colleague rather than the quoter.

4 Using a skilled variation of a well-known saying can be persuasive in a double way: it brings the support of the saying, and it shows that C. is a skilled wordsmith, able to revise the saying to good effect. It also demonstrates that C. can not just link what is being discussed to an appropriate saying but can actually create links with less appropriate sayings, and make them work to his or her will. This shows that C. is well in control of the saying, and also has an authority—that of a good thinker.

Further reading   Corbett (1977, 1990); Sonnino (1968)

RAPID SEQUENCES

Task

To present matters in swift sequence so that they impress with their quantity.

Description

It is grammatically possible to join words in rapid sequences without using the conjunction 'and.'

Persuasive value

C.s can pile up matters, as in

Ex. 1   There was trouble at work, fighting at home, illness, disasters of all kinds.

so that they are without any specified links, even the simple 'and.' C.s can omit the links and present the matters swiftly, to give them greater impact, both as individual items and as an accumulation of items. Because 'and' as a linking word is used to join matters which are considered as equivalents into a sequence, its presence means that A.s consider whether or not the linked items are actually equivalents: its absence means that this is not necessary, and A.s can concentrate on the items themselves.

Rapid sequences can be used for words, or phrases, or clauses, as in

Ex. 2   He had talent, charm, wit, efficiency, friendliness.

Ex. 3   He was on every committee, in every scheme, never in his office, always out on business.

Ex. 4   You need to do your homework, attend lectures, use the library, keep up with your assignments, study well for exams to be a successful student.

In Ex. 2, the steady beat of the rhythm that is created enables C. to press home the quantity of characteristics. In Ex. 3, the piling up of phrases, used with absolute terms in each phrase—'every,' 'never,' 'always'—with no pause for links or to mark the changes in grammar—from 'on every committee' to 'always out on business'—suggests something more than the sum of its parts (though this, of course, depends to some extent on the nature of the items themselves). It is possible that the accumulation is meant as critical; contrast the lower-key effect of

Ex. 5   He was on every committee and in every scheme. And so he was never in his office because he was always out on business.

Because C. uses a more relaxed pace in describing him, this attitude could be transferred to A.s. And along with the more relaxed pace, C. has explained the man's never being in his office by turning his absence into a reason for it.

In Ex. 4, the tasks for students are undoubtedly reasonable if looked at item by item, but by piling up the items in such quick succession, C. makes the list a very weighty one, and one that students could be depressed by.

Rapid sequencing can be used to good effect in narratives, where it can mirror quick successions of events, and render them quite dramatically, as in

Ex. 6 He came, he saw, he conquered.

Ex. 7 I sat down at my desk, the ideas came, I finished the essay in ten minutes flat.

The last example is probably intended to convince A.s of the speed of the essay-writing; it may not do so, however, if they know anything at all about writing.

See also **Accumulation**; **Narrative: choose**

Further reading   Corbett (1990); Sonnino (1968)

RAPPORT VERSUS REPORT: CHOOSE

Tasks

To understand the purpose of communication.
To improve communication between men and women.

Description

Men and women are often involved in miscommunication, for many reasons, but one of the most significant language reasons is that, generally speaking, each sex has a different goal when communicating with other people, and when they communicate across the sexes this can cause trouble.

Persuasive value

The essential difference in communicative purpose between men and women, again very generally, is that women talk and write in order to build and maintain bonds with others (i.e. rapport), while men talk and write in order to establish and maintain their independence from each other, and from women (i.e. report).

Consequently, women seek to establish common ground with others, often by sharing everyday life events, and they are particularly likely to share difficulties and problems they experience at work or at home as a way of bonding. Men, on the other hand, when talking or writing use it as opportunity to establish status, their own and that of others, to see it as a way of exercising social power, trying to dominate a group, holding the floor if possible, offering strong views, and firmly establishing their responses to others' strong views.

To the extent that this difference is true, it will have serious consequences for men's and women's perceptions of each other. The strong tactics used by men could be judged blunt and unfriendly by women, the absence of sharing troubles could be seen as being too distant, etc. On the other hand, women's extra politeness could be seen as social weakness by men, and their revelation of troubles and difficulties a sign of their lack of social ability.

Further reading   Tannen (1984, 1986, 1991)

READING: USE

Tasks

To understand how the reading process works in order to prepare an easily readable text.
To read more efficiently.

Description

Reading is hard cognitive work, since all that the reader has to use to understand a communication is what is actually presented in the text (*see* **Written communication: choose**). Readers make several assumptions about what they are doing while they are performing the reading act. They assume that they and the writer are engaged in a joint endeavor which is in the interests of both of them. They see themselves and the writer as belonging to a particular group which considers ideas in the same light, either as serious if the interaction is within a learning environment, or as entertaining in a leisure environment. They are either keen to learn new ideas and adjust old ones, gain explanations and insight, or they want to experience some favorite pleasure in their preferred kind of relaxation.

The process itself proceeds at the readers' own pace; that is, they can scan the text forward or back to suit themselves; they can skip sections if they wish to; stop to argue with a particular point; or return to a favorite passage to enjoy it again.

Contrary to many assumptions about the reading process being one in which readers proceed in a plodding manner word by word, line by line, paragraph by paragraph as they seek to discover how the writer has represented the material, readers actually process the text's representations in quite other ways.

1 They focus on what strikes them as of interest (e.g. vivid images) and concentrate on them, and can usually recall them later.

2 Because they often have a practical reason for reading, they note examples, sometimes much better than what they are intended to exemplify.

3 They pay attention only sporadically, for example as their minds digest a point, or they note an unusual idea which sets off a train of thought, etc.

4 They constantly analyze elements of the text, often in a quite sophisticated way, editing them or rewriting them to suit their own goals. (Hence the folk-saying 'People hear what they want to hear.') They are as likely to remember their own variants as to recall those of the writer. And they may well attribute their own version to the writer, without realizing it. In an example of this, a teacher gave out notes to her class which recommended them to make their sentences more active, by using more verbs and fewer abstractions, and this was recalled a week later by a mature student, one who had resisted the idea, as the teacher telling the class to be more 'flamboyant.' He distinctly remembered reading this, and was disconcerted not to find the word present in the notes.

5 Conversely, readers can search for underlying assumptions which they support, and may recall these as what C. wrote rather than what is evidenced in the text.

6 Readers do not normally read the text as a set of propositions, or a complex set of ideas, and if required to do so, as in composition classes, find it an unusual and difficult act. They read with a more general view to understanding the whole design purpose of the text rather than scrupulously attending to its details.

Persuasive value

These few comments on the very complex reading process may suggest that the difficulties faced by writers in trying to be read carefully and to be persuasive are almost insuperable. However, it seems better to know the difficulties and be prepared for misinterpretation than to assume one's words will have an easy passage into another's mind.

See also **Listening: use**

Further reading   Belsey (1980); Chafe (1985); Mulholland (1991); Olson, Torrance, and Hildyard (1985)

RECIPROCALS

Task

To bring two things into a relationship which is reciprocal.

Description

It is possible grammatically to bring together two or more things, people, or actions, etc., and suggest that they interact more or less reciprocally; that is, the two do the same thing as each other. As in:

Ex. 1 Mary and Peter love each other.

Persuasive value

C.s may wish to conceal or distort something about a joint action, and can use this tactic to do so.
1 The most important implication of this tactic is that both parties are truly equal, so that in Ex. 1, Mary loves Peter, and Peter loves Mary, to the same degree and in the same way. This use of the tactic means that the user need not show one person to differ (e.g. that Peter loves Mary in a different way from the way Mary loves him).
2 And the user also need not show that one or other of the people dominates the other, as in

Ex. 2 The media borrow each other's ideas.

where the implication is that no one medium is particularly prone to borrow from another, which may well not be true.
3 The user can use so general a term for the reciprocators, as in

Ex. 3 The staff cooperated with one another on the course.

that A.s assume that most if not all of the people who could be included in the term 'staff' are involved in the cooperation, and this may also not be true. It should be noted that the term 'cooperated' is also rather general, and supplies little detail on how or what was done.

Further reading   Corbett (1977, 1990); Sonnino (1968)

REFERENCE TO TEXTS

Tasks

To support an argument.
To support C.'s authority.

Description

C.s can supply references to other texts in support of (a) some aspect of their argument or (b) their position as communicator. They can give brief references, or quote at length from their contents. The principle on which such references act as persuasion is that if a recognized expert has the same idea as the present C. it suggests that the idea is valuable, and also that the C. is wise. (It is a debatable principle since authorities can be wrong. It is also, of course, possible that C.s can misread, misquote, or misuse their content.)

Persuasive value

The success of the reference will primarily depend on whether A. will accept the reference text as authoritative. Some people accept any printed authority, but reject any spoken text; some concede the power of scientific texts but reject literary ones; others accept no authority at all:

Ex. 1 A: The Union President said we should all . . .
       B: I don't care who said it, I don't agree.

Crucially, the reference should be of real relevance to the matter it is supposed to support. So, for example, a social-work account of family breakdowns should not be used to support an argument that young people today marry later than their parents did; it will simply confuse the two issues. Equally the reference should be of the right kind of authority: for example, to use a high-school encyclopedia as a medical authority when communicating with a specialist physician would be quite inappropriate. To be persuasive C.s should look for reference texts by someone with a high reputation and expert qualifications who is currently accepted within the community as having knowledge and wisdom. In particular, C.s should note the kind of authorities that A.s themselves refer to and look for similar ones.

There should not be conflict between the authority figure referred to and others in his or her field, since this reduces the power of their words to simply one opinion among many, so that A.s could easily retort with another.

Also, the texts should have a reputation as being unbiassed; and their material should be up-to-date. However, some A.s will be more swayed by a reference to someone who shares their bias, or be more impressed by an ancient, classical text written in scholarly language than a modern one written in technical language they do not fully understand.

The use of good references will demonstrate to A.s that C. is widely read, can make good use of what has been read, and has good research skills (i.e. that C. is an arguer to be reckoned with).

Further reading   Corbett (1977, 1990)

REFERRING TERMS: EXTERNAL

Tasks

To direct attention to some matter.
To make reference to something.

Description

There are 'pointing' words for use when a C. wishes to refer to something in the non-language world. They take as their base point the time and occasion on which they are used; so, for example, 'last week' means the week before the phrase is used, and 'there' means a place at a distance from the user. They can point to time, as in 'today,' 'soon'; or to place, as in 'here,' 'there'; or to the C., as in 'I,' 'we,' 'you,' 'they'; or to an object, as in 'this,' 'that,' 'these,' or 'those.'

Persuasive value

1 Their indeterminacy may be intentionally used in preference to such specifications as 'on the 5th of May,' or 'in the advertising department.' For example, 'I'll do it next week' allows the user more freedom than the specific 'by Friday noon.' Also, by avoiding the need to supply details, C. can avoid the revelation of opinion that would otherwise be required. When, for example, C. describes 'that person' in more specific detail, he or she might offer 'the Dean of Arts' or 'the man with the brown jacket drinking beer' or 'the man who made that good speech the other day.' All of these reveal something of C.'s opinion to and attitude both about the person described and in general. (C. notices the color of jackets, what people drink, remembers good speeches, and who was responsible for them—all these details tell something about how C. sees the world.)

2 Their vagueness assumes that A. shares C.'s world view. If A. does not, and reveals this (e.g. by asking for clarification—'What do you mean "over there"?'), it shows how thin the bond of shared experiences is. This may prove costly for some persuasive purposes.

3 By making C.'s position their base, they make C. the center of attention, indeed the center of the little world of that part of the communication. If A. uses C.'s terms in a response (e.g. where C. says 'our plan' and A. replies 'in your plan'), it shows acceptance of C.'s importance.

However, when it comes to be A.'s turn to communicate, the same terms will now refer to A. as basepoint. So the switch of speaker allows each participant to be the center of the world for a time. (This is a strong reason for the importance of fair shares at turntaking.)

N.B. There is a convention that the first person to refer to something as belonging to him- or herself is taken to be its rightful owner, so in

Ex. 1 A: Our idea was that we should . . .
  B: Er, as a matter of fact it was my idea . . .

B is left trying to reclaim possession, and this may require explanation, and may meet with resistance. However, if it is not done, and done quickly, the idea will be taken as A.'s.

Further reading Corbett (1990); Sonnino (1968)

REFERRING TERMS: INTERNAL

Task

To be clear what matter is being referred to in the text.

Description

There are terms which are used to refer to or to remind people of something in the text. They are shorthand ways of presenting the same material without having to repeat the same words each time. For example, there is no need to produce the sentence:

Ex. 1 John came in and John sat down, and John picked up John's favorite paper.

Instead one can use referring terms, and produce:

Ex. 2 John came in and he sat down, and he picked up his favorite paper.

There are two kinds of reference, those which point backwards to something earlier in the text, as in Ex. 1, and those which point forward, as in

Ex. 3 She's just got it ready now—lasagne!

Ex. 4 This should be fun—your favorite comedian is coming to the Cultural Centre.

The same words can be used in most cases, either for backward or forward reference—the pronouns, 'that/this,' and 'these/those.' Other words are specific to one direction or another—'above/below,' as follows,' and 'as in.'

The terms can substitute for one word, like 'he' for 'John'; or for a whole phrase, like 'it' for 'the new history book on the table'; or a whole sentence, like 'that' in

Ex. 5 A: The rain came down before I could get my laundry off the clothesline and into the house, so it got soaked.
   B: That's a pity.

And a term can substitute for a whole paragraph, a whole idea, even whole communication, as in

Ex. 6 I believe in the party's policy on . . . and on . . . and so that is my argument for voting for Bill Smith.

Persuasive value

The main communicative value of such terms is their efficiency, and if this is impeded then they are very counter-productive. The main problem is that of vagueness of reference, which can lead A.s astray in their understanding of the text. This can, of course, be rectified in speech, but not in writing where it is, as a consequence, more dangerous.

The vagueness can arise when there are several different things in the text to which the referring term could point back, as in

Ex. 7 Mary and Susan came in with Beth; it was her birthday.

'Her' could refer to any of the three women named, but there is a convention that in most instances the term will refer to the immediately preceding word to which it could refer, here Beth. If A. knows this convention then he or she will understand Beth is meant. However, if he or she is uncertain, there are two possibilities: one is to ask 'Whose birthday is it?' and the other, the one most often taken where the matter is an unimportant one (as it is here: it sounds like **sociable language**), is to respond with something minimal and hope that matters will become clear without having to ask about it. It should be noted, however, that a minimal answer could be interpreted by C. as unfriendliness, whereas in fact it is C.'s own vagueness that has caused it. If there were many of these instances in an interaction both participants could feel very uncomfortable, and their relationship become strained—a large outcome from such a small language problem.

Where the referring term points back to a large chunk of text, such vaguenesses can be compounded—A.s could wonder whether C. is referring to one item or another, or to all the items together. It could happen, however, that A. thought there was only one possible interpretation, while C. meant quite another, and they could continue for some time talking at cross purposes, misreading each others' communications without knowing it. If there is any danger of vagueness about referring terms C. should both take extra care with them, and check that A. has interpreted them correctly.

Forward reference is less confusing, provided that C. does supply what is referred to, and does so as soon as the referring term is used, with no intervening digression. The following is a bad example:

Ex. 8 There are three points to discuss, as follows (I am not giving them in any order of priority, which I would think quite inappropriate).

See also **Minimalism; Referring terms**: **external**

Further reading   Halliday and Hasan (1976); Leech and Svartvik (1975); Quirk, Greenbaum, Leech, and Svartvik (1985)

REFLEXIVE COMMENT

Tasks

To set or influence the agenda.
To change the activity in an interaction.

Description

To comment reflexively is to make explicit in words (i.e. to name) some aspect of communication activity: it is a comment in language on language.

In so commenting on the event currently in progress, C.s can influence either their own activity or those of particular others, or that of the whole group, including or excluding themselves. For example,

Ex. 1 So, what we've done today is to clarify the problem.

Ex. 2 O.K. I've dealt with the figures, now let's examine the personnel problems.

In Ex. 1 the comment represents the past activity as 'clarification'; in Ex. 2 it represents the current activity as 'dealing with the figures' and goes on to represent the next activity as 'examination of problems.' In Ex. 1 the activity includes C.; in Ex 2 the first clause refers to the communicator alone, while the second represents the whole group including the communicator.

Persuasive value

Reflexive comment is persuasive in two main ways.
1 It influences people to accept the representation it makes (e.g. in Ex. 1

to agree that the activity they have been engaged in was 'clarifying the problem'). This may be untrue or inadequate as a description, but if A.s wish to object they will have to exert themselves to put up an argument.
2 It influences people to accept that the past activity is in fact over and that a new activity is about to begin. As in Ex. 2 where they could be persuaded that since 'the figures have been dealt with,' they should proceed to the examination of personnel problems. It acts, that is, to persuade the group to accept C.'s declaration of the boundaries of their actions, the movement from one to another, which is a very powerful persuasion. If it is accepted, C. will control the whole development of the interaction.

Any member of an interaction can produce such comments about any part of the activity and attempt to have that representation accepted; if he or she succeeds, a degree of persuasive control has been imposed on the group.

Group control is particularly strong when the reflexive comment concerns activity in the future, and this is not easy to exercise. C. may have some external power (e.g. is Company President), but if not, the act of accepting his or her direction for the future grants a strong social power for that interaction. So useful a tactic is it that many reflexive comments are tried, often in polite question form, to allow for rejection of it without loss of face to the communicator:

Ex. 3 Since we have settled that, can we move on?

Further reading   O'Sullivan, Hartley, Saunders, and Fiske (1983)

REFUSE

Task

To refuse to do something requested of one without damage to bonding.

Description

When someone requests some act of another it is an F.T.A. in that it seeks to limit the freedom of action of that person, but it is also an F.T.A. for the person requesting it, since a refusal is a loss of face.

Persuasive value

Refusal is a difficult act to perform persuasively, because it is a blunt rejection of the other person's wishes, and it only comes about because the refuser does not want to do the thing requested. If the act requested is impossible to perform, then it can be rejected as impossible, with less face loss; but if it is quite possible, and the situation is just a clash of wills between two people, it is a very ego-threatening event.

While it is always face threatening to refuse someone's request, one can perform the refusal with more or less politeness. A blunt refusal, such as 'No,' or 'I won't,' with no modification to soften the rejection, can create antagonism, and so be counter-persuasive. A blunt refusal with some explanation or reason given, such as 'No, I can't, I'm busy,' is less threatening. But the most polite way to refuse is to give an apology, plus some explanation, and an acknowledgment of regret for the other's face loss, as in this extremely polite version:

Ex. 1 I'm afraid I can't. I'm sorry, but I am busy at the moment, otherwise I wouldn't turn you down like this. I know it is not friendly of me, but I can't help it.

See also **Face threats: recognize; Politeness** tactics.

Further reading Wierzbicka (1987)

REJECT ADVICE

Task

To reject advice without giving offense.

Description

It may be possible to ignore an offer of advice, but in most cases some response, either acceptance or rejection, is required by the offerer.

Persuasive value

The person giving the advice (a) presumes some degree of authority over the other, or (b) offers it because it will do some good for the other. In both cases a rejection must be tactfully worded so as not to belittle a justified authority or to refuse the goodwill.

If the advice is lightly or frivolously offered it can be ignored. But if the advice is seriously offered, the following set of possible rejections could be useful. They are arranged in order from most to least tactful.

1 Indicate that the circumstances to which the advice is directed have changed, or are not significant, or someone else is responsible for them. As in:

Ex. 1 A: Why don't you use the library to find the data you need?
       B: Well, we don't really need them any more, and besides, Mary is responsible for data work, not me.

2 Temporize by use of such phrases as 'Aha . . . hm . . .,' 'I'll bear that in mind,' or 'That's a useful thought.' However, 'Aha . . . hm' will be recognized as a form of rejection, partly because it is so brief. The others are **reflexive comments** and offer a thought about the advice rather than taking or rejecting it.
3 Question whether the advice would work, as in

Ex. 2 You said I should check the library for data, but I don't think the library holds the kind of data we need.

Such questioning involves criticism of the adviser's knowledge, so to offset it, this version includes a softening phrase, 'I don't think.'
4 Show emphatically that the advice would not work, but note this is strongly critical of the adviser's wisdom. As in:

Ex. 3 A: You can get that data you need from the library.
       B: That's an outdated notion; the library doesn't have it.

See also **Advise**

Further reading   Wierzbicka (1987)

REPETITION

Tasks

To highlight some matter.
To show feelings about some matter.
To delay a difficult communication task.
To show that one is actively listening.

Description

Repetition can take several forms: it can be an exact repetition, or a slight variation; it can be a word, phrase, sentence, or idea; and it can be of statements, questions, commands, or any other communicative acts. Repetition has several possible roles to play in communication.

Persuasive value

1 Repetition can be used to mark the start and close of any communication, or of any structural element in it, as in:

Ex. 1 O.K. So let's now turn to the first problem . . .
       O.K. So now let's turn to the second problem . . .

Repetition is a very noticeable act, and in using it at various stages throughout, C.s can often make a text seem more structured than it might really be.

2 Repetition can be an aid to understanding the material being represented if it is of difficult ideas or words. By hearing or reading these things over and over again, and in different textual surroundings, A.s will gradually learn their meaning, and do so in the most natural way possible, the way children pick up the meanings of words by their reiteration in different contexts. It is important, therefore, that what is repeated is representing something material to the meaning of the text, and not just a favorite phrase or saying. So, for example, it is more useful to A. to end a written report in this way:

Ex. 2 So, to go over the main points of my argument again: 1. the computer is a good one, 2. it is well priced, and . . .

rather than:

Ex. 3 So to conclude, I hope that I have shown that I have done what I said I would do in my opening paragraph, to argue for the new computer in the best way I could.

3 Repetition can highlight a matter, either by the use of slight variants, as in

Ex. 4 This is the crux of the problem: the increase of student numbers without any increase in faculty to teach them—the very rapid increase in numbers with no increase in faculty for four years.

or by exact repeats, as in

Ex. 5 We marked and marked and marked for three whole weeks.

In both cases the highlighting is done without the use of emotional terms, and although C. may well feel strong emotion and use repetition to have this understood, the appearance of the textual repetition is of thought—and in formal communications particularly, this is held in higher regard than emotion, and is therefore a better tactic.

4 C.s can use repetition of something previously communicated as a way of giving themselves time to prepare for a difficult act, as B does in the following:

Ex. 6 A: But what exactly will you tell the boss about this mistake?
      B: Well, as I've said before, it isn't the worst mistake we've made, we've done worse things before, and managed to survive. What'll I tell the boss? I'll just say . . .

B here repeats an earlier view, then says it again, then repeats A.'s question, all before giving an answer. From this amount of repetition, A can see how hesitant B is about answering. This may be useful information for A.

5 Repetition of a first speaker's words can be used by a second speaker to show he or she is actively listening, as in

Ex. 7 A: I think we'll have eggs for breakfast.
    B: Eggs for breakfast—that sounds good.

Some people find this too intrusive and unsettling, perhaps because it seems to 'take the words right out of my mouth,' that is to use my possession, my words, as if they belong to them.

6 Repetition can be used, almost paradoxically, in spoken reiterations of a negative word or phrase with a softening effect. Compare:

Ex. 8 A: Did you get the books you wanted?
    B: No.

with

Ex. 9 A: Did you get the books you wanted?
    B: No . . . no, unfortunately not.

The second version is less blunt than the first, though it would depend to some extent on **intonation**—if each no is as strongly said as the other, then it sounds like emphasis, while if the second is more muted it sounds like softening. This use of repetition occurs because there is a convention in talk that brevity is antisocial, and particularly where the speaker is negating what has been said.

In broader terms, people repeat jokes, slogans, proverbs, and familiar sayings. In these cases repetition is a powerful persuader, eventually causing society to tolerate or accept the repeated matter: it is said that if something is just repeated often enough it becomes truth.

See also **Accumulation; Minimalisation**

Further reading   Corbett (1977, 1990); Sonnino (1968)

REPORTING

Task

To repeat a message or to relate what has occurred, to give an account of something.

Description

To report is to inform by giving an account of something from one's own experience, or by restating others' information.

Persuasive value

Reports provide much of the groundwork for people's understanding of life's events, and provide more knowledge than personal experience does.

They can consequently have persuasive importance. People are understandably wary of those who offer reports, and will only accept them if the reporter can indicate his or her skills at the task. So C.s should present themselves as good at observing detail, at summarizing, as recognizing the assumptions and generalizations that might underlie superficial details, and as able to perform good categorizations of material. C.s also need to justify their role as reporter by showing they have some connection with the matters reported.

Reporting allows several opportunities to manipulate the content of a report, without in any way reporting untruths.

1 This can be done by omitting the circumstances in which something happened and distort the nature of the report. So by keeping silent on the communication context, on the mood or psychological state of those present, or even by omitting to mention all the people who were there, C.s can give an entirely biassed report of what occurred.

2 A report can omit everything apart from a particular matter. It can, for instance, not reveal that a perhaps provocative remark did not occur voluntarily, but was forced from the speaker. For example, it could report that Bill said 'That is unforgivable,' when in fact what happened was that Bill was asked a lot of questions about his opinion of something, to the last of which, 'Do you find that is hard to forgive?' he replied 'Well, yes, I suppose so.'

3 Reports can ignore passages of time, and intervening events, and suggest that two distant events occurred in juxtaposition, and change their meaning, as in 'We argued for a while then Mary said "I think you are all quite wrong," and she left the room.' In fact there might have been quite some time between Mary's speech and her exit, but C. reports it as if the two events were connected, as if she stormed out in disagreement.

4 All reports are selective, and summarize amounts of detail, and can therefore distort matters.

5 To ensure that one is reported properly, it is useful to supply some memorable summations of one's views which may tempt a reporter to just repeat them. Also one should make sure that the summations are very brief: it would appear that people's attention span is very short, and only a brief report is likely to be remembered.

See also the other **Report speech** tactics

Further reading   Freadman and Macdonald (1992); Quirk, Greenbaum, Leech, and Svartvik (1985)

REPORT SPEECH: DIRECTLY

Task

To report a written or spoken communication by another.

Description

A written or spoken communication can be reported by direct speech, by indirect or reported speech, or by 'free indirect speech.' Direct report begins with a verb of speaking or writing, then with quotation marks, then the exact words communicated must be given, with no alteration, and no omission.

Persuasive value

1 In direct speech, it is conventionally understood that C. is giving an accurate account of every word that the original communicator said or wrote. A.s will assume that it can be relied on. If it cannot, if C. has added or omitted something, and if the original communicator learns of this and if the matter is serious enough, the C. could be legally liable for the alteration, and could be charged with slander if it is in a spoken communication, and with libel if it is written.

This avenue of redress for incorrect reports shows how much importance society attaches to acts of communication. Society has many phrases which explain why this is so, for example, people say 'A person's word is his or her bond,' 'He or she is answerable for what they say or write,' and so on. So it is obvious enough why bad reporting should be so socially worrying. What can make it worse is that the original communicators may not hear of the misreporting, and so can act in ignorance that others have a particular perception of them as having said or written something specific. The false knowledge could affect others' reactions to them quite strongly.

2 C. can influence how the speech is perceived by making a careful choice of verb of speaking or writing for the speech act that was done. So C. can use 'said,' or 'complained,' or 'laughed,' and each would affect how A. understood what the original act meant.

3 C. can take the opportunity to emphasize his or her own role as a reporter, even while appearing to act as just a channel by which someone else's words are communicated. This can be done by using such introductory phrases as:

Ex. 1 Peter said, and I quote, 'We will accept the decision.'

Ex. 2 'I am certain of it' were his exact words, I guarantee it.

Ex. 3 If memory serves me correctly, he said 'We will agree to the plan.'

Note that Examples 1 and 2 will commit C.s to accuracy, but that Ex. 3 allows C.s to be less than accurate, and they have covered themselves in case of an attack on their accuracy.

See also the other **Report speech** tactics

Further reading   Leech and Svartvik (1975); Quirk, Greenbaum, Leech, and Svartvik (1985)

REPORT SPEECH: FREELY

Task

To report a written or spoken communication by another.

Description

Free indirect speech is a combination of direct and indirect report. Compare the direct, indirect, and free indirect speech report versions:

Ex. 1 I heard her say 'Are these the only ones you have?'

Ex. 2 She asked if these were the only ones we had.

Ex. 3 She gave me a look and said Good Heavens, are these the only ones we have?

The free indirect version can be dramatic, for example by quoting exactly any exclamations or colloquial phrases that were used, which are edited out in indirect speech reports (and even in direct reports), and is therefore very accurate in some details. It also contains something of the distancing that is found in indirect speech reports, by including some emphasis on the reporter, as in 'I heard her say' in Ex. 1.

Persuasive value

The free version is much used in feature journalism, because it allows so much flexibility to writers to communicate their own interpretations about the speech simultaneously with the speech. This makes it hard for A.s to separate the two and make their own judgment about the original and about the reporter's view. So in Ex. 3, the reporter suggests that 'she' did more than ask a question—she made a strong criticism, and merges the two. He or she may be exaggerating, but in using the free version will not be held to account for the exact words, as would happen in direct reporting.

The free version is also important persuasively because it blurs the distinction between what belongs to the speaker and what to the reporter. No quotation marks signal the original words, no boundaries are marked between the original and the reporter's speech, and indeed at times reporters make no distinction between what was said, and what they judge to have been thought, as in

Ex. 4 At the meeting we heard from Bill who did his usual 'I want the P.R. Section to be given credit.' Then Sandy said that she thought the campaign had run too long, and everyone sighed here we go again! Peter then took matters into his own hands for once and said 'It will stop when I say so and not before.' Wow, we thought, such strength of character!

A.s would need to take careful note of what is being directly reported and what not in such an account; the truth about what Bill and Sandy and Peter said, and what others said (did they all sigh, did they all think or say 'Wow' or 'such strength of character') is hard to know. It would be sensible to seek another report from someone else to check the value of this one before accepting it.

See also the other **Report speech** tactics

Further reading   Leech and Svartvik (1975); Quirk, Greenbaum, Leech, and Svartvik (1985)

REPORT SPEECH: INDIRECTLY

Task

To report a written or spoken communication by another.

Description

A written or spoken communication can be reported by direct speech, by indirect or reported speech, or by free indirect speech. In indirect speech the reporter alters the exact words of the original in certain conventional ways, shown below, using the following as an example of direct speech, imagining that it was said on Monday 5 May, and is being reported to A. some days later:

Ex. 1 Peter: 'I will be ready to meet you at any time this afternoon.'

1 Any first-person words (i.e. words like 'I,' or 'we') which indicate but do not specify the speaker should be converted into the name of the speaker, or into third person pronouns ('she,' 'he') if this will be enough for identification.
2 Any words which refer to other people may also need adjusting so that A. can know who exactly is meant, so 'you' would be altered to 'me' if it referred to the reporter, or to 'us' if it referred to the reporter and A., and so on.
3 Any words which indicate the time of the speech ('this afternoon') should be altered to some specific time words which could be understood by A. ('that day,' 'on that Monday afternoon,' 'on the afternoon of the 5th'). Note that time words used in the original speech may refer to its

present, past or future, and all need adjusting so that A. could understand them: so if Peter had said 'yesterday', this would become 'the day before', or 'Sunday' or '4th May'; while the word 'tomorrow' would become 'the next day,' or 'Tuesday, the 6th.'

4 C. will need to supply a verb of speaking or writing to record the nature of the speech act as originally performed: for example, 'said,' 'declared,' 'proposed,' or 'promised.'

So the example could be reported as either of the following quite accurately:

Ex. 2 He said that he would be ready to meet us at any time that afternoon.

Ex. 3 Peter said that he would be ready to meet the delegation at any time on that Monday afternoon.

Persuasive value

C.s can adjust or even distort what the original speaker said by incorporating something of their own interpretation or opinion of the speech. This can be done particularly through the choice of verb of speaking or writing. C. could use the neutral 'said' or 'wrote,' but also words like 'offered,' which weakens what Peter said, or 'promised,' which strengthens it, or 'claimed' or 'declared' each of which interprets it differently, and will have a different impact on A. If A. has no direct access to Peter this could be very effective.

See also the other **Report speech** tactics

Further reading   Leech and Svartvik (1975); Quirk, Greenbaum, Leech, and Svartvik (1985)

REPRIMAND

Task

To offer a serious adverse judgment to another.

Description

A reprimand is a formal negative judgment about someone. It is among the most face-threatening acts to offer to another because its goal is to criticize A., and if done badly can cause humiliation or resentment.

Persuasive value

To perform a reprimand efficiently and persuade A. to mend his or her ways, the following are essential conditions.

1 C. must have some authority over A. This could be by virtue of his or her work position. Occasionally A. gives authority to another to reprimand, by saying 'You have a right to be annoyed about this.'
2 C.'s own behavior should be fault-free; if not, A. could feel the act is unjust.
3 C. must be certain about the fault and that A. is to blame for it.
4 The reprimand should be performed in private; witnesses make it more humiliating for A.
5 The fault must be currently happening or have been done in the recent past. A reprimand for something done months before would be seen as unreasonable.

Since a reprimand is a punishment intended to cause, at the least, discomfort to A., C. should be prepared for A. to raise objections to any aspect of the act, and should have an answer ready.

If the reprimand is a particularly official one, it will be most persuasive if it is offered impersonally, as in 'Students should not allow their work to be copied, it is unprofessional and unethical conduct.' If C. adopts a more familiar tone this could weaken the official weightiness of the act, and if C. goes into details of the specific act mentioned, there is always a chance that A. can retort that that detail is wrong, and therefore lessen the effect of the reprimand.

N.B.   A reprimand is meant to be an institutional act, which C. performs as a representative rather than as an individual. This makes the act more authoritative, and more likely to taken seriously.

Further reading   Mulholland (1991); Wierzbicka (1987)

RESPOND TO COMPLAINT

Tasks

To note what caused C. to complain.
To respond appropriately to a complaint.

Description

If a complaint is of the sociable kind (*see* **Complain**) then A. should respond in a suitably sociable way. But if it is an expression of dissatisfaction with or censure of A., then A. must respond well to it in order to save face.

Persuasive value

1 Sociable complaints should meet with a friendly response, though this need not mean agreement with the substance or the tone of the complaint.

If, for example, C. made this complaint about a colleague, 'Bill's always talking. He's made me late again. Know what I mean?' and A. did not wish to agree, he or she could pick on the least troubling part of the complaint and perhaps respond 'I was nearly late myself. I got a phone call just as I left my office.' (Note: there is a power in a complaint which draws A. into agreement, and this may be misread by others as agreement with more than A. would wish: it is wise to hesitate before offering easy agreement.) If C.'s complaint appears merely to be seeking sympathy, then A. could note C. is feeling low, and use this knowledge.

2 In the case of more serious complaints, though ones not directed at them, A.s should note what the matter of the complaint is. This is because a complaint reveals something that gives C. unease and so it is always informative about some aspect of C.'s character, which may be useful in a later persuasion. In the complaint above, about Bill, C. expressed annoyance with being late, and A. could note this as a feature of C.'s response to the world. Or from C.'s saying 'Peter is so boring; he never says anything new,' A. can learn that C. wants to be kept interested.

3 In the case of complaints directed specifically at A.s, they need to defend themselves against potential face loss. This could be done by:

(a) anticipating the complaint and apologizing first;
(b) quietly and briefly and in formal tone accept responsibility in whole or in part;
(c) if the complaint is mistaken in some detail, A.s could accept responsibility for what is correct, and deny it for what is not;
(d) if the complaint is both correct and a major one, A.s could accept responsibility for it but seek to minimize it or to share the responsibility with others. A.s should not deny all responsibility unless they must, since this can all too easily sound untrue, and mark A. as untrustworthy. It is socially heroic to say 'the buck stops here';
(e) if the complaint is wholly wrong A.s could find it hard to respond: to defend the matter could sidetrack the interaction while to show that C. is mistaken may cause antagonistic debate. Yet leaving a false complaint unchallenged could destroy A.'s concentration or good will.

See also **Face threats: recognize**

Further reading   Mulholland (1991)

RESPONSES

Tasks

To reply to others to their satisfaction.
To reply to others while achieving one's own goals.

Description

An identifiably relevant response is required after every **initiating move**, whether question, statement, request, etc., and it will be constrained by the initiating act, in two ways: (a) its content and form are affected, and (b) anything that occurs after the initiating move will be taken as a response, whether intended or not, and interpreted as such. Convention requires that the responder achieve as much agreement with the initiator as possible (*see* **Preferred responses**).

Persuasive value

Because of the restrictions set by the initiator, the only opportunity the responder has to exert a persuasive influence is by maneuvering within the options provided.

1 Because agreement is the preferred response the initiator will recognize any degree of disagreement, however mild, as a deliberate choice. The responder needs therefore, just to hint quite unspecifically at disagreement, and the hint will be noted. This avoids an overt quarrel, as in

Ex. 1 A: I think we should do something about the lecture rooms.
      B: Oh? I quite like them.
      A: Well, I suppose they are not too bad.

2 There are signalling words and phrases which indicate disagreement without the need for any development of an opposition, thus enabling the user to reserve his or her position until he or she has a clearer idea of what would be more advantageous to say, as in

Ex. 2 A: Should we tell the boss about it? I think we should.
      B: Well . . . [*or* 'O.K. but,' 'Er . . .' *or* 'Oh?'].
      A: And so do the whole team in fact.
      B: Well, if everyone thinks so that's O.K. by me.

N.B. Even if a responder just says 'Mhm' it shows an absence of agreement, because 'Mhm' means 'carry on I'm listening,' and as a response that is unsatisfactory.

N.B. A responder can try a **reflexive comment** such as 'That's a difficult question,' or 'Let me think,' as an escape from the constraints imposed, but it would tell the initiator overtly that he or she has caused a difficulty, and this might be unwise for the responder to reveal.

3 The best option for responders to use, to reserve their position about what the initiator has offered, and to move the speech towards their own goals, is to begin in the mildest agreement possible, and then insert their own content, as in

Ex. 3 A: I think the first part of the report is the best.
　　　　B: Well, it depends on whether you want it to be clear or thorough.
　　　　　　I think it should be thorough.
　　　　A: Oh, I agree.

Further reading   Bilmes (1988); Clark (1980); Goffman (1981); Sacks (1987)

RESTRICTED CODE

Tasks

To show common ground with A.
To show there is no common ground with A.
To prevent offense to A.'s ego.
To give offense to A.'s ego.
To use clearly understood language.

Description

There are two important codes or ways of using language within English: using a restricted code which uses a small vocabulary and a narrow range of grammar; or an **elaborated code** which has a large vocabulary and uses the full grammar.

The restricted code is used when C.s can assume that they share with A. similar experiences, and a similar outlook on life. That is, it assumes and indeed depends on common membership of a group. It is the kind of language that puzzles eavesdroppers because they cannot understand what is being referred to.

The restricted code is given a low social status, and is seen as being useful mainly for sustaining social bonds, and for representing immediate and concrete experience. But this is to denigrate the value of both things. Nonetheless someone who can only communicate in this code will be regarded as socially undereducated.

People learn the restricted code first, as they form family and school bonds. It is marked by a preference for pronouns over complex noun phrases. For example, it would produce 'He's done it again' which relies on A. knowing what is being communicated, rather than 'The boy in the green shirt has finished his essay first again' which contains all the information necessary to understand it. The restricted code uses 'cover-all' words like 'he,' 'it,' 'thing,' or 'you know what,' and adjectives like 'O.K.,' 'great,' or 'fantastic,' rather than spelling out the details. It also prefers basic non-specific verbs like 'be,' 'do,' or 'have' to producing a fully represented action.

Persuasive value

1 Using the restricted code to focus on what is common between C. and A. consolidates a bond between them. So, two new colleagues might focus on their common newness and, by using restricted code, build a connection. It could be a useful counter to the awkwardness associated with being new.
2 If someone uses restricted code he or she may be trying to bond with others in a work interaction, which might signal that he or she is feeling isolated in some way; for example, because he or she has just been in opposition to the others' shared opinion.
3 Some people are uncomfortable with any sustained hypothetical discussion, or impersonal contact with others, and so may try to remind the others of the bonding between them, or to talk about lighter matters, in restricted code. Until their comfort is restored, they are unlikely to be persuaded of anything.

Further reading   O'Sullivan, Hartley, Saunders, and Fiske (1983)

RESTRICTIVE MEANING

Task

To indicate whether a matter that is being communicated is to be understood as being broadly meant, or with some restriction.

Description

To specify the meaning of a matter, so that it is not too broad to be clearly understood, C. can:

(a) add adjectives which specify details of its meaning;
(b) order the adjectives in certain ways;
(c) use modifying clauses (called 'restrictive relative clauses').

Respectively, examples of these are:

Ex. 1 'the apples' could be specified 'the juicy red apples'

Ex. 2 'the play' could be specified 'her first successful Broadway play'

Ex. 3 'the book' could be specified 'which she had spent three years writing sold well.'

Persuasive value

In examples like Ex. 1 the first version could well appear clear to those who receive it, but it is in fact so broad that they could have quite a different idea of 'apples' from the one meant by C.

In Ex. 2 the change from the first to the second version is even more specific than in Ex. 1, but is often mistaken, because people do not always realize that the order of the adjectives is crucial. The second version in Ex. 2 means the first play which has been successful on Broadway: it does not mean her first play, nor her first successful play, though either of these could be true. What C. produces is an order of words in which the adjective nearest to the noun 'Broadway' restricts the meaning most, and says that C. is talking only about her 'Broadway plays'; also, with respect to these, she has a successful one, and that it is her first of the successful Broadway plays. It is an important and useful way to specify meaning, but it does not always meet with understanding.

In Ex. 3, there is a modifying clause added to the 'book' so that C. is only talking about that specific book—the one that took three years to write—and not any of her others. If, on the other hand, C. meant not to be specific, but simply to supply an extra piece of information about the book, then this could be done, by adding commas on either side of the modifying clause, as in

Ex. 4 The book, which she had spent three years writing, sold well.

In this example, the commas act like brackets and the clause between does not in any way restrict the reference of 'the book.' Again, this difference in meaning is often missed, and the significance of the commas ignored.

Further reading   Leech and Svartvik (1975); Quirk, Greenbaum, Leech, and Svartvik (1985)

REVEAL THOUGHT PROCESSES

Tasks

To hint at the thought processes behind the representation of material.
To suggest to what extent C. believes in what is represented.
To prevent attacks on the views stated.

Description

People can state their views as if they are so obviously true and unarguable that no one could resist them, as in:

Ex. 1 It was a problem for him.

They can also express them more tentatively. One form of being tentative is to hint at how the views were arrived at, as in

Ex. 2 It was evidently a problem for him.

Ex. 3 It looks like it was a problem for him.

Ex. 4 It was presumably a problem for him.

Ex. 5 It appears to have been a problem for him.

Views can also be stated with great detail about how they came to be held, as in

Ex. 6 I have thought carefully about this, and while I am not prepared to say that the case is a bad one, I am prepared to say that it is not as good as the evidence suggests. And I mean 'evidence.' There is good evidence in . . . but there is also less verifiable evidence than I would like. So on the whole, taking all these things into account, I think he has a problem.

Persuasive value

1 In Ex. 1 C. presents the view as if there could be no doubt about it; it is just stated in absolute terms. It might not be accepted by its recipients, of course, but C. has left little choice for A. except to accept it or to reject it, and has raised no **topic** for A.s to pick up which might suggest that there is any doubt about it.
2 In Ex. 2, on the other hand, C. indicates a less absolute adherence to the view, and does this by showing how the view was arrived at, by some 'evidence.' That is, C. has stated that this view was arrived at after logical analysis, and so influences A. so that if A. wishes to object to the view, C. will want some counterevidence. What C. has done, therefore, is try to set the agenda for discussion if the view is resisted.
3 In Ex. 3 also, C. shows a weaker adherence to the view than in Ex. 1, in this instance indicating that the evidence on which the view rests is from personal experience, since the phrase 'looks like' suggests a direct, first-hand, concrete experience. To resist this A. will be influenced to respond in terms of the same kind of direct experience.
4 In Ex. 4 C. holds the view much less strongly, and has arrived at it by some 'presumption'; perhaps he or she has a general view into which the specific instance of the 'problem' seems to fit, and so deduces there is some probability that a problem exists. If A. resists the idea, he or she is being influenced to argue against the proposition in general terms.
5 In Ex. 5 C. holds the view in the weakest way, perhaps having acquired it from someone else; 'it appears' sounds like a report from someone with which C. is prepared to go along. If A. wishes to resist this view, he or she can do so knowing that C. is not committed to it, and could easily be brought to change if A. wanted to.
6 The piling up of details about the process of thought that lies behind a view can be so long and involved, as in Ex. 6, perhaps, that A.s would feel

intimidated from resisting the view. And C. is certainly suggesting indirectly that if A.s do wish to resist, they will have to provide as much detail about how they got to their contrary view.

N.B. It should be noted that while in speech the main evidential method is induction (the process of arriving at a view through specific examples from which generalizations are then drawn), in writing the favored choice is deduction (the process of using a generalization to explain and classify specific instances). Not only this, but induction is held socially to be a poorer reasoning method: there are many criticisms which describe it as being built on 'shaky ground' of 'merely anecdotal evidence,' and asking for 'hard' facts, arrived at deductively. This judgment is yet one more reason why speech is held in less esteem than writing, and why people's talk and practical experiences are regarded as less valuable than mental experience.

N.B. A.s should note that when a view is held only lightly there is no need to bring major arguments to bear against it, or to speak against it at length. To do this would show that A.s have not been noting the signs of commitment at all. Other signs of tentativeness are as in

Ex. 7 It is supposed to be a good hotel.

Ex. 8 It seems there is a new hotel being built.

Further reading   Sonnino (1968)

SELF-CORRECTION

Task

To highlight a particular word by using it as an explicit correction of an earlier word use.

Description

Where C.s have a specially important word they wish to use as a representation of some matter, and they wish to highlight it, they can first use another word, an appropriate but more neutral term, and then correct themselves and use the word they really want. As in:

Ex. 1 The main conclusions of the report were very useful, though indeed it would be more appropriate to call them not conclusions but recommendations.

Ex. 2 I thought it was a splendid party. Well, actually, it was a very particular kind of party; a family celebration, in fact.

Ex. 3 I went to the staff development lecture last week, though really it was an exercise in self-indulgence rather than a lecture.

Persuasive value

C.s can do several things through this tactic .

1 In Ex. 1, by presenting the two versions side by side, C. can focus on some feature missing in the first version but present in the second (i.e. by setting up a contrast), and direct A.s' attention to it. A.s should consider what 'recommendations' have that 'conclusions' do not have. Note that in making this particular change C. is changing the very perception of the report itself, into one which makes recommendations.

2 In Ex. 2, C. focusses on the difference between a general term 'party' and one particular type of party, one with the features of 'family' and 'celebration.' It might be worth asking whether the name 'party' was ever really right for a 'family celebration,' but this may be glossed over as A.s consider the differences between the two things. Did C. intend this to happen?

3 In Ex. 3 C. explains his or her criticism of an event by naming that the event was supposed to be 'a lecture' and showing how it fell short of this and became 'an exercise in self-indulgence.'

N.B.   In any instance where C. corrects a word use, it is possible that it is a genuine case of using a word and then realizing it has some fault, but it is equally possible that the first word was used knowing what the effect of correction would be.

See also **Self-repair**

Further reading   Jefferson (1974, 1987); Sonnino (1968)

SELF-DEFENSE

Task

To defend oneself against real or expected attacks.

Description

To offer some defense when others have attacked something in C.'s communications, some idea raised, some attitude shown, some criticism offered, etc. Defense could also be offered in order to prevent a predicted attack.

Persuasive value

There are several tactics to adopt; the choice of which one to use, or the decision to use more than one, will depend on the seriousness of the attack, the social power of the attacker, and how much C. him- or herself is affected by the attack. (Note that how heavily C. defends him- or herself will reveal how important the matter is, and this may be usable for persuasion against C.) The following tactics are in no order of priority:

(a) The charges can be denied, in general or in detail, and this can be done more or less objectively.
(b) The charges can be admitted but C. could show that they are not serious.
(c) C. could either admit or deny the charges and go on to cite what relevant positive qualities he or she has, and so defuse the importance of the attack.
(d) C. could admit the charges but claim they were an honest mistake, or done by accident.
(e) Others could be shown to be like C. in the matter about which he or she is attacked, but, C. could claim, they were not attacked; that is, C. has been singled out unfairly.
(f) C. could claim that he or she had a good motive in doing the thing attacked, and should be given credit for that.
(g) (This one is weaker defense.) C. could make a general attack, claiming maliciousness or hostility is the motive behind the attacks.
(h) (This one is also weak.) Blame others, and claim they did the thing which is being attacked; this usually attracts criticism or dislike, because people prefer some defense that acknowledges that, as the popular saying puts it, 'the buck stops here'.
(i) (Only to be used in dire emergencies.) Attack the attackers as fools or liars, etc. This will undoubtedly cause hostility, and make it difficult to preserve enough rationality to continue with effective communicating.

Further reading   Corbett (1990); Sonnino (1968)

SELF-INTERRUPTION

Task

To interrupt the flow of one's own speech with least damage.

Description

On occasions speakers and writers can interrupt themselves as they communicate by offering something which breaks the flow or thread of communication.

Persuasive value

There are three main types of self-interruption.
1 An exclamation of emotion plus some sudden change of topic or mood, as in

Ex. 1 So then I went to the library and—Damn! . . . I've forgotten to take that book back to Mary.

Such exclamations are often followed by a pause during which C. remembers what has been forgotten. While this is happening A. is left in suspense, and could be irritated by this. To hold the floor in this way and not to speak is to be very dominant over those present and should not be overdone.
2 Self-corrections can be interruptions, as in

Ex. 2 Our competitors, I beg your pardon, our fellow students at Radcliffe, are . . .

Here C. makes a mistake in the representation of content and immediately seeks to repair it. Repairing in this instance is only a matter of damage control since once said, the mistake has been heard and noted and cannot be unsaid.
3 A subset of self-correction exists in which C.s make interactional mistakes, as in

Ex. 3 So here it is, Bill, if I may call you Bill.

Here C. fears he or she has taken a too friendly approach when talking to someone in a superior position. Note that it is almost impossible for Bill to refuse without being rude.
4 C.s can elaborate on or qualify a term used, as in

Ex. 4 I found a new book in the library; well actually it wasn't a book so much as a new magazine, on literary criticism.

Such breaks in flow are rarely acceptable in writing because they betray a lack of revision which would have incorporated the detail in its proper place. They are more acceptable in speech, but only if the matter supplied in the interruption is of some interest to A. In Ex. 5 this would not be so:

Ex. 5 I went to the doctor on Monday about my arm, or was it Tuesday, or Wednesday, no it was Monday. Anyway . . .

See also **Interruption of other**; **Parenthesis**; **Self-repair**

Further reading   Bennett (1981); Mulholland (1991)

SELF-REPAIR

Tasks

To repair one's mistake.
To avoid loss of face.
To avoid having someone else show one has erred.

Description

Both C.s and A.s prefer that speakers and writers correct their own mistakes, because it avoids loss of face for the one who has erred, and it eliminates the need for such a socially difficult task as correcting someone.

Persuasive value

1 To perform a self-repair one must know that a mistake has occurred. So C.s should monitor their words, and also note any **body language** signs that A. has noticed an error. To have an error pointed out involves loss of face in that C. has not seen what A. can see. It is therefore a socially awkward act for A.s to perform, and there are ways of doing so more or less tactfully. The most tactful method is to give a questioning glance, or to offer a brief sound, say 'Uh,' where C. might expect the agreement sound 'Mhm.' A slightly less tactful method is to repeat the mistaken word or phrase, as in

Ex. 1 A: I thought Mary sang well at the party.
      B: Mary?

(where 'Mary' is the wrong name), or by adding 'I thought it was Sandra.' The least tactful way is to point out the error, correct it, and criticize A. for committing it, as in 'Mary! It was Sandra, you idiot!'

N.B. Choosing to correct another is to make a fuss, and one who does this should be sure that that is a good thing to do. It may well be taken as very antisocial to correct A in Ex. 1 if it is just a slip of the tongue (or mind?). If B knows that it was Sandra, and further, knows that A knows it, then to correct A shows a desire to humiliate. A would note this, and it could have bad consequences for the future persuasive power of their relationship.

2 To respond when corrected, the most neutral way is to show that it was just a superficial mistake, as in 'Did I say "Mary"?' or to offer a mild apology, 'Sorry, Sandra.' If A wishes to show a degree of annoyance, this could be done by adding 'Of course I meant Sandra.' If A wishes to go further and show anger, he or she could say 'Of course it was Sandra. It couldn't have been Mary—she was on holiday at the time and anyway she

can't sing.' Anger is clear in the way A shows that it was just a slip, and by the sheer quantity of unnecessary information added, forces it home to B that it might have been wiser to have said nothing rather than listen to a long explanation.

See also **Social convention of quantity**

Further reading   Schegloff, Jefferson, and Sacks (1977)

SENTENCE STRUCTURE: COMMAND/REQUEST

Task

To use the sentence structure of command/request to the best advantage.

Description

Sentence structure consists of a number of slots. For example, in command/request the basic slots are verb (V), object (O), complement (C), and adverbial (A). To these can be added the name of the person commanded, usually as first slot. So a basic command/request could take the following form:

Ex. 1 Name   V   O   C   A
       Peter, show your school report to your father now!

Persuasive value

The most important considerations in planning what to put into the slots in commands/requests are those concerned with face and politeness. Since this speech act is such a threat to A.'s self-esteem, and is such a curtailment of A.'s freedom of action, it needs careful handling if the relations between C. and A. are not to be damaged.

   Ex. 1 is bluntly produced, and so could be how his mother might perform it, but even with her acknowledged power over Peter she could have produced it more gently, as in

Ex. 2 Peter, come on dear, show your father your report.

In the first example the bluntness, and the fierceness of the 'now!' that ends it, suggests that she is exasperated with something in the situation. Most command/requests are not offered with such clear power.

   In fact, many of these acts are not just offered because the person performing them wants something done, but because he or she is trying to win power in the interaction. If someone tries to command, and is allowed to do so, and others obey, then that person has won a battle for superiority, however temporary it may be. Many interactions have such acts within them, and they should be noted with care since accepting them awards authority to the commander, and this may be used to some purpose once won.

As a corollary to this, if the command/request is obeyed although it has been offered with little by way of politeness, then that commander has won a great victory; whereas if he or she had to use a good deal of tact and politeness, then the victory is lessened by the amount of work it has taken to achieve.

See also **Face: sustain**; **Face threats**: **recognize**; **Politeness** tactics; the other **Sentence structure** tactics

Further reading Davidson (1984); Leech and Svartvik (1975); Quirk, Greenbaum, Leech, and Svartvik (1985)

SENTENCE STRUCTURE: QUESTION

Task

To use the sentence structure of questions to the best advantage.

Description

Sentence structure consists of a number of slots, For example, in questions the basic slots are verb (V), subject (S), object (O), complement (C), and adverbial (A)—though not all slots need be filled. So, a standard question could take this form:

Ex. 1 V   S   (V)   O   C   A
      Did Peter sell his car to Jim today?

Persuasive value

C.s should think carefully about what choices they make for each slot. And since questions act as a strong constraint on what A.s can answer, C.s should note what constraints they are producing. (*See* **Preferred response**.)

1 In Ex. 1, one constraint on A. is that he or she will have to make some answer as to whether Peter did or did not sell the car today. The options are 'yes,' 'no,' today,' or 'not today,' etc., and a few closely related ones—'Well not exactly sold, but Jim paid a deposit so it is going to be sold.'

2 C.s should consider whether their question will pose any face loss to A. as he or she answers it. In Ex. 1, is there any social disadvantage in selling

or not selling a car? For example, would A. care about the appearance of (mild) failure to sell? Does A. identify closely with his or her brother Peter? Would A. enjoy telling something to a disliked brother's disadvantage? And, importantly, is there any social disadvantage in A.'s having to return a negative answer to a question from C.? If C. had any doubt about any of these things, and was just asking for sociability anyway, then a more sociable, and less face-risky act would be to form the question in this way.

Ex. 2 How did your brother get on trying to sell his car?

If the goal is just sociability, and C. considers that A. could be made uncomfortable with any version of the question, then it should be left unasked.

See also the other **Sentence structure** tactics

Further reading   Lakoff (1973); Leech and Svartvik (1975); Quirk, Greenbaum, Leech, and Svartvik (1985)

SENTENCE STRUCTURE: STATEMENT

Task

To use the sentence structure of statements to the best advantage.

Description

Sentence structure consists of a number of slots. For example, in statements the basic slots are subject (S), verb (V), object (O), complement (C), and adverbial (A) (though not all of them need be filled). So a basic sentence could be:

Ex. 1   S   V   O   C   A
     Peter sold his car to a friend on Friday.

Each slot holds a 'sense unit'; that is, a matter which C. wishes to make public and tell to another person.

Persuasive value

1 In each slot, C.s should take care to use a sense unit which A. will understand: for example, in Ex. 1, does A. know Peter as 'Peter,' or 'brother of C.,' or not know him, in which case C. should use 'my brother Peter.'

2 C.s should choose a term which gives an accurate representation of the sense unit as C. perceives it: for example, in Ex. 1, C. should think whether 'sold' is exactly right, or whether 'exchanged' or 'bartered,' or 'sold for a profit,' would be more truthful; each would be understood differently by A.

3 C.s should choose the right amount of information for any particular A.: for example, in Ex. 1, C.s should decide between 'his car,' and 'his VW sedan,' and 'his 1967 VW "Bug" sedan.' The choice should depend on A.'s knowledge of, or interest in, cars.

4 C.s should consider what degree of friendliness they wish to show: for example, in Ex. 1, whether to say 'My older brother Peter who is studying science,' which assumes A. knows little about Peter, and also keeps a fair degree of distance between the two interactants. (It could be rudely distancing as a way of putting the matter, if A. could respond 'I know your brother, I've met him at your house often.' This suggests that C. has forgotten A.s visits, and this is unfriendly.) C. could, however, produce a very different sentence, 'My crazy brother Pete has just sold his beat-up old car to an equally crazy friend,' where the degree of informality in the language, and the description of the brother as 'crazy' and owning a 'beat-up old car,' show C. is willing to expose both him- or herself and family with all their faults, which is a more friendly act.

5 C. ends the statement with 'on Friday.' Adverbial slots need not be filled, and before filling them C.s should ask what purpose would be served by doing so. In this case, is 'on Friday' crucial to A.'s understanding of the event, or is it just a fact about the event and C. gives it for completeness? This particular instance seems to pose no problem, but occasionally people spend a lot of energy in supplying adverbials unnecessarily, and only succeed in boring their readers, as in

Ex. 2   Peter sold his car to a friend on Friday, about 3 o'clock. No, I tell a lie. It was around 4.15. Well, it may have been a bit later, but it was roughly about then anyway.'

See also the other **Sentence structure** tactics

Further reading   Leech and Svartvik (1975); Quirk, Greenbaum, Leech, and Svartvik (1985)

SET A REFRAIN

Tasks

To make a point memorable.
To link different parts of the communication to a specific point.
To present the text as structured.

Description

C.s can repeat exact phrases at intervals during their communications in order to make the content of the phrase memorable, or to link material with the main point, or to give an impression of structural form. The classic example is Mark Antony's funeral oration in *Julius Caesar*, where he repeats the ironic statement 'So are they all, all honorable men.' One by one he deals with various aspects of the men's behavior towards Caesar and at the end of each one repeats the refrain to keep his audience's focus on what links all the items together.

A more modern refrain might be as in

Ex. 1 We must take stock of our options in this recession. . . . First, we must take stock of the staffing needs. . . . Second, we must take stock of the overseas trading possibilities . . . and third, we must take stock of our efficiency levels.

Persuasive value

The refrain focusses attention on some goal of the user: in Ex. 1 that A.s do a certain action ('take stock') and even though they may wish to bring up other issues in such a broad coverage as the example shows, C. has set the limits of relevance by the refrain—and if someone brings up something different, C. can easily show it is out of order. The presence of a refrain shows that C. is in control of the structure of what is being communicated, and so that he or she is a good guide to follow.

Refrains can be very persuasive in that they signal divisions in the material, and may do so in misleading ways. A.s might prefer other divisions, and wish to have these discussed, but the pounding rhythm of the refrain suggests that the speaker is very insistent on the way the material has been treated, and will react badly to change, even if A.s can manage to insert their views. A strong refrain creates a communicative rhythm like a dance rhythm in which it is difficult to alter the beat or change the music.

There is a pleasure to be gained from recognition of the refrain as it recurs, and in time it can even be echoed by those present. One particular kind of refrain is the running gag in which an ongoing joke is steadily built up throughout a communication and which has proved entertaining on many occasions. In one Victorian melodrama the hero keeps repeating the phrase 'The mills of God grind slowly but they grind exceeding fine,' till by the fourth repeat the audience is ready to join in and delightedly shouts it out in unison with the actor.

Further reading Sonnino (1968)

SIDE SEQUENCES

Tasks

To avoid making an immediate response.
To change the topic or speech activity of a talk.
To digress in talk.

Description

The **exchange of speech** is rigorously governed by conventions of connect-edness, but these can be broken, for example by side sequences. A side sequence is a digression which breaks the connection between initiating move and response, and because it can occur unpredictably can prove disconcerting.

Ex. 1 A: So we went out last night to the movies.
　　　 B: What did you see?
　　　 A: *Rain Man*.
　　　 C: Anyone want another coffee?
　　　 A: No thanks . . . I enjoyed it.

Here C. produces an 'aside' which is neither on the topic of the previous utterance nor any kind of response to it.

Persuasive value

1 Side sequences with socially friendly purposes like the one in Ex. 1 are frequent. They often appear to be motivated by the good of the others—here offering them a coffee. But even such friendly side se-quences are recognized as intrusions by those offering them, as witness such accompanying phrases as 'Pardon me' or 'Excuse me, but would you like a coffee?' (And note that the criticisms of poor service in res-taurants and hotels often mention the intrusiveness of the waiters, and most people declare that the best service [i.e. side sequence] is the least obtrusive.)

2 Other side sequences are less obviously for the good of the others. When a latecomer to a meeting offers his or her apologies within another's speech exchange rather than waiting till a more opportune moment, and particu-larly when the apologies are lengthy or highly dramatized, he or she is likely to be judged as a bad communicator for not recognizing that a distraction is being caused.

3 A subset of side sequences are of the following type:

Ex. 2 A: It was a good resort Bill wrote.
　　　 B: Resort?

A: Sorry. Report. It was a good report Bill wrote.

This is not an **inserted sequence**, with the second speaker seeking clarification before responding to the initiating move, but rather it appears a gratuitous correction of a mere slip of the tongue. As a criticism it will make A. uncomfortable, and perhaps hostile; the error it focusses on is a superficial one, and raising it may persuade A that B is not listening to the essence of what is being said.

Further reading   Coulthard (1985); Goodwin (1981); Jefferson (1972); McLaughlin (1984); Nofsinger (1991)

SILENCE

Tasks

To manage interaction well.
To avoid silence.
To understand a silence.

Description

Silence is usually a negatively perceived social act, whether it occurs in talk, or in writing, or between interactions. Its significance is different in each case. In talk it signals mismanagement of **turntaking**, except in the most intimate of talk, where it is a sign of close accord. In writing, by not supplying an expected representation of some matter, it is interpreted as active avoidance or some problem of understanding the matter. When it occurs between interactions, especially where bonding is weak, it shows neglect.

Persuasive value

It is in talk that silence has the greatest complexity of effects, and it can happen, or be used deliberately, for some important reasons.
1 Its position in talk is important in determining its value. Where it occurs at the end of a turn, silence shows a lapse in interaction. It can indicate that no one has anything to say—which may reflect adversely on them, or on the previous speaker. It can show that no one likes the topic, or wishes to give the **preferred response**, or is embarrassed or annoyed by, or in some way resistant to, something in the speaker's performance, perhaps excess emotion, or power exertion. People show by silence that they wish to reserve something to themselves rather than share it with those present. They may indicate that something is wrong with the bonding of the group. Silence is always noticeable, and has an effect, and if it continues for any

time it can indicate a complete breakdown in relationships. A brief silence (a second or so) between turns is acceptable, but even this if repeated can indicate problems.

A silence or long pause within a turn can indicate to listeners that the speaker has a hesitation about the next matter to be mentioned, and they will interpret this as they wish. It may be seen as a problem of relationship with the listeners, or as a difficulty in articulation of the content, as a dramatic way of emphasizing a matter, or as an arrogant way to make others hang on in a waiting position for what is to come.

Where one single person remains silent for a long time this will create a sense of mystery about his or her character, about the motives for the silence, and generally about his or her goals. It can disconcert, antagonize others, and cause resistance to anything the silent one might do or say in the future. The presence of a silent person may make others unwilling to join in the talk out of fear for what the silence means—in case it means an adverse judgment, such as contempt.

Further reading   McGregor and White (1986); McLaughlin and Cody (1982)

SLOGANS

Task

To provide familiar phrases from media or advertising to reinforce an attitude.

Description

Slogans are widely disseminated phrases which are repeated throughout the range of media communications for a brief spell, and become familiar to the whole community as they are so frequently repeated, as in

Ex. 1 Put a tiger in your tank.

Ex. 2 I like Ike.

Ex. 3 I ♥ N.Y.

Ex. 4 Coke. The real thing.

Persuasive value

The source of slogans in the commercial and advertising world condemns them for many who prefer that if language is borrowed, is taken up just as others have designed it, it be borrowed from a more respectable source.

But although many slogans are commercially, and some are politically, generated, they can take on a life of their own as ordinary people use them for their own purposes.

1 When they are used just as they are, the same words and intonation as in the original advert or media program, they can be used as a sign of shared experience: not that all people drink Coke, but that people all over the world are exposed to Coke advertisements. They can therefore form a suitable topic for sociability instances and one that is safe in the sense that it is not personally focussed. However, their use, and constant reuse, means that whatever meanings they contain are incorporated into the world view of those using them. So, for example, since many ads show youthful women and men with beautiful bodies cavorting joyfully on the beach, these people and their activities become a symbol of what is admired and what is (or should be) enjoyable in society.

2 Used just as they are, however, they can meet with criticism from those who despise popular culture and the consumerist world, and their use would be very non-persuasive with such people. They would, for example, be out of place in formal settings and in serious encounters, where quotations from great writers would be more appropriate.

3 They may be viewed with less dislike if they are adapted by the people repeating them. That is, if people show originality in using them. This could be by changing the wording, as in Ex. 3 using 'I ♥ my dog' or using them as witty jokes in unusual contexts; that is, adapting them to circumstances, not just repeating them as the advertisers would like. The essence of using slogans well lies in this: making something useful and relevant to a particular circumstance from their prefabricated quality, and giving them novelty and original treatment.

See also **Sociable language**

Further reading   Atkinson (1984)

SOCIABLE LANGUAGE

Tasks

To create and maintain social bonds between people.
To repair damage to social bonds between people.

Description

Sociable language is language whose main aim is not the representation of matters but rather sociability. It is obviously and wholly non-representational, as in

Ex. 1 A: Hello, doctor.
   B: How are you Mrs. Smith?
   A: Fine thanks. How are you?
   B: Good. Now then, what's the problem?
   A: I feel terrible, doctor.

Although A says that she feels 'fine' then immediately says that she feels 'terrible,' this is accepted without comment, because both know that the first 'How are you?' is sociable language used to show friendliness; it is not asking for a representation of her health.

It can appear wholly referential, as in

Ex. 2 A: Well, look, I think we'll just have to agree to differ on this. [pause] Did you get away for the weekend?
   B: Yeah, we went to the beach and had a lovely time.

Here A.'s question raises the real topic, the beach weekend, but is still understood by both as primarily sociable—because it comes immediately after an argument, in which the social bond is strained, and needs to be made strong again.

Sociable language can be recognized by:

(a) poorer articulation and blander voice qualities;
(b) the topics used, which are a set of culturally accepted routines— the weather, last night's news/T.V., the failings of the boss/politicians, etc.;
(c) its location at the beginning and end of the interaction, and at any shift in action during it.

Persuasive value

1 It can be used to establish a bond, or to maintain, reinforce, or repair it.
2 Its absence or reduction can damage a bond. So also can a refusal to join in sociable language interaction with the other participant(s).

N.B.   Although the examples given here are from speech, sociable language also occurs in writing. Note that the formal salutations 'Dear Sir,' and 'We should be grateful for a reply at your earliest convenience, Yours faithfully,' contain some sociability, in that they use non-referential words like 'Dear,' 'Sir,' 'grateful', and 'faithfully.'

See also **Interaction: begin**; **Interaction closure** tactics; **Sociable language: topics**

Further reading   Levinson (1983); Mulholland (1991)

SOCIABLE LANGUAGE: TOPICS

Task

To set, maintain, or to change the social bond.

Description

Although sociable language is not referentially focussed, it is usually 'about' something: it can refer to C., or A. or to some more neutral topic, as in:

Ex. 1 Gosh, I'm feeling tired this morning.

Ex. 2 You are looking good/tired this morning.

Ex. 3 It's a lovely day today.

A person's choice of which kind to use is often purely routine but it has a strong social impact.

Persuasive value

1 By referring to oneself, C.s reveal general aspects of their preoccupations and opinions, as well as more specifically their current mood and attitude to the interaction. For example, it can show C. to be frivolous: 'That reminds me, I heard a great joke last night,' or grudging: 'I hate these business meetings.' It can also show C.'s sense of social distance from A., as in 'My office is working flat out at the moment.' Using 'my office' rather than 'I,' and choosing a collegial rather than a personal topic, C. shows a friendly but personally remote distance from A.

People note others' routines of social language and from them build a profile of their sociability, which can be used to persuasive effect. It does not follow, of course, that people using mainly self-focussed sociability will necessarily respond well to ego-boosting tactics, but they might.

2 By referring to the other person, C.s can still reveal something of themselves, but they also reveal their sense of role and social status with respect to A., as in: 'You look stressed, are things getting on top of you?' That is, 'you look as if you cannot manage your job, and I am clever enough to notice this.' It may sound like sympathy, but even so it leaves C. in a superior position to A., even when they are peers. Consider the first speaker's power plays in this casual chat before a meeting:

Ex. 4 A: Have you seen Bill?
       B: Er, is that the President?
       A: Oh, sorry, I forgot you don't know him.

Here A boasts that he or she knows the President as 'Bill' and that B does not. (The apology may or may not be sincere.)

3 By a neutral topic, C.s and A.s can delay self-revelation. Neutral topics are safe because they are non-committal, but not always. Consider the following:

Ex. 5 A: It's a lovely day, isn't it? Really good rain.
         B: It's a miserable day; it hasn't stopped raining.

where A's positive and B's negative views clash unsociably.

See also **Sociable language**; **Sympathize**

Further reading   Levinson (1983); Mulholland (1991)

SOCIAL CONVENTION OF MANNER

Tasks

To achieve a social act which is understood by A.
To be clear enough in manner to be understood by A.

Description

There are four social conventions that enact the **cooperative principle**. The social convention of manner states that to be cooperative with A., C.s must be clear enough for A. to understand them, and to do this they should use their knowledge of A's language experience, and must use it well.

Persuasive value

The convention seems very simple, though difficult to obey in practice, but its power is a more complex affair than this suggests.
1 Obviously, any departure from clarity (as A. judges it) could cause the communicated matter to be misinterpreted, or cause A. to judge C. adversely, as a poor communicator, as not having prepared his or her thoughts properly, or as arrogant (if the message is in unfamiliar terms), or as obstructionist in denying A. the chance to know and understand.
2 If A.s sense that C. is trying to be clear, but using an inappropriate standard of clarity, perhaps addressing A. as an adult addresses a child, or a child addresses an adult, or as an antagonist or colleague and not properly as a friend, they could see this as poor-quality clarity, and resist what C. is saying.
4 More importantly, because A.s know the convention, and expect clarity, it works to make them sense when a simple matter is presented unclearly, and they will seek for a reason. And it is in this way that the convention is interpretively useful. If, for example, C. seems unable to make a simple request, but says 'I was wondering if you could possibly tell me what time is

it?' A.s will note the signs of unclarity and deduce that C. has some difficulty in making the request, and from the kind and degree of unclarity will make some estimates of what is causing the problem.

5 Equally importantly, if C.'s language does appear to be clear, and nothing else but clear, with no signs of social rapport between C. and A., just a piece of information, then A. may interpret this badly, as a denial of his or her selfhood, interests, etc., and resist the information. Most communicative interactions involve social factors as well as informative ones and they usually incorporate something of sociability; even in a brief formal memo:

Ex. 1 To Research Staff: *Sorry* it is such short notice but *we* must have a
        meeting on 24th, 9:30 A.M., room 15. J.

A.s may not notice the presence of bonding signs, but they are sure to notice their absence. The only occasions when clear information alone is acceptable are some work-related instances where urgency is a priority, and in emergencies. A.s feel comfortable responding to them.

Further reading   Brown and Levinson (1987); Leech (1983)

SOCIAL CONVENTION OF QUALITY

Tasks

To achieve a social act which is understood by A.
To be seen as truthful.

Description

There are four social conventions that enact the **cooperative principle**. The social convention of quality states that C.s should tell the truth, and only say what they have evidence for.

Persuasive value

1 If C. appears to be telling the truth (as A. understands it), and to be doing nothing more than this, A. will realize that C. is offering information, no more than that, and is doing so in a neutral manner. A. will therefore take the information provided, and either accept or reject it, but more than this, will perceive C. to be not particularly sociable, and to be treating A. just as a receptacle for ideas, not as a human being. College lectures can often be just this kind of informative communication, without any recognition of the students as human beings. To be treated in this way is acceptable in small doses only; if it continues C. would be characterized as antisocial.

2 If C. appears not to be telling the truth, perhaps exaggerating or

underplaying it (*see* **Ironic understatement/overstatement**), then A. should be roused to consider why. So, for example, if C. were to say 'I've got a million books to take back to the library,' A. knows this could not be true. The social convention of quality has obviously been broken. If C. says it with a friendly smile and a pleasant tone of voice, then it is unlikely that C. is intending to tell a lie to mislead A. Instead A. should assume that the convention has been broken for some socially cooperative purpose—in this case, to share an experience which C. knows A. has also been through, to ask for sympathy, without being explicit about it, or in some other way be linked in social bonding with A. The greater the break with the convention the greater C.'s need for cooperation.

If A. knows the statement is false, but instead of working out why, treats it as a lie, and responds 'But you can't take more than four books out at a time, did you cheat to get them?' A. is wrong not to realize that the convention exists to be a means of measuring what else is involved in the communication C. has made. Even if A. responded to the lie not with an accusation of cheating, but with an innocent query, 'Oh, can you have a million books out at a time?' it would be a failure to recognize the true meaning of the C.'s apparent lie. A much better response, which accepted the social meanings, would be to say 'I hate carrying heavy loads,' or 'Do you want me to drive you there?'

Further reading   Brown and Levinson (1987); Leech (1983)

SOCIAL CONVENTION OF QUANTITY

Tasks

To achieve a social act which is understood by A.
To supply enough information to be useful to A.

Description

There are four social conventions that enact the **cooperative principle**. The convention of quantity states that C.s should make their contributions as informative as necessary for each stage of the interaction, and not more informative.

Persuasive value

It can obviously be difficult to be as informative as A. needs, since it requires a clear perception of A.s' knowledge and goals.

Ex. 1 A: Where are you from?
       B: England.
       A: I know that, but where in England?

Ex. 2 A: Where are you from?
      B: Well I was born in a little village in the north of England about twenty miles from Burnley.
      A: Oh you are from England are you?

The term 'information' needs to be defined in this context. Take the following example, said where A and B and Mary are classmates, and A and B are having coffee:

Ex. 3 A: Mary hasn't finished her essay.

For the utterance to make sense it assumes some information is already known to B: who Mary is, what an essay is, and that it must be finished. If this information has been incorrectly omitted, B will have to find it out (e.g. by asking 'Who is Mary?' or 'Which essay?' etc.) i.e. ask about the specifics of the topic. He or she is unlikely to ask 'What is an essay?' or query what it means to finish one, since this is general knowledge. The 'new' information A supplies lies in the combination of 'Mary' and 'her essay' and her 'not finishing' it.

At this stage B could think he or she understands the information, so asks 'Why is this amount of information being offered to me, now, and by this person?'. Assuming the cooperative principle, A must feel it is of value to B. If it seems mainly known information, perhaps it is meant to be primarily sociable. B could think 'Does A think it relevant because I dislike Mary and enjoy hearing criticism about her? Could the new information about Mary and her essay be thought relevant to me because A knows I too have not finished my essay and wants me to feel better knowing that someone else is in same situation? This appears less likely; the more standard way of giving that kind of information would be "Mary hasn't finished her essay either." If A knows I have finished my essay, is it intended to make me feel good because I am better than Mary?'

See also **Sociable language**

Further reading Brown and Levinson (1987); Leech (1983)

SOCIAL CONVENTION OF RELEVANCE

Tasks

To achieve a social act which is understood by A.
To show relevance to the topic, or the interactional purposes.

Description

There are four social conventions that enact the **cooperative principle**. The convention of relevance states that C.s should make their contribution to an interaction relevant to the topics and purposes of the event. Relevance especially applies to the relation between one communicative act and the next.

Persuasive value

Ex. 1 A: It's started raining
        B: Oh dear! My laundry is on the clothesline!

In such an example it would be understood by A that B is obeying the maxim of relevance, because there is an easy progression of inferences to follow which show how this is so: rain makes things wet, laundry is put on the clothesline to dry, rain will spoil the drying process. The connection may be harder to follow in

Ex. 2 A: There's a lovely shirt in that store window.
        B: Don't tell me, I'm broke.

but it is still possible—shirts are in store windows to be bought and sold, buying them costs money, B has no money and so cannot take an interest in the shirt. However, whereas in the first example the easy relevance is used to show bonding, in the second example the harder to follow relevance is used to be unfriendly. It is basically true to say that the less obviously relevant a response is the more it shows some kind of social trouble. In Ex. 2 we see a rejection of A's topic, and we must assume that B intended to do this, but it is done obliquely, B does not just say 'How boring, I am not at all interested in talking about shirts.' What B does is hide behind the social convention of relevance: he or she shows a reasonably high degree of irrelevance in order to be unfriendly rather than be directly rude.

The convention is also a useful way of performing difficult social acts, like requests or demands. So, if A wished to have B close the door, and felt that he or she had no right to request it, or that it would prove a nuisance for B, the request could be put indirectly, as a breaking of the convention of relevance, by for example, suddenly saying 'Goodness it is cold in here, is that door open?' B would search for its relevant meaning—working out 'Why is this being said at this time and to me?' B might stop there, and think the utterance is just friendly, and respond by agreeing. (Oblique requests always risk being misunderstood.) But if B continued, and started thinking what it might really mean, he or she might notice the door is at hand, that A frequently asks B to do things like close doors, and so on, and B might eventually close the door.

See also **Politeness: use indirection**

Further reading   Brown and Levinson (1987); Leech (1983)

SOUNDS AND SENSE

Tasks

To focus attention on a matter.
To focus attention on C.'s language skills.
To set a tone.
To reinforce the chances of a good response.

Description

1 Sounds can imitate the sense of what is being represented (called 'ono-matopoeia' in classical rhetoric):

Ex. 1 The mutterings and grumblings of the mutinous staff members.

2 In quite a different way, words can be chosen which have similar sounds but different meanings, and the similarity in sound be used to yoke matters which have little real connection (called 'paronomasia' in classical rhetoric):

Ex. 2 The supervisors, and sundry loony advisers, have been involved in
      this.

Persuasive value

1 By using onomatopoeia, C. can set two cognitive processes working in tandem in A.'s mind. The sounds make A. search the memory for experiences which 'fit' the sounds, and for the word meanings. If the word choice is good, the two processes should coalesce to produce one thoroughly well perceived notion, with experiential evidence to support it. A. may still reject the notion, but this will not be because it was misunderstood.

Sentence structures also imitate meanings, as when a slowly developing sentence echoes a slow process that is being represented by it, or when a staccato series of words imitates a quickly moving series of events.

Sound imitation can serve also another purpose: to affect the tone for an interaction. So harsh, gutteral sounds suggest a mood of anger, haste, etc., while sibilants and an abundance of long vowel sounds can indicate mildness, or calm. Using sound to set tone can either reinforce what will be represented in the words or clash with them to some effect. So, for example, if C. has a harsh action to perform, like a brusque command, he or she could mitigate it by softness of sound in the words chosen to represent it.

2 Sounds can also be used quite differently, to suggest similarity between matters which have little real connection. The sounds signal the connection without accounting for it, or explaining it. This can be useful if C. wishes to join unlike ideas together and have them jointly perceived by A., as in

Ex. 2 where the phrases 'supervisors' and 'sundry loony advisers' are made to be matched. In this way C. can show how he or she perceives 'supervisors'—not as superiors in charge, but as foolish 'loony' unattached 'sundry' people who advise.

Further reading   Corbett (1990); Sonnino (1968)

SPOKEN COMMUNICATION: CHOOSE

Tasks

To consider the choice between written and spoken communication.
To select the best mode of communication where there is a choice between speech and writing.

Description

Spoken communication is very different from writing in the following respects:

(a) C. is present, delivering the text.
(b) The material presented should be more or less known by A.
(c) Information is given in smaller and less complex units than in writing.
(d) The words and grammar used are chosen at speed, so the words are not always used precisely, with their dictionary meanings, and the grammar is often messy and uncontrolled.
(e) There is little sense of design structure in the text.
(f) The text and the whole communication activity are transient (unless recorded).

Each mode of communication requires quite different skills.

Persuasive value

In human experience speech is learnt before writing, and its features set the pattern for people's expectations of communication. In spoken interactions people know who is talking, share a context with them, and expect the communication to have practical value. Also, they expect spoken interaction to involve solidarity, agreement, and cooperation between the participants; that is, all the most comfortable possibilities where people are gathered together. These expectations should always be taken into account if C.s are to achieve any part of their goals for an interaction. Therefore, the greater the maintenance of bonding and a sense of shared common ground between speakers, the more successful the event will be for any persuasion within it. A spoken interaction can also work as pre-persuasion to some other event in the future. So opportunities for speech with others should never be despised as chat or small talk.

Speech is a far more prevalent mode of communication than writing, and is used by all members of the community, not just the higher-status ones. Perhaps as a consequence of these two facts, speech is held in lower social regard than writing. If a particular speech turns out to be important (for example, if an elderly person tells an interesting tale of pioneer days), someone will suggest that it is too good for the impermanence of speech and should be accorded the status and permanence of writing.

To take up points (a)–(f), respectively, described above:

1 C. is present.

(a) This means that he or she can add to the words and grammar the dimensions of **intonation** and **body language**, making a threefold communication. Each can enhance the meaning of the others and can make meanings more intense, emphasized or complex. For example, C. could speak using words in their literal meaning but add a wry facial expression which undermines the literal, as in

Ex. 1 I wouldn't dream of coming late to work.

where C. wishes to suggest the opposite meaning, that he or she has dreamed of it but may or may not have done it.

(b) C.'s presence means that he or she can adapt the speech as required to A.'s reactions, and do so as soon as they occur. C. can decide, for example, to elaborate if A. looks puzzled, or to cut the speech short if A. looks bored. And A.s expect this, and can even use their reactions to force C. to change what he or she is saying.

2 A.s expect that the bulk of the ideas, facts, and events presented as material in speech should either be familiar or at least fit into their general conceptions of the world: they do not want much that is startlingly new or odd. In speech, unlike writing, A. expects to agree with C. to a high degree. Some new material is welcome for interest's sake, particularly if it relates well to old, known material, but A.s do not want too much of it. Speech, in fact, consists of a good deal of repetition from day-to-day of ideas, and even phrases and sentences—people repeat their favorite stories, state their favorite opinions and so on, over and over again. And this is not only tolerated but expected: it makes A.s feel comforted to hear the familiar talk and so to know that the world is much the same as it always was.

3 Absorbing information in speech is difficult because it is constrained by the speed of C.'s delivery. A.s can therefore comfortably manage only a small unit of information in their short-term memories and C.s should pace their information with this in mind. (*See* **Information flow**.)

4 Words have to be chosen at high speed during spoken interaction, as C.s respond to the speech of others. This means that words are usually from the most familiar, well-used vocabulary of everyday talk; the ones, that is, with the broadest range of meanings and little precision. A.s can 'understand' something of the meaning of these easily, though what exactly they understand is uncertain. They will be displeased if too many unusual or difficult words are used because they take longer to absorb, and require more thought, all at high speed.

The grammar too is produced and has to be understood at speed and consequently should show less of the complexity of writing—more coordinated sentences and fewer subordinated ones, fewer elaborate noun phrases, etc.

5 Individual speakers cannot control the structural design of their contributions to speech in an interaction because they are engaged in dialog, which means that others will interfere with their plans and intrude their own. Speakers can and should, however, plan to control each utterance they make. (*See* **Spoken communication: design**.)

6 Knowing that speech is transient could lead C.s to feel confident that their words will not become public property beyond the event. It is a foolish confidence; speech is reported just as writing is, with much less accuracy, and little possibility of verification. It will entirely depend on the reporter's memory, and is unlikely to show the contribution made by intonation and the non-verbal modes. If therefore it is important to be reported well, C.s should circulate a written version of their contributions to the event.

See also **Body language**; **Express personal involvement**; **Intonation**; **Restricted code**; **Voice quality**; **Written communication: choose**

Further reading Chafe (1985); Olson, Torrance, and Hildyard (1985)

SPOKEN COMMUNICATION: DESIGN

Task

To design a spoken text so that it achieves C.'s goals.

Description

A.s expect that most of the following features will be present in a spoken text:

(a) some revelation of C.'s self;
(b) an appearance of spontaneity;
(c) the information is in small and discrete units;

(d) no overall design plan but well-designed utterances;
(e) **intonation** support for design purposes;
(f) frequent use of **sociable language**;
(g) recognition that all present may wish to speak.

Persuasive value

A.'s expectations must be met if the communication is to be persuasive. (In the discussion below, the model interaction is collegial, informal talk. The comments need to be adjusted if they are to be applied to either very casual talk or very formal meetings.)

1 C.s are required to give (or they may pretend to give) a glimpse into the way their minds work as they speak. That is, they reveal themselves as hesitating, changing their mind (and words), they are seen making choices, etc. Except in the most formal interactions A.s expect, and want, to hear this apparent preparation for speech within the finished product. They will respond badly to speakers who are too polished and formal. C.s can use this preference to advantage if they need to produce complex meanings, for example by offering several versions of a thing, as if hesitating which to choose, while really intending all the versions to be understood together: for example,

Ex. 1   It's a matter of procedure, well, more or less procedure, but I suppose it's also dependent on what they reply, I think . . .

Here C. represents 'it' as a procedural matter, but has some reservations, and these depend on a reply, so finally he or she is still uncertain about it. All of this apparent confusion may be exactly what C. wishes to convey.

2 A.s not only dislike polished performances in speech but they also dislike utterances which pay no attention to the immediate context in which they occur, particularly if they ignore those people present: Queen Victoria is said to have objected to talking to Prime Minister Gladstone because he always addressed her as if she was a public meeting. Utterances should therefore incorporate the circumstances of the event, and should appear to arise spontaneously from the immediate context of the inter-action, and not be prepared in advance. (The best jokes are the ones which do this, while prepared one-liners of the kind used by some comedians are less-valued in interactive speech.)

However, some preparation is obviously necessary in order to achieve the speaker's goals; but it should not consist of a plan for one's whole contribution to an event, let alone a plan for the whole event, including the acts of others. Signs of this kind of control will be viewed negatively by others. Suitable preparation should involve thinking about what topics to raise, or avoid, what speech acts to perform, and what responses to make to anticipated acts by others.

3 Any new ideas, opinions, or facts that C.s wish to contribute to spoken interaction should be minimal. As an informal guide, most lecturers would consider that only four new ideas should be communicated in an hour. At a micro-level, some research suggests that the amount of information people can hold in their short-term memories is roughly the amount of information that can be represented in seven words. This is an approximate guide only; it is useful in that it indicates that a very small amount of information can be absorbed at a time. For example, in the following pair of utterances by Mary, the first caused information overload problems which the second one rectified by padding out the information over a longer stretch.

Ex. 2 Mary: Come in. You need to fill in one of those forms then check the board for a class time that suits you then come and see me.
       Student: Pardon?
       Mary: Come in O.K.? The first thing you need to do is fill in one of those forms—the ones on the table, O.K.? Then see the board here and have a look at it to see which class time suits you. For example you could do the first one on Monday, see? Then come along here and see me.
       Student: Oh. Right.

4 Each utterance should connect with those before it (*see* **Exchange of speech**), and should be designed to expect a following utterance from someone present. It should also contain signals of its approaching end so that others can know when to take the floor. It should be of a comparable length with the ones before it; conversations build up a kind of rhythm of utterance length as they proceed, and speakers should follow the pattern if they wish to be perceived as a friendly interactant.

5 **Voice quality** and **intonation** can be used to enhance the features of the text, providing emphasis, establishing cohesion, and showing relationships between parts of the material. They also assist in signalling the approaching end of an utterance. In speech a flat monotone and unvarying intonation will not just bore A., but, because no help in interpretation is offered, will render the text difficult to understand. So the preparation for an important spoken interaction should also involve rehearsing the intonation to be used.

6 Since people consider that speech should be addressed to the maintenance of sociability, some effort should be made to insert **sociable language** to some degree (see Ex. 2, where most of the padding is sociable). C.s can choose whether to concentrate it at the start and close of the interaction or to keep a modicum of it running throughout, or both. The choice should to some extent copy the way others are using it, for sociability. (*See also* **Listening: active.**)

7 Spoken interaction is rarely a monolog, and so A.s expect to be able to take a turn. They will therefore be unsympathetic towards anyone who denies them this right, by speaking too long or by speaking in 'written' language or on abstruse topics so they cannot join in the discussion and so are inhibited from taking their fair turn.

See also **Spoken communication: choose**; the **Turn** tactics; **Written Communication: choose**;

Further reading   Chafe (1985); Olson, Torrance, and Hildyard (1985)

STATE

Task

To produce an opinion, idea, or fact, which is formulated as a statement to be accepted as true information.

Description

Statements have special qualities:

(a) they are assumed to be true and provable;
(b) they are understood to be offered just for consideration;
(c) they are seen not as persuasive in intent, but to be something which is communicated in order to be on public record;
(d) they are taken to be offered dispassionately.

Persuasive value

All these assumed qualities have a strongly persuasive impact.
1 Since a statement is taken to be offered as true and to be produced only for consideration, A.s are likely to accept it more easily, and while they may not altogether agree with it, nevertheless they could report its contents so these become widely known, and hence be influential in setting the framework within which people think.
2 Since it is assumed to be offered as 'just' information which is worth putting on public record, A.s may take it at face value. But this assumption, that there is such a thing as 'just' information, is foolish. Every piece of information arises from a personal choice of what to say and how to say it; and that choice is influenced by cultural and other social factors; and arises from some motive or another. It follows, then, that every informative statement is to some degree or another less than objective. And what it represents is available to exert a particular influence on those who receive it.

A.s are likely to accept statements at face value because of their long socialization to statements as a way of imparting information. People have memories of schooldays during which their heads were filled with state-ments, like 'There are seven days in the week,' 'Christopher Columbus sailed the ocean blue in 1492,' etc., all of which were accepted without evidence of any kind. And this happened in part because it is thought that teachers are motivated by nothing other than what is best for the education of their pupils, and so are just supplying information disinterestedly. If communicators can build on these memories, and sound like disinterested teachers, then their statements could well be very influential, and be accepted without question. However, if communicators sound tentative, or emotionally involved, or urgently persuasive, then the statement will be received more hesitantly.

Making a statement has therefore the potential to be as persuasive as any other speech act of more obvious influence. Its power to some extent, of course, depends on the content of the statement's information.

If the information is already known by A.s, it would be accepted as reinforcing their knowledge; if it requires them to make a slight adjustment to their knowledge this may be quite acceptable also. If it has cognitive value in that it gives an overview of details already known, or shows relations between things which A.s had not previously noticed, or if it serves some useful classifying purpose, etc., it may prove influential as it causes adjustments to A.s' thinking.

If, however, the information is strange or new, or if it demands a realignment of what is already known (e.g. 'turned my views upside down,' 'knocked my world sideways') it may meet with resistance, but on the other hand it may just prove very influential.

When about to make a statement, C.s should try to think along these lines to understand what effect it will have on A.s, and how A.s will view the person who produces that effect on them: there is a well-known folk-saying about people disliking messengers who tell them bad news, and it applies equally to those who make disturbing statements.

See also **Command/request**; **Questioning**

Further reading   Mulholland (1991); Wierzbicka (1987)

STATISTICAL SUPPORT

Tasks

To support an argument.
To support C.'s authority.

Description

C.s can refer to statistical figures which support their point, or enhance their position as a communicator.

Persuasive value

The statistics will only be persuasive if A. understands them; many people cannot 'read' Bell curves, block diagrams, or pie charts, or even percentages. So C.s should carefully consider the best way to make the figures readable, given the likely expertise of A. But even if C. fails to make them throughly understandable this need not mean that using figures is persuasively useless; their very presence in the text could mark it as 'expert' or 'authoritative' and so persuade some A.s.

It is vital that all A.s should note how they are being persuaded by statistics. They should check the figures to see what exactly they are saying. They should note whether they come from an unbiassed source, whether they are up to date, and most importantly whether they actually support the point. And, they should check them to see what has been left out that might be significant. If a statistic implies that because two million people bought Smith's Soap the product must be good, it is worth asking the question 'How many people bought it twice?'

Also it is important to consider how the statistics were found—if the figures are based on phone polls, or questionnaires (which may contain loaded questions), or just asking people in the street for their views, they are evidence for nothing. In a recent evaluation of university teachers it was found that many who scored highly across all the other questions failed when students were asked 'Does this teacher motivate you to work hard?' Apparently students felt that motivation is self-produced and nothing to do with the teacher. The low score on this question reduced the teacher scores significantly, and if queries had not been raised about why the low mark was occurring it would have given a false impression that the teachers were poor motivators.

In some cases statistics, however well gathered and communicated, are quite irrelevant as support: for example, in a debate about health-care funding, if a C. says 'only 0.23 per 1,000 babies die of this disease, so we should not fund research on it,' A.s could quite properly retort that even one baby's death is too much; the statistic ignores the human aspects of what it is showing.

Further reading   Corbett (1977, 1990)

STEREOTYPES

Task

To make a matter easily recognizable.

Description

Society has a set of representations in language for people, groups, and events, that are standardized or stereotyped. They contain value judgments about the thing represented, and their frequency of use causes them to become fixed perceptions, which are mainly unconscious but none the less powerful. For example, there are stereotypes of gender, or of occupational groups, like politicians or housewives, and the value judgments of them are automatically produced: if the word 'blonde' is used it is usually prefixed with 'dumb'; academics live in 'ivory towers,' etc. There are also stereotypes of such events as riots or courtroom 'battles.' They are useful shorthand generalizations, but because they are value laden, and attract automatic support or rejection, they can be problems.

In professional discourse, stereotypes also exist (e.g. of meeting procedure, of bureaucratic writing, or interdepartmental rivalries) and these are fixed perceptions which we all share.

Even though people may be aware from personal experience of exceptions to a stereotype, they may resist adapting or losing it. So if someone who has a stereotype of youth as rebellious meets a young man who is conspiciously conformist, he or she could refuse to accept the evidence, and believe that the youth is hiding his rebellion, or has yet to come to the rebellious stage, or is the exception which proves the rule.

Persuasive value

1 Stereotypes help communication by packing a lot of meaning into one or two words; for example, 'typical bureaucrat' represents a thoroughly understood and agreed notion.
2 But this help has to be paid for: they can prevent new ideas or innovative proposals from receiving proper attention if these (or the people offering them) do not fit some stereotype. So, for example, if the minute secretary at a meeting came up with a good idea, the stereotype of his or her role as merely a recording instrument could mean that the idea received less than its fair share of attention. (Or, of course, if the idea were taken up, its source may well be forgotten, or the idea attributed to someone else.)
3 If C. and A. do not share stereotypes then miscommunication is likely, and so is an awareness of social or ideological difference which may be counterproductive.
4 If C.s feel that their own topics or activities could clash with A.'s stereotypes of them attention should be given to countering this, or else their communication will simply not be taken in let alone accepted.

5 On the other hand, if what is communicated fits the stereotype, then A. may understand it as 'typical' and not attribute it specifically to C. as a person. It will then be hard for C. to retain personal ownership of any idea offered.

Further reading   Sonnino (1968)

SUBSTITUTES FOR NAMES

Tasks

To reveal general attitude or mood.
To show specific attitude to the person to be named.

Description

To substitute a phrase for a name.

Persuasive value

Where a C. wishes to emphasize his or her attitude towards a person, but to do so covertly, it can be incorporated into the communication by substituting a phrase for the name of the person.
1 The person's social role (or one of his or her social roles) or characteristic behavior could be used, as in 'our friendly neighborhood police officer' (for a colleague with police tendencies) or 'our mine of information on the regulations' for a colleague who is well informed.
2 The person's status either in general social terms or with respect to the participants could be used, as in 'Sir has called another meeting,' or 'The boss has sent us another memo.'
3 The person's office, profession, qualifications, could be used, as in 'The Registrar is calling for nominations,' 'Our Personnel Officer is on the phone,' or 'Scientists spend too much of the University's money.'
   The C. can in these and other ways indicate his or her views or opinions. It is achieved partly by what the word choice represents but also by the associations it brings with it. In particular the tone of C.'s viewpoint can be effective.
4 There is a special set of names called 'nicknames' which also incorporate attitudes; they differ from the others above by being more intimate. They may refer to personal qualities like body weight, 'Fatty,' or the wearing of glasses, 'Four-eyes.' They may be a corruption of the person's name, or, a favorite, a baby's lisping version of the name, etc. The use of such names

marks the users as part of a close group, family, school class, etc., and can act to exclude others who don't recognize who is being the focus of communication.

Further reading   Sonnino (1968)

SUM UP

Task

To produce a brief covering comment on a complex matter.

Description

To sum up a complex matter, or a set of events, as it comes to an end, and to reduce it to one single assertion.

Persuasive value

The amount of material in the complex matter that must be left out means that C. has a high degree of flexibility about the way he or she interprets the material, and therefore also how it is summed up. This means that C. can impose a less than fair meaning on the material, and so be persuasive. This can also happen because the summing up itself can be quite loosely linked to the material it is about. And finally the fact that a summing up can be an assertion, and need not be a recapitulation of events or topics, means that C.'s choice of assertion presents a major opportunity for persuasive influence.

All that is required of a summing up is that it show a serious attempt to say some one thing that will best capture the essence of the matter. It must also be put in a strikingly phrased way (many summations are rather like **proverbs** in form), so that it can be held in memory longer than the events it describes. Typical examples are:

Ex. 1   It was just another of those meetings where little was done and a lot was said.

Ex. 2   The best way to sum up the interviewing process is to say that many were called but few will be chosen.

Further reading   Wierzbicka (1987)

SYMPATHIZE

Task

To show fellow feeling with others over some trouble they have.

Description

To share another's emotional state, particularly the states of misery, distress, fear, or pain. It can also be a demonstration of fellow feeling for someone feeling weak, oppressed or poor. It represents at its best the appreciation of someone who has had similar experiences and so can understand and not judge adversely the low state of another.

Persuasive value

Most people appreciate sympathy as a demonstration of close bonding, and because it supports their self-esteem that others should show a fellow feeling with them. It makes them feel less isolated in their low state that others can try to share their feelings or situation. However, it is a very difficult act to perform well, partly because those to whom it is directed are in a low state, are emotional or stressed or in pain, etc., and their sensitivity to slights is heightened. It is also difficult because it almost always arises out of a situation in which the sympathizer is better off than the other, and this imbalance in social position is difficult to handle well. This is particularly so when the sympathy is offered as an **initiating move**, as in

Ex. 1 You are looking rather depressed this morning, are you O.K.?

Ex. 2 I heard you were ill, are you feeling better?

In Ex. 1, C. could annoy or irritate A. if A. does not feel that he or she is 'looking rather depressed,' and will not see the act as one of sympathy but as an attempt to reduce A. socially. Even the attention represented by C.'s noticing A.'s appearance and the time taken to ask after his or her health will not offset that first mistake in reading A.'s appearance.

In Ex. 2, C. reveals that people have been speaking about A. while he or she was not present, and while this may meet acceptance as a sign of bonding, it might also affect a sensitive A. badly as being gossip, perhaps malicious gossip, about him or her. If this first part of Ex. 2 is received well, however, there might still be problems with the second part, though this is less likely. If A.'s situation is one which will not improve in the short term or at all, then the question 'Are you feeling better?' may be too intrusive, since it will require A. to either lie and reply 'I'm better thanks,' or to tell the truth, 'No, nor am I likely to be; I have a major illness,' which he or she may well not want to reveal.

To ask for sympathy is seen as a antisocial act, since it is felt that it should be generously given, not required of people, and it is likely to meet a bad response.

Further reading   Mulholland (1991); Wierzbicka (1987)

TELLABLE TOPIC: CHOOSE

Tasks

To maintain a bond.
To choose a topic of interest to others.
To meet social obligations to supply information to others.

Description

A tellable or newsworthy topic for an encounter is one that suits all the factors involved in the event: the setting, goals, participants, timeframe, and channel (speech or writing). It should also be relatively new.

Persuasive value

1 If a topic is entirely suitable it can produce an enjoyable interaction and so a good framework within which to be persuasive. If it is unsuitable, as, for example, an intimate anecdote in a formal meeting, it will present C. as either ignorant of the conventions or deliberately breaking them.
2 Every interaction, provided it is not by chance, is assumed to have a goal, so whoever initiates the event will be entitled to set the first topic, to fit his or her goal (and will be peeved if not allowed to do this).
3 When a topic is not considered newsworthy enough, this can be reflected in such phrases as 'She never has anything new to say,' or 'What has that got to do with me?' They indicate that the topic should be new, and in some degree relevant to A.s' lives. It should never be totally familiar except when people are engaging in **sociable language**. It need not be of immediate relevance but should be something detailed and useful enough to be worth storing until it has relevance. So the topic should be offered with enough detailed information and explanatory power to be of use.
4 For some topics there is a convention which requires that a specific person raise them, and this is reflected in such a phrase as 'Why didn't he tell me himself instead of making you do it?'
5 An important tellability convention places people under compulsion to tell A. of a matter if they know it has immediate consequences for A., and to do so in time to be useful. So, for example if Mary knows that her colleague Bill is looking for a new car, and she sees one fitting his requirements, Mary must tell him, and tell him soon. She is expected to go to some trouble to do so, as much trouble as the closeness of their working relationship suggests. For example, she should tell him first thing next day at work; there would be no need to ring him that night if they never communicate outside the work environment. The convention works on the assumption that Mary may be found out as knowing something which

would help Bill and not passing it on. If Bill discovered her lapse, he would take it as a mark of unfriendliness, and could be made hostile by it.

6 A similar convention stipulates the order of people to whom a tellable matter should be told. For example, if a son got engaged, he must tell his parents first, then friends, perhaps next his Aunt Flo and then immediately Aunt Emmy since either one of them would be hurt to hear the news first from the other. If by chance a friend were told before the parents, they would be told to 'keep it to yourselves until I've told my parents.'

Further reading   Coulthard (1985); Mulholland (1991); Nofsinger (1991)

TESTIMONY OF OWN EXPERIENCE

Task

To prove some matter which is new to others by citing one's own experience as evidence.

Description

When some information is thought likely to be new to A., and therefore in need of evidential support, one method is to give testimony from one's own experience as a guarantee that the information is true. As in:

Ex. 1 During the Second World War, in Britain butter was rationed to two ounces a week—I remember it quite clearly, I used to spread my ration thinly on my slice of bread so that it would last the week, while my sister would gobble hers on just one slice and then make do with margarine.

Persuasive value

If C.s are depending solely on their own experience as testimony, it is crucial that the experience is given in some detail, and that it is clear, vivid, concretely detailed, and presented in such a way that it creates a link with A.'s very different experience. So in Ex. 1 C. is clear about facts, 'two ounces,' and not something as vague as 'only a tiny bit'; not only states that he or she remembers, but proves it; gives evidence not just from own actions but also from his or her sister's, with the implication that she could be asked to vouch for it. The idiosyncratic detail of the sister gobbling her ration has what people call the ring of truth about it, by which they mean that they could imagine themselves doing the same thing. And in giving two contrasting ways of dealing with butter rations, C. allows A. to get involved with thinking how they would eat their butter, and by taking this narrative of experience into their own lives they themselves give support to the testimony and so can accept it as true.

The hardest testimony from personal experience is where the experience is so different from that of those receiving it that they cannot recognize any possible options for themselves were they to have the same experience. As in:

Ex. 2   I was driving along and came round a corner and I nearly ran into this car crash. I stopped the car and rushed across. There was a terrible smell of gasoline and I thought the car would go up in flames, but I managed to get this baby out of the passenger door, but then the whole thing erupted.

A.s hearing this could well find it hard to imagine themselves doing such an heroic act, and so could find it difficult to accept the hero's testimony, not because they distrust him or her necessarily, but because it is beyond their sense of themselves and how they relate to experience.

Further reading   Corbett (1977, 1990); Sonnino (1968)

'THEREFORE'

Task

To suggest that some things add up to an inevitable conclusion.

Description

'Therefore,' when it comes at the end of a series of matters—ideas, facts, or opinions—has the meaning 'and so it follows from these reasons that this conclusion is true.'

Persuasive value

The very presence of the word 'therefore' can be enough to make the preceding matters into reasons for something, and the following matter into the inevitable conclusion to be drawn from those reasons. As a consequence its persuasive power is very strong. It can be used quite legitimately to show that a process of reasoning has reached its conclusion, but it can also be used with intent to deceive.

It can deceive in two ways: by making the preceding matters, which may be a list of quite unconnected things, into reasons which come together to suggest a conclusion; or by naming a false conclusion, one which does not arise from those reasons, or which is not the only conclusion to be drawn from them.

Ex. 1 We need our graduates to feel that their university is the best there is, and we also need to design our courses so they are more attractive to students. Therefore we need to employ a firm of publicity consultants: I would suggest Smith and Brown. They have done good work for a couple of businessmen I know.

A further problem to consider whenever the word 'therefore' is used is that it may falsely suggest that because some things have occurred before some matter, they have caused that matter. It is a classical logical fallacy to assume that just because there is a time relationship between two things that there is a logical connection, and one of cause and effect, so in the following example it would be illogical to assume that the first thing caused the second:

Ex. 2 Mary was in town, playing hooky from her work, and she had just had lunch in this café when she was run over by this man driving down the street. It was bound to happen: if you play hooky you must expect dire consequences.

See also **Begging the question**; **'Either–or' fallacy**

Further reading   Quirk, Greenbaum, Leech, and Svartvik (1985)

TITLE CHOICE

Tasks

To guide people in their interpretation.
To influence their understanding of a text.

Description

The title chosen for a text signals to intending readers the topics, themes, and tone they will find in it.

Persuasive value

Whatever is chosen as the title is a metonym for all that the communication contains, and as such can influence how the whole text is understood. The title frames the interpretation (i.e. it constrains A. to a frame of mind, and to a way of processing the material), one which C. hopes is conducive to acceptance of the content.

Ex. 1 *Principles of Pragmatics*

As a book title, this tells the reader that the text will focus on ideas, 'principles,' and yet at the same time will deal with pragmatic (practical) matters. Also the word 'pragmatics' resembles words like 'mathematics,' and suggests that C. will present the practical matters as a subject which could be studied as mathematics is studied. This title contains very different notions from, say, *Handbook of Persuasive Tactics*, which by using 'Handbook' shows the text is of practical, 'hands-on' value, and the subject is 'tactics' (i.e. the specific use of persuasive methods, not abstract notions of persuasion).

A title may cause readers not to read on because it promises nothing of interest. But a false promise will cause them to read in expectation of something that the text will not supply, and consequently their sense of the content and theme, etc., will be seriously distorted, and will persuade them of nothing except that the writer is a cheat. Chapter and section titles also need care for the influence they can exert. Titles can also exist, and exert influence, in spoken communication, as statements of theme, as in

Ex. 2 We need to talk about the difficulties of postgrad students.

where C. guides the discussion by naming it 'talk' not 'make a decision,' or 'make recommendations,' and calls the situation of postgraduates the 'difficulties,' not 'situation,' or 'distress,' etc.

See also **Metonymy**; **Paragraph design**; **Topic** tactics

Further reading   Brown and Levinson (1987)

TOPIC

Tasks

To make good use of subject matter in a communication.
To find a suitable subject for communication.

Description

Topic is a significant aspect of communication and needs careful handling, and there are many tactics in this book addressed to this problem. There are conventions or rules for topic use in both speech and writing: rules for what would constitute a good topic; rules for handling topic conflict; and conventions for ensuring that a topic is coherently treated, etc.

Persuasive value

The most general convention about topic is that there must be one, and it must be shared by those participating. It is only in **sociable language** that topic can be less than vital, and even then there must be some kind of topic if the sociability is not to be very boring. Communication must be 'about something' if it is to please all parties to it. Equally, the parties have to agree on a single topic they will all use, at least for a time. It is a total failure of communication if people speak to each other and pay no attention to the others' topics. In some parts of the community this behavior would be judged as insane, or the person doing it as having some kind of learning difficulty.

The best topics are those judged to be appropriately 'tellable,' that is with some relevance to the interests of the people involved.

They can be selected because they interest the speaker or writer, but this may meet with resistance unless he or she is a good communicator and manages to create an interest in them. They can be selected for their connection with the actions or events of the communicator's life, and this may interest others, particularly if there is some reason why they must get to know the person.

They can be selected to relate to the other participants' lives, as in such topics as sport, or a family matter, or professional matters, or something connected with their work or education.

They can arise from things said in the particular interaction, and so have a very relevant aspect; or they can be drawn from people's moods in the interaction, and so be very directly of interest to them. A topic initiator can build on previous communications the others are known to have had. And so on.

The crucial thing is that the topic must be something of relevance, or the others will not accept it and will seek to introduce one of their own. This will not just produce topic conflict, but will be a personal conflict too, and can be damaging to the relationship between C. and A.

In spoken interaction, topics are often trialled during the introductory sociable part, until one is judged acceptable by all or most of those present. They do not necessarily agree on a proposition about the topic, but they do agree that that topic could form the basis of their interaction. Topics will be accepted when all those present either feel that they could make a contribution to them, or are willing to listen while others discuss them.

Other factors which might affect the topic choice are the situational aspects, such as the social distance between the participants, their moods, any hierarchical differences, and any anticipated difficulties which might arise from the socially 'dangerous' topics, such as sex, culture, politics, religion, and so on.

See also '**By the way**'; **Informing**; **Narrative** tactics; **Tellable topic: choose**; **Title choice**; the other **Topic** tactics.

Further reading   Button and Casey (1985); Leech and Svartvik (1975); Mulholland (1991); Nofsinger (1991)

TOPIC: CHANGE

Task

To mark the change from one topic to another.

Description

In order that a line of thought can be followed, A.s need to be given notice of any changes in topic direction and of the start of any new topics. These are usually marked in writing, as in

Ex. 1 Moving now to the second issue I raised . . .
To turn now to a point of some concern . . .
The third principle for us to consider is . . .
Another point to be considered is . . .

and in speech by

Ex. 2 A: I went on holiday as you know. Well it was a disaster from the start . . .
B: Now where was I? Oh, yes. This new computer paper is really awful . . .
C: Hey listen, we need to send that letter to the Dean.

Persuasive value

In all these examples there is nothing to suggest that the next topic differs in value or priority from the last; in this case A. will therefore assume they are to be taken as equivalent in importance. If, on the other hand, C. wants to represent one topic as of more or less importance than the others being communicated, then it could be so signalled, in the hope that A. would accept the signal without questioning whether it is really appropriate for that topic, as in

Ex. 3 To turn now to the most important issue . . .
Another, lesser, point to be considered is . . .
And I suppose we should say a word or two about . . .
And in order to complete the picture we probably need to say a few words about . . .

One of the hardest topic changes to effect successfully is the change from an embarrassing subject. The topic change needs to occur without showing that its cause is embarrassment, or else there will be even more embarrassment as the previous topic user realizes what he or she has done. If the embarrassing nature of the preceding topic is explicitly mentioned, this just makes that in itself the next topic, and there has been no real change. If the change is too blunt, with no link to the preceding topic, this could signal a strong need to change, and the user could ask why. The best tactic is probably first to respond to the awkward topic, and while still holding the floor hark back to the topic preceding the awkward one, using a linking phrase like

Ex. 4 A: The blister exploded then, and the smell of gangrene spread slowly across my lunch.

       B: Yuk! How awful! But talking of explosions, it reminds me I had a narrow escape the other day . . .

See also the other **Topic** tactics

Further reading   Button and Casey (1985); Mulholland (1991)

TOPIC COHERENCE: EXTERNAL

Tasks

To establish topic coherence.
To avoid topic incoherence.

Description

Topic coherence has two aspects, one internal to the text and the other external. External coherence is what people understand about communication material from their knowledge of the world—life's events, childhood and adulthood, work and play, sport and art, the psychology of humans, literature and science, etc. In effect their whole cultural experience is brought to bear when they receive a communication, and they use it to assess what the material might mean, to interpret what the act of communication is, and estimate what goals the communicator has, and decide how best they should respond to these.

Although many members of a community will share a good deal of this kind of experience, they will develop different interests in different parts of it, sport in preference to art, literature in preference to science, etc. And this interest will also affect how they interpret topics.

To be effective communicators, therefore, writers and speakers need to be able to assess the degree and kind of cultural experience their audiences have, and what their interests are. This is why it is difficult to talk with people from other cultures, or from different age groups, or with different degrees of knowledge about a particular subject. It is why it is hard to communicate with strangers and easy to do so with one's family and friends. Luckily, small talk exists for people to use to acquire some of this information, and it is often used for this purpose.

Even with some small talk among old friends, topic mistakes can be made. For example, two old schoolmates might meet after one has gone to college and the other is in paid employment. The college friend might assume that the other knows about and is interested in student life, assignments and deadlines, lectures and libraries, while the employed friend might assume that the other is knowledgable about supermarket shopping, train timetables, bosses, and so on. Topic failure in this external sense occurs when a listener says 'I don't understand what you are saying,' or a reader discards a text thinking it is written for some other kind of reader.

Persuasive value

External topical incoherence is so major a factor in interpreting and understanding texts that if it fails, the whole intention and persuasive goals of the communicator will also fail.

See also the other **Topic** tactics

Further reading   Button and Casey (1985); Leech and Svartvik (1975); Mulholland (1991); Nofsinger (1991)

TOPIC COHERENCE: INTERNAL

Tasks

To establish topic coherence.
To avoid topic incoherence.

Description

Topic coherence has two aspects, one internal to the text and the other external. To show how internal topic coherence works, a sample of a student essay is supplied below, with each clause numbered.

1 The display of coins in the museum is set up (1a) so that they can be seen clearly and properly and (1b) the viewer knows exactly what they are (1c). 2 To aid viewers in their understanding of the coins, a book, or catalog, is provided to explain them. 3 To identify the coins, each has below it a small piece of flexible plastic with a number printed on it. 4 With only the number under the coin, a lot of space is saved as the coin's life history can be referred to the book provided, instead of it being written beneath or beside the coin, and taking up a great deal of room in the display.

The first sentence has three clauses:

(1a) The display of coins in the museum is set up

(1b) so that they can be seen clearly and properly and

(1c) the viewer knows exactly what they are.

The topics in 1a are in this order: 'display', 'coins', 'museum', 'set up'. Using a general knowledge of the world, and of museums in particular, a reader would know that there is a close connection between 'display' and 'coins', and both connect as a single unit to the museum which is a larger entity of which they are part. The next topic is 'set up', which is more closely connected to the 'display' and 'coins' unit since it is specific to them and not to the whole of the larger entity 'museum'. But as written, the linear sequence of the clause places 'museum' next to 'set up,' and not next to what it is closest to, 'the display.' It would be more coherent, from a topical point of view, if the clause were rewritten:

The display of coins is set up in the museum.

or

The museum coin display is set up.

The second clause, (1a), begins with the topic 'they,' referring to coins, and continues with 'see,' 'clearly,' and 'properly.' It would seem more topically coherent to bring repetitions of a single topic ('coins' and 'they') closer together, but this would be not be possible with either the first or the second rewritten example above:

The display of coins is set up in the museum so that they can be seen . . .

or

The museum coin display is set up so that it can be seen . . .

However, a better version is possible if the first clause is rearranged:

The museum has set up a display of coins so that they can be seen . . .

Here, as it turns out, the rewriting has also brought together 'display' into fairly close connection with 'see,' and these two topics are closely cognitively linked, and this is now reflected neatly in the text.

The latter part of the second clause contains the topics 'clearly' and 'properly.' One question to ask of any coordinated words is whether there is enough of topical interest in connecting these two things, and indeed, in this case whether there is enough topical interest in using both ideas. If no social value can be found in the presence of the two, then one should be omitted. (This account is ignoring such possibilities as that the writer is pacing the information carefully and padding out the text at this point.)

The third clause (1c) uses the topics 'viewer,' 'know,' 'exact,' and 'they.' There are topical links between 'viewer' and 'see' in clause (1b) and between 'they' and 'coins' in clause (1a). In each case the links are repetitious, or tautologous. But here this is a means of topic coherence, in that 'viewer' is a transformation of 'see' into the agent who sees, and so brings this topic into the account, and 'they' is a close link back across to the first clause, and a way of maintaining the topic of the 'coins' across an intervening clause.

It is perhaps unnecessary to go through the rest of this brief text in this kind of detail, but there are a few useful questions to ask of the later sentences. Why is the topic 'flexible' (or even 'plastic') introduced, since they do not link with the 'see' topic, but set up a new one, 'touch'? Why has 'spacesaving' suddenly appeared as a topic by sentence 4? It is in no way predictable from (or linked with) earlier topics. It could be that the writer wishes to begin a totally new topic, but to do so will startle the readers, and could puzzle them as they look for a reason why the first topic is now being dropped.

Persuasive value

Readers of written texts process what they read as they read it, and do so in something like the analytic method used here. So it is worth the time of writers who wish to have their texts understood, and their material accepted, to spend some time drafting the linear sequence of the text to take account of topic coherence.

See also the other **Topic** tactics

Further reading   Button and Casey (1985); Leech and Svartvik (1975); Mulholland (1991); Nofsinger (1991)

TOPIC CONFLICT

Tasks

To recognize topic conflict.
To avoid topic conflict if intent on persuasion.

Description

Topic conflict is a strong resistance to another's topic use, far stronger than is the case in **topic movement**. In the most extreme case, the second speaker makes no connection at all with the topics mentioned by the first speaker, and starts a totally new one; in most cases, however, the conflict consists of each speaker keeping to his or her own topic and reiterating it, and not taking up the topic raised by the other.

Persuasive value

The extreme case causes worry and ego loss, and is a poor environment in which to try persuasion. For example:

Ex. 1 Mary: Did you see the film on T.V. last night?
       Lisa: I fell off my bike today.

So rare is this kind of topic conflict that Mary will spend some time trying to find a link, even of the most tenuous, since if she does not she will have to admit that Lisa is paying no attention at all to her—which means loss of face for Mary, or that Lisa is angry. If Lisa has replied 'I fell off my bike yesterday,' and could be seen as taking up the 'time' topic Mary set (i.e. 'yesterday'), Mary would be relieved to find at least this connection between her initiation and Lisa's response. She might try to work out what the chain of thought is between falling of a bike and watching or not watching T.V., and if she could come up with something would feel more comfortable about the interaction since it would show that they are engaged in talk together, and not just two people talking to themselves.
    Topic conflict is usually less extreme than this; a typical example is:

Ex. 2 Bill: I had to get my car fixed yesterday.
       John: My new bike is a real success.
       Bill: It was the brakes, and cost a fortune.
       John: I never have any trouble with my bike.

Here the major topics raised by Bill are 'I,' 'car,' 'fixed,' and 'yesterday.' John keeps only to 'I' when he refers to 'my' bike, and while there is a faint connection between the car and the bike because both are modes of transport, there is far more that differentiates the two speakers' topics. If they continued to keep talking, Bill about the car and John about the bike, one about his transport's failure and the other about his transport's success, there would be a breakdown in topic, and this would affect their relationship. The event has become a competition rather than a cooperation.

See also the other **Topic** tactics

Further reading   Button and Casey (1985); Leech and Svartvik (1975); Mulholland (1991); Nofsinger (1991)

TOPIC MOVEMENT

Task

To use topic movement and development to advantage during an interaction.

Description

There are two main aspects to note about topic movement in an inter-action: it is acceptable that it 'drifts' in speech, though it must be logically ordered in writing; and in speech it can meet conflict which can drastically affect its movement.

Persuasive value

In writing, topic movement should be marked as logically ordered. It should begin from some point which makes a clear start to an account or other communication genre. That is, it must not be so dependent on things prior to itself that its beginning is unclear, otherwise A.s will not be able to understand it. If it needs a good deal of explanation to separate it from its circumstances it is not a good topic. The topic should proceed by logical stages to some point at which it can be ended without a good deal of explanation of what might happen afterwards.

In speech, topic movement is made more difficult because there is usually more than one speaker who wishes to affect the topic and its movement. It is usual for there to be such weak topic links that speakers can easily ask 'How did we get onto this topic?' but the links exist, and speakers can usually trace them back to the starting topic.

As a typical example of reasonably friendly topic drift, the following shows something of the way topics move, and in so doing shows something of how relationships between the speakers develop and change. Such developments should be watched closely for what they can show of a participant's attitude, or mood, so that persuasion can be suitably planned.

Ex. 1 Bill: I liked Dustin Hoffman in *Rain Man*.

       John: Oh did you? I liked Tom Cruise.

       Bill: No, I think Hoffman is a better actor.

       John: I think Cruise is good too, and he should have won the Oscar.

       Bill: Never. Anyway I thought *Rain Man* was marvellous.

       John: Oh, me too, it was great.

Bill raises three potential topics – 'liking,' 'Dustin Hoffman,' and '*Rain Man*.' John takes up the 'Hoffman' topic and opposes it, mentioning the other main actor 'Cruise' who formed a close-knit pair with Hoffman in the movie. The link is tenuous, but clearly there. They are both on the same topic, though they are disagreeing about it. Bill then returns to his first topic of 'Hoffman' but includes 'Cruise' obliquely when he compares the two in 'a better actor.' John returns to his own topic of 'Cruise' but keeps to Bill's topic of comparing the two. He then introduces a new topic, the 'winning the Oscar.' Bill takes this up, disagrees with who should have won it, and turns again to part of his first topic set, '*Rain Man.*' John, for once, accepts the topic and agrees with him on both the topic and his opinion of it.

The topic here occurs in the sociable part of an encounter, and was presumably chosen as likely to help Bill and John to show solidarity and agreement. It does not do so: though both share the same topic they use it for disagreement. Bill finally recognizes this, as can be seen through his use of the word 'Anyway' which usually indicates the speaker is going to change something about the communication, and probably for a social purpose, as here. (Other signals of topic problem are '**By the way**' and 'That reminds me.') Since the Hoffman/Cruise topic is proving divisive, Bill changes it to the movie '*Rain Man*' from his first speech move, in the hope that this might prove more sociable. They will continue to try topics until they either reach one on which they can agree or at least talk amicably about, or until they realize the interaction will not be sociable or amicable. At that point they may end the whole encounter or get straight down to business.

If Bill hopes to persuade John of something during that encounter, he has had several signs that John is not in a friendly mood, has adopted an oppositional stance, and is hence unlikely to be swayed to agree with Bill. Bill might be well advised to leave his persuasion to another day.

See also **Genre; choose**; the other **Topic** tactics

Further reading Button and Casey (1985); Leech and Svartvik (1975); Mulholland (1991); Nofsinger (1991)

TRIPLETS

Tasks

To heighten a phrase.
To focus attention on a representation.

Description

It is the use of a list of three recognizably similar ways of representing a matter, as in

Ex. 1 We would like to thank Ken for his commitment to the Department, his devotion to our ideals, and his endeavors for staff and students.

Ex. 2 We need to examine our policy: its ideas, presentation, and implementation scheme.

Ex. 3 We must work, work, and still work till we get it done.

The three items can be variants, as in the first two examples, or three identical phrases, as in Ex. 3.

To constitute a triplet, the three items usually act as one grammatical entity—clauses within a sentence, as subject or object of a clause, and so on—as in

Ex. 4 [clauses] They will have to work fast, and work well, and work together, to achieve their goal.

[subjects] Our plans, our schemes, our future viability, depend on this.

[adverbs] She is absolutely, without question, and without compromise, our best worker.

Persuasive value

Using a triplet works in two ways: it emphasizes (a) by repetition, or (b) by creating a recognizable pattern. The **repetition** is aimed to get A. to accept and remember a representation; while the pattern acts to focus A.'s mind on the connectedness of the three matters and so have them considered as one complex whole. This may covertly join three quite dissimilar things.

The form is very common, and this lends the triplet a sense of familiar completeness, which is lacking in two- or four-part lists. (The evidence for this is the way C.s try hard to produce a third element, occasionally having to resort to such poor versions as in 'The words, phrases, . . . or whatever, all need attention'; while a four-part list, because it is perceived as one too many, is often interrupted by another speaker who expected the standard triplet.)

Triplets help A.s to handle the ideas in them cognitively better than unlinked items.

N.B. They also help in the smooth transition of speaking turns, by signalling completion with the third item, and so allowing A. to begin his or her turn at that point.

Further reading   Atkinson (1984)

TURN: REFUSE

Tasks

To keep the floor while speaking.
To deny others the speaking turn.

Description

While holding the floor a speaker may deny others a turn in several ways:
1 He or she can announce a long turn either by genre choice or by showing

that the turn will contain several parts. The generic signal tells listeners roughly what to expect by way of length – so, for example; narratives are structured in recognizable ways, and their ends can be predicted. Where a speaker uses words like 'first, . . . second, . . .' or 'I wish to make three points,' listeners know roughly what to expect, and certainly know when not to butt in.

2 He or she can reject attempts by others to take turns, by such phrases as 'Hold on,' 'Let me finish,' or 'Just a minute.'

3 Thought ends can be held off till the last possible moment, by using periodic sentences where the completion of the sense is held up until the very end, as in

> Ex. 1 Because the new equipment is not yet operational, and therefore the report is delayed (though I hope it will not take much longer), we must not take on any new, or indeed revive any old, plans until we have cleared the decks.

contrasted with

> Ex. 2 With our plans now established we could proceed (.) with the project (.) though we should make sure they understand the deadline (.) and that the staff are busy (.) and that's my opinion (.) but I'd be interested in yours (.) Bill (.)

where each (.) signals a possible thought end.

4 Word speed can be increased, and pauses omitted.
5 Eye contact with others can be refused.
6 Physically a speaker can dominate the floor with sweeping gestures, loudness of voice, etc.

Persuasive value

Anyone resisting for long others' attempts to speak, or refusing to recognize their own dominance of the floor, will be perceived as arrogant, with adverse consequences for his or her goals. There are familiar phrases in which this is encoded, in as 'He never stops talking,' 'You just can't get a word in edgeways with her,' etc.

Moreover, what is being said while others are jockeying for the speaking position will be lost in the others' anxiety or annoyance. Attention will be focussed on the turn change, rather than on the turn content.

See also **Genre: choose**; **Narrative: choose**; **Sentence structure**

Further reading   Coulthard (1985); Goodwin (1981); McLaughlin (1984); Nofsinger (1991); Sacks, Schegloff, and Jefferson (1978)

TURN: REQUEST

Task

To achieve an opportunity to speak.

Description

While another is speaking a listener may offer signs that he or she wishes to gain the floor. The signs are:

(a) catching the speaker's eye, which is conventionally necessary before anyone can speak;
(b) using **body language**: for example lean forward, raise hand, increase nods, as ways of self-focussing and physically moving to center stage;
(c) increase rate and volume of support noises;
(d) speak simultaneously or finish the speaker's utterance, stutter a beginning, overlap using own words, or interrupt in a pause;
(e) explicitly ask permission to speak (*see* **Metaquestions**), as in 'May I say something here?' or 'May I ask a question?' (*see also* **Name: call**);
(f) or use any combination of these things.

Persuasive value

To interfere with another's right to a complete turn is a major social gaffe, and can lead to relationship damage (immediately in a bad case—for example, when the speaker is very nervous, has been denied a turn until this point, is emotional about the content, etc.—otherwise the damage can develop over time). It may be forgiven where a bond is strong enough to support such damage, as in close families, or between long-standing colleagues, or, of course, in emergencies. However, people have strong antagonisms to those who manage their turn requests badly, judging them as turn-greedy, or disruptive. There are many standard phrases which encode this, as in 'He never lets me finish,' or 'She is always butting in,' or 'I hate the way she finishes my sentences for me.'

The more signals of a turn request that are given, and the earlier in the other's turn they come, the more the requester will need to justify him- or herself when speaking. This could take the form of an apology, or emphasis on the interest and value of the content, or a good excuse, as in 'Sorry to butt in like that, but I have to go soon and you need to know that . . .,' etc.

If the turn that is interfered with is of particular interest to the audience, and is being seriously delivered, and then the turn requester's speech turns out to be of little interest and frivolous, these contrasts will work against his or her persuasiveness.

See also **Listening: active**; **Turntaking**; **Turn: yield**

Further reading   Antaki (1988); Nofsinger (1991); Sacks, Schegloff, and Jefferson (1978)

TURN: SELECT NEXT SPEAKER

Tasks

To direct who speaks next.
To control the floor though not as speaker.

Description

The person who holds the floor can nominate the next speaker. This can be done either by calling his or her name, as in 'So far so good. What about you, Fred?' or by directing a statement specifically to someone, as in 'We need a comment from our Personnel Officer on this.' The nomination can be increased by using **body language**: for example, directing the gaze to one person, touching someone, or turning the body in his or her direction.

Persuasive value

Even though C. vacates the speaking position he or she can continue to control the interaction to some degree by selecting a speaker to take the next turn who is likely to support C.'s point of view. It may also have the effect of excluding someone else who wishes to speak, and this too may suit C.'s purposes.

The control can include constraining the next speaker's topic or attitude, for example, by setting up and making it impossible for A. to avoid producing a particular **preferred response**, as in 'You agree with this, don't you Bill?' or 'With your special interest in this you'll have to accept this, won't you Mary?' The control can be disguised a little by making it more generally offered, as in 'No sensible person could possibly object to this. Bill?'

N.B.   This control could be applied even without nominating Bill to speak next: it could nominate the topic and attitude whoever speaks.

Further reading   Coulthard (1985); Goodwin (1981); McLaughlin (1984); Nofsinger (1991); Sacks, Schegloff, and Jefferson (1978)

TURN: YIELD

Tasks

To show end of speaking turn is approaching.
To nominate next speaker.

Description

At some point speakers must either yield the turn gracefully or have it taken away from them. To yield it, they make clear that the end of their last thought unit is approaching, by various means, as follows.

1 They ask a question, which invites someone else to speak in answer, and they may add the name of the person they want to be the next speaker.

2 They complete a grammatical structure.

3 They let their words gradually die away, as in 'and so on,' 'so it was all sort of . . . er . . .'

4 They offer an overt sign of closure, in such phrases as 'and finally, . . .' or 'which all amounted to . . .,' or 'and that's that,' or in an aphorism of the summarizing kind 'which all amounts to a hill of beans,' or 'so, there is nothing new in the world after all.'

5 A change in **voice quality** or **intonation**, a marked slowing down of speech, a voice stutter, or drawl can also mark the end of a turn.

6 **Body language** can signal completion, as speakers change their eye contact (from stare to intermittent glance, or vice versa). They also move or lean back, and cease their gestures, all of which signal a physical vacating of the 'floor' for the next speaker.

Persuasive value

Where the floor holder selects the next speaker, that person is thereby given a prior right to the next turn. He or she must then take the floor or be known as reneging on an obligation. It is a strong compulsion, and even if to speak is embarrassing or bothersome it must be done. If anyone else usurps this turn it would be taken as antisocial and their words would meet with a bad reception.

Where no one is selected, anyone can try for the next turn. The first speaker should win, but if two speak simultaneously, then the one with courage to prolong the speaking till the other drops out will win. Over time one who too consistently is first, or courageous, will be judged as greedy. If, however, the greedy speaker proves to be good value, the greed may be forgiven.

If no one takes up the yielded turn, after a reasonable time, it reverts to the floor holder. However, judgments of what is a 'reasonable' time can differ across the sexes and between cultures, and between slow and fast thinkers.

The persuasive effect of turn yielding arises from how well or badly turns are managed at each turn point. Success may go unnoticed but failure, in whatever form, will distract from the next speaker's content, which will adversely affect its reception and hinder the fair consideration of what he or she wishes to say and do.

Further reading   Antaki (1988); Nofsinger (1991); Sacks, Schegloff, and Jefferson (1978)

TURNTAKING

Tasks

To maintain smooth exchange of turns at speaking.
To avoid silence.

Description

In conversation, unlike interviews or debate, convention allows every person the right to speaking turns if they so wish, but there are no rules as to how often they can speak or how long a turn should be, nor is there an order of speakers.

To cope with this freedom, society has evolved a system of conventions to ensure the circulation of the speaking turn, frequent changes of speaker, and smooth transitions from one turn to another. The operation of these conventions provides for many persuasive effects, quite irrespective of the content of what is spoken, because what they do at each turnpoint affects all others present.

Persuasive value

The main conventions and their effects are as follows.

(a) One speaker speaks at a time (though occasional joint turns occur, produced, for examples by married couples). So interruptions and frequent demands for the floor are antisocial, and bring discredit to the interrupter. (*See* **Turn: request**.)
(b) Floor holders have obligations not to speak too long. 'Too long' is measured by such things as the interest of speech content, the social authority of the speaker, the wish of others to speak, and whether a speaker has already had more than a fair share in the interaction. If others judge that the speaker is being greedy, this will affect their general response to his or her content. If a particular turn is too long its content will be lost, along with any intended effects, as listeners become bored. (*See* **Turn: yield**.)
(c) Floor holders can directly call on some one person to be the next speaker. This power can embarrass someone who has nothing to say, though it can help someone shy who finds it hard to get a turn. (*See* **Turn: select next speaker.**)
(d) Turns should follow immediately upon one another, without **silence**. Speakers are therefore obliged to give signs of the approach of their

turn end, and listeners must be alert for their chances to take the floor. (*See* **Turn: yield**.)

The conventions are regulative; that is, they can be, and frequently are, broken. But their power is such that a broken convention is noticed and interpreted by others. So, for example, one who speaks too long is designated 'a bore,' a strong social criticism. An acknowledged bore will find it hard to persuade anyone of anything thereafter. So also, one who never takes a turn is called 'shy' or 'standoffish,' and this will be an adverse factor in his or her future persuasions.

N.B. Turntaking is not primarily a matter of personalities or relationships, but it is a system of turn allocation over and above such individual matters, although it is affected by them. Behavior in turntaking will produce personality or relation judgments, but does not depend on their prior existence.

Further reading Antaki (1988); Nofsinger (1991); Sacks, Schegloff, and Jefferson (1978)

UNDERSTATEMENT

Task

To reduce the importance or significance of a matter.

Description

Downgrading a matter can be done by (a) **word choice**, or (b) omission, or (c) sentence structure manipulation. To understate something needs a word which represents the thing well enough so that A. recognizes what is being referred to. Omission will only work if it would not be noticed. Sentence structure will only work if the sentence does not strike A.s as odd, and cause them to think about the form, and what it might be doing to the matters represented in it.

Persuasive value

1 If the understatement is too strong, A. may resist it and may even seek for fairness to the matter by responding with an overstatement, as in

Ex. 1 A: The delay has only caused slight damage to our chances of winning the contract.
     B: 'Slight damage!' It has ruined them!

The following, milder versions, are more likely to be persuasive as understatements:

Ex. 2 Bill has submitted the report.

as a version of

Ex. 3 Bill produced the report

or

Ex. 4 Bill was in charge of the report submission.

The power of these understatements rests on the relative social values given to the terms 'submitting,' 'producing,' and 'being in charge.'

Equally C. could downgrade 'business trouble' for example, by saying a customer 'is making a few complaints about us'; where 'few' understates the quantity while 'complaint' undervalues the nature of the trouble, making it sound unimportant.

2. Omitting mention of something is a very severe understatement, because it gives A.s no opportunity to resist or defend the matter: if they do not notice it they could accept the view. So, by omitting to mention good things about colleagues C. can keep these off the agenda. However, when such things are already on the agenda then C.'s omission will be noticed and will be interpreted in some other way.

3. Sentence structure can be manipulated to diminish the value of a matter. Consider these variations for example:

Ex. 5 The document was produced on time by Mary.

Ex. 6 Mary produced the document on time.

Ex. 7 The document was produced by Mary on time.

In Ex. 5, final position in the sentence gives Mary the most attention. Ex. 6 puts her in the weakest position while Ex. 7 loses her in the middle of the account.

See also **Ironic understatement/overstatement**

Further reading   Corbett (1977, 1990); Sonnino (1968)

'UNLESS'

Task

To use the word 'unless' satisfactorily.

Description

The word 'unless' can be a very difficult one to use as a clause initiator. Like other negation terms it can be confusing if its scope is not clearly defined. It is easy when its scope is a simple clause, as in

Ex. 1 I'll do this unless I hear otherwise.

Ex. 2 Unless you start that typing soon it will be too late.

Its meaning in both these examples is 'if not,' and so they could be rewritten as:

Ex. 3 I'll do this if I do not hear otherwise.

Ex. 4 If you do not start that typing soon it will be too late.

But its scope may be less clear, and it can prove confusing, as when it is used in official forms, as in

Ex. 5 Unless you are in receipt of a supplementary pension, or are over eighty years old, you should not apply for special benefits.

Here the problem lies in the fact that there are two clauses to which the 'unless' applies, and they are of different grammatical structure. The reader has to backtrack from the second clause to see how the 'unless' applies to being or not being over eighty years old. In addition, the problem is compounded by the presence of another negative 'not' in the last clause. To produce a better version, and one which is likely to produce correctly completed forms, the negative words should have been reduced as far as possible in the text, to result in something like:

Ex. 6 If you are in receipt of supplementary pension you should not apply for special benefits. If you are over eighty years old you should not apply for special benefits.

The following example was set as a test of reasoning in a logic examination:

Ex. 7 Unless there are fewer than seven days in the week, leave this space blank.

Further reading   Quirk, Greenbaum, Leech, and Svartvik (1985)

VALIDATION OF MATERIAL

Tasks

To indicate clearly the degree of reliability of one's material.
To show how firmly one believes in one's material.
To show how generally applicable one's material is.

Description

Although C.s usually offer their material as if it were absolutely true or widely accepted, they can vary from this on occasion. When they are less than sure about what they are representing they can express this uncertainty. There are terms which indicate their attitudes: for example,

Ex. 1 There were possibly fifteen people there.

Ex. 2 Students should normally have four Grade A results in order to graduate.

Ex. 3 It is generally true that cats cannot be trained to obey commands.

Ex. 4 We might be able to do that by Friday.

Ex. 5 I'm sure we can manage that.

Persuasive value

In each of these examples a different aspect of the material is being left invalidated, and this should be noted.
1 'Possibly' suggests that C. does not firmly believe in the matter.
2 'Normally' represents the material as true for most cases but there can be exceptions (which C. wishes to indicate to A.).
3 'Generally' indicates that C. considers the information is true but is prepared for A. to offer a rebuttal.
4 'Might' shows that C. has a hesitation about the general applicability of what is represented.
5 Paradoxically, the presence of 'I am sure' may mean that C. is not sure. Contrast Ex. 5 and:

Ex. 6 We can manage that.

N.B.   In speech the phrase could be given sufficient intonational support for it to be clearly a strengthening of C.'s certainty.

N.B.   Different validating phrases are thought suitable for speech or writing. In the informality of speech there is a preference for 'maybe' or 'might,' while in writing there is a preference for the more formal 'possibly,' 'undoubtedly,' 'certainly.' The preferences arise because writing, as the more precise and careful mode, is concerned not just with absolute validity or lack of it, but with degree of validity.

See also **Intonation**; **Spoken communication: choose**; **Voice quality**; **Written communication: choose**

Further reading   Corbett (1990); Sonnino (1968)

VOICE QUALITY

Tasks

To demonstrate emotion.
To add emphasis by using the voice.
To hold an audience interested.

Description

1 The vocal forms we know as sob, whisper, chuckle, giggle, and laugh can obviously add emotion to a communication. And they can be used with a range of intensity, from very noticeably to a subtle hint.
2 The other voice characteristics—breathy, husky, resonant, falsetto— provided they are deliberately used, and are not a person's permanent voice quality, can be used to draw attention to a particular part of the communication.

Persuasive value

1 Vocal forms can be seriously or jokingly used, as, for example, the giggle accompanies a joke-telling, or can be a sign of serious embarrassment; the exaggerated sob can dramatize a tale; or whispering can be used as a sign of fear, as of being overheard by a threatening person, or mystery.
2 They can reinforce the representation of a matter, to make sure that it is noticed, or can act as counterpoint to it, to give the matter some complexity of meaning. So, for example, a hint of laughter can alter a seriously worded statement and give it some added depth and ambiguity.
3 Because some of the voice qualities are very subtly delivered, they rely on a good deal of shared communications to be noticed. So a group of friends could 'read' the vocal signs and respond to them, while a stranger would not be able to. If therefore they were used a good deal, they could mark those who belonged to the group and those who did not.
4 Without some voice-quality variation an utterance is monotonous, and in some places, perhaps, difficult to interpret. Those who can use some of the emotional voice qualities are easier to listen to, so people will listen longer, and as a result there are more opportunities to be persuasive.
5 Some voice qualities, combined with certain words and phrases, can identify the code used by a specific group in society, as for example, the droning voice of a clerical minister, the husky voice of a rap singer, the falsetto men use when they wish to imitate a woman's high pitch. These signs can be used along with the rest of the identifying signs whenever a C. wishes to codeswitch.

See also **Codeswitching: role-playing in difficult tasks**

Further Reading   Beattie (1983); Crystal and Davy (1969)

WEAK EXPRESSIONS

Tasks

To present oneself as strong.
To notice weakness in others.

Description

Some turns of phrase act as clear signs of nervousness or a lack of self-assertiveness.

Persuasive value

1 C.s should present themselves as holding strong opinions or as being confident about what they are communicating, if they are to persuade A. They should, that is, avoid using weak expressions, since A.s are unlikely to be impressed by any opinion or persuaded to agree with any proposition about which even its utterer is not confident. So the following kinds of phrase should be avoided:

Ex. 1 I have the feeling it's right.

Ex. 2 I rather think he's done it.

Ex. 3 I think it's a matter of waiting till we hear.

Ex. 4 I suppose we could leave it for the moment.

In Ex. 1 the choice of 'feel' is weaker than 'think,' just because the first refers to emotions, while the second refers to thoughts, which are held in higher regard. In Ex. 2 'rather' implies a hesitation about thinking, an uncertainty. In Ex. 3 'it's a matter' removes the thought expressed from C.'s own responsibility, and so weakens his or her commitment to it. In Ex. 4 'suppose' is a weak version of 'think.'

2 C.s should not explicitly disclaim the opinion they are about to offer, since this is unlike to persuade A. to accept it. As in:

Ex. 5 I probably should not do this, but I'll argue the case.

Ex. 6 I am not sure, but I think it is true that . . .

3 C.s should not pause or make hesitation signs about expressing a view, as in

Ex. 7 Er . . . Um . . . Well . . . I think we could do it.

4 C.s should not use strong emotion as they write or speak, unless this is the accepted mode of communicating by all involved. Even if C. holds a belief passionately, its representation should suggest this, but the manner in which it is spoken or written should not. Too much expressed emotion is taken as a sign of irrationality, and will not be persuasive where some signs of reason should be presented.

N.B   C.s should observe when A.s use weak expressions in order to spot the moments when they are less sure about what they are communicating.

Further reading   Brown and Levinson (1987); Goffman (1959)

'WELL'

Tasks

To soften spoken disagreement.
To indicate a change of communicative action.

Description

'Well' is usually described as an exclamation of surprise or a sign of disagreement or of the start of speech.

Persuasive value

Good interaction is based on the connectedness of one communication with another, as one utterance follows another. Indeed, it is a major assumption that each act must be coherently linked with the one preceding it (*see* **Exchange of speech**). So people offering unlinked acts will cause misunderstandings and be perceived as communicatively inept, and this can affect how people receive their subject matter. Successful linkage is crucial as a condition for persuasion, and failure will adversely affect it. 'Well' helps maintain coherence.

1 It can be used to mark, and help listeners adjust to, a change of viewpoint as a new speaker begins, where it can mean 'Prepare for a change of viewpoint.'

2 It can be used as a phase marker to signal a change in interactional activity, to show that a speaker wishes to move from one phase, and to get others to agree:

Ex. 1 Well now, I think we should start talking about how to plan our trip or we'll never make it.

3 It can be used to preface and soften unwelcome or dispreferred responses. It can warn the first speaker to be prepared to withdraw the thrust of the **initiating move**, as in the invitation:

Ex. 2 A: Do you want to read this book? It's very good.
        B: Well, I am rather busy at the moment.

It softens a negative response to a request, as in

Ex. 3 A: Can I borrow a couple of apples please?
        B: Well, I've only got two left.

4 It can soften an even more serious dispreferred response, one which rejects the assumptions on which the speaker bases his or her offering, as in

Ex. 5 A: It is a beautiful day for gardening.
       B: Well, it would be if it were not so hot.

Those who get a lot of 'well's from others should perceive that they are having little success in that interaction, and either make a radical shift in approach or make the best of a bad job and withdraw till another, more auspicious occasion.

See also **Paragraph design**; **Preferred response**; **Phase change**; **Referring terms: internal**

Further reading   Schegloff (1982); Schiffrin (1980,1987)

WORD CHOICE

Tasks

To have a view of the world accepted.
To understand another's view of the world.

Description

Words represent matters—ideas, objects, people, events, etc.—as these are perceived by C. Each word aims to bring C.'s perception into the mind of A. and have it accepted as worth thought, or even as a better view than A.'s own. C.s, therefore, choose those words which they consider best represent a matter, and, importantly, are most likely to cause A. to share C.'s perception of it.

Words are chosen, consciously or subconsciously, for several reasons:

(a) They embody C.'s views, beliefs, opinions, and attitudes about some matter.
(b) They reflect C.'s attitude to the mode, and genre of the communication used, as well as the specific interaction.
(c) They suit C.'s sense of the relationship between themselves and A.; for example, whether it is distant or close, awkward or relaxed, serious or joking, formal or casual and whether it is hierarchical or between peers. Words also reveal therefore what judgments C. holds about A.'s social position or abilities.

Persuasive value

C.s bring their interpretation of the world to the attention of A. As A. digests it, both in general and in specifics, it is categorized alongside other views A. has of the world, and is assessed as fitting them or not. If it fits, A. might think 'I understand what C. is saying'; if it does not, A. might think 'that's not right,' or 'People don't do things like that,' or 'I can't accept that at all.' C.s must hope to choose words which make the view represented by them likely to be familiar to A. and therefore acceptable. (Note: this is particularly so when a matter is likely to confict with A.'s worldview: it will need careful disguising in A.'s own terms.)

It should be noted that once C. has brought the representation of a matter into the public domain it is almost impossible to deny it or to have it forgotten: once words are spoken they are gone beyond C.'s control. One cannot 'un-communicate.'

Examination of others' preferred word choices can enable one to see what worldview they hold, and C.s should build on this to help them choose the right words to achieve acceptance. Most people are habit-ridden in their choices of words, so the more people communicate, and the more of their words a C. has access to, the easier the choice can be.

Also, words act as clues to any reservations or hesitations or, conversely, to any enthusiasms, people have about what they are currently doing in the interaction. They can hint at the degree of certainty or discomfort, or conversely any enthusiasm, people might have about communicating this matter in this way to this person on this occasion.

N.B. It is this habitual use of words, and what they tell us of the person who uses them, that enables us to say about a reported communication 'That sounds just like Mary,' or to make predictions like 'Fred is bound to bring up the "efficiency" factor again, he always does.'

N.B. Words are not always the individual choice of the user, but could be prescribed by the organization or profession, on behalf of which the person is communicating, so what they reveal should be attributed to him or her as a representative as well as a person, and ultimately to the institution, which he or she represents.

Danger Note that the habitual choice of words is true for C.s too, so it would be worth a little self-examination to see whether good choices are being made. If a C. notices that he or she says 'sorry' too often, and so presents as a person frequently in the wrong, this habit should be corrected. If C. realizes that he or she frequently uses the phrase 'I can't remember . . .' a less damaging substitute should be found, such as 'I'll check that . . .'

See also **Genre: choose**

Further reading Dutch (1966); Gluck and Patai (1991); Quirk, Greenbaum, Leech, and Svartvik (1985)

WORD COMBINATIONS

Tasks

To represent something in a very familiar way.
To show that C. is like A.
To show opinions obliquely.

Description

Society has some language routines which bring together certain words so frequently that in time they appear to be inevitably linked. Typical examples refer to physical things like 'bacon and eggs,' and 'glass' and 'water'; or they are phrases which express social perceptions like 'he "fell silent" or 'her story didn't "ring true"', and 'she'll "make" someone a "good wife"'. So frequently used are these combinations that they pass unnoticed except that A.s feel that the communication is comfortingly familiar. And so powerfully linked are they that anyone who varies from them, as by asking for a 'cup of water,' can cause confusion if it is noticed, or it may well be not noticed at all, and what will be produced will be a glass of water.

Persuasive value

1 A C. can take advantage of the sense of inevitable linkage by, for example, simply using a lot of such combinations with the result that he or she will be perceived as an integrated member of the group.
2 C.s can also take advantage of the combinations to get a reputation for wit quite easily, by simply varying slightly one of the terms. If done in an unthreatening way (i.e. not requiring A. to expend a lot of energy to understand what is happening or to follow the new meaning), C.s can make themselves sound quite original. For example, where A. would expect to hear the familiar adage 'They married young,' C. could substitute 'They married old,' or for 'Out of sight out of mind,' 'Out of hearing out of mind.' A. could well enjoy the twist of meaning C. has imparted to the familiar phrase. Many instances of such (mild) wit exist, particularly where a combination phrase has to be used very frequently; then people seem to feel the need to vary it a trifle. So such well-worn combinations as 'many thanks' and 'thanks very much' might be altered to 'muchos gracias' or 'thanks muchly.'

However, such variations on the tried and true combinations risk being misunderstood if something of major significance is represented through them. Then they may simply cause confusion as A. tries to work out what the new version means, how it is related to the old, and why C. has chosen to introduce a variation at all.

3 By using one part of a strong combination in the 'wrong' place, as in 'I see it is feeding time at the Smiths' house,' where 'feeding time' is usually combined with some representation of animals, like 'feeding time at the zoo,' C. can suggest, without being direct about it, that the Smiths eat like animals.

Further reading   Leech and Svartvik (1975); Quirk, Greenbaum, Leech, and Svartvik (1985)

WORDS: ACCEPTABILITY

Tasks

To use words which will be acceptable to A.s.
To recognize that word usage is a matter of concern to many people.

Description

New words or new meanings and new ways of using old words are the focus of much social debate, and people hold strong opinions about them. C.s should take this into account since the 'wrong' use of a word will damage their chances of being persuasive. People vary in what they hold to be acceptable about word usage, depending on their age, sex, and social status. They also have a strong sense about what words are permissible in different kinds of communications: what is allowed in informal speaking is not acceptable in formal writing; genres within speech or writing have their own proper words; and words can be differently chosen when the relationship between C. and A. is closer or more distant.

Persuasive value

If C. uses a 'wrong' word it creates 'noise'; that is, it causes a disturbance in the communication process. On hearing or reading it, A. halts to think about its wrongness, and as a consequence is disturbed from comprehending what C. is trying to communicate. It would certainly impede A. from attending to the next part of the text while all this thought is going on. If it is a word use that A. feels strongly about, the hiatus in attention could be a major one, and an important point could be missed. More, if A. feels very strongly about the misuse, his or her response to C. will be badly affected. At the least A. will become aware that there is a difference between them about word use, and, more likely, A. could extend this to a difference in social class or age or general valuations of language.

   Word acceptability as a social issue is far more important that it might appear at first sight. University departments of English are asked each day to adjudicate in disputes over word usage, and there are countless letters to the editors of newspapers about word choices; it is obviously of major concern to many people. And they are nearly always negative about other ways of using words than they themselves do; so they say 'You can't say that, can you?' or 'This isn't a word, is it?' At its heart, the question of word acceptability is not just about using the word 'infer' instead of the word 'assume'; it is about valuing education and class and social status differently. And it is about a longing for security and the retention of old values in a world of change and new values. People who ignore others' preferences in word usage do so to the detriment of persuasion.

See also **Word choice**; **Word combinations**

Further reading   Corbett (1977, 1990); Sonnino (1968)

WRITTEN COMMUNICATION: CHOOSE

Tasks

To consider the choice between written and spoken communication.
To select the best mode of communication where there is a choice between speech and writing.

Description

Written communication is a very different mode from speech and requires quite different skills. It has the following features which distinguish it from speech:

(a) There is no C. present alongside the text.
(b) The material is expected to be new, and to be in logical order.
(c) The information can be supplied in lengthy units.
(d) The words used are to be read precisely as the dictionary defines them.
(e) There is a design structure to the text.
(f) The writer's major goal is to argue for a particular interpretation of the world as correct.

Persuasive value

In general terms, writing is more highly regarded than speech. This assessment comes not only from the near-permanence of writing, but also from the fact that only a relatively few members of society, the highly placed ones, actually write (though, of course, most members can read). This socially high status for writing is currently being maintained even in a computer-dominated world. There is a marked social division between those who know nothing about computers at all or just play with them, and those who can write using them, and, most elite of all, can write their own programs for them. So choosing writing over speech allows C. to give this cachet to the text; but note that it will also be judged by these high standards.

To take up the particular points described in (a)–(f) above, respectively:
1 The absence of a physical C. means that A.s will seek to find C. within the writing, and will look for signs of personality or character in it. C.s should therefore design the text to incorporate some versions of themselves where this suits their goals.
2 The content will be judged by a general social sense of its worthiness as a member of the canon of written texts. So its content has to meet with the higher standards of writing, and must certainly be more 'important' in some way or another than is necessary for speech. For example, in universities staff will take less account of what they say in lectures than they will of what they write in articles, and it is a high accolade if someone says of a lecture 'that is worth writing up for publication.'
3 The amount and complexity of information contained in a unit—phrase, clause, sentence, paragraph—can be appreciably more than in speech. And as a corollary to this, the units can be longer. The density and length are possible because the written form both enables C. to compose the text carefully and also allows A.s to scan the text whenever they wish, to read it at their own speed, and to pause to digest anything difficult.
4 Because C.s are assumed to have had time to prepare the text carefully, its vocabulary will be treated more seriously than in speech. That is, A. will be judgmental about the precision with which words are used, the appropriateness of their associated meanings and their suitability to the tone of the text and to its goals.
5 At macro-level, the text should manifest signs of design and logical structure; some evidence that C. has thought the whole project out in advance, made linkages, achieved coherence, and paced the **information flow** well so that A. can easily process it. At micro-level, the sentences should be varied in design, complex in pattern, and dense in material: in effect their design features should be worth the effort taken to follow them.
6 The goals of writing involve the representation of material—opinions, facts, events, and so on—and only to a minor degree do C.s seek to create a bond with A.s.

A.s expect that written texts have these features and will judge any specific text accordingly. Their absence could prevent the persuasive impact of even the most interesting and useful material.

See also **Elaborated code**; **Express personal involvement**; **Information: add**; **Spoken communication: choose**; **Words: acceptability**; **Written communication: design**

Further reading   Chafe (1985)

WRITTEN COMMUNICATION: DESIGN

Task

To design a written text so that it achieves C.'s goals.

Description

A.s expect that most of the following features will be present in a written text:

(a) some representation of the (physically absent) C.;
(b) some new information to enlighten A.;
(c) some clues to the attitude C. expects them to take to the text;
(d) some signs of genre;
(e) some interest or entertainment;
(f) some overall sense of plan or structure.

Persuasive value

As a text is drafted and revised it must address A.'s expectations that these features will be present. (In the discussion below, the model written communication is an informal report. The comments need to be adjusted if applied to informal texts or official reports.) A. will read the text and feel discomfort with it or resistance to it if the expectations are not met. There is evidence from speech where A.s have the chance to give feedback to the C. that they often question the absence of these features, as in such queries as:

1 'But how do you feel personally about student unrest?'—where A. wants to hear a voice not an institution;
2 'So what? I know that, tell me news'—where A. wants something new to think about;
3 'Why are you telling me that? What am I supposed to do with it?'—where A. needs something to show what role he or she should adopt to the material, or perhaps to the utterance;
4 'Is this a joke or what?'—where A. cannot tell how to interpret the material because no genre clues have been given;
5 'That's boring'—where A. needs some entertainment to justify listening;
6 'So where is all this taking us?' 'So? If that's what you meant to say, why did you mention that other thing, for heaven's sake? Stick to the point'—where A. needs some guidance as to the goal of the utterance.

Written texts need to incorporate all these features and so must be much more complex, densely packed and, therefore, well designed, than spoken texts. If producing all the features listed above seems a difficult task, the two main features to select are:

(a) structural design, which must be well thought out and executed. Unless this is done, even if every individual sentence is perfect in itself, the text will not be properly understood, and will not be judged well unless each part fits (and A.s can see that it fits) into a grand design. A well-designed text is one which can be easily summarized or which lends itself well to note-taking;

(b) A.s expect some new information from written texts; however, this will be difficult for them to understand unless it is well supported with explanations, examples, analogies, and logical ordering. It is one of the important ways in which writing differs from speech that while speech can build on its shared context and use it to assist interpretation, writing is denied this help. Writers may be anonymous, they may have lived in another time or place and so be very different from A. Therefore A.s will be at a loss to understand their material unless it is carefully planned and executed to accommodate any differences of view, knowledge, or experience that its readers might have, and provide some help which can substitute for the way the shared context of speech helps speakers to understand what they hear.

See also **Express personal involvement; Genre: choose; Spoken communication: choose; Written communication: choose**

Further reading Olson, Torrance, and Hildyard (1985)

'Y'KNOW'

Tasks

To discover what is shared knowledge.
To check that others accept the speech so far.
To indicate a change in type of information offered.

Description

1 In talk 'Y'know' can mark moments where C. feels the matters being mentioned need approval before he or she continues. It means in effect 'Are you with me so far?'
2 The phrase may signal that the speaker doubts whether the preceding or the following information is shared.

Persuasive value

1 A listener should note the appearance of a 'Y'know' because it indicates a moment of uncertainty for the speaker. Perhaps it is a feeling that the topic is going wrong, or the level of explanation is too high or too low. Or

perhaps it is a check that the listener agrees so far with what is being said. Perhaps it is a sense that the listener's attention is drifting away. Speakers should therefore also note when they use the phrase in order to avoid revealing their uncertainties.

2 If taken up by the listener, 'Y'know' provides a chance for A.s to alter C.'s output to suit their own interests, as in

Ex. 1 A: So I spoke to the new Student President. Y'know Sandy Brown
won the election?
B: Yes. She's good. I'm glad she did.
A: Well anyway. Sandy said . . .

By showing that the speaker has mistaken B's knowledge of the matter, B can cause A to adjust (the sign of this here is 'Well anyway').

3 Too many 'Y'knows' in a speaker's words suggests too many moments of uncertainty, and marks the speaker as lacking in self-confidence. This is true also for 'Y'knows' which occur where the speaker could not possibly believe that the topic is a problem for the listener, as in 'Y'know it was raining yesterday again, and y'know the wind was really blowing hard.'

4 Whenever C. uses the phrase it provides a chance for A. to take up the talking role and run with his or her own topic. After all, 'Y'know' appears to seek a response, and while giving it A. can try to change anything about the talk that he or she wishes.

5 Where C. offers a 'Y'know' and A. really needs help to understand what is being talked about, then A. has an obligation to seek help at that point. Not to do so could cause C. to go on talking and not be understood, which is inefficient, and is also rude because it makes a fool of C.

Further reading   Schegloff (1982); Schiffrin (1980, 1987)

Further reading:
List of reference texts

The texts listed here are of two kinds:

(a) those which relate to a broad range of rhetorical aspects of language;
(b) those which have a narrow focus on a specific set of language tactics.

The first kind are marked by a final asterisk*.

Antaki, C. (ed.) (1988) *Analysing Everyday Explanation*, London: Sage.
Argyle, M. (1975) *Bodily Communication*, London: Methuen.*
Atkinson, J.M. and Heritage, J. (eds) (1984) *Structures of Social Action: Studies in Conversation Analysis*, Cambridge: Cambridge University Press.
Atkinson, M. (1984) *Our Masters' Voices: The Language and Body Language of Politics*, London: Methuen.
Beaman, K. (1984) 'Coordination and subordination revisited: syntactic complexity in spoken and written narrative discourse,' in D. Tannen (ed.) *Coherence in Spoken and Written Discourse*, Norwood, N.J.: Ablex, 45–80.
Beattie, G. (1983) *Talk: An Analysis of Speech and Non-verbal Behavior in Conversation*, Milton Keynes: Open University Press.
Belsey, C. (1980) *Critical Practice*, London: Methuen.
Bennett, A. (1981) 'Interruptions and the interpretation of conversation,' *Discourse Processes* 4: 171–88.
Bilmes, J. (1988) 'The concept of preference in conversation analysis,' *Language in Society* 17: 161–81.
Brown, P. and Levinson, S. (1987) *Politeness: Some Universals in Language Usage*, Cambridge: Cambridge University Press.*
Button, G. (1987) 'Moving out of closings,' in G. Button and J.R.E. Lee (eds) *Talk and Social Organisation*, Clevedon: Multilingual Matters, 101–51.
Button, G. and Casey, N. (1985) 'Topic nomination and topic pursuit', *Human Studies* 8: 3–55.
Chafe, W.L. (1985) 'Linguistic differences produced by differences between speaking and writing,' in D.R. Olson, N. Torrance and A. Hildyard (eds) *Literacy, Language, and Learning: The Nature and Consequences of Reading and Writing*, Cambridge: Cambridge University Press.
Chaffee, S.H. (1991) *Communication Concepts 1: Explication*, Newbury Park, C.A.: Sage.
Chiaro, D. (1992) *The Language of Jokes: Analysing Verbal Play*, London: Routledge.
Cicourel, A. (1972) 'Basic and normative rules in the negotiation of status and role,' in D. Sudnow (ed.) *Studies in Social Interaction*, New York: Free Press,

229–58.

Clark, H. (1979) 'Responding to indirect speech acts,' *Cognitive Psychology* 11: 430–77.

—— (1980) 'Polite responses to polite requests,' *Cognition* 8: 111–4.

Clark, H.H. and French, J.W. (1981) 'Telephone goodbyes,' *Language in Society* 10: 1–19.

Corbett, E.P.J. (1977) *The Little Rhetoric*. New York: John Wiley.*

—— (1990) *Classical Rhetoric for the Modern Student*, 3rd edn, New York: Oxford University Press.*

Coulthard, M. (1985) *An Introduction to Discourse Analysis*, new edn, London: Longman.*

Craig, R.T. and Tracy, K. (eds) (1983) *Conversational Coherence: Form, Structure, and Strategy*, Beverly Hills: Sage.

Crystal, D. and Davy, D. (1969) *Investigating English Style*, London: Longman.*

Davidson, J. (1984) 'Subsequent versions of invitations, offers, requests, and proposals dealing with potential or actual rejection,' in J.M. Atkinson and J. Heritage (eds), *Structures of Social Action: Studies in Conversation Analysis*, Cambridge: Cambridge University Press, 102–28

Dillon, G.L. (1981) *Constructing Texts: Elements of a Theory of Composition and Style*, Bloomington: Indiana University Press.*

Downes, W. (1983) *Language and Society*, London: Fontana.*

Dutch, R.A. (ed.) (1966) *Roget's Thesaurus of English Words and Phrases*, Harmondsworth: Penguin.*

Ervin-Tripp, S. (1976) 'Is Sybil there?: The structure of American English directives,' *Language in Society* 5: 25–66.

Fairclough, N. (1989) *Language and Power*, London: Longman.*

—— (1992) *Discourse and social change*, London: Polity Press.

Fowler, H.W. (1983) *A Dictionary of Modern English Usage*, 2nd edn, Oxford: Oxford University Press.*

Freadman, A.S. and Macdonald, A.J. (1992) *What is This Thing Called 'Genre'?* Queensland: Boombana.

Giles, H. and Smith, P. (1979) 'Accommodation theory: Optimal levels of convergence,' in H. Giles and P. Smith (eds) *Language and Social Psychology*, Oxford: Basil Blackwell.

Gleitman, L. (1965) 'Coordinating conjunctions in English,' *Language* 41: 260–93.

Gluck, S.B. and Patai, D. (1991) *Women's Words: The Feminist Practice of Oral History*, New York: Routledge.

Goffman, E. (1959) *The Presentation of Self in Everyday Life*, New York: Anchor Books.*

—— (1981) *Forms of Talk*. Philadelphia: University of Pennsylvania Press.

Goodwin, C. (1981) *Conversation Organization: Interaction between Speakers and Hearers*, New York: Academic Press.

Goodwin, M.H. (1982) ' "Instigating": Storytelling as social process,' *American Ethnologist* 9: 799–819.

Halliday, M.A.K. (1978) *Language as a Social Semiotic*. London: Edward Arnold.*

Halliday, M.A.K. and Hasan, R. (1976) *Cohesion in English*, London: Longman.

Jacobs, S. and Jackson, S. (1981) 'Argument as a natural category: The routine grounds for arguing in conversation,' *Western Journal of Speech Communication* 45: 118–32.

Jefferson, G. (1972) 'Side sequences,' in D. Sudnow (ed.) *Studies in Social Interaction*, New York: Free Press, 294–338

—— (1974) 'Error correction as an interactional resource,' *Language in*

Society 3: 181–99.

—— (1978) 'Sequential aspects of story telling in conversation,' in J. Schenkein (ed.), *Studies in the Organization of Conversational Interaction*, New York: Academic Press, 219–48.

—— (1979) 'A technique for inviting laughter and its subsequent acceptance/declination,' in G. Psathas (ed.) *Everyday Language: Studies in Ethnomethodology*, New York: Irvington, 79–96.

—— (1987) 'On exposed and embedded correction in conversation,' in G. Button and J.R.E. Lee (eds) *Talk and Social Organisation*, Clevedon: Multilingual Matters, 86–100.

Kress, G. and Hodge, R. (1993) *Language and Ideology*, 2nd edn, London: Routledge.*

Lakoff, G. and Johnson, M. (1980) *Metaphors We Live By*, Chicago: University of Chicago Press.

Lakoff, R. (1973) 'Questionable answers and answerable questions,' in B. Kachru (eds) *Papers in Honor of Henry and Renee Kahane*, Urbana: University of Illinois Press, 453–67.

—— (1990) *Talking Power: The Politics of Language*, New York: Basic Books.*

Larson, R.L. (1968) 'Discovery through questioning,' *College English* 30: 126-34.

Leech, G. (1983) *Principles of Pragmatics*, New York: Longman.*

Leech, G. and Svartvik, J. (1975) *A Communicative Grammar of English*, London: Longman.*

Leith, D. and Myerson, G. (1989) *The Power of Address: Explorations in Rhetoric*, London: Routledge.

Levinson, S.C. (1983) *Pragmatics*, Cambridge: Cambridge University Press.

Lyons, J. (1981) *Language, Meaning and Context*, London: Fontana.

McGregor, G. and White, R.S. (eds) (1986) *The Art of Listening*, London: Croom Helm.

McLaughlin, M.L. (1984) *Conversation: How Talk is Organized*, Newbury Park, C.A. Sage.

McLaughlin, M.L. and Cody, M.J. (1982) 'Awkward silences: Behavioral antecedents and consequences of the conversational lapse,' *Human Communication Research* 8: 299–316.

Mandelbaum, J. (1989) 'Interpersonal activities in conversational storytelling,' *Western Journal of Speech Communication* 53: 114–26.

Mulholland, J. (1991) *The Language of Negotiation: A Handbook of Practical Strategies for Improving Communication*, London: Routledge.*

Nash, W. (1980) *Designs in Prose: A Study of Compositional Problems and Methods*, London: Longman.

—— (1985) *The Language of Humour: Style and Technique in Comic Discourse*, London: Longman.

Nofsinger, R.E. (1991) *Everyday Conversation: Interpersonal Commtexts 1.* Newbury Park, C.A.: Sage.*

Olson, D.R., Torrance, N. and Hildyard, A. (eds) (1985) *Literacy, Language, and Learning: The Nature and Consequences of Reading and Writing*, Cambridge: Cambridge University Press.

O'Sullivan, T., Hartley, J., Saunders, T. and Fiske, J. (1983) *Key Concepts in Communication*, London: Methuen.*

Owen, M.L. (1983) *Apologies and Remedial Interchanges*, The Hague: Mouton.

Pomerantz, A. (1984) 'Agreeing and disagreeing with assessments: Some features of preferred/dispreferred turn shapes,' in J.M. Atkinson and J. Heritage (eds) *Structures of Social Action: Studies in Conversation Analysis*, Cambridge: Cambridge University Press, 57–101.

Quirk, R., Greenbaum, S., Leech, G. and Svartvik, J. (1985) *A Comprehensive Grammar of the English Language*, London: Longman.*

Redfern, W. (1984) *Puns*, Oxford: Basil Blackwell.

Ritchie, L.D. (1991) *Communication Concepts 2: Information*, Newbury Park, C.A.: Sage.

Sacks, H. (1974) 'An analysis of the course of a joke's telling in conversation,' in R. Bauman and J. Sherzer (eds) *Explorations in the Ethnography of Speaking*, Cambridge: Cambridge University Press, 337–53.

—— (1987) 'On the preferences for agreement and contiguity in sequences in conversation' [from a tape recording of a public lecture originally delivered in 1973], in G. Button and J.R.E. Lee (eds) *Talk and Social Organisation*, Clevedon: Multilingual Matters, 54–69.

Sacks, H., Schegloff, E.A. and Jefferson, G. (1978) 'A simplest systematics for the organization of turn-taking for conversation,' in J. Schenkein (ed.) *Studies in the Organization of Conversational Interaction*, New York: Academic Press, 7–55.

Schegloff, E.A. (1980) 'Preliminaries to preliminaries: "Can I ask you a question?",' *Sociological Inquiry* 50: 104–52.

—— (1982) 'Discourse as an interactional achievement: Some uses of "uh huh" and other things that come between sentences,' in D. Tannen (ed.) *Analyzing Discourse: Text and Talk*, Washington, D.C.: Georgetown University Press, 71–93.

Schegloff, E.A. and Sacks, H. (1974) 'Opening up closings,' in R. Turner (ed.) *Ethnomethodology: Selected Readings*, Baltimore: Penguin, 233–64.

Schegloff, E.A., Jefferson, G. and Sacks, H. (1977) 'The preference for self correction in the organization of repair in conversation,' *Language* 53: 361–82.

Schiffrin, D. (1980) 'Meta-talk: Organizational and evaluative brackets in discourse,' in D. Zimmerman and C. West (eds) *Language and Social Interaction*, special edn of *Sociological Inquiry* 50: 199–236.

—— (1985) 'Everyday argument: The organization of diversity in talk,' in T.A. van Dijk (ed.) *Handbook of Discourse Analysis,* Vol. III. Discourse and Dialogue, London: Academic Press, 35–46.

—— (1987) *Discourse Markers: Studies in Interactional Sociolinguistics 5*, Cambridge: Cambridge University Press.

—— (1991) 'Cooperative conflict,' in A. Grimshaw (ed.) *Conflict Talk*, Cambridge: Cambridge University Press.

Shoemaker, P.J. (1991) *Communication Concepts 3: Gatekeeping*, Newbury Park, C.A.: Sage.

Sonnino, L.A. (1968) *A Handbook to 16th-Century Rhetoric*, London: Routledge.*

Tannen, D. (1984) *Conversational Style: Analyzing Talk among Friends*, Norwood, N.J.: Ablex.

—— (1985) 'Relative focus on involvement in oral and written discourse,' in D.R. Olson, N. Torrance and A. Hildyard (eds) *Literacy, Language, and Learning: The Nature and Consequences of Reading and Writing*, Cambridge: Cambridge University Press.

—— (1986) *That's Not What I Meant!*, New York: William Morrow.

—— (1991) *You Just Don't Understand: Women and Men in Conversation*, Sydney: Random House.

Wiemann, J.M. and Harrison, R.P. (eds) (1983) *Nonverbal Interaction*. Newbury Park: Sage.

Wierzbicka, A. (1987) *English Speech Act Verbs: A Semantic Dictionary*, Sydney: Academic.*

Bibliography

The texts listed here are of two kinds:

(a) those which relate to a broad range of rhetorical aspects of language;
(b) those which have a narrow focus on a specific set of language tactics.

The first kind are marked by a final asterisk *.

Bolinger, D. and Sears, D.A. (1968) *Aspects of Language*, New York: Harcourt Brace Jovanovich.*

Brown, G. and Yule, G. (1983) *Discourse Analysis*, Cambridge: Cambridge University Press.*

Cameron, D. (ed.) (1990) *The Feminist Critique of Language*, London: Routledge.

Craig, R.T. (1986) 'Goals in discourse,' in D.G. Ellis and W.A. Donohue (eds) *Contemporary Issues in Language and Discourse Processes*, Hillsdale, N.J.: Lawrence Erlbaum, 257–73.

Dillon, G.L. (1986) *Rhetoric as Social Imagination: Explorations in the Interpersonal Function of Language*, Bloomington: Indiana University Press.

Ellul, J. (1965) *Propagandas: The Formation of Men's Attitudes*, New York: Vintage Books.

Fisher, R. and Ury, W. (1981) *Getting to Yes: Negotiating Agreement without Giving In*, Boston: Houghton Miflin.

Goffman, E. (1967) *Interaction Ritual: Essays on Face-to-Face Behavior*, New York: Pantheon Books.

—— (1971) *Relations in Public*, New York: Harper & Row.

—— (1974) *Frame Analysis*, New York: Harper & Row.

Gumperz, J.J. (1982) *Discourse Strategies*, Cambridge: Cambridge University Press.*

Hodge, B. (ed.) (1983) *Readings in Language and Communication for Teachers*, Melbourne: Longman Cheshire.

Jordan, M.P. (1984) *Rhetoric of Everyday English Texts*, London: George Allen & Unwin.

Kreckel, M. (1981) *Communicative Acts and Shared Knowledge in Natural Discourse*, New York: Academic Press.*

Labov, W. and Fanshel, D. (1977) *Therapeutic Discourse: Psychotherapy as Conversation*, New York: Academic Press.

Morris, G.H. and Hoper, R. (1980) 'Remediation and legislation in everyday talk: how communicators achieve consensus,' *Quarterly Journal of Speech* 66: 266–74.

Nash, W. (1986) *English Usage: A Guide to First Principles*, London: Routledge &

Kegan Paul.*
Ricks, C. and Michaels, L. (1990) *The State of the Language: 1990s Edition*, London: Faber & Faber.*
Silverman, D. and Torode, B. (1980) *The Material Word: Some Theories of Language and its Limits*, London: Routledge & Kegan Paul.
Stubbs, M. (1983) *Discourse Analysis*, Chicago: University of Chicago Press.
Watzlawick, P., Beavin, J.H. and Jackson, D.D. (1967) *The Pragmatics of Human Communication*, New York: Norton.